Collateralized Debt Obligations: Structures, Strategies & Innovations

Edited by
Arturo Cifuentes
and
Brian P. Lancaster

Published by
Wachovia Capital Markets, LLC

Published by Wachovia Capital Markets, LLC
One Wachovia Center
301 S. College St.
Charlotte, NC 28288

Publisher's Cataloguing-in-Publication Data

Cifuentes, Arturo.
Lancaster, Brian P.

Collateralized debt obligations: structures, strategies & innovations/ Arturo Cifuentes and Brian P. Lancaster. — Charlotte, NC: Wachovia Capital Markets, 2004.

p. ; cm.
ISBN: 0-9760983-0-X

1. Collateralized debt obligations. 2. Debt. 3. Credit derivatives. 4. Credit. 5. Derivative securities. 6. Risk management. I. Lancaster, Brian P. II. Title.

HG6024.A3 C54 2004   2004111811
332.63/2--dc22   CIP

Printed in the United States of America
08 07 06 05 04 • 5 4 3 2 1

Collateralized Debt Obligations: Structures, Strategies & Innovations

Preface

The collateralized debt obligation (CDO) market has grown tremendously in the past five years, in terms of both size and innovation. This growth has been propelled by the attractiveness of the product, or perhaps more accurately, this technology. Consistent with this growth, we have seen a continuous flow of new market participants, plus a never-ending sequence of structural innovations. With that as background, we have attempted with this book to fulfill two goals. The first is to provide the new investor (or new market participant) with a brief introduction to the key aspects of CDO technology. The second objective is to keep more seasoned participants abreast of what we think is new or innovative, or just important. The chapters are relatively independent from one another and can be read in any order. The introductory chapter provides the necessary foundation to grasp the topics addressed in the more advanced sections. Experienced CDO players should probably skip the introduction and jump to whatever chapter they feel attracted to. In the conclusion, we speculate a bit about certain aspects of this market that we feel need some fresh thinking.

Several colleagues have made important contributions to this volume. We are grateful to Steve Altemeier, Bill Brown, Manish Desai, Daphne Fan, Shanker Merchant, Bob Ricci, Michael Rose, Michael Thompson and Yu-Ming Wang for their participation. We are also grateful to Jeanne M. Deitz, Michael D. Evans, Jim Pierpoint, Anik Ray and Jennifer Yount for their help during the preparation of this volume. Finally, we also wish to acknowledge the contributions of two former members of our organization: Nichol Bakalar and Jeff Prince.

Arturo Cifuentes, Editor
Brian P. Lancaster, Editor

About the Editors

Dr. Arturo Cifuentes joined Wachovia Securities in July 2003 as managing director and head of CDO Research. Before joining Wachovia Securities, Cifuentes co-headed the Structured Products group at Triton Partners and co-managed the Triton Opportunities Fund I, a $330 million "CDO of CDOs" (a leveraged fund that invested in CDO bonds) that was rated by Moody's Investors Service, Inc., and Standard & Poor's Corp. (S&P). Previously, he held a managing director position with the Structured Finance department of AMBAC and a senior vice president position at Moody's.

Cifuentes is widely credited with developing an important part of the core methodology used by Moody's to rate CDOs. While at Moody's, from 1996–1999, he rated more than 50 CDOs, including many pioneering transactions. In addition, he has contributed to the development of many analytical techniques that are commonly used in the structured-finance arena and has lectured extensively on many financial topics in the United States and overseas.

From 1984 to 1995, Cifuentes held scientific and engineering positions at the IBM T.J. Watson Research Center and The MacNeal-Schwendler Corp., an engineering software firm. He is also an accomplished journalist and prolific academic lecturer in engineering and applied mathematics. He has authored one book, three book chapters, more than 40 technical and scientific articles plus many op-ed pieces in English and Spanish. He has also held faculty positions at the University of Southern California, California State University and the University of Chile.

Cifuentes received a Ph.D. in applied mechanics and an M.S. in civil engineering from the California Institute of Technology, an MBA in finance (Stern Scholar Award) from New York University and a degree in civil engineering from the University of Chile.

Brian P. Lancaster, the head of structured products research, joined Wachovia Securities as managing director and head of CMBS Research in July 2001. Before joining Wachovia Securities, Lancaster was a managing director at Bear, Stearns & Co. Inc. from 1990 to 2001. From 1987 to 1990, he was a vice president at Chemical Securities Inc., and from 1984 to 1987 he was a senior economist both at the Federal Reserve Bank of New York and the Bank of England in London. From 1996 to 1999, Lancaster served as an adjunct professor of finance in Columbia University Business School's MBA program, where he taught courses on the capital markets. He has also lectured at the University of Pennsylvania's Wharton School of Business and New York University's

Stern School of Business. Lancaster was voted to *Institutional Investor's* All-America Fixed-Income Research Team in 2001, 2000 and 1999 and was awarded CMBS Analyst of the Year honors in 2003 by *Real Estate Finance & Investment* newsletter, an Institutional Investor publication. Lancaster holds an MBA in finance from New York University; a masters of international affairs from Columbia University, where he was selected as an international fellow; and a B.S. in economics from MIT. He has been a contributing author to five textbooks on the capital markets and commercial real estate as well as co-editor of the first edition of this book, previously titled *Collateralized Debt Obligations: Structures and Strategies.* Lancaster is a member of The Counselors of Real Estate, an editorial board member of the Counselors' journal, *Real Estate Issues,* and an advisory board member of CMBS Forum. He has also published numerous articles in industry and academic journals including *The Financier, The Securitization Conduit, Journal of Housing Finance* and *CMBS World,* where he is a managing editor.

Contributors

Steve Altemeier is a director at Wachovia Securities and the head of the Synthetic Corporate Deal Management team within the Structured Credit Products Group. Altemeier was at Bank of America and predecessor institutions for seven years before joining Wachovia Securities in June 2002. For the past six years, he has focused primarily on creating structured credit derivative transactions for institutional investors. Altemeier has a B.S. in mathematics from Vanderbilt University and an MBA from the Owen Graduate School of Management.

William J. Brown is a director and manages the Loan Arbitrage Group within Structured Credit Products. The team's activities span leveraged loans, middle-market commercial loans, small business loans (SBA sponsored and conventional), high-yield bonds and structured securities. The Loan Arbitrage Group conducts three primary activities: Counterparty Management oversees approval of structured "evergreen" facilities for loan product and the ongoing monitoring/due diligence of counterparties; Corporate Credit Trading conducts loan principal activities relating to middle-market commercial loans and rated leveraged loans; and Structured Credit Trading manages synthetic financing programs (CDS and TRS) for rated leveraged loans, high-yield bonds and structured securities. Brown has 10 years of capital markets experience and joined Wachovia Securities from NationsBanc Montgomery Securities LLC, where he focused on the securitization of consumer assets. Brown's other work experience includes NationsBanc-CRT, Associates Corp. of N.A. and Merrill Lynch. Brown graduated from Southern Methodist University with an MBA and a BBA in accounting.

Manish Desai joined the Structured Products Research Group as a CDO research analyst in April 2003. Desai is primarily responsible for overseeing the CDO surveillance effort, coordinating and publishing a weekly market commentary on the structured products sector and assisting senior analysts with the writing of the group's primary research. Before joining the group, he was an analyst in the Asset-Backed Finance Division at Wachovia Securities, focusing primarily on corporate high-yield CDOs and commercial asset-backed securitizations. Desai holds a B.S. in mathematical sciences and a B.A. in biological sciences from the University of North Carolina at Chapel Hill.

Daphne Fan is an associate in the Structured Credit Products Group, mainly focused on the structuring and modeling of synthetic and cash corporate transactions. Fan joined Wachovia Securities as an associate working on the origination of CDO transactions. She has a B.S. in management information systems from Tongji University and an MBA from the Kenan-Flagler Business School.

Shanker Merchant is a managing director in the Structured Credit Products group of Wachovia Securities. He focuses his efforts in the development of new CDO products and alternative investments. Before joining Wachovia Securities in late 1997 to develop the nontraditional mortgage-backed securities business, Merchant worked as a managing director at Prudential Securities in the corporate finance, asset-backed securities and mortgage-backed securities areas. Before this, Merchant worked at Citicorp as a vice president in the investment banking, merchant banking and international banking areas. He holds an MBA from Columbia University.

Michael E. Rose, Ph.D., is a director in financial analytics. He received his doctorate in applied mathematics from the University of Chicago in 1978. Since then, he has been a professor of mathematics at Tulane University in New Orleans and has worked in the reservoir simulation groups of several major oil companies in Houston and London. He has been in the financial services industry since 1984, specializing in developing financial software based on mathematical models, focusing on interest rate and credit derivatives.

Yu-Ming Wang, as managing director of Wachovia Securities' Structured Credit Products Division, is responsible for all aspects of Wachovia Securities' cash flow and synthetic CDO businesses. These platforms include origination, structuring, marketing and trading of corporate CDOs, repacks, synthetics and middle-market CLOs. Before joining Wachovia Securities, Wang co-founded Structured Credit Partners, LLC, an industry pioneer in the management of arbitrage repack CDOs with nine transactions totaling $4.4 billion in issuance currently under management. Structured Credit Partners became a wholly owned subsidiary of Wachovia Corp. in August 2001. Before co-founding Structured Credit Partners, Wang was the portfolio manager responsible for managing approximately $2 billion of asset-backed securities and commercial mortgage-backed securities portfolios at CGA Investment Management. Before joining CGA, Wang was a portfolio manager at General Reinsurance, where he managed approximately $2.0 billion in mortgage assets and approximately $1.1 billion in preferred equities against major market indices. Before joining General Reinsurance, Wang was a fixed-income trader at FGIC Capital Market Services. Wang received a bachelor's degree from MIT and an MBA from New York University.

Chapter 1

Introduction to CDOs

BACKGROUND

Collateralized debt obligations, traditionally referred to as CDOs, constitute one of the most interesting innovations that have appeared in the structured-finance arena in recent years. Generally speaking, the term *CDO* refers to a certain class of securities for which the performance is linked to the credit performance of a specific pool of assets. Within a given CDO, there are several securities (liabilities) characterized by a specific risk/reward profile that is based on their position within the capital structure.

Alternatively, one can think of CDO technology as a method for creating a family of synthetic bonds, each with a different risk profile and supported by sequential claims on the cash flows emanating from a given collateral pool. In other words, this technology allows one to redistribute the credit risk of a specific pool of assets and create a number of securities with different credit risk characteristics. Depending on the priority of their claims on the collateral pool cash flows, these securities can range from very safe to highly speculative. It is important to realize that the CDO *only* redistributes the total credit risk associated with the pool of assets among the newly created securities. The overall risk remains the same, that is, the CDO neither increases nor reduces the total credit risk associated with the initial pool of assets.

BASIC ELEMENTS OF A CASH FLOW CDO

The basic structure of a CDO, or more precisely, the so-called cash flow CDO, is better explained with the help of Exhibit 1.

The collateral pool (assets) consists of a diversified group of securities, in this case bank loans, which pay an average coupon of LIBOR plus 280 bps. The number of loans can generally vary between 50 and 100, although there is no specific rule stating any fixed number. These loans,

Exhibit 1: Typical Structure of a Cash Flow CDO

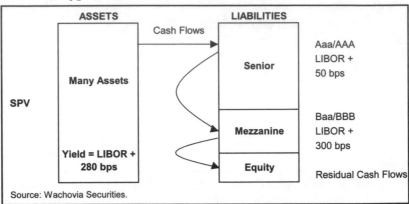

Source: Wachovia Securities.

which, in this example, have an average rating around B1/B+, are subjected to credit risk; in other words, they may default, a situation that—depending on the recovery rate after the default—can result in minor or major losses within the collateral pool.

The liability structure consists of three tranches: 1) a senior tranche (class A), normally rated AAA/Aaa; 2) a mezzanine tranche (Class B), normally rated BBB/Baa; and 3) an equity tranche, which is typically unrated.

The cash flows generated by the collateral pool, which, in all likelihood, will be affected by defaults over the life of the transaction, are distributed sequentially starting with the Class A notes, then the Class B notes and, finally, the equity. Obviously, the Class A notes (having the first claim on the cash flows) are the safest and command a high credit rating from the rating agencies. These notes, therefore, receive a lower coupon—for instance, LIBOR plus 50 bps. The Class B notes, enjoying the second claim on the cash flows, are somewhat riskier than the Class A notes but are less risky than the equity. They might receive, for example, a coupon of LIBOR plus 300 bps. Finally, the equity, which is in a "first loss" position, bears most of the risk associated with the pool. In compensation for this risk, the equity has a huge upside potential—should the collateral pool perform well (i.e., not suffer many defaults) the equity is entitled to all excess cash. On the other hand, if the pool does not generate enough cash to pay all of the liabilities, the equity is the first to be affected by the shortfall. The return on the Class A and B notes, however, is capped at the notes' respective coupon rates.

This is a simplified version of a CDO structure. Variations of this basic concept, as well as a more detailed discussion of the different aspects of these transactions, are discussed later in this chapter. Obviously, some natural extensions of this idea include a liability structure with more (or fewer) tranches, combinations of fixed- and floating-coupon assets and liabilities asset classes other than bank loans. However, Exhibit 1 captures the essential elements.

Finally, in terms of credit risk distribution, it is clear that the CDO structure manages to reallocate (or re-tranche) the credit risk associated with the initial pool by affording the three tranches different "protection" levels. Broadly speaking, CDO technology allows one to create securities ranging, in terms of credit risk, from very safe to very speculative, regardless of the characteristics of the reference pool.

These transactions generally have expected lives of 7–12 years. In terms of their evolution over time, CDOs go through three stages: 1) a ramp-up period, 2) a reinvestment period and 3) amortization. Most CDOs do not purchase all of the assets they need to build the collateral pool at the time of close. Although the proceeds from the debt issuance are readily available, the portfolio manager might not be able to purchase the entire portfolio at once. Thus, in most cases, during a period that could be as short as a few weeks or as long as several months, the collateral pool actually consists of a combination of cash and debt securities. As times goes by, all of the cash is eventually invested in additional securities for the collateral pool. This marks the end of the ramp-up period.

Once the transaction is "fully ramped," there is a period of roughly 3–6 years, the reinvestment period, during which the collateral manager is permitted to reinvest all principal proceeds in additional debt securities. In other words, the goal is to maintain a collateral pool with the same (or higher) par amount than the initial portfolio.

Finally, following the reinvestment period, the transaction enters the amortization phase, during which principal proceeds are used to retire the notes sequentially.

MOTIVATION AND REQUIREMENTS

One may wonder what the motivation is for doing a CDO, and further, what the conditions are under which a CDO works. Let us begin by tackling the second issue.

The first condition is that

(Portfolio Weighted Average Yield) – (Weighted Average Cost of All Liabilities) – (Expenses Associated with Arranging CDO) > 0

A more refined version of the preceding statement is that

> (Portfolio Weighted Average Yield) – (Weighted Average Cost of Debt) – (Expenses Associated with Arranging CDO) must be "positive enough" (i.e., leave sufficient residual cash flows) to make the equity position attractive.

In short, the equity investors (after making some assumptions regarding potential defaults) should have a reasonable probability of getting a return compatible with the risk profile of that position. Generally speaking, people refer to this condition as "arbitrage" (a misnomer, for this is not a risk-free situation) and make statements such as "the arbitrage that makes a CDO feasible is not present now..." or "the arbitrage is very attractive for the equity piece now..." A more accurate statement is to speak of the "funding gap" (between assets and liabilities).

A second requirement, more operational that conceptual, is to have enough data available to evaluate the risk/reward aspects of the proposed CDO. This refers to the ability to predict (in a statistical sense) the cash flows generated by the asset pool. More precisely, there are three basic pieces of information that one needs:

- The probability of default of the assets
- Recovery values (in case assets default)
- Portfolio correlation (or the degree of diversification of the collateral pool)

These requirements are discussed later in more detail.

In terms of the investor's motivation to participate in a CDO, it all depends on the position in the capital structure and the investor's risk appetite. However, all investors share collectively one benefit: a diversified exposure to a pool of assets (something that might be difficult to achieve individually) in addition to a "low" funding cost, locked-in at the onset of the transaction. The low funding cost needs to be explained. In the CDO, the cost of funding is, somehow, "subsidized" by the senior tranche (AAA/Aaa rating in general). Because this tranche constitutes a significant portion of the liability structure, its low coupon results in an overall low funding cost relative to other alternatives. For example, if the investors were to borrow money from a bank to fund the purchase of the portfolio, the cost would clearly be higher, as bank funding costs, up-front fees and bank profit margins are factored in.

In a way, the CDO allows for the creation of "customized" securities with different risk/reward profiles for investors with different needs, at a low (and constant) funding cost. In addition, the securities offered by the CDO have characteristics typically not found in securities available in the open market. Finally, the rated notes issued by a CDO offer more attractive spreads compared with those of conventional bonds with comparable ratings. This explains why investors find this product attractive.

MARKET EVOLUTION

The first CDO was structured in 1988 by Drexel, Burnham and Lambert and was backed by a collateral pool consisting of high-yield ("junk") bonds. Accordingly, at the time these transactions were known as CBOs (collateralized bond obligations). In due time, after the technology was extended to securitize bank loans, the CLO (collateralized loan obligation) made its debut in the structured products market. At present, the preferred term is simply *CDO*, and it refers generically to any transaction structured using this technology regardless of the nature of the asset pool.

In terms of size, this market has grown significantly since its inception and today exceeds $100 billion per year in issuance (Exhibit 2).

Exhibit 2: Size of the Domestic CDO Market

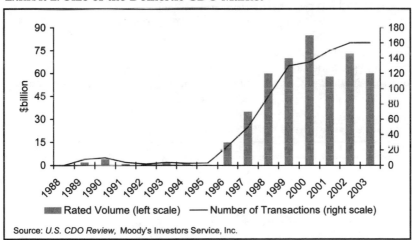

Source: *U.S. CDO Review*, Moody's Investors Service, Inc.

The list of the types of underlying assets backing CDOs has also expanded since 1988 and currently includes bank loans, emerging market debt, middle-market loans, project finance debt, REITs, trust preferred securities (TruPS), high-yield bonds and others. In short, it seems that any asset for which cash flows can be predicted (in a statistical sense) has managed to find its way into a CDO. (Exhibit 3 shows the evolution of the asset classes.) In addition, in recent years, transactions known as resecuritizations (a.k.a. CDO of CDOs or CDO-squared) have become common. These are CDOs in which the assets consist of tranches from previous securitizations, for example, mezzanine tranches from CDO transactions and B-pieces from MBS deals.

Exhibit 3: Evolution of the Assets Employed in CDOs

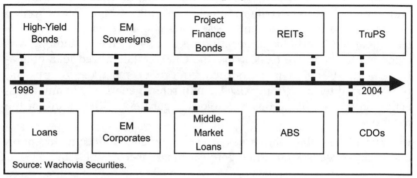

Source: Wachovia Securities.

In terms of the types of structure, CDOs have also evolved considerably from the conventional cash flow schematic depicted in Exhibit 1 (Exhibit 4). Further innovation has led to the issuance of synthetic CDOs, balance-sheet transactions, single-tranche (customized portfolio tranched securities, or CPORTS) transactions, market value CDOs, fund-of-fund structures, CDOs with money market tranches and others. Some of these varieties are discussed later in this chapter.

Exhibit 4: Evolution of CDO Structures

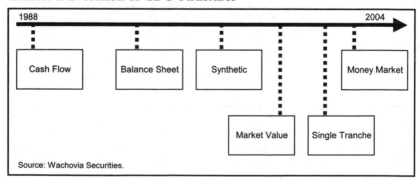

Source: Wachovia Securities.

CASH FLOW CDO WATERFALL

The cash flow distribution scheme outlined in Exhibit 1 needs to be explained in more detail. Although the basic concept shown in that exhibit is correct (cash flows are distributed based on the tranche seniority), the details are more complex. The rules for CDO cash flows distributions are spelled out in the so-called priority of payments section of the indenture (the legal document that governs the transaction). These rules are also collectively referred to as the waterfall. In summary, the waterfall explains, in a fairly detailed fashion, the manner in which principal and interest are distributed.

Before discussing the waterfall, we need to introduce an important concept — the cash diversion test. Although the different notes issued by the CDO are afforded different levels of protection depending on seniority (that is, the priority assigned to each tranche's claim on the cash flows), these priorities are further modified by the cash diversion tests under certain circumstances. Briefly, if a cash diversion test is violated, cash flows (interest or principal generated by the collateral pool) are redirected to more senior tranches instead of passing straight to the next tranche. The most common cash diversion tests are the overcollateralization (OC) and the interest coverage (IC) tests. The OC test is also commonly referred to as the par value test or the par coverage test.

The OC test is defined in terms of the OC ratio. In reference to Exhibit 1, we can distinguish between two OC ratios: the senior OC ratio and the mezzanine OC ratio. They are defined as follows:

Senior OC ratio = NUM / DEN

where

NUM = (Performing Collateral Par Value) + (Cash) + (Defaulted Collateral Par Value) × (Recovery Rate)

and

DEN = Class A Par Value.

Analogously, the mezzanine OC ratio is defined as follows:

Mezzanine OC Ratio = NUM / DEN

Where NUM is defined as before and

DEN = (Class A Par Value) + (Class B Par Value).

If the OC ratio is higher than the OC trigger, the test is considered "in compliance" and no cash flows are diverted. The triggers are determined taking into consideration the values of the ratios at close, but also provide some leeway (i.e., "cushion") for collateral pool deterioration.

For instance, if the initial senior OC ratio has a value of 1.4, it would not be uncommon for the senior OC trigger to be set up at 1.2. (The exact determination of the OC and IC triggers is dealt with later in this chapter.)

The IC tests (senior and mezzanine) are calculated in a similar fashion.

Senior IC Ratio = NUM / DEN

where

NUM = (Performing Collateral Par Value) × (Collateral Weighted Average Coupon)

and

DEN = (Class A Par Value) × (Class A Coupon).

Analogously, the mezzanine IC ratio is defined as follows:

Mezzanine IC Ratio = NUM / DEN

Where NUM is defined as before and

DEN = (Class A Par Value) × (Class A Coupon) + (Class B Par Value) × (Class B Coupon).

If the IC ratio is higher than the IC trigger, the test is in compliance and no cash flows are diverted. The same holds for the mezzanine IC test.

Using these elements, we can describe the waterfall. In reality, there are two waterfalls. One waterfall specifies the distribution of principal payments, and a second one specifies the distribution of interest payments. Exhibit 5 summarizes a generic version of each waterfall. Of course, there are many variations of this theme, but the essential elements are captured in Exhibit 5.

The purpose of the waterfall is to protect the most senior investors, at the expense of the most subordinated pieces, in the event that the transaction experiences an "excessive" number of defaults. What constitutes an "excessive" number of defaults is defined by the triggers. If the triggers are "tight" (i.e., likely to be tripped with a few defaults) the structure offers more protection to the most senior pieces, because cash will be diverted to amortize these notes rather quickly. In contrast, "loose" triggers (i.e., more defaults are needed to violate the covenant) tend to offer less protection to the senior tranches. In these cases, the subordinated tranches will not experience cash flow interruptions unless the number of defaults is somewhat higher. Either way, the purpose of the test is the same: to accelerate the amortization of the liabilities (in order of seniority) and delever the transaction once the pool deteriorates beyond a certain level. There are no "right" (or "wrong") values for the OC and IC

Exhibit 5: A Typical CDO Waterfall

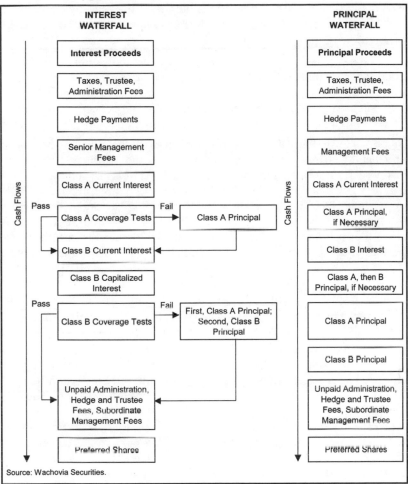

INTEREST WATERFALL	PRINCIPAL WATERFALL

Interest Proceeds — Principal Proceeds

Taxes, Trustee, Administration Fees — Taxes, Trustee, Administration Fees

Hedge Payments — Hedge Payments

Senior Management Fees — Management Fees

Class A Current Interest — Class A Curent Interest

Pass / Fail — Class A Coverage Tests → Class A Principal

Class A Principal, if Necessary

Class B Current Interest

Class B Interest

Class B Capitalized Interest

Class A, then B Principal, if Necessary

Pass / Fail — Class B Coverage Tests → First, Class A Principal; Second, Class B Principal

Class A Principal

Class B Principal

Unpaid Administration, Hedge and Trustee Fees, Subordinate Management Fees — Unpaid Administration, Hedge and Trustee Fees, Subordinate Management Fees

Preferred Shares — Preferred Shares

Cash Flows

Source: Wachovia Securities.

triggers. These are simply tools that are used to control the cash flows and, in turn, design tranches with different risk profiles.

In summary, the "protection" afforded to the different tranches issued by the CDO depends on their seniority, the cash diversion tests (which might or might not interrupt the cash flows available for a certain tranche according to the degree of deterioration suffered by the asset pool) and—finally—the excess spread. The excess spread is simply the difference between the average coupon paid by the collateral and the weighted average coupon paid to the liabilities (the funding cost).

INTEREST RATE RISK

So far, the discussion has been focused on credit risk—that is, the likelihood that the collateral pool performance might be affected by defaults. Ideally, the CDO performance should only be driven by credit events (defaults). After all, the thought behind the CDO concept is to permit investors to gain credit exposure to a diversified pool.

In principle, if there is a fixed-floating mismatch between the assets and liabilities the CDO notes might be exposed to interest rate risk. Suppose, for example, a situation in which the assets pay a fixed coupon (say, $c = 11.4\%$) and the liabilities (Classes A and B) are funded at LIBOR dependent rates, for instance, LIBOR plus 50 bps and LIBOR plus 300 bps, respectively. Clearly, changes in the LIBOR environment might stress the cash flows available to serve the debt, regardless of the credit performance of the pool of assets. Specifically, as the value of LIBOR increases, the transaction's ability to tolerate defaults decreases. Although interest rate risk is generally low compared with credit risk, it cannot be ignored, especially because CDOs are designed with up to 12–15 year maturities. Thus, there is a clear need to mitigate this risk.

The most common approach to managing the interest rate risk in a CDO is to use either a cap or a swap. First, consider the cap. Exhibit 6 shows schematically a simple CDO with only two tranches (a senior note plus equity). The cap fees are typically paid up-front, but they could be paid over time (within the waterfall, but enjoying a high priority). The cap notional amount is generally less than the full notional collateral amount and can amortize after the reinvestment period. The diagram in Exhibit 6 is straightforward: in the event LIBOR were to exceed the strike rate, the cap counterparty injects cash to supplement the cash generated by the pool, thereby mitigating significantly the interest rate risk and leaving the CDO exposed primarily to credit risk (defaults), as was originally intended.

The implementation of a hedge strategy using a swap is described in Exhibit 7. Again, the swap notional amount might vary over time, and generally decreases after the reinvestment period, somehow mimicking the amortization schedule of the pool. The swap payment (from the CDO to the swap counterparty) is normally fairly senior in the waterfall.

Evidently, these are only the basics. A wide variety of hedge strategies can be implemented using different combinations of caps and swaps

Exhibit 6: CDO with a Cap

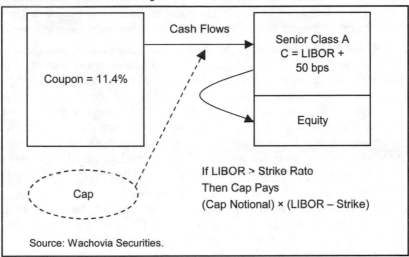

Source: Wachovia Securities.

Exhibit 7: CDO with an Interest Rate Swap

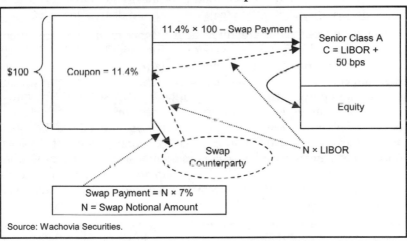

Source: Wachovia Securities.

with various strike rates and/or notional amounts. Finally, investors should be mindful of onerous hedge arrangements that could tax excessively the CDO in the event that there are many defaults. In other words, these unwise hedges can make a bad situation (many defaults) worse by taking away a significant portion of the cash flows under certain LIBOR scenarios.

PARTICIPANTS IN A CDO TRANSACTION

The major actors in a CDO transaction are the investors, but other players perform important roles. This section describes these roles in greater detail.

Investment banker. The responsibility of the investment banker is to structure the transaction. This involves several undertakings, including determining the precise architecture of the CDO (e.g., the composition of the capital structure, the hedge strategy and waterfall provisions), placing the notes and finding equity investors, negotiating the requirements/characteristics that are set by the rating agencies to achieve particular ratings for the notes issued and providing (in many cases) a warehouse facility to help with the collateral acquisition process (before closing).

Asset (or collateral/portfolio) manager. The role of the manager is twofold. First, he selects the initial portfolio of assets. This occurs either during the ramp-up period (shortly after closing) or during the warehouse period (before the closing). Second, he trades the portfolio during the life of the transaction (within the guidelines set by the indenture) to preserve the quality of the portfolio and, ideally, to avoid (or at least minimize) credit deterioration (e.g., defaults and distressed sales).

Rating agencies. There are three active agencies in the structured-finance arena: Moody's Investors Service, Inc., Standard & Poor's Corp. (S&P) and Fitch Ratings. The rating agencies perform collateral manager due diligence, review the legal documents governing the transactions and, most important, run several quantitative analyses. These quantitative analyses are designed to evaluate the performance of each class of notes under several asset pool default scenarios. In addition, the rating agencies participate actively in negotiating certain aspects of the legal documents with the banker, sometimes imposing specific provisions aimed at protecting the noteholders. Finally, the rating ultimately assigned to each tranche is a reflection of the credit risk associated with such tranche based on all of the factors mentioned previously.

Trustee. The role of the trustee is to safekeep the assets and monitor the manager's trading activities. The CDO indenture spells out some specific rules regarding trading, and the trustee should, at least in theory, monitor compliance with these rules. In addition, the trustee is responsible for issuing periodic reports describing the status of the CDO—including a description of the collateral pool securities, compliance with the coverage and collateral quality tests, cash payments allocated to each tranche and expenses incurred by the CDO.

Hedge counterparty. As explained before, a CDO might enter into a swap or cap agreement (or several combinations of these) to mitigate interest rate risk. The hedge counterparty is just the other leg of the swap. Occasionally, a CDO might enter into a basis swap to "smooth" the timing of the cash flows generated by the collateral (suppose, for instance, that the assets make semiannual payments and the liabilities receive quarterly coupons) or a currency swap.

Monoline insurer. Some CDO transactions, either because the strength of the collateral pool is not sufficient (or is perceived to be insufficient by certain investors or the rating agencies), find it necessary to enlist the help of a third party to provide certain investors (normally the senior bondholders) an extra assurance that their cash flows will not be impaired. These third parties are the monoline insurers (e.g., AMBAC, MBIA, XL and FSA) These institutions, after reviewing in detail all of the aspects of a CDO, agree, in exchange for a fee, to step in should the collateral pool fail to generate enough cash to pay the tranche afforded this protection. Obviously, to be an effective participant in this market the monolines must maintain a high credit rating (generally AAA/Aaa, or at least AA/Aa) because their insurance policies are only as good as their own financial strength. Hence, the monolines are constantly monitored by the rating agencies. In addition, an extra advantage of having a monoline in the transaction is the extra level of due diligence that this brings to the CDO (on top of the oversight provided by the rating agencies).

Exhibit 8 depicts more graphically the roles played by all these participants.

OTHER TYPES OF CDOS

Exhibit 1 outlined the basic structure of the cash flow CDO. In recent years, this basic concept has provided the foundation for many innovative variations. In what follows, we review some of the extensions of the basic concept.

Synthetic CDO. The synthetic CDO is the most important and popular variation of the original structure. It is, in reality, a mixture of CDO technology and credit default swaps; this concept has been extremely popular among European investors. The basic idea is explained in Exhibit 9.

At the root of this arrangement is a sponsor who seeks protection in case a large pool of assets (the "reference pool") experience losses as a result of credit events. The mechanics are straightforward. First, the $100 collected from the issuance of the notes is invested in AAA/Aaa

Exhibit 8: CDO Market Participants

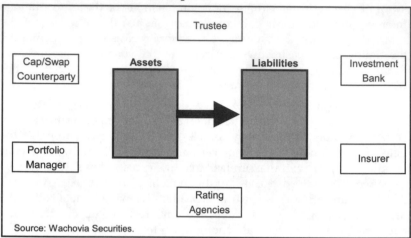

Source: Wachovia Securities.

(i.e., very safe) securities that will normally yield a LIBOR coupon and will have a total par amount of $100. The sponsor (the institution buying credit protection) pays an additional premium in return for this protection, which, in turn, is used to supplement the cash coupon (LIBOR) generated by the AAA/Aaa securities to cover the notes' interest payments. If there are no defaults during the life of the transaction, the AAA/Aaa securities are liquidated and the proceeds are used to pay down the CDO liabilities. In these transactions, assets and liabilities all have identical "bullet-like" amortization profiles.

Should defaults occur, some of the AAA/Aaa assets are liquidated to compensate the sponsor for the loss. At the same time, an amount equal to the loss is written down from the par value of the liabilities, starting with the first loss portion at the bottom of the capital structure. For instance, assume a reference asset defaults, generating a $3 loss. This means that, after compensating the sponsor for the $3 loss (by selling $3 worth of AAA/Aaa assets), the equity par amount is reduced (written down) from $10 to $7. Eventually, as the losses might pile up over time, all of the equity and possibly even the mezzanine piece could see its notional amount reduced significantly or, in a worst-case scenario, wiped out completely.

In summary, if no defaults occur, the investors (senior, mezzanine and equity) ultimately receive 100% of their principal, plus the periodic interest payments made by the protection buyer. In case there are defaults,

Exhibit 9: Synthetic CDO General Structure and after a Default

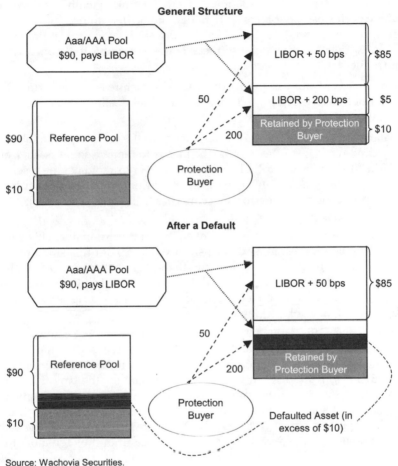

Source: Wachovia Securities.

the sponsor is compensated for the loss at the expense of the investors who progressively see the notional amount of their notes decrease.

This is only the basic idea. Of course, there are more nuances in practical terms. For example, the equity is frequently not "sold" to investors, but rather retained by the sponsor. This means the sponsor is covered only if the defaults exceed some specific level (the size of the equity). The question of what constitutes a default is not as straightforward as it seems. It must be defined in a detailed fashion in the transaction legal documents and generally refers to one of the following: bankruptcy, failure to pay, restructuring, acceleration and repudiation or moratorium. Again, many variations of these basic definitions are possible. Finally, the correct value of the loss, after an asset defaults, can be determined in a number of ways. In general, either a cash or physical settlement approach is used. A detailed discussion of these issues is beyond the scope of this introduction.

An attractive feature of the synthetic CDO structure is that it permits the sponsor to seek credit protection without actually selling the loans. Thus, client-bank relationships are not jeopardized.

Balance-sheet CDO. This is a CDO done with the sole purpose of obtaining capital relief; in other words, the idea is to remove some assets from the institution (in general, a bank) balance sheet to avoid having reserves tied up to those assets. In a few cases, an additional motivation has been to improve the bank's performance metrics (e.g., return on assets).

In the conventional cash flow CDO, the assets are sold to the CDO (actually, to a trust) and are "de-linked" from the originator. This could certainly be the case in a balance-sheet CDO, and in this situation the transaction would operate identically to the example shown in Exhibit 1. The only difference, compared with the conventional CLO, is that in the balance-sheet transaction all of the loans are typically originated by one institution: the bank seeking capital relief.

Alternatively, the assets might not be sold to a trust, but rather, segregated internally ("earmarked"), and thus they remain on the bank's balance sheet. This situation is referred to as a linked structure and is described in Exhibit 10. In this case, it is crucial for the bank to obtain assurance that it will be granted capital relief (because the assets are actually not sold). From the point of view of the investors, this transaction operates similarly to the CDO depicted in Exhibit 1. The only consideration is the need to have an assurance from the regulators that in the event the bank were to become insolvent, the assets of the CDO will not become part of the bank's bankruptcy proceedings. Or, presumably, if the sponsoring bank has a good credit rating (AA/Aa or higher) the investors might gain comfort knowing that the potential failure of the institution is unlikely and, in practical terms, their credit risk exposure is only to the loans in the transactions and not to the performance of the bank itself.

Market value CDO. Again, this CDO works similarly to the conventional cash flow CDO except for one significant modification—the OC test is specified using the market value of the collateral pool instead of the par value. This means the portfolio manager (and trustee) is required to

Exhibit 10: Balance-Sheet CDO, Linked and De-Linked Structures

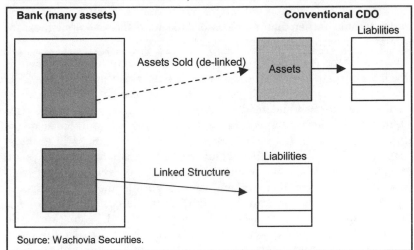

Source: Wachovia Securities.

monitor constantly the market value of the assets. For certain types of assets, typically illiquid assets, the manager is given some latitude. In dishonest hands, this feature could be abused. On the other hand, when dealing with liquid assets, there is less room to manipulate the OC test calculation. The capital structure of the market value CDO is based on the so-called advance rate concept. The advance rate expresses, in reference to the market value of the collateral pool (and after taking into account features such as the nature of the assets, their ratings and maturities), the amount of debt those assets can support. If the OC ratio is violated, the manager is required to sell some securities to pay down the most senior notes and bring the transaction back into compliance.

Static CDO. In this case, there is no manager and the collateral pool selected at the onset of the transaction does not change, except by natural amortization or events of default. In addition, some CDOs are referred to as lightly managed in the sense that the manager is permitted only a few trades per year, or is allowed to trade only under specific circumstances.

LEGAL ISSUES

The centerpiece of the CDO structure is the trust. Strictly speaking, although one might say that the CDO issues notes, the reality is that the notes are issued by a trust. In other words, a trust (also known as a special-purpose vehicle, or SPV) is the legal entity that owns the assets and issues the liabilities. The trust is a bankruptcy-remote entity for which the sole purpose is to hold the assets, and it cannot engage in any other activity (other than those associated with the CDO) such as, for example, entering into swap agreements.

In terms of the legal documents, the most important legal document is the indenture. In essence, the indenture is the "constitution" of the CDO and articulates, in excruciating detail, all of the rules governing the transaction. Investors should read — and, most important, understand — this document because although the indentures retain common elements from transaction to transaction, the scope of the variations in terms of important details are significant and crucial to grasp. More to the point, the indenture specifies in detail 1) the definition of collateral debt securities (i.e., the assets that can, and cannot, go into the collateral pool); 2) the waterfall and the precise definition of the cash diversion tests; 3) the trading rules, that is, what the manager can (and, again, cannot) do in terms of replacing (selling and buying) securities in the pool, reinvesting principal payments, the treatment of interest and principal proceeds and 4) investor's rights and, particularly important, voting rights in case the manager is to be replaced or removed.

In addition, investors should consider the provisions stated in the collateral management agreement, the swap confirmations and the surety policy (in case there is a monoline insurer).

BASIC QUANTITATIVE CONCEPTS

Different CDO market participants employ different methods to assess the risk/reward characteristics of a potential CDO tranche. These methods can go from dangerously simple to unnecessarily complex. That said, at the root of whatever method one employs, there are three basic elements that need to be addressed: 1) the default probability of the assets, 2) recovery rates and 3) portfolio correlation (or portfolio diversification). These are the building blocks of all possible quantitative approaches.

Default probability of the assets. This is the most important variable to estimate, for it is the one that has the most influence on the pool's performance and, therefore, the different notes' performance. The default probability of an asset depends on two factors: the tenor of the asset (easy to know) and its credit quality (more difficult to assess). The credit quality can be estimated using the ratings assigned by the rating agencies, credit default swap prices, KMV analysis, fundamental analysis (a euphemism that reflects somebody's opinion based on the entity's balance sheet and industry outlook) or simply a combination of all these pieces of information plus whatever insight the analyst might add. In addition, many companies use proprietary models that allegedly do not have the flaws of the techniques mentioned. In any event, once a probability of default is assigned to an asset, it can be used in a modeling effort, or it can be used to calculate an average probability of default that describes the portfolio as a whole with a single number. Exhibit 11 provides some reference information regarding default probability values based on credit ratings. In most models, the default probability — either at the asset level or pool (aggregate) level — is treated deterministically, that is, characterized by one number. In reality, of course, this variable is stochastic.

Exhibit 11: Typical Default Probability Values Based on Ratings for Some Selected Categories

Investment-Grade Ratings				Speculative-Grade Ratings			
S&P/ Fitch	Moody's	Moody's 10-Year Default Rates	Interpretation	S&P/ Fitch	Moody's	Moody's 10-Year Default Rates	Interpretation
AAA	Aaa	0.01	Highest Quality	BB+	Ba1	9.4	Likely to Fill Obli-
AA+	Aa1	0.10		BB	Ba2	13.5	gations; Ongoing
AA	Aa2	0.20	High Quality	BB-	Ba3	17.7	Uncertainty
AA-	Aa3	0.40		B+	B1	22.2	High Risk
A+	A1	0.70	Strong	B	B2	27.2	Obligations
A	A2	1.20	Payment	B-	B3	34.9	
A-	A3	1.80	Capacity	CCC+	Caa1	47.7	Current
BBB+	Baa1	2.60	Adequate	CCC	Caa2	65.0	Vulnerability
BBB	Baa2	3.60	Payment	CC	Caa3	80.7	to Default
BBB-	Baa3	6.10	Capacity	C	Ca	100.0	In Bankruptcy
				D	D	100.0	or Default

Source: Moody's Investors Service, Inc.

Recovery rate (or value). This is simply the value of an asset after it has defaulted. This information is also important in any modeling effort for the severity of the loss (the amount actually lost in a default event) is represented by the par value of the asset minus the recovery rate. Recovery rates are in general easier to estimate because there are more data. The values are a function of the seniority of the asset and the jurisdiction in which the entity issuing the security is domiciled. Exhibit 12 provides some idea of these values. Again, these are stochastic variables (there is some evidence that beta distributions are a reasonable characterization of the stochastic behavior of recovery values). That said, most market participants treat this variable as deterministic.

Exhibit 12: Typical Recovery Values for Some Common Assets

Loan/Bond Seniority	Median Default Rates	Mean Default Rates	Standard Deviation
Sr. Sec. Loans	73.0%	68.5%	24.4
Sr. Unsec. Loans	50.5%	55.0%	28.4
Sr. Sec. Bonds	50.0%	51.6%	26.9
Sr. Unsec. Bonds	31.0%	36.1%	25.0
Sr. Sub. Bonds	27.0%	32.5%	23.9
Sub. Bonds	29.0%	31.1%	21.4
Jr. Sub. Bonds	16.9%	24.5%	19.7

Source: Moody's Investors Service, Inc.

Correlation. Portfolio correlation, that is, the extent to which the default behavior of all of the assets in the pool "move in tune with one another," is by far the most difficult variable to estimate. The difficulties are caused by many factors. First, default correlation, which is the correlation we are interested in estimating, is difficult to observe (not enough data) especially for high-quality assets because defaults are rare. Second, the few data available are often contradictory. Correlation also changes over time. Finally, the experience of using other variables (e.g., equity prices) as a proxy to estimate default correlations is mixed at best. To make matters worse, correlation is not one number that one must estimate; it is *several* numbers. In fact, correlation is captured by a matrix, an N × N matrix in the case of a portfolio of N assets. The diagonal of the matrix consists of 1s, and it is symmetric, thus, in the case of portfolio of N assets, $(1/2)$ N (N – 1) coefficients must be estimated. For example, a 10-asset portfolio (a fairly small portfolio by any standard) would require one to estimate $(1/2)$ 10 × 9 = 45 correlation coefficients.

That said, any investor making an assessment of a potential CDO position must make an assumption regarding portfolio asset correlation. One common simplification that almost all market practitioners have embraced is to define the correlation between two assets as a function of the industries (or geographical region) that characterize each asset. In this context, it is assumed, for instance, that the correlation between any bond issued by a telecommunications company and any bond issued by a mining company is always the same: a constant number specified a priori and dictated by the two industries.

In principle, there are two schools of thought when dealing with correlation: 1) the diversity score approach pioneered by Moody's and 2) the full correlation matrix approach. The idea of ignoring correlation altogether, a practice regrettably adopted in the past by some misguided souls, has been discarded.

Moody's diversity score. The idea behind the diversity score is to replace the actual collateral pool (e.g., a heterogeneous pool of assets in terms of par value, default probability recovery rate) with a homogeneous pool consisting of DIV assets and having all of the same characteristics. The question, of course, is how to choose DIV—the number of equal size (par amount) assets—that collectively replicate the loss behavior of the original pool[1].

Let us introduce some notation. Let $\rho_{i,j}$ represent the correlation coefficient between asset i and asset j (specified by the industry to which these assets belong); p_i denotes the default probability of asset i, and F_i denotes the par amount of asset i. It can be shown that that if we choose DIV as

   DIV= A / B

where

$$A = \left(\sum_i p_i F_i \right) \left(\sum_j q_j F_j \right)$$

$$q_j = 1 - p_j$$

and

$$B = \sum_i \sum_j F_i F_j \rho_{ij} \sqrt{p_i q_i p_j q_j}$$

the homogeneous portfolio of DIV assets replicates the mean and the standard deviation of the loss distribution of the original (heterogeneous) portfolio.

Several comments are in order. First, although the formula is general in the sense that no assumptions have been made in terms of the correlation values, $\rho_{i,j}$, Moody's has further made the simplification that the correlation for assets in the same industry is about 17%, whereas the default correlation for assets in two different industries is 0%. (Moody's uses different correlation coefficients for CDOs backed by nontraditional

---

1. A. Cifuentes et al., "Buying and Selling Credit Risk," Chapter 8, in *Credit Derivatives*, RISK Books, London, 1998.

asset classes such as tranches of asset-backed securities [ABS] and commercial mortgage-backed securities [CMBS]). Thus, one could use the diversity score approach with whatever correlation assumptions one deems reasonable.

Second, as powerful as it is, the diversity score has some limitations. In general, it does not capture well the behavior of "unbalanced" (heterogeneous) portfolios. For example, a pool in which one asset accounts for 15% of the portfolio and all others account for about 2% each might not be suitable for a diversity score characterization. Finally, when using the diversity score approach, the collateral pool, in terms of its other attributes (e.g., recovery rates and default probabilities) is characterized using average values.

A simplified version of the diversity score calculation is given below.

$$DIV = A / B$$

where

$$A = \left(\sum_i F_i \right)^2$$

and

$$B = \sum_i \sum_j F_i F_j \rho_{ij}$$

For most practical purposes, this second formula is adequate.

The higher the diversity score (DIV), the more diversified the collateral pool. In general, a value higher than 50 provides, for most practical purposes, enough diversification. The use of the diversity score concept in a modeling context is dealt with later in this chapter.

Correlation matrix approach. In this context, the entries in the correlation matrix are determined by the industries to which the two assets belong. With this characterization, one is forced to use a Monte Carlo simulation to model the default behavior of the pool of assets.

In general, most practitioners specify the so-called asset correlation as a function of the two industrial sectors involved. Then, taking into account the probability of default of each asset, one estimates the default probability correlation. This is done, in most cases, using a combination of Cholesky decomposition and copula approach. This approach is discussed in more detail in a previous publication.[2] Exhibit 13 shows some typical default correlation values between certain industrial sectors, just to give a sense of the range of these coefficients. At present, there is a great deal of debate as to what the correct asset correlation values are. This debate will likely continue for the foreseeable future. In any event, investors should be wary of the frequently false sense of accuracy that is attributed to anything that has the name "Monte Carlo" in it, especially if the Monte Carlo is based on dubious correlation assumptions.

Exhibit 13: Commonly Used Correlation Values

Average Probability of Default	Implied Inter-Industry Default Correlation (Average)			Implied Intra-Industry Default Correlation (Average)		
	Moody's	S&P	Fitch	Moody's	S&P	Fitch
1%	0.00%	0.00%	3.20%	17.00%	6.30%	5.30%
2%	0.00%	0.00%	4.90%	17.00%	7.80%	8.30%
3%	0.00%	0.00%	5.60%	17.00%	9.20%	9.20%
4%	0.00%	0.00%	8.60%	17.00%	9.60%	10.20%
5%	0.00%	0.00%	9.20%	17.00%	10.60%	11.00%
10%	0.00%	0.00%	9.00%	17.00%	13.70%	13.70%
15%	0.00%	0.00%	11.70%	17.00%	15.20%	16.10%
20%	0.00%	0.00%	13.10%	17.00%	16.40%	17.60%
30%	0.00%	0.00%	14.50%	17.00%	18.70%	18.90%

Source: Fitch Ratings, Moody's Investors Service, Inc., and Standard and Poor's Corp.

THE RATING AGENCIES' APPROACH

The rating agencies, due to their role as quasi-regulators, enjoy a tremendous amount of power over the structured-finance market in general, and the CDO market in particular. With the advent of Basel II, this power will likely be enhanced. Broadly speaking, the rating agencies, by assigning a specific rating to a CDO tranche, determine whether certain institutions can invest in such an instrument, what capital reserves the investor must set aside (in case the note in question defaults) or simply whether the investment banker will be successful in finding suitable investors, because certain participants would, under no conditions, consider an unrated note. In addition, there is a high correlation between the interest a note must pay to entice investors and the rating of such note. Subsequent upgrades or downgrades by the rating agencies might

2. See a) Chapter 10 or b) *Default Correlation and Its Effect on Portfolios of Credit Risk*, Fitch Ratings, February 2003. Two additional useful articles are *On Default Correlation—A Copula Function Approach*, David Li, The RiskMetrics Group [www.riskmetrics.com] or *Random Variables, Joint Distribution Functions and Copulas*, A. Sklar, Kybernetica 9, 1973, pages 449–460.

force sales (certain investors cannot hold assets with a rating below certain levels), affect prices and influence the secondary market liquidity of a tranche. Moreover, in some extreme cases, the rating agencies might refuse to rate a transaction. In practical terms, this can kill the transaction.

The qualitative aspect of issuing a rating involves assessing the competence of the collateral manager, making sure that the legal structure (trust) is sound from a taxation and bankruptcy remoteness point of view and that the provisions in the indenture, management agreement, swaps agreement, etc., protect the interests of the bondholders.

From a quantitative viewpoint, the idea is to ensure that each of the notes in the liability structure meets certain specific requirements. The specific requirements depend on the rating agency, and the agencies are different conceptually and operationally. We describe briefly the key points of each agency analysis. In what follows, we assume the banker (and ideally the collateral manager) has access to what is generically referred to as a cash flow model. In this context, a cash flow model refers to a computer model that receives as input the cash (principal and interest) generated by the collateral pool and then, by replicating all of the provisions in the waterfall, calculates the amount of cash distributed to each tranche. This model is deterministic in the sense that the assumptions regarding what constitutes a likely default scenario (or the likelihood that such a scenario could happen) are handled outside the model.

The methods employed by the rating agencies are described briefly below.

Moody's. This approach is based on the diversity score concept (explained before) and the binomial expansion method, also known as the BET method.[3] The idea is to determine the expected loss associated with each tranche. Moody's ratings are based on the expected loss concept, and as long as the expected loss for a given tranche falls within a certain prescribed range (which also depends on the tenor of the note) the tranche in question is assigned the corresponding rating. The expected loss (EL) is calculated using the following equation:

$$EL = \sum_{j=0}^{DIV} P_j L_j$$

---

3. A. Cifuentes and G. O'Connor, *The Binomial Expansion Method Applied To CBO/CLO Analysis*, Moody's Investors Service, Special Report, December 1996.

where DIV denotes the diversity score, L_j is the loss suffered by the tranche under consideration in case there are j defaults, and P_j designates the probability that the collateral pool could have j defaults. Such probability, P_j is calculated (using the binomial formula) as follows:

$$P_j = \binom{DIV}{j} p^j (1-p)^{DIV-j}$$

where p is the average default probability of the pool (based on the Moody's rating of each individual asset).

The loss (L_j) for each scenario is determined using the cash flow model and obviously takes into consideration not only the waterfall but also the recovery rates assigned by Moody's. In short, this approach decomposes the collateral pool into DIV uncorrelated assets, and by computing the loss (for the note under study) under 0, 1, 2, ..., DIV defaults, attempts to cover all the possible default scenarios. Exhibit 14 summarizes this process.

S&P. S&P's approach is based on the probability of default concept (as opposed to expected loss). S&P has developed a computer model known as CDO-evaluator (aptly nicknamed the Black Box), which takes as input the characteristics of each of the assets in the collateral pool (e.g., S&P rating, par amount and maturity). The output is the so-called scenario default rate (SDR). Each target rating is characterized by a different SDR. In this case, the user's (banker or manager) cash flow model is used to determine the maximum collateral pool cumulative default rate (CDR) that does not result in a loss for the tranche under study. This default rate, known as the break-even (B/E) rate, must be less than the SDR to obtain the desired rating. The Black Box uses a Monte Carlo simulation technique. S&P employs a correlation matrix in which assets in different industries are assumed to have zero correlation, and assets in the same industry always have the same asset correlation (30%). Exhibit 15 summarizes this process. S&P has made the CDO-evaluator available to all market participants. However, a full description of the architecture of the Monte Carlo method used by the CDO-evaluator (or the source code) has not been made. Sometimes investors and bankers have found this a little unsettling because, as is often the case with any black-box system, one has difficulty identifying the variables that have a greater influence on the output. This could be somewhat frustrating when structuring a CDO with specific goals in mind.

Exhibit 14: Moody's Investors Service, Inc., Approach for Rating CDOs

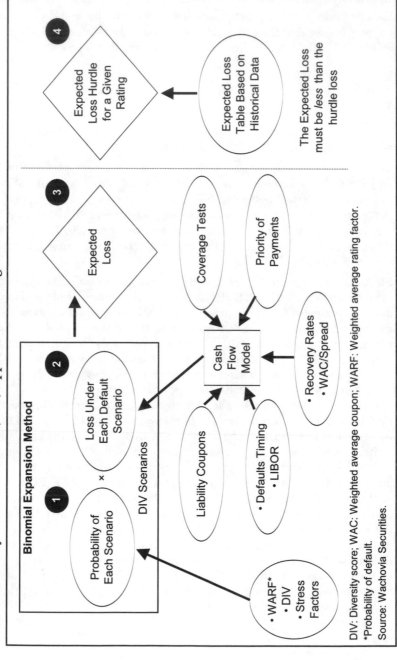

DIV: Diversity score; WAC: Weighted average coupon; WARF: Weighted average rating factor.
*Probability of default.
Source: Wachovia Securities.

Exhibit 15: Standard & Poor's Corp. Approach for Rating CDOs

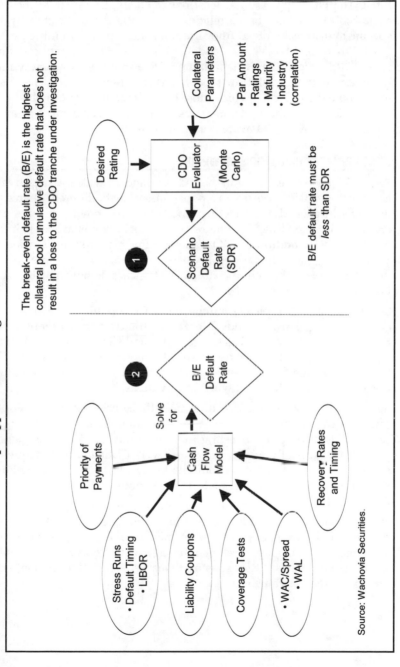

The break-even default rate (B/E) is the highest collateral pool cumulative default rate that does not result in a loss to the CDO tranche under investigation.

Source: Wachovia Securities.

Fitch. The Fitch approach, at least conceptually, is similar to the S&P approach except that the correlation assumptions are dictated by the specific industries involved (they are not constant) and, in this case, the Black Box (called the Vector Model), produces both the rating default rate (RDR), which is equivalent to the SDR, and the asset recovery rates to be used with the cash flow model. The cash flow model is then used to compute the B/E rate, which must be less than the RDR to obtain the desired rating. Exhibit 16 summarizes the method. The comments made regarding the S&P CDO-evaluator apply here also.

CDOS FROM THE INVESTOR'S VIEWPOINT

As explained before, investors buy CDO tranches with the objective of gaining diversified exposure to a pool of assets, with different degrees of leverage. In general, the CDO tranches offer risk/reward profiles that are difficult to replicate with more conventional bonds available in the open market. In addition, CDO tranches offer higher spreads, vis-à-vis bonds having the same ratings. Investors, in turn, give up some liquidity because, due to their complexity, CDO tranches do not enjoy the same liquidity as a conventional bond.

Senior tranches are typically purchased by CP conduits, SIVs, insurance companies and pension funds. Mezzanine tranches attract more or less the same investors, as well as hedge funds and CDOs of CDOs. Finally, equity tranches—which are treated as alternative investments—are also bought by hedge funds, pension plans, insurance companies, endowments and private (high net worth) individuals.

Senior and mezzanine investors buy their notes directly. Equity investors can certainly do that, and they often do it. However, more recently, the concept of investing in CDO equity via a fund is gaining popularity, especially with newcomers. Also, CDO equity is frequently structured as a combo note (a combination of CDO equity and senior or mezzanine note) or as a principal-protected note.

In addition to the characteristics mentioned at the beginning of this chapter (matched funded leverage at low funding cost), CDOs enjoy the benefits of the watchdog role performed by the rating agencies, the advantage of having a professional manager with credit expertise on the assets in question and little exposure to market value ("liquidation") risk (except for market value CDOs.)

Exhibit 16: Fitch Ratings Approach for Rating CDOs

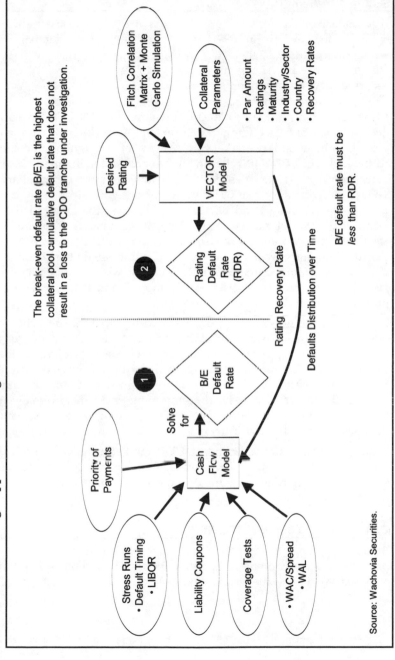

The break-even default rate (B/E) is the highest collateral pool cumulative default rate that does not result in a loss to the CDO tranche under investigation.

B/E default rate must be *less* than RDR.

Source: Wachovia Securities.

SECONDARY MARKET

A secondary market for CDO tranches was virtually nonexistent in 1988 but began to take shape in 1999. It got started slowly, focusing mainly on senior pieces. In 2000, there was consistent two-way flow with Bear, Stearns & Co., Inc., Lehman Brothers Holdings Inc. and Wachovia Securities playing an active role. Finally, this market took off with gusto after Pacific Investment Management Co. (PIMCO) liquidated the former Abbey National portfolio in 2003.[4] Today, all major CDO dealers are involved in secondary trading to some extent. An additional factor in the growth of the secondary market was the wave of downgrades that affected the high-yield CDO tranches in 2000 and 2001, forcing many institutions and vehicles to sell their positions to avoid onerous capital charges. Today, the secondary market is more robust, with stronger liquidity even for mezzanine (B and BB) pieces. That said, the market is by no means mature. Volume has surged to approximately $300 million–$500 million per month (precise figures are difficult to verify) and includes both tranches in "good standing" and those that are distressed. There is also a limited market for CDO equity, which, incidentally, and just by way of comparison, is slightly more liquid than, for example, private equity.

In addition, the growth in secondary trading has been propelled, no doubt, by an increase in market transparency, as trustee reports are available electronically and standardized computer runs have made it easier to make first approximations in terms of performance comparisons. Also, investors have become more sophisticated, and the use of complex computer models has become more widespread. Finally, the increase in liquidity has led investors to perceive CDO tranches as more than just buy-and-hold instruments.

Major participants in the secondary CDO market include certain hedge funds, specialized distress debt funds, CDOs of CDOs, opportunistic special situation funds, insurance companies, banks, conduits and money managers. In short, this is no longer a niche market.

EVALUATION OF A CDO INVESTMENT

Broadly speaking, the evaluation of a potential CDO investment encompasses two stages: preliminary evaluation and in-depth quantitative analyses. We discuss them in more detail below.

---

4. The notional amount of this portfolio was probably in the $5 billion–$10 billion range.

Preliminary evaluation. This stage, which is rather qualitative in nature, can be broken down into four tasks.

- **Asset/portfolio considerations.** This involves making an independent assessment of the portfolio credit quality, that is, looking beyond the ratings provided by the rating agencies. In fact, one important factor investors should be concerned about is the possibility of having "misrated" assets, that is, assets that could be a lot riskier than indicated by the credit ratings. Also, investors should look at portfolio concentrations (or the degree of diversification), pricing and CCC/Caa assets. In terms of the CCC/Caa assets, it is critical to make an assessment of their immediate default likelihood and recovery values.

- **Manager evaluation.** This is an important factor, especially for equity investors. All things equal, the relevance of the manager is inversely proportional to the investor's seniority in the capital structure.

  In terms of objective factors, investors should focus on the structure of the organization (key personnel and retention agreements) and financial situation (sources of revenue, the likelihood that revenue could be interrupted, future capital commitments/expenses and key financial ratios). Also, previous experience with CDOs and the asset class considered in the transaction, as well as the performance of previous transactions (portfolio par losses, trading gains/ losses and record against relevant indexes) should be taken into account. Finally, the technical self-reliance of the manager must be evaluated, based in part on in-house systems/models, third-party software and compliance/back-office procedures.

  Among the chief subjective factors are the manager's motivation for doing the transaction and the degree of expertise on CDO technology, with particular emphasis on the manager's understanding of the transaction "mechanics" — including trading limitations, cash diversion tests, treatment of defaulted securities and reinvestment provisions. In addition, the manager should be able to explain the rationale behind the acquisition of each asset and any previous trading decisions, and also demonstrate the ability to make independent, "against the flow" decisions, as well as some degree of nimbleness. An investment process clogged with memos and committees is not always a sure recipe for avoiding disasters.

  In addition, investors should examine what, for the lack of a better name, we describe as character issues: trading patterns exhibited by previous CDOs managed by the same people/organization, past interpretations of indenture provisions that give latitude to the manager and, in short, the willingness to make good long-term decisions for the benefit of a transaction instead of focusing on short-term goals (e.g., receiving the subordinated manager fee).

Finally, some investors are overly concerned with whether the manager of the CDO has taken an important equity position in the transaction at hand ("has skin in the game"). Evidence suggests that this concern is misguided, for there is no evidence indicating that CDOs in which the manager did not invest at the equity level have performed any better or worse than others.

- **Structural considerations.** This refers to understanding the provisions in the indenture, which are, essentially, the rules of the game for the transaction under consideration. The definition of an eligible asset, trading restrictions, waterfall structure, controlling class language, basket limitations, reporting requirements, the definition of OC and IC tests, trigger levels and collateral quality tests are all among the most important of these provisons.

- **Legal/other issues.** This refers to reviewing the documentation and legal opinions to understand the taxation issues, event of default definitions, liquidation and voting rights, true sale opinions and the management agreement, particularly provisions regarding replacing the manager. Also, the responsibilities of the trustee should be clearly understood.

In-depth quantitative analyses. This step assumes that the investor, somehow, has made an independent assessment of the three key elements that characterize the credit risk of the pool, namely, the probability of default of the assets, the recovery rates and the portfolio correlation. Also, it assumes the investor has access to a cash flow (e.g., waterfall provisions and hedge) model of the transaction.

First, the investor should carry out a sequence of "What-If" scenario analyses (essentially a series of analyses that do not take into account any probabilistic dimension) simply to detect possible weakness of the transaction, or more precisely, the tranche(s) under scrutiny. The goal is to detect, for example, which percentage of the collateral pool needs to default before the cash flows to the tranche under study are shut off, or to determine what could happen to the tranche if certain "weak" (high credit risk) assets default rather quickly (shortly after closing the transaction). Also, the "cushion" in the OC and IC tests should be analyzed (i.e., the number of defaults necessary to violate the triggers). Finally, the sensitivity of the tranche performance with respect to changes in the interest rate (LIBOR) environment must be investigated. A tranche that is too sensitive to changes in interest rates might indicate a bad hedge arrangement. In essence, the concept here is to capture as much information as possible regarding the tranche in question by looking at many "representative" scenarios. Of course, what constitutes a "representative" scenario (ideally, a scenario that reveals a weakness of the transaction) is a matter of personal judgment and experience.

The second family of analyses should incorporate a probabilistic dimension (the likelihood that a given default scenario could occur). This could be done using a Monte Carlo simulation or a binomial expansion technique (either a la Moody's or other variations of it[5]). In any case, the goal is the same: to estimate the mean (and ideally, the standard deviation) of some relevant performance variable (e.g., the IRR of the tranche, loss and payback period) An important component of this step is the stability analysis of the tranche. The idea here is to identify the variables that are the most influential in the performance of the tranche and quantify the effect of a change in these variables on the ultimate performance of the tranche. This is critical, for frequently one must struggle with insufficient (or worse, contradictory) data. A final word of caution: Monte Carlo analyses based on dubious correlation matrices (or without a stability analysis) are often deceiving. They can give an appearance of accuracy to what is actually nothing but numerical toxic waste.

The third and final step (a step almost always forgotten) is to look at the potential CDO investment in a portfolio context. One must ask, "How does this investment fit with the rest of the investor's holdings? Does it add enough diversification? Is it highly correlated with other previous investments?" Finally, there is the price issue—an investment only makes sense at a certain price.

---

5. An important variation of the typical Moody's BET is described in *The Double Binomial Method and Its Application to a Special Case of CBO Structures* (A. Cifuentes et al., Moody's Investors Service, Inc., Special Report, March 1998). An expansion of the BET method using stochastic recoveries is described in *Analyzing the Risk of Structured Credit (CDO) Tranches: The Modified Binomial Expansion Method* (A. Cifuentes et al., Triton Partners Research Report, September 2000). Finally, it should be mentioned that the BET method is general in the sense that the diversity score (DIV) can be computed with whatever correlation assumptions the investor might find appropriate.

CONCLUDING REMARKS

CDO technology has proved to be resilient and innovative. That probably explains why, more than 15 years after their entrance into the capital markets, CDOs still remain a central fixture of the structured-finance arena. What the future brings is unknown. What is certain, however, is that CDOs are flexible enough that, instead of disappearing, they will continue to transform themselves and create interesting structures and new challenges along the way.

The objective of this chapter has been to introduce the basic concepts of CDO investing to an audience unfamiliar with this topic, chiefly, new investors. Many colleagues and competitors have already written competent *Introduction to CDOs* pieces. With that in mind, it might be difficult to justify the need for yet another introduction to the topic, so we will not try. After all, the main motivation for writing anything, we think, is the self-centered conviction that one has something interesting to say. We just hope that at least somebody might find our attempt useful in some sense, maybe because we explained something in a slightly different fashion, or perhaps because we gave something a slightly different twist. To the extent that some readers might feel motivated to learn more about CDOs after going through our exposition, we will feel rewarded. Finally, we hope that in a few years, a much younger CDO practitioner will write a more complete and more innovative—that is, a much better—Introduction to CDOs.

CDO Market Sectors

Chapter 2

Understanding Commercial Real Estate CDOs

EXECUTIVE SUMMARY

Since the first issue in 1999, commercial real estate collateralized debt obligations (CRE CDOs) have emerged as one of the most attractive asset classes in the CDO market. CRE CDOs are debt obligations typically collateralized by a combination of commercial mortgage-backed securities (CMBS) and senior unsecured real estate investment trust (REIT) debt.[1] This chapter chronicles the rapid growth of the $13 billion CRE CDO market, the factors driving such growth, the market's performance, issuer motivations in sponsoring CRE CDOs (with specific examples) and key factors for investors to consider in the purchase of CRE CDOs. We also analyze the relative value of CRE CDOs versus other fixed-income instruments, arguing that they benefit from the overly conservative nature of the rating agencies' methodologies. Finally, we stress different types of CRE CDOs in light of the historic performance of the CRE markets and in so doing provide the investor with a methodology to discriminate among CRE CDOs.

A BRIEF HISTORY OF THE CRE CDO MARKET

As in the CMBS market, the Russian debt crisis in the fall of 1998 was a milestone in the CRE CDO market. In addition to causing significant losses for unhedged originators of unsecuritized CMBS collateral, it led to the demise of some of the most significant CMBS B-piece[2] buyers, most notably CRIIMI MAE. These highly leveraged investors would typically finance their purchases of CMBS B-pieces and subordinated debt, at least in part, with short-term repo financing. The Russian debt

---

1. Some CRE CDOs, such as CREST G-Star 2001-1, may have CRE whole loans as collateral although this is not as common.
2. B-piece is the market moniker for subordinate debt that protects higher-rated asset classes from losses.

crisis triggered margin calls, caused remarkable price volatility in the fixed-income markets and led to a significant repricing of risk. More significantly, it led to the demise of heavily leveraged books with duration and/or basis mismatches (including CMBS B-piece buyers). The departure of key B-piece buyers compounded CMBS price volatility and prolonged the recovery period. However, it also created fertile ground for the development of the real estate CDO market. Real estate CDOs filled a key need primarily because they are a non–mark-to-market, long-term financing vehicle backed by B-pieces of CMBS trans-actions. The old issues of margin calls, price volatility and the mismatch of short-term financing were eliminated. Indeed, it is no coincidence that many current B-piece buyers, such as Arcap, Blackrock, GMAC and Lennar, now use CDOs as a long-term, non–mark-to-market financ-ing vehicle.

Thus, although CDOs backed by corporate debt and emerging market debt (in that order) had existed for several years,[3] CRE CDOs did not emerge as an asset class until October 1999, when Moody's Investors Service, Inc., published its rating methodology for CDOs backed by commercial real estate.[4] Since then, CRE CDO issuance has nearly doubled each year to $13 billion outstanding across 28 deals (Exhibit 1).

Exhibit 1: CRE CDO Issuance by Year

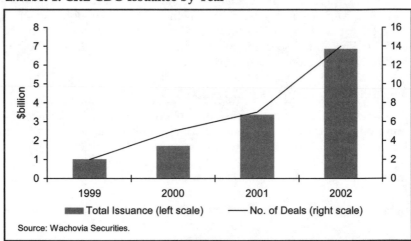

Source: Wachovia Securities.

3. ABS CDOs had existed for less than a year when CRE CDOs emerged.
4. See Moody's Structured Finance Special Report, *The Inclusion of Commercial Real Estate Assets in CDOs*, of Oct. 8, 1999, by H.Z. Remeza, J. Gluck and E.J. Choi.

In 2002 alone, nearly $7 billion was issued even as CMBS issuance declined over the previous year.

WHAT ARE CRE CDOS?

A CRE CDO is a special-purpose vehicle[5] (SPV) that finances the purchase of CMBS, REIT debt and other CRE assets by issuing, in 144A and "Reg. S" offerings, rated liabilities and equity (Exhibit 2). CRE CDOs are most frequently done as static pools[6] but can also be actively managed. The benefits and implications of each are key considerations for an issuer. A static pool does not permit trading of the underlying collateral except in the case of an impaired security (generally defined as a security that has been downgraded or defaulted). Static pools qualify for off-balance-sheet treatment by being structured as qualified special-purpose vehicles (QSPVs).

Actively managed deals allow a manager to express views by trading the contributed collateral, which may allow the manager to achieve additional returns vis-à-vis a static deal. Managed deals are typically not structured as QSPVs yet are still generally off-balance-sheet vehicles. Static pools are typically 100% "ramped up" or funded at closing (e.g., all the collateral securities have been purchased). Actively managed deals usually have a high percentage of assets purchased (greater than 75%) but are not necessarily fully "ramped up" in order to provide the manager flexibility in identifying relative value.

The sponsor, or collateral manager, of a CRE CDO, identifies the assets that will be sold into the trust and is paid an ongoing fee to monitor the performance of the collateral portfolio. Because of limitations placed on the collateral administrator by SPV guidelines, collateral bonds can only be sold when certain predefined events occur (referred to as trigger events) and any principal proceeds received by the trust cannot be used for reinvestment. Instead, proceeds must be applied to the redemption of the most senior class of notes outstanding.

CRE CDOs are generally quarterly pay transactions. Typically, the bond tranches rated A3/A- and higher are issued as floating-rate liabilities,

---

5. Located in the Cayman Islands.
6. A static pool CDO is collateralized by a pool of securities that remains predominantly unchanged over time. The asset manager of a static pool CDO may only sell a security if it has defaulted or is "credit impaired," and may at no time purchase new collateral into the portfolio. Static pool CDOs are fully ramped as of the transaction's closing date and are attractive because they allow investors to fully underwrite the portfolio before the closing date.

Exhibit 2: CRE CDO Diagram

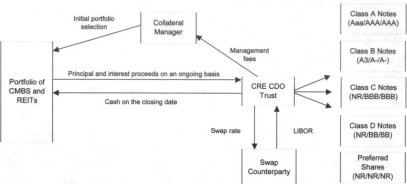

Source: Wachovia Securities.

whereas all other bonds are issued as fixed-rate liabilities. Because the vast majority of the collateral is fixed rate, a fixed-floating swap must be entered into by the trust with a counterparty acceptable to the rating agencies (Exhibit 2). In addition, because the REIT bonds are semiannual pay, the trust also will generally enter into a timing swap to match the REIT payments with the payments on the liabilities of the CRE CDO.

The CRE CDO bond tranches rated above BB generally receive "will" opinions[7] for debt for tax purposes and are ERISA-eligible; the tranches rated BB and below (with the exception of the equity) generally receive "should" opinions[8] and are restricted as to the amount that can be purchased with ERISA-eligible funds (24.9% of the tranche can be purchased with ERISA money). The senior notes in CRE CDOs are usually listed on an exchange, such as the Irish Stock Exchange Limited.

BORROWER MOTIVATIONS LEAD TO THE TWO BASIC TYPES OF CRE CDOS

CRE CDO issuers generally fall into one of two groups: B-piece buyers and special servicers who need to obtain non–mark-to-market financing for subordinate CMBS (financing transactions) and money managers

---

7. A "will" opinion refers to the tax opinion issued by deal counsel with regard to the liabilities issued by a CDO. The opinion states that a security will be treated as debt for U.S. income tax purposes and is generally issued for a CDO's investment-grade tranches. Investors should consult their accountants for further details.

8. Similar to a "will" opinion, a "should" opinion deals with the U.S. income tax treatment of a security issued by a CDO. The "should" opinion generally is issued with regard to the BB and B rated liabilities, tranches that, due to their subordinate position in the capital structure, may be viewed as equity interests in the CDO.

seeking increased assets under management (asset management transactions). As noted previously, B-piece buyers' and special servicers' needs were the initial impetus for the creation of CRE CDOs and continue to be a powerful force in the market. However, money managers make up an important and rapidly growing second group.

The CRE CDO issuer's motivation generally drives the capital structure of the transaction, as the ratings of the CMBS collateral determine the subordination levels for the rated debt tranches and thus the return profile for the equity. The CMBS portion of financing transactions is primarily rated below investment grade and can include the nonrated, first-loss B-piece of CMBS transactions. Although generally below investment grade, the collateral composition of financing transaction type CRE CDOs can vary considerably (Exhibit 3). For example, one of GMAC's CDOs, CREST G-Star 2001-1 shown in Exhibit 3, has a weighted average rating factor (WARF)[9] of 885. On the other hand, LNR CDO 2002-1 contained more than 64% of single-B and below, a WARF of 2157 and no REIT debt.

Exhibit 3: Collateral Composition of CRE CDOs—Financing Transactions

Deal	Collateral Contributor	WARF	% below BB	AAA Class Size	% REIT
G-Force 2001-1	GMACCM	2790	60%	16%	0%
CREST G-Star 2001-1	GMACCM	885	3%	72%	50%
CREST G-Star 2001-2	GMACCM	640	0%	76%	60%
LNR CDO 2002-1	LNR	2157	65%	12%	0%
Anthracite RE CDO	Anthracite	1290	29%	41%	22%
G-Force 2002-1	GMACCM	1874	41%	35%	0%
O-Otar 2002-1	GMACCM	641	6%	75%	48%

Source: Wachovia Securities.

Reflecting their historic role in the formation of the market, financing transactions closed to date total almost two-thirds of the real estate CDO market, or about $7.7 billion, and include those shown in Exhibit 4.

9. Moody's idealized cumulative default rate (ICDR) matrix serves to gauge expected cumulative default rates for corporate credits depending on Moody's rating and a given period of measurement (i.e., five years). The Moody's applicable weighted average rating factor (WARF) is derived from the ICDR matrix by taking the expected 10-year cumulative default rate for a credit and multiplying by 10,000. For instance, the 10-year expected cumulative default rate for a credit rated Baa2 is 3.60%, which equates to a Moody's WARF of 360. For a complete display of Moody's ICDR matrix and further information, see Appendix B.

Exhibit 4: Commercial Real Estate CDOs—
Financing Transactions Issued as of Dec. 31, 2002

Closing Date	Issuer	Collateral Manager	Type	Size ($million)	Original WARF	% AAA
9/01/99	Fortress Commercial Mortgage Trust 1999-PC1	Fortress	Financing	500.00	893	65%
10/01/99	DRT 1999-1	Wells Fargo	Financing	518.76	469	72%
3/31/00	Diversified REIT Trust 2000-1	Wells Fargo	Financing	287.15	474	68%
5/15/00	Mach One CDO 2000-1	Bank One	Financing	310.00	1,582	56%
4/05/01	G-Force 2001-1	GMACCM	Financing	861.79	2,790	16%
4/07/01	Ajax One, Ltd.	ING Barings	Financing	375.00	861	67%
9/06/01	CREST G-Star 2001-1	GMAC I.A.	Financing	500.00	885	72%
12/18/01	CREST G-Star 2001-2	GMAC I.A.	Financing	350.00	640	76%
4/22/02	G-Star 2002-1	GMAC I.A.	Financing	311.95	641	75%
5/16/02	CREST 2002-IG	Structured Credit	Financing	660.00	450	78%
5/29/02	Anthracite RE CBO I	BlackRock	Financing	515.92	1,290	41%
6/20/02	G-Force 2002-1	GMACCM	Financing	1,104.99	1,874	35%
7/09/02	Lennar CDO 2002-1	Lennar	Financing	800.63	2,157	12%
10/10/02	JER CDO 2002-1	J.E. Roberts Cos.	Financing	206.45	2,104	NA
12/10/02	Anthracite RE CBO II	BlackRock	Financing	363.42	1,290	52%
				7,666.06	1,311	52%

Fortress: Fortress Investment Group LLC; ING Barings: ING Barings Capital Corp.; Lennar: Lennar Partners, Inc.;
Structured Credit: Structured Credit Partners, LLC.
Source: Wachovia Securities.

G-Star 2001-1, a financing transaction for GMAC, is illustrative of the benefits of real estate CDOs for borrowers. Through this transaction, GMAC was able to obtain an advance rate superior to that available in the repo market on its below-investment-grade CMBS portfolio. This attractive advance rate is achievable in part because of the diversity that the contributed REIT collateral provides to the aggregate portfolio. In addition, GMAC retained the vast majority of the capital structure below the BBB rated liability tranche, as do most issuers of financing transactions (an attractive feature to many investors). The CRE CDO market

Exhibit 5: Capital Structure for G-Star 2001-1 Financing Transaction

Class	Amt. ($million)	% of Capital Structure	Moody's Rating	S&P Rating	Fitch Rating	Rated Spread/ Coupon	Original WAL (years)
Class A Notes	360	72.0%	Aaa	AAA	AAA	L + 47 bps	8.1
Class B-1 Notes	60	12.0%	A3	A-	A-	7.08%	9.8
Class B-2 Notes	15	3.0%	A3	A-	A-	L + 120 bps	9.8
Class C Notes	20	4.0%	Ba2	BB	BB	9%	11.4
Class D Notes	15	3.0%	B2	B	B	9%	11.8
Preferred Shares	30	6.0%	NR	NR	NR	NA	NA
Total	500	100.0%					

Source: Wachovia Securities.

enabled GMAC to achieve off-balance-sheet leverage, increasing its capital availability and diversifying its risk position while enhancing the yield on its below-investment-grade CMBS portfolio. The capital structure for G-Star 2001-1 is shown in Exhibit 5.

Asset management transactions, the other primary type of real estate CDO, total about $4.3 billion closed to date, or just under one-third of CRE CDOs outstanding, and include those shown in Exhibit 6.

Exhibit 6: Commercial Real Estate CDOs — Asset Management Transactions Issued as of Dec. 31, 2002

Closing Date	Issuer	Collateral Manager	Type	Size ($million)	Original WARF	% AAA
10/26/00	Duke Funding I	Ellington	AUM	300.00	648	87%
11/02/00	CREST 2000-1	Structured Credit	AUM	500.00	415	79%
12/06/00	Sutter RE 2000-1	Wells Fargo	AUM	325.00	982	75%
4/05/01	Pinstripe I CDO	Alliance	AUM	484.00	329	66%
11/15/01	Putnam CDO 2001-1	Advisory Group	AUM	300.00	366	82%
2/12/02	Storrs CDO Ltd.	Babson	AUM	398.50	423	81%
3/28/02	Newcastle CDO	Fortress	AUM	500.00	677	74%
5/22/02	TIAA RE CDO 2002-1	Teachers	AUM	500.00	585	75%
9/19/02	CREST Clarendon Street 2002-1	MFS	AUM	300.00	579	76%
11/20/02	G-Star 2002-2	GMAC	AUM	397.50	365	87%
11/26/02	Charles River CDO	TCW	AUM	300.00	412	88%
				4,305.00	**518**	**78%**

Alliance: Alliance Capital Management L.P.; AUM: Assets under management; Babson: David L. Babson & Co., Inc.; Ellington: Ellington Capital Management, LLC; Fortress: Fortress Investment Group LLC; Putnam: The Putnam Advisory Group; Structured Credit: Structured Credit Partners, LLC.
Source: Wachovia Securities.

A good example of an asset management transaction and the benefits to its issuer is CREST Clarendon Street 2002-1, on which MFS Investment Management (MFS) acted as collateral administrator. MFS, a predominantly total return mutual fund manager, was able to increase its assets under management while broadening its investor base, both in terms of geography (approximately one-third of the transaction was placed with European investors) and investor type (institutional versus retail).

Because CRE CDOs, like all cash flow CDOs,[10] are not marked to market, and because CREST Clarendon Street 2002-1 is a static pool that allows limited ongoing collateral administrator flexibility, MFS was able to

10. A cash flow CDO is a non–mark-to-market vehicle (either static or actively managed) that issues rated, term liabilities and first-loss equity in order to finance portfolios predominantly consisting of corporate and/or structured credit products.

focus on the roles of up-front underwriter and ongoing credit monitor rather than that of active trader. As with most asset management transactions, CREST Clarendon Street 2002-1 primarily consisted of investment-grade collateral (about 80%), resulting in the capital structure seen in Exhibit 7, of which MFS retained a percentage of the equity.

Exhibit 7: Capital Structure for CREST Clarendon Street 2002-1 – An Asset Management Transaction

Class	Amt. ($million)	% of Capital Structure	Ratings	Subordination	Original WAL (years)
Class A Notes	228	76.0%	Aaa/AAA	24.0%	7.3
Class B Notes	39	13.0%	A3/A-	11.0%	9.9
Class C Notes	15	5.0%	NR/BBB	6.0%	10.0
Class D Notes	10	3.3%	NR/BBB	2.7%	10.7
Preferred Shares	8	2.7%	NR/BB-*	NA	NA
Total	300	100.0%			

*Rated with respect to return of notional amount only.
Source: Wachovia Securities.

THE INVESTOR PROFILE: WHO BUYS REAL ESTATE CDOS

The universe of CRE CDO investors includes traditional CMBS conduit buyers seeking relative value, floating-rate international buyers and investors in other types of CDOs. As evidence of the widespread participation in the market, more than 80 institutional investors have purchased Wachovia's CRE CDOs. Although there is no readily attainable data on investors for the entire real estate CDO market, we believe investors in Wachovia's CRE CDOs, which account for more than 25% of CRE CDOs outstanding, are reasonably indicative of the investor breakdown. Almost two-thirds of CRE CDOs are purchased by financial institutions, such as banks, whereas another 25% are purchased by insurance companies (Exhibit 8). Money managers (7%) and a variety of other investors make up the balance.

Individual institutional investor patterns of CRE CDO investments may vary. Exhibit 9 shows a general breakdown of which financial institutions have bought what types of CRE CDO tranches. For example, although insurance companies and structured investment vehicles (SIVs) generally purchase the fixed- and/or floating-rate senior notes rated A or better, financial institutions (generally banks) have purchased these tranches but also lower-rated tranches down to BBs as well.

Some CMBS investors have bought lower-rated CRE CDOs than they typically would in a CMBS deal. Their reasons range from the superior

Exhibit 8: CRE CDO Investor Breakdown

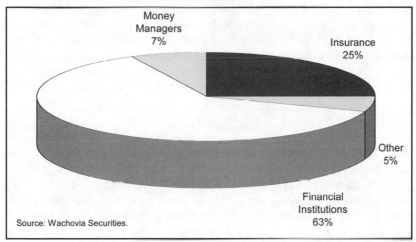

Money Managers 7%

Insurance 25%

Other 5%

Financial Institutions 63%

Source: Wachovia Securities.

diversity offered by CRE CDOs over CMBS, the reputations of the CRE CDO sponsors and the fact that CRE CDO sponsors often keep a portion of the equity. Indeed, in deals backed by lower-rated collateral (i.e., higher WARFs) the sponsors usually retain all of the equity.

Exhibit 9: Who Buys CRE CDOs

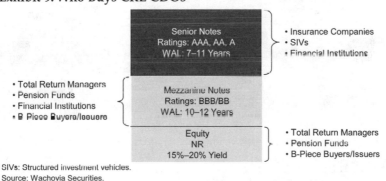

Senior Notes
Ratings: AAA, AA, A
WAL: 7–11 Years

• Insurance Companies
• SIVs
• Financial Institutions

• Total Return Managers
• Pension Funds
• Financial Institutions
• B-Piece Buyers/Issuers

Mezzanine Notes
Ratings: BBB/BB
WAL: 10–12 Years

Equity
NR
15%–20% Yield

• Total Return Managers
• Pension Funds
• B-Piece Buyers/Issuers

SIVs: Structured investment vehicles.
Source: Wachovia Securities.

A number of institutional investors prefer pure-play CRE CDOs. Pure-play CRE CDOs are backed exclusively by commercial real estate rather than a mix of asset types, such as asset-backed securities (ABS) and CMBS. Intuitively, this makes sense as many investors' risk management groups are split by asset type (e.g., real estate groups and ABS groups), making the underwriting of homogenous collateral more efficient. Although it is difficult to say that this preference unequivocally trans- lates into tighter pricing on pure-play deals, CREST Clarendon Street, a pure-play CRE CDO with a WARF of 579, achieved pricing in late August 2002 of LIBOR plus 48 bps on the floating-rate 7.3-year AAA and swaps plus 135 bps on the single-A fixed-rate tranche, which was regarded by market observers at the time as good.

Geographically, the investor base in Wachovia's CRE CDOs is nearly evenly split between U.S. domestic (48%) and international investors (52%) with a slight bias to the latter (Exhibit 10). Of the international investors, the British account for almost half (47%), followed by the Germans (34%), who are traditionally strong CRE investors. Belgian (4%), Austrian (4%) and Irish (3%) investors account for much of the European balance, however, investors from other European countries have also participated. Investors from around the world are included in the "Other" category, with Asian investors accounting for a growing share of the market.

Exhibit 10: Geographic Breakdown of CRE CDO Investors

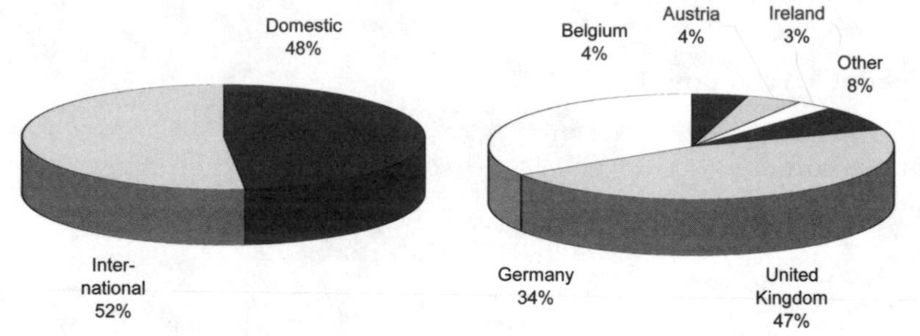

Domestic 48%

International 52%

Belgium 4%

Austria 4%

Ireland 3%

Other 8%

Germany 34%

United Kingdom 47%

Source: Wachovia Securities.

INVESTOR CONSIDERATIONS

Understanding WARF and D-Scores

Two key concepts investors need to understand in evaluating CRE CDOs (and other CDOs) are a deal's diversity, or D-Score,[11] and the WARF of a deal, both Moody's concepts. The D-Score is Moody's measure of the

11. For a more detailed explanation of how the D-Score is derived, see Appendix A.

diversity of the CDO collateral. The WARF is a measure of the riskiness of the collateral. The WARF for each deal is derived numerically from Moody's idealized corporate default rate (ICDR) matrix[12] by taking the expected 10-year cumulative default rate for a credit and multiplying by 10,000. For instance, the 10-year expected cumulative default rate for a credit rated Baa2 is 3.60%, which equates to a Moody's WARF of 360. Moody's ICDR matrix serves to gauge expected cumulative default rates for corporate credits depending on Moody's rating and a given period of measurement (e.g., five years). These two factors (WARF and D-Score) are important because they are the primary determinants of the subordination levels for CRE CDOs. The higher the WARF and the lower the D-Score (diversity), the greater the subordination level and vice versa.

WARFs and D-Scores: Are CRE CDOs Unfairly Penalized?

We believe Moody's current incorporation of its WARF and D-Score methodologies for CRE CDOs (and the corresponding methodologies used by Fitch and S&P) is conservative, perhaps overly conservative. As noted above, the WARF and D-Score of a deal drives the deal's subordination levels. One of Moody's fundamental assumptions is that CMBS and REITs are, by their nature, diverse and therefore default probability correlations among each CMBS and REIT industry group should be relatively high. For example, as shown in Moody's correlation matrix for CRE CDOs (Exhibit 11) Moody's assumes significant levels of correlation for various CMBS and REITs. In contrast, Moody's correlation matrix for corporate CDOs (not shown) assumes zero correlation among the various corporate sectors and 14% correlation between corporate assets within the same sector.

Intuitively, one would think that the more diverse, the lower the correlation, not the higher. Moody's reasoning is that because there are so many different properties backing CMBS and REIT cash flows that due to the law of large numbers, there is little diversification benefit from combining the tranches of different CMBS and different REIT debt in a CRE CDO. Moreover, they give little diversification "credit" for the different vintages of the CMBS in a CRE CDO even though research has historically demonstrated otherwise.[13] Finally, the ICDR is based on an empirical study of corporate defaults, which have historically been far in excess of CMBS defaults.

---

12. For a complete display of Moody's ICDR matrix, see Appendix B.
13. "The timing and total defaults of a cohort (or vintage) are highly dependent on its position in the real estate cycle." "Commercial Mortgage Defaults 1972–2000," by H. Esaki, *Real Estate Finance*, Winter 2002.

Exhibit 11: Moody's Correlation Matrix—Commercial Real Estate Sectors

	ABS-CMBS						REITs							
	Conduit	Conduit BIG*	CTL	CTL BIG*	Large Loan	Large Loan BIG*	Hotel	Multi-family	Office	Retail	Industrial	Health-care	Self-Storage	Diversified
ABS-CMBS Conduit	12.0%	14.5%	9.0%	11.0%	9.0%	11.0%	7.0%	7.0%	7.0%	7.0%	7.0%	7.0%	7.0%	8.0%
ABS-CMBS Conduit BIG*	14.5%	17.0%	11.0%	13.0%	11.0%	13.0%	7.0%	7.0%	7.0%	7.0%	7.0%	7.0%	7.0%	8.0%
ABS-CMBS CTL	9.0%	11.0%	18.0%	21.5%	9.0%	10.0%	6.0%	6.0%	6.0%	17.0%	6.0%	6.0%	6.0%	7.0%
ABS-CMBS CTL BIG*	11.0%	13.0%	21.5%	25.0%	10.0%	11.0%	6.0%	6.0%	6.0%	17.0%	6.0%	6.0%	6.0%	7.0%
ABS-CMBS Large Loan	9.0%	11.0%	9.0%	10.0%	18.0%	21.5%	6.0%	6.0%	6.0%	6.0%	6.0%	6.0%	6.0%	6.0%
ABS-CMBS Large Loan BIG*	11.0%	13.0%	10.0%	11.0%	21.5%	25.0%	6.0%	6.0%	6.0%	6.0%	6.0%	6.0%	6.0%	6.0%
REIT Hotel	7.0%	7.0%	6.0%	6.0%	6.0%	6.0%	18.0%	6.0%	6.0%	6.0%	6.0%	6.0%	6.0%	8.0%
REIT Multifamily	7.0%	7.0%	6.0%	6.0%	6.0%	6.0%	6.0%	18.0%	6.0%	6.0%	6.0%	6.0%	6.0%	8.0%
REIT Office	7.0%	7.0%	6.0%	6.0%	6.0%	6.0%	6.0%	6.0%	18.0%	6.0%	6.0%	6.0%	6.0%	8.0%
REIT Retail	7.0%	7.0%	17.0%	17.0%	6.0%	6.0%	6.0%	6.0%	6.0%	18.0%	6.0%	6.0%	6.0%	8.0%
REIT Industrial	7.0%	7.0%	6.0%	6.0%	6.0%	6.0%	6.0%	6.0%	6.0%	6.0%	18.0%	6.0%	6.0%	8.0%
REIT Healthcare	7.0%	7.0%	6.0%	6.0%	6.0%	6.0%	6.0%	6.0%	6.0%	6.0%	6.0%	18.0%	6.0%	8.0%
REIT Self-Storage	7.0%	7.0%	6.0%	6.0%	6.0%	6.0%	6.0%	6.0%	6.0%	6.0%	6.0%	6.0%	18.0%	8.0%
REIT Diversified	8.0%	8.0%	7.0%	7.0%	6.0%	6.0%	8.0%	8.0%	8.0%	8.0%	8.0%	8.0%	8.0%	13.0%

*Below investment grade (BIG).

Source: Moody's Investors Service, Inc.

The D-Score and the WARF are important because they are the two major drivers of subordination in CDOs. Because rating agency methodologies assume CMBS and REITs are more correlated than corporates, a corporate CDO with low-quality collateral could have the same level of subordination for its AAA tranche as a CRE CDO with much better quality collateral.[14]

For example, a typical assets-under-management (AUM) CRE CDO will have a WARF of approximately 400–600 (between Baa2 and Baa3) and a D-Score of 8–10 (low diversity). This type of transaction would likely be able to attain a AAA tranche equal to approximately 80% of its entire capital structure, or 20% subordination to the AAA tranche. A corporate CDO with a WARF of about 2200 (B1), much lower quality collateral, could have a D-Score of 45–55 (highly diversified) and thus would also be able to achieve a AAA tranche equal to 80% of the deal, or 20% subordination. As is readily apparent, although the CRE CDO collateral has a much lower default probability (measured by its WARF) than the corporate collateral, the corporate CDO achieves a comparably sized AAA tranche because the rating agencies assume corporate collateral is so diverse.

Looked at from another perspective, if a CRE CDO had low-rated collateral with a WARF of 2200, like the corporate high-yield CDO, Moody's would require as much as 65% subordination to the AAA versus 20% for a high-yield corporate CDO with the same 2200 WARF because of the CRE CDO's low diversity score (8 D-Score).

Although a complete refutation of Moody's methodology is beyond the scope of this chapter, the following analysis is indicative of why we believe this approach to rating CRE CDOs is overly conservative. In Exhibits 12 and 13, we show the break-even cumulative underlying collateral default rates necessary to "break" or cause discount margin impairment on the AAA rated and A- rated notes of a typical high-yield corporate CDO and a CRE CDO. We also show the break-even level of cumulative defaults necessary to "break" or cause yield impairment on the BBB rated notes of each CDO.

As is apparent, the cumulative default rates necessary to break the high-yield corporate CDO are higher than those needed to break the CRE CDO (see column 4 in Exhibits 12 and 13). One might think at first glance

14. Moreover, of the small number of industry groups (11) Moody's assigns for REITs and CMBS, only about eight are common, reducing their diversity score even further. The other three groups, healthcare REIT, hotel REIT and diversified REIT, are used less commonly.

that the high-yield corporate CDO is the more robust deal because the AAA tranche sizes are similar and the CRE CDO has less equity than the high-yield corporate CDO. However, as shown in column 5 in each exhibit for each deal, the CRE CDO has a much higher multiple of ICDR[15] than the high-yield corporate CDO at each tranche level. Moody's ICDR is the expected-case estimate of how many cumulative defaults the respective portfolios should experience given the weighted average life (WAL) and WARF of the collateral. For example, the AAA bond in the high-yield corporate CDO breaks at a cumulative default rate of 64.8%, which is approximately four times Moody's ICDR of 16.2%. The results show that the CRE CDO bonds are 1.5–3.1 times as strong as the high-yield corporate CDO bonds (column 4 in Exhibit 14).

Exhibit 12: High-Yield Corporate CDO — Break-Even CDR

Typical High-Yield Transaction*

Class Rating	Asset WAL	ICDR	Cumulative Default Rate	As a Multiple of ICDR	Tranche Size
AAA	3.3	16.2%	64.8%	4.0x	67.0%
A-	3.9	17.8%	53.1%	3.0x	10.7%
BBB	4.1	18.3%	48.8%	2.7x	3.5%

*Assumptions: 1) Collateral: 100% B2/B rated high-yield bonds; 2) Weighted average price: 91%; 3) Weighted average coupon: 10.75%; 4) Moody's diversity score: 45; 5) Annual fes and expenses as a percentage of total collateral amount: 0.48%; 6) Defaults: Begin 0.5 year from closing date at the rates shown; 7) Immediate recoveries; 8) Constant annual prepayment rate: 10%; and 9) Reinvestment period: five years.
Source: Wachovia Securities.

Exhibit 13: CRE-CDO — Break-Even CDR

CRE CDO

Class Rating	Asset WAL	ICDR	Cumulative Default Rate	As a Multiple of ICDR	Tranche Size
AAA	7.7	4.5%	55.6%	12.3x	76.0%
A-	7.8	4.6%	29.6%	6.4x	13.0%
BBB	7.9	4.6%	18.5%	4.0x	5.0%

Source: Wachovia Securities.

15. For a complete display of Moody's ICDR matrix, see Appendix B.

Exhibit 14: CRE CDO Quality versus Corporate High-Yield CDO Based on Moody's ICDR

Class Rating	High-Yield Transaction ICDR Multiple (HYM)	CRE CDO ICDR Multiple (CRE CDO Multiple)	CRE Multiple/HYM
AAA	4.0x	12.3x	3.1x
A-	3.0x	6.4x	2.1x
BBB	2.7x	4.0x	1.5x

Source: Wachovia Securities.

CRE CDOs versus High-Yield Corporate CDOs: Other Considerations

CRE CDOs also offer a number of beneficial features that high-yield corporate CDOs lack. CRE CDOs, unlike high-yield corporate CDOs, offer investors two levels of subordination: structural and asset level. For example, the BBB tranche of a hypothetical real estate CDO (Exhibit 15) has 6% subordination at the structural level. Assuming this real estate CDO was backed 100% by BB+ CMBS, the CDO tranche would benefit further from the initial 7% subordination of the BB+ CMBS tranches at the asset level. As a result, before a real estate CDO tranche becomes impaired, subordination on the underlying CMBS must first be eaten through by losses on the underlying loans. Indeed, the CMBS tranche itself can withstand losses on the underlying loans before experiencing losses of its own. Thus, real estate CDO equity, unlike high-yield corporate CBO equity, can withstand relatively stressed loan level losses without impairment due to the subordination of the underlying CMBS collateral.

Exhibit 15: Dual Subordination of a CRE CDO

Underlying CMBS		RE CDO	
Rating	Subordination	Rating	Subordination
BBB+	12%	AAA	25%
BBB+	10%	A-	10%
BBB-	9%	BBB	6%
BB+	7%	BB	3%
BB	5%	Equity	NA

Initial Subordination   Secondary Subordination

Source: Wachovia Securities.

Exhibit 16: Corporate CBO Transaction Matrix (1996–2001)

One-Year	Aaa	Aa1	Aa2	Aa3	A1	A2	A3	Baa1	Baa2	Baa3	Ba1	Ba2	Ba3	B1	B2	B3	Caa1	Caa2	Caa3	Ca/C	W/R
Aaa	94.63%		0.67%																		4.70%
Aa1		80.95%		14.29%																	4.76%
Aa2	0.50%		86.57%	3.98%	2.49%	1.99%	0.50%	0.50%	0.50%												2.99%
Aa3				88.68%	7.55%		1.89%			1.89%											
A1					66.67%	16.67%	8.33%														8.33%
A2						89.47%	5.26%														5.26%
A3							91.67%	4.17%				2.08%									2.08%
Baa1								85.71%										14.29%			
Baa2									93.38%	2.21%	0.74%	2.21%		1.47%							
Baa3										82.67%	3.47%	5.94%	1.49%	1.49%	0.99%	0.99%	0.99%				1.98%
Ba1											60.00%	10.00%			20.00%			10.00%			
Ba2												83.33%		1.67%	3.33%	1.67%	1.67%	1.67%	1.67%	3.33%	
Ba3													92.31%	2.56%	1.28%					1.28%	1.28%
B1														71.19%		6.78%	10.17%	1.69%	5.08%	5.08%	
B2															55.56%	11.11%	11.11%			22.22%	
B3																85.29%	2.94%	2.94%		8.82%	
Caa1																	30.00%	20.00%	10.00%	40.00%	

Source: Moody's Investors Service, Inc., "Credit Migration of CDO Notes, 1996–2001."

Moreover, unlike a high-yield CBO, the collateral in real estate CDOs is backed by tangible assets (the underlying properties) helping to support higher recovery rates when defaults occur. For example, various studies have shown average historic CRE loss severity rates of 31%–38%.[16] In contrast, in the past few years corporate bond loss rates have generally been closer to the recovery rates of CMBS (60%–70%).[17] Corporate bonds also have greater event risk than CMBS.[18]

CRE CDOs versus Corporate CDOs: Downgrades to Date

Although only a few years of performance history exist, the outperformance of CRE CDOs over corporate CDOs is telling. Although no CRE CDOs have been downgraded, significant numbers of high-yield corporate CDOs have been downgrades (Exhibit 16).

The relative performance of the collateral (Exhibits 17 and 18) has been important in the solid performance of CRE CDOs versus high-yield corporate CDOs. However, we believe the rating agencies' conservative approach to CRE CDOs, as well as the other factors noted previously, have played a key role in the outperformance of CRE CDOs and will continue to do so in the future.

Investor Considerations: CRE CDOs versus CMBS

One of the biggest attractions of CRE CDOs to CMBS mezzanine investors is the extra spread offered by CRE CDO mezzanine tranches. Similar-rated single-A CRE CDOs typically trade 50 bps wider than similarly rated CMBS, whereas CRE CDO BBBs trade approximately 75 bps–100 bps wider. Although some of this certainly represents the lower liquidity in mezzanine CRE CDOs, a portion of it represents limited investor understanding of mezzanine CRE CDOs—a perceived complexity premium, if you will. We would expect the extra spread offered by mezzanine CRE CDOs to narrow over time.

---

16. Source: "Commercial Mortgage Defaults: An Update," by H. Esaki, *Real Estate Finance,* Winter 2002. It is important to note that these severities are averages for all commercial real estate. Different property types typically exhibit significantly higher and lower severities. For example, hotels often exhibit average severities of around 50%, whereas apartment properties typically have 20% severities. However, CMBS have only had about 10% hotels historically. Following the events of 9/11, hotels have made up an even smaller percentage of CMBS deals.
17. Source: Moody's Investors Service, Inc.
18. Event risk in the CMBS market up until the World Trade Center disaster in New York City had been virtually nonexistent other than several acts of fraud. However, in most cases in the CMBS market, with some notable exceptions, loans have been insured against terrorism.

Exhibit 17: CMBS Transition Matrices (1991–2001)

	AAA	AA	A	BBB	BB	B	CCC - C	D
One Year								
AAA	100.00%							
AA	11.76%	88.24%						
A	1.45%	9.30%	89.16%	0.09%				
BBB	1.06%	1.55%	5.35%	91.62%	0.21%	0.07%	0.14%	
BB	0.40%	0.51%	1.01%	4.65%	92.73%	0.61%		0.10%
B	0.11%	0.22%	0.22%	1.00%	3.99%	92.58%	1.88%	
CCC - C					2.17%	3.26%	92.39%	2.17%
Two Year								
AAA	100.00%							
AA	19.41%	80.59%						
A	4.70%	13.17%	81.99%	0.13%				
BBB	2.04%	4.09%	9.19%	83.54%	0.57%	0.34%	0.23%	
BB	0.79%	1.59%	1.27%	7.95%	86.65%	1.75%		
B	0.34%	0.51%	1.02%	1.87%	6.46%	84.86%	4.76%	0.17%
CCC - C			2.08%		4.17%	12.50%	77.08%	4.17%

Source: Fitch Ratings, "Structured Finance Rating Transition Study."

Exhibit 18: Corporate Transition Matrices (1991–2001)

	AAA	AA	A	BBB	BB	B	CCC - C	D
One Year								
AAA	95.80%	3.84%	0.18%	0.18%				
AA	0.10%	92.32%	7.23%	0.31%		0.03%		
A	0.08%	3.03%	92.36%	4.20%	0.17%	0.02%	0.10%	0.04%
BBB		0.25%	5.38%	89.53%	3.34%	0.76%	0.44%	0.29%
BB			0.18%	6.88%	83.57%	4.73%	2.95%	1.70%
B				0.41%	9.47%	84.77%	3.50%	1.85%
CCC - C						12.30%	63.93%	23.77%
Two Year								
AAA	92.08%	7.28%	0.43%	0.21%				
AA	0.08%	86.35%	12.83%	0.70%	0.04%			
A	0.10%	6.16%	86.14%	6.84%	0.43%	0.03%	0.13%	0.18%
BBB	0.05%	0.28%	10.70%	81.94%	4.76%	0.94%	0.85%	0.47%
BB		0.12%	0.73%	10.68%	79.00%	4.25%	2.79%	2.43%
B			0.27%	2.41%	13.40%	79.62%	2.41%	1.88%
CCC - C						27.87%	63.93%	8.20%

Source: Fitch Ratings, "Structured Finance Rating Transition Study."

Although pricing on AAA- rated CRE CDOs tracks that of AAA- rated CMBS (see How CRE CDOs Trade for the relative performance of AAA CRE CDOs versus AAA CMBS), investors are attracted to CRE CDOs versus CMBS for other reasons. As in the case of CRE CDOs versus corporate high-yield CDOs, CRE CDOs offer CMBS investors an extra level of structural subordination.[19]

Investors also favorably regard the fact that the collateral behind CRE CDOs is more diverse than the collateral backing CMBS. A CRE CDO typically includes bonds of 15–25 CMBS conduit deals and a similar number of unsecured REIT bonds, which collectively have more than $100 billion of real estate supporting the bonds. This compares with the typical CMBS conduit deal that typically has approximately $1 billion of loans supporting the transaction and no REIT debt. As a result, CRE CDOs are more granular than CMBS deals, as the largest collateral positions rarely constitute more than 5% of a deal. In contrast, CMBS conduit deals frequently have single loans that constitute 7%–15% of the deal. Because CRE CDOs are backed by a number of different deals, the collateral is not only diverse across a greater variety of real estate loans than the typical CMBS but also, and most important, across a variety of vintages — a key determinant of commercial mortgage defaults.[20]

Advantages and Disadvantages of REIT Debt Inclusion

The REIT portion of CRE CDOs is nearly always investment grade and frequently constitutes 30%–50% of a deal. Notably, CMBS conduit deals, which contain no REIT debt, rarely have more than 15%–20% of investment-grade loans. In most CRE CDOs, REIT senior unsecured debt is included in the collateral portfolio to enhance the diversity and therefore the stability of the transaction. Moody's has only three principal

19. The vast majority of CMBS collateral consists entirely of whole loans with no structural subordination. However, a few loans backing CMBS are occasionally split into an "A" and a subordinated "B" note with only the "A" note being placed in the CMBS deal and the subordinated "B" note being held by a third party outside the deal. However, the vast majority of CMBS collateral consists entirely of whole loans with no structural subordination.

20. Vintage is a key component of commercial real estate defaults as it determines when in the real estate cycle a commercial loan is originated. For example, a loan originated when rents are at a peak and vacancies low may exhibit more stress than one originated at the bottom of the cycle. Although rating agency and B-piece discipline have forced underwriters to originate loans more conservatively at all times, in the real estate cycle vintage is still likely to be an important factor affecting defaults. For an analysis of the variation in defaults experienced by commercial real estate loans originated in different vintages, see "Commercial Mortgage Defaults 1972–2000," by H. Esaki, *Real Estate Finance,* Winter 2002.

CMBS categories it uses in its diversity score model, and thus the inclusion of REITs, for which there are eight categories for the purposes of diversity scores, reduces the aggregate portfolio default probability because REITs are appropriately assumed to be less correlated with CMBS. The primary purpose of including individual REITs is not to enhance the yield of the asset portfolio but rather to reduce the overall portfolio variance. However, the universe of investment-grade equity REITs that are appropriate for a CRE CDO (typically, healthcare and hospitality REITs are viewed as being too rating volatile for CRE CDOs) includes only 40–50 companies. Because inclusion of REITs outside of this universe creates an adverse selection problem, most CRE CDOs exhibit relatively substantive overlap across their REIT portfolios. Although we view this as an issue worthy of being addressed, we feel strongly that the benefits of including REITs in CRE CDOs greatly mitigate any overlap concerns.

The positive credit fundamentals exhibited by the majority of investment-grade REITs and the debt covenant packages that mandate that such fundamentals be preserved are the primary reasons why there has never been a default by an investment-grade equity REIT. The weighted average debt to total assets for an investment-grade REIT is usually about 50%, whereas all REITs covenant to maintain debt to total asset ratios lower than 60% (and secured debt to total assets of less than 40%). This compares favorably with the average loan-to-value (LTV) of loans included in CMBS conduit transactions, which is typically 65%–75% and we believe more than compensates investors for the unsecured nature of REIT debt.

In addition, unlike CMBS, the portfolio of properties owned by a REIT can continually change, as management teams have the ability to reduce/increase exposure to out-of-favor/attractive markets and properties. REIT asset portfolios are also generally of higher quality (based on property values) than those of CMBS.

The Benefits of Overcollateralization (OC) and Interest Coverage (IC) Tests

In addition to levels of structural subordination, CRE CDOs provide another level of protection that CMBS do not offer, overcollateralization (OC) and interest coverage (IC) tests. These performance tests further enhance interest and principal payments. When a CRE CDO breaches either an OC or IC trigger, collateral interest proceeds that otherwise would have been used to pay interest on the subordinate notes are used, along with any collateral principal proceeds, to redeem senior notes in an amount sufficient to bring the breached test or tests back into compliance. Such interest diversion preemptively deleverages the transaction, thus reducing its risk profile while benefiting the senior noteholders.

Although this would create negative convexity for the senior notes if they were fixed, 80% of the deal is floating rate and senior. Therefore, this is typically not an issue as the bonds being paid down after the breach of a trigger will likely be floaters.

This mechanism can create situations in which the subordinate notes are forced to capitalize interest, or PIK, which is acceptable pursuant to the terms of such subordinate notes and does not constitute an event of default. The protection afforded to the senior notes in a CRE CDO by the OC and IC triggers is also available to the subordinate notes once the senior notes have been redeemed in full.

Investor Considerations: CRE CDOs versus ABS CDOs

Beyond the fact that CMBS collateral has thus far outperformed ABS collateral, CRE CDOs exhibit greater average life stability and better convexity characteristics than ABS CDOs because of the significant prepayment protection in CMBS collateral.[21] Some ABS collateral, such as home equity ABS, has greater prepayment sensitivity and negative convexity.

CRE CDO PROTECTION: A HISTORIC CONTEXT

Rather than dwell on the protections afforded by CRE CDOs in the context of the solid performance of the CRE and CMBS markets for the past several years,[22] we thought it more conservative to look at those protections in the context of the more severely stressed CRE markets of the 1980s and early 1990s.

As noted previously, CRE CDOs, due to borrower motivations, are generally backed by, on average, investment-grade CMBS and REIT collateral (BBB- or higher) in the case of AUM CRE CDOs or non-investment-grade collateral in the case of many financing

---

21. The vast majority of CMBS, particularly those issued after 1998, have strong prepayment protection in the form of lockout, Treasury defeasance, yield maintenance agreements and other prepayment penalties.
22. For a current in-depth analysis of the CMBS and commercial real estate markets and their outlook, see Wachovia Securities' CMBS and Real Estate research reports, *The Outlook for CMBS and Commercial Real Estate* (October 2002) and *The Outlook for Commercial Real Estate by Property Sector* (October 2002).

transactions. In the case of CRE CDOs backed by investment-grade CMBS, such as many AUM CRE CDOs, the subordination levels of the lowest investment-grade CMBS collateral in those CRE CDOs in nearly all cases would be sufficient to absorb the average 10-year historic CRE losses experienced over the past three decades. The average 10-year cumulative default rate for CRE loans according to an update of a prominent and widely referenced study was 18.4% beginning in 1972[23] (Exhibit 19). Using the severity calculations in that study, the average cohort lost 4.9% of its original balance.[24] Because BBB- CMBS subordination levels range from 5% to 10% and BBB CMBS subordination levels range from 6% to 12%, "investment-grade CMBS would be protected against the average loss of commercial real estate origination cohorts of the last 30 years"[25] (Exhibit 20).

Exhibit 19: Lifetime Default Rates by Origination Cohort (by loan count)

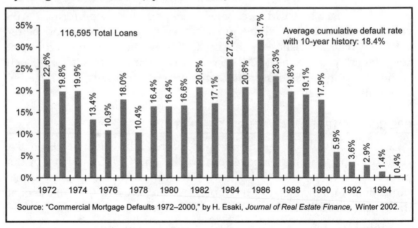

Source: "Commercial Mortgage Defaults 1972–2000," by H. Esaki, *Journal of Real Estate Finance,* Winter 2002.

23. Source: "Commercial Mortgage Defaults: An Update," by H. Esaki, *Real Estate Finance,* Winter 2002.
24. To calculate losses, the study found that 59% of loans entering default were eventually liquidated, 39% were restructured and 1% became current again. Foreclosed loans were found to have a 34% severity rate (including interest, expenses and principal) and the assumption of 17% severity was made for restructured loans—the latter assumption sometimes being disputed with some market participants believing that restructured loans have close to a 0% severity and others arguing that it should be higher. Given the assumptions, the loss of 4.9% is calculated as follows (18.4% × .59% × .34%) + (18.4% × .39% × .17%) = 4.9%.
25. Source: "Commercial Mortgage Defaults: An Update," by H. Esaki, *Real Estate Finance,* Winter 2002.

Exhibit 20: Historic Losses versus CMBS Tranche Subordination

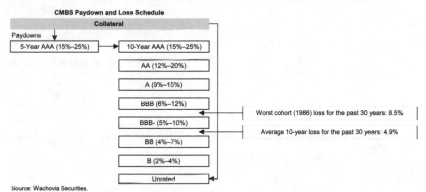

Source: Wachovia Securities.

In short, the investment-grade CMBS collateral backing CRE CDOs, in and of itself, without the additional structural subordination and excess spread of the real estate CDO, should be sufficient to absorb average historic losses as calculated previously. Moreover, even if we assume losses hit the extraordinarily high 8.5% level experienced by the 1986 cohort wiping out the BBB- subordination we would still be afforded the structural subordination in the deal to protect the higher-rated real estate CDO tranches. This does not mean that some CRE CDO tranches would not experience losses in this case, but rather that the losses would be mitigated by the additional subordination in the structure. Moreover, more seasoned CMBS tranches have higher subordination levels due to deleveraging, increasing the ratings threshold that would be pierced by the level of defaults cited above.

A METHODOLOGY TO DISCRIMINATE AMONG CRE CDOS

To provide the investor with a useful tool to help determine relative value and apply the historic losses and severities noted previously to specific deals and situations, we stressed two deals, CREST Clarendon Street 2002-1 and G-Force 2002-1, with the scenarios shown in Exhibit 21. "Curve" is the level and timing of annual defaults and severities as defined in the study[26] and the gross default rate (GDR) is based on Moody's ICDR for REITs. For different scenarios, we assume various multiples of the curve to increase or decrease the stress. Indeed, this is a

26. Source: "Commercial Mortgage Defaults: An Update," by H. Esaki, *Real Estate Finance*, Winter 2002.

common methodology employed by many CRE CDO investors to determine the strength of a CRE CDO.

Exhibit 21: Stress Methodology Assumptions

	CREST Clarendon Street 2002-1	G-Force 2002-1
Scenario 1	Base Case	Base Case (0 Defaults)
	0% GDR	0% GDR
Scenario 2	CMBS: 0.5x Curve	CMBS: 0.5x Curve
	REIT: 0% GDR	
Scenario 3	CMBS: 1.0x Curve	CMBS: 1.0x Curve
	REITs: 2.86% GDR (Moody's ICDR)	
Scenario 4	CMBS: 1.5x Curve	CMBS: 1.5x Curve
	REITs: 5.97% GDR (ICDR + 1 St. Dev.)	
Scenario 5	CMBS: 2.0x Curve	CMBS: 2.0x Curve
	REITs: 9.08% GDR (ICDR + 2 St. Dev.)	
Scenario 6	CMBS: 1.5x Curve	NA
	REITs: 2.86% GDR (Moody's ICDR)	
Scenario 7	CMBS: 2.0x Curve	NA
	REITs: 2.86% GDR (Moody's ICDR)	

GDR: Gross default rate; ICDR: Idealized cumulative default rate.
Source: Wachovia Securities.

The AAAs of CREST Clarendon Street 2002-1, which are backed mostly by investment-grade collateral with a WARF of 579, remain completely intact in Scenarios 2 and 3, where we assume stresses equal to or half of the historic averages found in the study (Exhibits 22 and 23). The same is true for the AAAs of G-Force 2002-1, which are backed by lower-quality collateral with a WARF of 1874 (Exhibit 23). However, the higher quality of the CREST Clarendon Street CRE CDO becomes apparent if we look at the mezzanine classes. Here, under one times the historic stress, the BBs of CREST Clarendon Street 2002-1 remain intact, whereas the BBBs of G-Force 2002-1 are hit.

As we increase the stress levels further in Scenarios 4–7, the robustness of CREST Clarendon Street 2002-1 becomes more apparent. Indeed, its BBs remain intact under Scenario 4 when the AAAs of G-Force 2002-1 begin to erode.

Although this type of analysis is useful for CRE CDO investors to distinguish between the quality of CRE CDOs, it is a conservative stress scenario. These stresses assume the same level of defaults and the timing of defaults occur simultaneously across all of the different CMBS deals

Exhibit 22: CREST Clarendon Street 2002-1 Default Stresses

Scenario	Tranche	WAL	DM/Yield	Principal Win	Principal Loss
1	AAA	7.31	0.48%	6/05–6/12	—
	BB	10.42	10.12%	9/12–12/13	—
2	AAA	7.39	0.48%	6/05–6/12	—
	BB	11.77	10.12%	3/13–12/13	—
3	AAA	7.46	0.48%	9/03–6/12	—
	BB	11.21	10.11%	9/13–12/13	—
4	AAA	7.55	0.48%	9/03–9/12	—
	BB	12.47	10.05%	12/13–3/16	—
5	AAA	7.63	0.48%	9/03–9/12	—
	BB	NA	-5.39%	NA	100%
6	AAA	7.58	0.48%	9/03–9/12	—
	BB	11.95	10.07%	12/13–12/15	—
7	AAA	7.70	0.48%	9/03–9/12	—
	BB	16.28	-1.01%	NA	100%

Source: Charter Research and Wachovia Securities.

Exhibit 23: G-Force 2002-1 Default Stresses

Scenario	Tranche	WAL	DM/Yield	Principal Win	Principal Loss
1	AAA*	8.04	0.46%	7/10–6/11	—
	BBB	10.70	8.31%	11/12–3/14	—
2	AAA	8.43	0.46%	7/10–4/12	—
	BBB	13.12	8.31%	8/15–11/16	—
3	AAA	9.62	0.46%	7/10–2/15	—
	BBB	NA	8.37%	NA	100%
4	AAA	10.91	-1.17%	8/10–3/25	23%
	BBB	NA	-23.57%	NA	100%
5	AAA	10.65	-7.25%	12/10–3/25	70%
	BBB	NA	-31.19%	NA	100%

*Represents "long" AAA of capital structure. G-Force 2002-1 also includes a AAA rated money market tranche that constitutes 16% of the capital structure.
Source: Charter Research.

backing the CRE CDOs. We know from history that defaults and losses of different CRE properties in different states, let alone vintages, do not occur at the same time.

Furthermore, this assumption of simultaneous defaults and losses more negatively affects CRE CDOs with lower-rated collateral and higher subordination, such as G-Force 2002-1. If defaults and losses simultaneously rise to a level that breaches all of the subordination levels of all of the underlying CMBS collateral and consume all of the tranches making up the CRE CDO, then no level of secondary structural subordination in the CDO will protect the CRE CDO tranches. Thus, the lower collateral subordination characteristic of lower-rated CMBS collateral is more easily breached and the low-rated collateral tranches are entirely consumed by defaults and losses as we simultaneously increase defaults and losses. In reality, we know that defaults and losses of different CMBS may or may not occur at any time and indeed may never occur in some cases. In this more realistic scenario, lower-rated higher-subordination collateral will likely fare better than indicated in the aforementioned stress tests. It is also important to note that running one set of assumptions for all real estate loans ignores three key factors in commercial real estate: vintage, location and property type.

HOW CRE CDOS TRADE

In 1999 and 2000, CRE CDOs priced behind high-yield bonds, leveraged-loan CDOs and ABS CDOs, however, as performance diverged and CRE CDOs outperformed, spreads on corporate-backed CDOs and ABS CDOs began to lag. Currently, CRE CDOs trade 10 bps–15 bps tighter than leveraged loan and ABS CDOs. Floating-rate CRE CDOS trade at LIBOR plus 47 bps–50 bps versus LIBOR 60 bps–65 bps for leveraged loans and ABS CDOs. The difference is more dramatic further down the yield curve. BBB CRE CDOs trade as much as 50 bps–75 bps tighter than leveraged-loan and ABS CDOs.

The relative value of CRE CDOs is also notable in secondary trading. CRE CDO AAA bonds trade on top of new issue pricing (e.g., 48DM) with a tight bid/ask spread that is somewhat wider than AAA conduit CMBS (e.g., 1 bp–2 bps). On the other hand, high-yield and ABS CDO AAA product typically trade 8 bps–10 bps wider than new issue product with an 8 bps–10 bps bid/ask as the deal ages beyond one or two quarters.

Secondary trading volume in CRE CDOs has been increasing, particularly in 2002, however, it remains a less liquid market than the CMBS conduit market. Nevertheless, according to our trading desk, floating-rate CRE CDOs, particularly the AAA and A classes, have similar if not better liquidity than CMBS large-loan floating-rate bonds. We expect liquidity in CRE CDOs to continue to improve as the sector matures further and transparency improves.

For example, transparency both at primary issuance and thereafter has improved noticeably in many static pool transactions, allowing investors to re-underwrite each bond in the portfolio before making a purchase decision. Ongoing surveillance and modeling on third-party systems such as Trepp, Charter and Intex, have helped facilitate tighter pricing relative to CMBS and substantial secondary trading support for CRE CDOs (Exhibit 24).

Exhibit 24: U.S. Corporate Bond Defaults

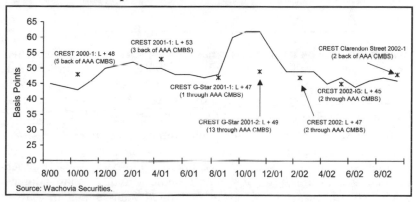

Source: Wachovia Securities.

PERFORMANCE TO DATE OF THE CRE CDO SECTOR

Since the inception of the CRE CDO market in 1999, the corporate bond market has faced a marked deterioration in credit that has resulted in increased default rates and decreased recovery rates. Since 1999, the Moody's Corporate Default Index has averaged 3.3%, versus a 10-year trailing average default rate of 1.97%. Although the Moody's Corporate Default Index peaked at 5.34% in July 1991, in February 2002 it reached a recent high of 4.89%. The U.S. Speculative Grade Index has been even more volatile. The average since 1999 has been 7.52% compared with a 10-year trailing average of 4.73%. The recent high for this index was in February 2001 at 11.43%; although still shy of the 13.00% registered in July 1991, it is dramatically higher than recent averages.

Exhibit 25: U.S. Corporate Bond Defaults

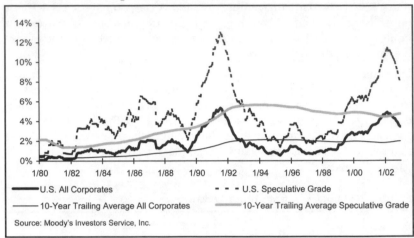

Source: Moody's Investors Service, Inc.

In addition, the volume of defaults has increased. The average per issuer default was $844 million in 2002 compared with $390 million in 2001 and $287 million in 2000. At the same time, corporate recovery rates have lagged. Over the past two years, recoveries for senior unsecured bonds have averaged 23% versus 40% in the three years before that.

Although we are starting to see some improvement in the corporate bond sector, high default rates and low recovery rates have put many of the high yield bond–backed and investment grade–backed CDOs under substantial pressure. In the first nine months of 2002, Moody's down-graded 407 tranches of 146 CDOs in the United States alone. This activi-ty exceeds all prior years combined. Based on Moody's watch list for downgrades, negative rating actions will likely continue. As of Sept. 30, 2002, 87 CDO deals and 167 CDO tranches were on watch for down-grade, primarily in the high-yield CBO sector.

Given the volatile state of the corporate CDO market, the performance of CRE CDOs during this same period stands in stark contrast. As discussed earlier, there have been no CRE CDO downgrades to date. This is a direct result of the performance stability of CRE securities. Earlier in this chapter, we showed the rating migration stability that CMBS have exhibited. This explains why, based on a broad sample of 15 CRE CDOs issued between November 2000 and July 2002, the WARF migration average was approximately 1% (990 WARF–1000 WARF). The diversity score exhibited similar robustness, which is partially due to the static pool nature of the CRE CDO transactions. In an environment in which equity in many high-yield and investment-grade CDOs has been locked out due to a breach of a cash flow diversion trigger, CRE CDO equity has averaged cash-on-cash returns of 16%–20% based on our random sample.

CONCLUSION

CRE CDOs have emerged as one of the most attractive asset classes in the CDO market. Although still a young market, the solid performance thus far has been encouraging. The strong performance of the underlying collateral (i.e., CMBS and REITs) has been important, however, the rating agencies' particularly conservative approach to CRE CDOs has and should continue to benefit the sector. We hope this guide will serve as a useful point of entry and analytical framework for investors to discover the opportunities offered by this new and rapidly growing fixed-income sector.

APPENDIX A: MOODY'S D-SCORE[27]

Moody's assumes the default risk of ABS in different sectors is more highly correlated than that of two corporate credits in different sectors. The Moody's Alternative Diversity Score model was developed to analyze bonds from sectors with correlated default risk. Each bond in the portfolio is assigned a default probability and expected loss rate based on its rating, WAL and applicable Moody's recovery rate. The diversity score model is based on matching the mean and standard deviation of the portfolio's expected loss profile.

The formula used to calculate the alternative Diversity Score is as follows:

$$D = \frac{\left(\sum_{i=1}^{n} p_i F_i\right) \left(\sum_{i=1}^{n} q_i F_i\right)}{\sum_{i=1}^{n}\sum_{j=1}^{n} \rho_{ij} \sqrt{p_i q_i p_j q_j} \left(F_i F_j\right)}$$

where n equals the number of bonds in the portfolio; bond i has a face value of F_i, a default probability of P_i and a survival probability of Q_i ($Q_i = 1 - P_i$); and the correlation coefficient between bonds i and j is P_{ij} (the correlation coefficient is based on the Moody's default correlation matrix (provided earlier in this chapter).

Using this formula, the entire collateral pool can be expressed as D homogenous securities with uncorrelated default risk. This new pool has the following characteristics:

Average face value $= \left(\sum_{i=1}^{n} F_i\right) \Big/ D$

Average default probability $= \left(\sum_{i=1}^{n} p_i F_i\right) \Big/ \left(\sum_{i=1}^{n} F_i\right)$

---

27. Source: Moody's Investors Service, Inc.

APPENDIX B: MOODY'S WEIGHTED AVERAGE RATINGS FACTOR

The weighted average rating factor (WARF) is a Moody's concept that is used to estimate the expected loss of a given pool of assets. The WARF is calculated based on the Moody's Rating Factor Table (Exhibit 26) and the weighting of each security in a portfolio by its par amount. The lower the WARF, the fewer defaults the structure must withstand, resulting in greater leverage. For example, under Moody's stress scenarios, a portfolio with a WARF of 2720 will be stressed to withstand 27.20% cumulative defaults over a 10-year period.

Exhibit 26: Moody's Rating Factors

Rating	Rating Factor	Rating	Rating Factor
Aaa	1	Ba1	940
Aa1	10	Ba2	1350
Aa2	20	Ba3	1780
Aa3	40	B1	2220
A1	70	B2	2720
A2	120	B3	3490
A3	180	Caa1	4770
Baa1	260	Caa2	6500

Source: Moody's Investors Service, Inc.

Once the threshold in a structure has been breached, the asset manager must improve or maintain the WARF in all subsequent trades. Generally, this means the asset manager will either sell the asset that caused the breach and replace it with a higher-rated asset (but with potentially lower par) or sell a different asset and replace it with another higher-rated asset to lower the WARF.

Exhibit 27 shows shows typical WARF scores for select CDO types.

Exhibit 27: WARF Scores for Select CDO Types

CDO Type	WARF	Equivalent Rating
Plain Vanilla CDO	2500–2720	B1/B2
ABS CDO	260–610	Baa1–Baa3
Balance Sheet CDO	600–1600	Baa3–Ba3

Source: Moody's Investors Service, Inc.

Exhibit 28: Moody's Idealized Cumulative Default Rates

Year	1	2	3	4	5	6	7	8	9	10
Aaa	0.00005%	0.00020%	0.00070%	0.00180%	0.00290%	0.00400%	0.00520%	0.00660%	0.00820%	0.01000%
Aa1	0.00057%	0.00300%	0.01000%	0.02100%	0.03100%	0.04200%	0.05400%	0.06700%	0.08200%	0.10000%
Aa2	0.00136%	0.00800%	0.02600%	0.04700%	0.06800%	0.08900%	0.11100%	0.13500%	0.16400%	0.20000%
Aa3	0.00302%	0.01900%	0.05900%	0.10100%	0.14200%	0.18300%	0.22700%	0.27200%	0.32700%	0.40000%
A1	0.00581%	0.03700%	0.11700%	0.18900%	0.26100%	0.33000%	0.40600%	0.48000%	0.57300%	0.70000%
A2	0.01087%	0.07000%	0.22200%	0.34500%	0.46700%	0.58300%	0.71000%	0.82900%	0.98200%	1.20000%
A3	0.03885%	0.15000%	0.36000%	0.54000%	0.73000%	0.91000%	1.11000%	1.30000%	1.52000%	1.80000%
Baa1	0.09000%	0.28000%	0.56000%	0.83000%	1.10000%	1.37000%	1.67000%	1.97000%	2.27000%	2.60000%
Baa2	0.17000%	0.47000%	0.83000%	1.20000%	1.58000%	1.97000%	2.41000%	2.85000%	3.24000%	3.60000%
Baa3	0.42000%	1.05000%	1.71000%	2.38000%	3.05000%	3.70000%	4.33000%	4.97000%	5.57000%	6.10000%
Ba1	0.87000%	2.02000%	3.13000%	4.20000%	5.28000%	6.25000%	7.06000%	7.89000%	8.69000%	9.40000%
Ba2	1.56000%	3.47000%	5.18000%	6.80000%	8.41000%	9.77000%	10.70000%	11.66000%	12.65000%	13.50000%
Ba3	2.81000%	5.51000%	7.87000%	9.79000%	11.86000%	13.49000%	14.62000%	15.71000%	16.71000%	17.66000%
B1	4.68000%	8.38000%	11.58000%	13.85000%	16.12000%	17.89000%	19.13000%	20.23000%	21.24000%	22.20000%
B2	7.16000%	11.67000%	15.55000%	18.13000%	20.71000%	22.65000%	24.01000%	25.15000%	26.22000%	27.20000%
B3	11.62000%	16.61000%	21.03000%	24.04000%	27.05000%	29.20000%	31.00000%	32.58000%	33.78000%	34.90000%
Caa1	17.38160%	23.23413%	28.63861%	32.47884%	36.31374%	38.96665%	41.38538%	43.65696%	45.67182%	47.70000%

Year	11	12	13	14	15	16	17	18	19	20
Aaa	0.01211%	0.01438%	0.01682%	0.01941%	0.02215%	0.02502%	0.02802%	0.03114%	0.03438%	0.03771%
Aa1	0.13067%	0.15933%	0.19101%	0.22571%	0.26340%	0.30402%	0.34755%	0.39389%	0.44298%	0.49474%
Aa2	0.24924%	0.30428%	0.36521%	0.43201%	0.50464%	0.58303%	0.66707%	0.75664%	0.85159%	0.95177%
Aa3	0.64366%	0.76341%	0.89248%	1.03046%	1.17691%	1.33136%	1.49334%	1.66236%	1.83794%	2.01958%
A1	1.03796%	1.22241%	1.41960%	1.62873%	1.84897%	2.07946%	2.31936%	2.56781%	2.82399%	3.08707%
A2	1.43226%	1.68140%	1.94672%	2.22700%	2.52103%	2.82756%	3.14538%	3.47326%	3.81003%	4.15456%
A3	2.33195%	2.67955%	3.04214%	3.41796%	3.80533%	4.20263%	4.60833%	5.02099%	5.43926%	5.86190%
Baa1	3.23138%	3.67740%	4.13723%	4.60857%	5.08925%	5.57728%	6.07084%	6.56825%	7.06800%	7.56872%
Baa2	4.13080%	4.67524%	5.23233%	5.79918%	6.37317%	6.95194%	7.53335%	8.11551%	8.69674%	9.27554%
Baa3	7.69682%	8.48789%	9.27384%	10.05209%	10.82050%	11.57735%	12.32125%	13.05114%	13.76618%	14.46580%
Ba1	11.26178%	12.29939%	13.31414%	14.30373%	15.26650%	16.20137%	17.10772%	17.98528%	18.83411%	19.65450%
Ba2	14.82673%	16.11089%	17.35444%	18.55537%	19.71250%	20.82540%	21.89418%	22.91943%	23.90204%	24.84320%
Ba3	19.61340%	21.07935%	22.47361%	23.79821%	25.05569%	26.24889%	27.38084%	28.45466%	29.47346%	30.44031%
B1	24.39863%	26.04633%	27.59125%	29.03949%	30.39727%	31.67075%	32.86586%	33.98824%	35.04322%	36.03575%
B2	29.18386%	31.01331%	32.70888%	34.28076%	35.73886%	37.09262%	38.35087%	39.52182%	40.61297%	41.63118%
B3	37.47788%	39.85510%	42.05837%	44.10091%	45.99560%	47.75471%	49.38972%	50.91127%	52.32914%	53.65224%
Caa1	49.97284%	52.06250%	53.94014%	55.63419%	57.16872%	58.56416%	59.83781%	61.00440%	62.07650%	63.06482%

Year	21	22	23	24	25	26	27	28	29	30
Aaa	0.04114%	0.04467%	0.04827%	0.05195%	0.05571%	0.05953%	0.06340%	0.06734%	0.07132%	0.07535%
Aa1	0.54907%	0.60588%	0.66505%	0.72649%	0.79008%	0.85570%	0.92324%	0.99259%	1.06362%	1.13622%
Aa2	1.05700%	1.16709%	1.28183%	1.40102%	1.52444%	1.65187%	1.78308%	1.91783%	2.05591%	2.19709%
Aa3	2.20682%	2.39916%	2.59616%	2.79735%	3.00231%	3.21061%	3.42185%	3.63564%	3.85161%	4.06941%
A1	3.35629%	3.63087%	3.91009%	4.19326%	4.47973%	4.76888%	5.06013%	5.35292%	5.64676%	5.94118%
A2	4.50576%	4.86257%	5.22402%	5.58917%	5.95716%	6.32715%	6.69840%	7.07021%	7.44192%	7.81294%
A3	6.28774%	6.71572%	7.14485%	7.57423%	8.00305%	8.43057%	8.85613%	9.27911%	9.69898%	10.11526%
Baa1	8.06919%	8.56831%	9.06510%	9.55869%	10.04834%	10.53337%	11.01320%	11.48734%	11.95536%	12.41689%
Baa2	9.85064%	10.42090%	10.98534%	11.54315%	12.09362%	12.63616%	13.17027%	13.69557%	14.21174%	14.71853%
Baa3	15.14956%	15.81722%	16.46864%	17.10380%	17.72276%	18.32566%	18.91270%	19.48411%	20.04017%	20.58119%
Ba1	20.44690%	21.21193%	21.95029%	22.66278%	23.35021%	24.01346%	24.65339%	25.27090%	25.86685%	26.44210%
Ba2	25.74424%	26.60664%	27.43195%	28.22175%	28.97766%	29.70125%	30.39409%	31.05770%	31.69353%	32.30300%
Ba3	31.35819%	32.22996%	33.05837%	33.84603%	34.59540%	35.30881%	35.98843%	36.63632%	37.25439%	37.84443%
B1	36.97045%	37.85159%	38.68311%	39.46862%	40.21146%	40.91468%	41.58109%	42.21327%	42.81358%	43.38419%
B2	42.58272%	43.47323%	44.30785%	45.09121%	45.82751%	46.52055%	47.17375%	47.79022%	48.37277%	48.92396%
B3	54.88868%	56.04583%	57.13036%	58.14828%	59.10505%	60.00560%	60.85438%	61.65543%	62.41242%	63.12865%
Caa1	63.97860%	64.82576%	65.61319%	66.34686%	67.03196%	67.67305%	68.27416%	68.83881%	69.37014%	69.87094%

Source: Moody's Investors Service, Inc.

Chapter 3

Middle-Market CLOs:
What's in a Name?

INTRODUCTION

Fueled by the exodus of traditional bank lenders and the success stories of non-bank specialty finance companies, the middle-market (MM) sector, comprising loans to private companies with $5 million–$50 million in EBITDA, has become a topic of great interest. During the past few years, the MM sector has attracted the attention of numerous "opportunity" funds and traditional asset managers. Most recently, several established private equity groups (PEGs) and various start-ups have signaled their intent to enter the fray through the use of the business development company (BDC) model, an investment vehicle uniquely designed for mezzanine and equity investing in the MM sector.

The array of market participants now spans traditional bank lenders, specialty lenders, opportunity funds and asset managers. Each of these groups employ differing funding sources, motivations and credit skills. These variables have acted as the catalyst for noteworthy financial innovation and market segmentation, particularly with respect to the manner in which the market parcels and funds investment risk.

These events have littered the loan market with numerous types of loans and ambiguous terminology describing their relative slices of the capital structure. This chapter is intended to provide insight with regard to events affecting the MM sector, some clarity relating to these new loan types and a look beyond current trends toward likely outcomes.

MARKET EVOLUTION

Flight to liquidity. Bank consolidation spanning the past decade and less than effective loss-leader strategies employed by bank lenders have driven many banks away from the MM sector in pursuit of liquidity and fee income. As a result, many leveraged finance groups now focus on larger, broadly syndicated loans to borrowers with $50 million or more in EBITDA, leaving loans to smaller borrowers with their general banking groups. Unlike corporate lending groups employing specialized industry teams, most general bank lenders are geographically focused and tend to pursue *relationship* lending versus *event-driven* transactions (e.g., PEG activity). This gap has created a shortfall of capital and served as the catalyst of opportunity for lenders catering to the MM sector.

Interest rate environment. Historically low interest rates have driven corporate borrowers to refinance higher cost debt over the past three-plus years. As the economic environment started showing signs of recovery toward the end of 2002, borrowers began accessing the high-yield bond markets at record levels.

Exhibit 1: Historical Domestic High-Yield New Issuance (1994–2003)

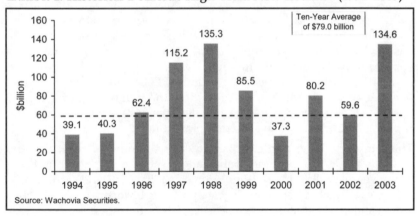

Source: Wachovia Securities.

As corporate borrowers refinanced, banks experienced significant roll-off in their loan portfolios. The reduction in their loan portfolios was exasperated by the migration toward larger borrowers and intense competition, compressing bank loan spreads to historically tight levels. As a result, many loan managers, particularly those using collateralized loan obligation (CLO) vehicles for funding, were unable to achieve equity returns necessary to entice investors and were forced to the sidelines while determining the best alternative path.

Anticipation of Basel. Implementation of the Basel Committee's newest Capital Accord (Basel II) is not expected until 2007, but commercial banks have spent considerable time preparing for its impact. At the broadest level, Basel II is designed as a risk-sensitive approach for determining bank capital requirements (i.e., higher-risk assets attract more capital). The current proposal highlights the need for banking institutions, absent substantial historical performance data, to solicit external confirmation of their loss given default (LGD) assumptions. In preparation of these requirements, many larger commercial banks have been sharing loan data (e.g., financial accounting and performance statistics) relating to their MM loan portfolios with the rating agencies.

This wealth of data has assisted Fitch Ratings (FITCH), Moody's Investors Service, Inc.(Moody's) and Standard & Poor's Corp. (S&P) to develop proprietary credit scoring models targeting the MM sector. FitchRisk's CRS MARS 5.3 and S&P's CreditModel™ are designed for private companies with $50 million plus in revenue. Moody's estimated default frequency (EDF) RiskCalc™ 3.1 can be used for private borrowers with in excess of $100,000 in total assets.

Search for yield. The oversupply of capital pursuing larger, broadly syndicated loans forced many loan managers to find creative ways to enhance their equity returns. In many instances, their efforts were characterized as little more than stretching on credit. Few loan managers (e.g., Denali Capital LLC) have developed the required infrastructure and successfully included MM loans in traditional CLO vehicles. Many syndicated loan managers now include nominal buckets, typically 5%–10%, for MM loans in their CLOs.

Tight bank loan spreads have pushed several loan managers to respond in one of the following manners: 1) establish broadly syndicated loan funds using synthetic financing (e.g., total return swaps) and nominal setup costs when compared to traditional CLOs, but these structures are typically subject to market value triggers, 2) stretch deeper in the capital structure (e.g., last-out and second lien loans) and 3) participate in relatively smaller "club" transactions for borrowers with $25 million–$50 million of EBITDA. The latter two strategies should be limited to lenders with appropriate infrastructure and underwriting guidelines designed for more intensive credit analysis. Participants in these credits will also require the balance-sheet capacity to work through troubled credits rather than relying on market liquidity. Investors should closely scrutinize participants in the MM sector to understand their motivation and ensure that they have the capacity to work through troubled credits.

Recent wave of activity. During the past 12 months, the market has seen in excess of $7.5 billion of registration statements filed for public BDCs.[1]

---

1. See Wachovia Securities equity analyst Joel Houck's May 24, 2004, report, *BDC/RICs: A New Era in Mezzanine Finance.*

BDCs are closed-end funds designed for mezzanine and equity investing in private companies (70% of their assets must be in qualifying investments, e.g., private companies). Most BDCs operate as regulated investment companies (RICs) and avoid federal taxation, requiring distribution of not less than 90% of their taxable income to shareholders. BDCs have the added benefit of being able to leverage up to 1:1 debt to equity. The addition of leverage results in a relatively lower blended cost of capital (generally in the 7%–9% range) and, coupled with permanent equity alleviating the need to manage their portfolio to an *event horizon*, makes the BDC a formidable investment vehicle for the MM sector.

SENIOR SECURED LOANS

Senior secured loans, asset-based or cash flow, should be conservatively underwritten assuming firm valuations applicable through all business cycles. Primary workout strategies include two paths: 1) liquidation of assets (asset-based loans) and 2) pressuring equity investors to refinance or infuse additional capital (cash flow loans). Most companies, excluding those in industries such as media, should reflect enterprise values in the range of 5.0–6.0x for LTM EBITDA, calculated with nominal benefit for addbacks or anticipated synergies. Loans underwritten at more aggressive levels provide subordinate investors little incentive to support borrowers experiencing difficulty as their investment might have no value. Deviations from conservative standards often amount to bets on the future and are more consistent with investments benefiting from equity upside. Senior lenders seldom receive payment-in-kind (PIK) interest and rarely benefit from equity "kickers" (e.g., warrants or equity ownership). Accordingly, they are not compensated to endure workout strategies commonly pursued by subordinate lenders including replacement of management or equity "cramdowns."

The days in which the market could be generically defined in terms of senior secured or subordinated debt has passed. An array of new entrants to the MM sector has resulted in substantial market segmentation and driven the evolution of numerous loan types including "stretch" senior, "last out" senior and second lien/B-notes. The development of these loan types has littered the market with conflicting interpretations. In the absence of market accepted terms, the following definitions are an attempt to provide general parameters in an effort to narrow these concepts to manageable definitions.

Asset-based loans (ABLs) are generally revolving facilities tied to a borrowing base and secured by first liens on accounts receivable, inventory or equipment. Advance rates are applied against orderly liquidation

Exhibit 2: Historical Debt/EBITDA Multiples

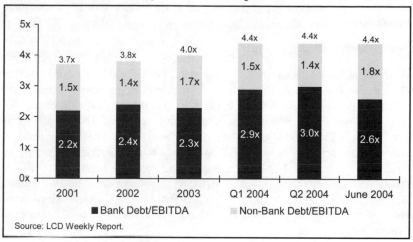

Source: LCD Weekly Report.

value (OLV) typically not to exceed 85%, 50% and 80%, respectively. Lock boxes are commonly used for greater cash control. The fluid nature of the borrowing base and relatively lower credit quality of these borrowers highlights a greater risk of fraud, requiring lenders to have substantial infrastructure and controls to monitor the collateral base. When properly managed, ABL facilities should result in the lowest LGD of all loan types despite the borrower's relatively lower credit quality. These loans are often competitively priced in the LIBOR plus 250 bps–325 bps area. Their labor-intensive nature and thin margins have historically limited this market to banking institutions with specialized lending groups and larger specialty lenders.

Traditional senior loans may be structured as revolving or term facilities, frequently to support the borrower's working capital requirements. These loans are often underwritten to loan-to-values (LTV) in the 40%–60% range and benefit from first liens on all of the borrower's assets. This group can be further divided into two groups: 1) general bank loans and 2) event-driven loans.

General bank loans are typically limited to non-event-driven transactions in low volatility industries with historical cash flows spanning several years. These loans are typically at LTVs of 40%–50% and frequently benefit from substantial asset coverage. The perceived low risk of these loans often results in loss leader pricing in hopes to entice the sale of other bank products (e.g., cash management and lock box services). Pricing for general bank loans ranges in the LIBOR plus

250 bps–300 bps area. When evaluated apart from the ancillary income and on a stand-alone basis, many of these loans would trade well below par.

Event-driven loans are typically associated with some material event (e.g., acquisition or recapitalization) and often involve PEG sponsors. Additional layers of complexity frequently come in the form of material changes to the borrower's business operations or management adjustments, but there is an added benefit in the initial due diligence and ongoing oversight provided by the equity sponsor. These loans are typically at LTVs of 50%–60%. Additional leverage and cash flow volatility often attract lenders with particular industry expertise and result in premium pricing of 100 bps or more over general bank loans. PEGs frequently point to their purchase price as an indication of market value, but it typically reflects numerous forward-looking assumptions and may not be reflective of firm valuations looking through several business cycles.

"Stretch" senior loans may include revolving or term facilities and are frequently related to event-driven strategies including growth or acquisitions, possibly stemming from PEG activity. These loans benefit from first liens on all of the borrower's assets, but will represent higher leverage up to 65% LTVs. It is important to reiterate that these loans are not subordinate to other lenders, but may evidence slightly higher LGDs than ABLs or traditional senior loans due to their higher leverage. Pricing ranges from LIBOR plus 400 bps–550 bps. Due to the complexities and "stories" often surrounding these loans, they are largely the domain of specialty lenders and larger opportunity funds.

"Last-out" senior loans are typically term facilities needed to fund expansion or some other event, possibly relating to PEG activity. These loans are second in liquidation to another lender, but will share in the first lien from a documentation standpoint and have LTVs up to 60%. They are typically found in conjunction with ABL facilities and benefit from residual claims to receivables, inventory and equipment. Standstill provisions often allow ABL lenders to pursue remedies following payment default, but payment blockage for nonpayment defaults would be unusual. Last-out lenders commonly push for excess cash flow sweeps, covenants on total debt and fixed charges, limitation on amendments without 100% vote and restrictions on the release of collateral. Pricing ranges from LIBOR plus 450 bps–650 bps. Given the relative collateral position of these loans and corresponding yield premium, they tend to be pursued primarily by specialty lenders and opportunity funds.

Second lien/B-notes are similar in nature to "last out" senior loans, but differ in terms of documentation and leverage. Second lien/B-notes are usually documented apart from the senior loan, typically an ABL facility, due to the ABL lenders' concerns relating to adequate protection in the event of a bankruptcy proceeding. They frequently have LTVs slightly higher than "last out" senior loans, reaching as high as 70% LTVs. Standstill provisions and payment blockage are common. Second lien/B-note lenders may press for rights and remedies similar to "last-out" lenders, but their higher leverage and premium pricing would make this unusual. Pricing covers a broad range, typically relating to borrower size, from LIBOR plus 550 bps–850 bps and frequently includes PIK to reduce pressure on cash flow. These loans are substantially more credit-intensive and have historically been the domain of investors willing to perform more equity-like analysis in pursuit of yield (e.g., Ableco Finance LLC and American Capital Strategies, Ltd.).

Exhibit 3: Senior Secured Loan Types

Loan Type	Pricing (LIBOR +)	Lien	Collateral Position	LTV	Payment Blockage	Stand Still	Same Doc	Equity "Kicker"
Senior Secured								
Asset-Based	250 bps–325 bps	1st	1st	NA*	No	No	NA	No
Traditional Senior								
General Bank	250 bps–300 bps	1st	1st	50%	No	No	NA	No
Event Related	350 bps–400 bps	1st	1st	60%	No	No	NA	No
Stretch	400 bps–550 bps	1st	1st	65%	No	No	Yes	No
Last Out	500 bps–650 bps	1st	2nd	60%	No	60+	Yes	No
Second Lien/								
B-Notes	550 bps–850 bps PIK	2nd	2nd	70%	Maybe	90+	No	Maybe
Subordinated Debt	Mid-teens	2nd or Unsecured	2nd+	85%	180+	180+	No	Likely

*Loan amounts are typically calculated as advance rates (e.g., 50% of inventory, 80% of receivables, 85% of equipment) against "orderly liquidation value."
Source: Wachovia Securities.

Interaction between second lien/B-notes and first lien (i.e., ABL, traditional senior loans, last-out loans and stretch senior loans) facilities are governed by intercreditor agreements and typically focus on three key issues: 1) influence on any post-bankruptcy plan of reorganization, 2) dilution of collateral coverage and 3) exercise of remedies. Negotiated terms may vary substantially and are often influenced by the relative importance of each lender to the success of the transaction. Although these loans are usually documented separately from the first lien facility, it may actually be easier for the lender to negotiate provisions the borrower would not otherwise afford the broader bank group.

First lien lenders often pursue post-default strategies including collateral liquidation and may run contrary to the second lien provider's interests. This conflict will influence most first lien lenders to exclude second lien lenders from the negotiation table or being in a position to block the plan of reorganization. It would be uncommon for the second lien lender to have this right, but balance is frequently achieved by inserting the ability of the second lien provider to take out the first lien facility and increase its control in workout situations.

Collateral dilution frequently arises when first lien lenders upsize their facilities, amend key terms (e.g., interest rate, covenants or advance rates), release collateral or provide debtor-in-possession (DIP) financing. Many of these issues can be addressed through covenants on total debt, but the ability to provide DIP financing or nominal "over advances" are often contemplated. Amendments relating to key intercreditor provisions should require 100% vote of all note holders.

Standstill provisions restrict second lien lenders from pursuing remedies for some period of time and are fairly common. The first lien lender will look for some window of time to work with the borrower on an out-of-court restructuring or sale without the second lien provider exercising its remedies and forcing the borrower into bankruptcy. The likely result is a standstill period of 60–120 days.

MARKET PARTICPANTS

Following the bank merger craze of the past decade and subsequent acquisition of several large specialty lenders (e.g., Associates Corp. of North America was acquired by Citigroup Inc. and Heller Financial, Inc., was acquired by General Electric Co.), the MM sector experienced a substantial drought of capital. According to the Federal Deposit Insurance Corp. (FDIC), the number of commercial banks declined from 12,343 in 1990 to 7,712 as of March 31, 2004. Although merger activity has generally slowed (82 mergers YTD 2004 versus an average of 500 annually during the 1990s), recent transactions of noteworthy size should result in a continuation of this trend (e.g., J.P. Morgan Chase & Co./Bank One Corp. and Bank of America Corp./Fleet Bank N.A.).

Market participants can generally be divided into five categories: 1) asset managers, 2) BDCs, 3) opportunity funds, 4) specialty lenders and 5) traditional bank lenders. Depending on their legal form (i.e., internal versus external management), BDCs could arguably fall into the specialty

Exhibit 4: Lenders with Substantial Middle-Market Focus

Asset Managers
- Ares Management LLC
- Callidus Capital Management, LLC
- Denali Capital LLC
- Golden Tree Asset Management, LP
- GSC Partners
- Orchard Paladin Management, LLC

Business Development Companies
- Allied Capital Corp.
- American Capital Strategies Ltd.
- Apollo Investment Corp.
- Gladstone Capital Corp.
- MCG Capital Corp.
- Technology Investment Capital Corp.

Opportunity Funds
- AbleCo Finance LLC
- Amaranth LLC
- Back Bay Capital Funding LLC
- Citadel Investment Group, L.L.C.
- Contrarian Capital
- Dymas Capital Management Co., LLC
- Farallon Capital Management, LLC
- Fortress Investment Group
- Guggenheim Investment Partners
- D.B. Zwirn Capital Management
- Silver Point Capital
- Soros Capital Management LP

Specialty Lenders
- Antares Capital Corp.
- CapitalSource, Inc.
- GE Capital Corp.
- Madison Capital Funding, LLC
- Merrill Lynch Capital Group
- NewStar Financial, Inc. (fka Novus Capital)
- ORIX Capital Markets, LLC

Traditional Bank Lenders
- Bank of America Corp.
- J.P. Morgan Chase & Co. (Bank One Corp.)
- Wachovia Corp.
- Wells Fargo & Co.

Source: Wachovia Securities.

lender or opportunity fund category. Recent market activity and flexibility to pursue various slices of the capital structure, either directly or through the use of wholly owned portfolio companies, warrants separate consideration for BDCs.

Presently, there are six BDCs focused on the MM sector, but recent filing of registration statements by several established private equity firms has garnered significant attention.

Exhibit 5: Recent Business Development Company Registration Statement Filings

	Initial Filing Date	Stated Filing	Status
Blackridge Investment Corp.	4.14.04	$650 million	Withdrawal request 7/16/04
Evercore Investment Corp.	4.14.04	$300 million	Pending
Porticos Capital Corp.	4.14.04	$200 million	Delayed
Marathon Capital Finance Corp.	4.16.04	$200 million	Pending
Prospect Street Energy Corp.	4.16.04	$207 million	Pending
Triarc Deerfield Investment Corp.	4.19.04	$500 million	Pending
Orchard First Source, Inc.	4.20.04	$460 million	Pending
Ares Capital Corp.	4.20.04	$450 million	Pending
THL Investment Capital Corp.	5.04.04	$500 million	Pending
Gores Investment Corp.	5.06.04	$250 million	Pending
Gleacher Investment Corp.	5.11.04	$500 million	Pending
Other Filings	NA	$1,500 million	Pending
		$6,647 million	

Source: Securities Exchange Commission and Wachovia Securities.

Pending filings represent an aggregate potential capital raised of almost $5 billion directed at the MM sector. Coupled with maximum allowable leverage, about $10 billion of capital could enter the market in pursuit of MM loans. The likely result is partial displacement of traditional private mezzanine and equity funds. When viewed in the context of historical capital raised in these sectors, the net effect appears less dramatic.

Although the number of market participants has dramatically increased in the past few years, we believe the absolute dollars serving the MM sector is still relatively depressed compared with historical levels. Equally important is the trend of market segmentation whereby participants are focusing on specific slices of the capital structure. Few market participants have the balance-sheet capacity to execute one-stop financings for relatively larger (i.e., $25 million–$50 million EBITDA) financings.

Exhibit 6: Mezzanine and Private Equity Capital Raised

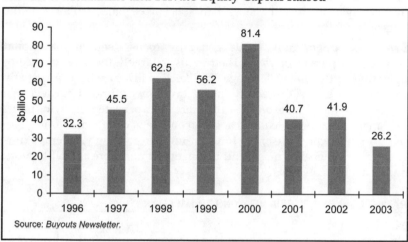

Source: *Buyouts Newsletter.*

Commercial banks continue to remain absent from the MM sector and pursue "barbell" strategies. The primary focus has remained the combination of broadly syndicated loans to borrowers with $50 million or more in EBITDA and relationship lending associated with smaller borrowers (i.e., $5 million–$50 million in EBITDA) through their geographically focused general bank groups.

Several loan managers have dipped their toes in the MM sector, but most have been precluded from underwriting MM loans due to trade or business issues restricting CLOs from directly originating loans. The high level of granularity required by traditional CLOs has further limited their ability to take down meaningful loan sizes and drive lending transactions. These restrictions have limited meaningful market participation to only the largest loan management platforms with the ability to spread larger loan participations across multiple CLO vehicles.

Specialty lenders have predominantly focused on the $25 million–$50 million EBITDA slice of the market, enjoying a healthy CLO appetite to pursue distribution strategies. This portion of the MM sector has seen the greatest level of spread compression as underwriters compete fiercely for syndication income to enhance profitability. The handful of lenders pursuing loans to relatively smaller borrowers (e.g., $5 million–$25 million in EBITDA) has experienced relatively less spread compression and should continue to benefit until general bank groups learn to adapt their geographic focus to PEG sponsor loans requiring industry expertise. Even fewer specialty lenders have pursued the ABL market. The thinner margins and labor-intensive nature of ABLs has historically restricted this market to specialized bank affiliates or the largest specialty lenders.

BDCs and opportunity funds generally focus deep in the capital structure in pursuit of yield. Their focus is largely the consequence of operating with limited leverage. Unlike the BDCs, which are legally restricted to 1:1 debt to equity, many investment funds limit leverage by choice. Most investment funds are compensated in two parts: 1) management fees calculated as a percentage of capital under management and 2) some share of the fund's return. Accordingly, leverage runs counter to the goal of most fund managers to put more capital to work and generate larger fees.

RATING AGENCY CRITERIA RELATING TO MM LOANS

MM loans were first introduced to CLO vehicles in the late 1990s. The challenges in rating these early transactions were mitigated by investment-grade servicers (e.g., Wells Fargo & Co.) or diverse collateral pools including broadly syndicated loans (e.g., Antares Capital Corp.). The first CLO backed 100% by MM loans (MM CLO) was brought by American Capital Strategies and consisted almost entirely of mezzanine loans. These transactions were similar to balance-sheet CLOs in motivation, but uniqueness of the structure and collateral drove rating agencies to take varying approaches. S&P evaluated MM CLOs out of their new assets group, whereas Moody's applied commercial ABS methodology. Fitch's experience in Europe's small to medium enterprise (SME) securitization market led them to apply a more traditional CLO methodology. In all cases, each loan was individually reviewed for default probability, recovery estimate and lag to recovery.

Four years and multiple transactions later, all of the rating agencies rate MM CLOs out of the CDO groups and apply traditional CLO methodology, highlighting the need to review each loan and determine rating estimates and recovery rates at the loan level. Development of proprietary credit scoring models has provided greater transparency and opened the door to enhanced transaction surveillance. These models may also be used by MM lenders to evaluate liquidity by estimating treatment of the loan for inclusion in CLO vehicles. S&P has formalized this link and published guidelines outlining the application of CreditModel™ to evaluate MM loans for inclusion in CLOs.

Relative to traditional CLO structures, rating agencies have blessed MM CLOs with significantly more efficient capital structures. This benefit is largely derived from the financing motivation and relatively tighter structures including reserve accounts for delinquent loans (generally defined as 60-plus days past due), tighter overcollateralization triggers set at 100% and substantial excess spread available to support the transaction. Recent transactions benefit from structural developments including money market tranches and pro rata amortization[2] of principal.

Rating agency recovery rates for modeling CLOs focuses on documentation and the lender's lien position (e.g., first lien, second lien or unsecured). Relative to loans benefiting from the first lien, lenders with second lien positions are perceived to be further from the table during workout discussions. Those lenders participating in the in the last-out, senior and second lien markets would be well advised to understand this differentiation and its ramifications for obtaining financing in the capital markets. Exhibit 7 outlines base-case recovery assumptions for modeling MM loans for inclusion in CLOs and may vary significantly from actual agency recovery assumptions:

Exhibit 7: Rating Agency Base-Case Recovery Assumptions

	Recovery Rate	Lag	Comments
Fitch			
Asset-Based Loans	60%–75%	NA	Influenced by facility structure and servicer strength
First Lien Senior	60%	NA	
Second Lien/Unsecured	40%	NA	
Subordinate	20%	NA	
Moody's*			
First Lien Senior	40%–60%	1–2 Years	Higher recovery rates applied to lower-rated liability tranches
Second Lien/Unsecured	30%–55%	1–2 Years	
Mezzanine	0%–30%	1–2 Years	
S&P			
Senior Secured	50%–60%	2–3 Years	50% during Years 1–2, 50% at Year 3
Senior Unsecured	25%–50%	2–3 Years	50% during Years 1–2, 50% at Year 3
Subordinate	15%–28%	2–3 Years	50% during Years 1–2, 50% at Year 3

*Moody's CDO methodology assumes relatively higher recovery rates for lower-rated liability tranches and will be dependent on the difference between Moody's Obligation Rating (i.e., the specific loan facility) and Moody's Default Probability Rating.
Source: Fitch Ratings, Moody's Investors Service, Inc., and Standard & Poor's Corp.

ABL facilities still receive relatively punitive treatment in light of their historical performance. Development of credit scoring models, primarily focused on estimating borrower default probability, has little

2. Pro rata amortization of principal is subject to loan performance. Recent structures employ equity "lock-outs" at 25% pool factors and switch to sequential pay at 10% pool factors.

application for asset-based facilities. These borrowers tend to be of lower credit quality, but the loan's strong collateral coverage and tight structures should result in relatively low LGDs. The difficulty for rating agencies to assess ABLs result from their labor-intensive nature, revolving structures using borrowing bases and the need for continual collateral monitoring. These characteristics highlight the need for strong servicers and conflict with agency stress scenarios assuming default by the loan servicer. Accordingly, ABLs have historically received relatively conservative recovery rate assumptions not reflective of their historical levels and more in line with senior secured cash flow loans.

OUTLOOK

Interest in MM loans is unlikely to decline in the near future. The exodus of bank lenders has only been partially offset by recent entrants to the market and the shortfall will likely be compounded by recent bank merger activity. These events continue to create additional opportunity in the MM sector. As economic conditions improve, further bank consolidation is likely and merger-and-acquisition (M&A) activity should pick up. These events will exacerbate the shortfall of capital targeting the MM sector.

Continued bank consolidation and economic strengthening will highlight the shortfall of capital available for MM loans and entice additional non-bank lenders to enter the market.

Recent bank consolidation has reduced the number of active participants in the ABL market. Thinner pricing and the challenges of funding these loans in traditional CLOs have limited the amount of new capital available to the ABL market. The disconnect between rating agency methodology and historical performance of the ABL sector will continue to restrict traditional CLOs from pursuing the ABL market.

The limited number of ABL lenders and challenges funding these loans using capital markets vehicles is expected to translate to favorable risk/reward profiles. Lenders with diverse funding sources (e.g., medium-size specialty lenders and larger opportunity funds) should be drawn to the ABL market.

The application of Basel II is not targeted until 2007, but banks are busy preparing for its impact. Absent substantial historical data, banks must look to third-party (e.g., rating agency) estimates of LGD on their MM loan portfolios. Rating estimates for MM loans will likely entail use of their credit scoring models and mapping bank credit scales to the corresponding agency ratings. The tendency of these models to heavily

Exhibit 8: Transactions with Material Concentrations of Middle-Market Loans

Closing Date	Transaction	Servicer/Manager	Size ($million)	Structure	Collateral
8/04/98	Foothill Income Trust, L.P.	FIT GP, L.L.C.	760.0	Managed	Mix
8/30/99	First Source Financial (Caymans), L.P.	First Source	2,181.3	Managed	Mix
12/14/99	Antares Funding L.P.	Antares/Mass Mutual[1]	600.0	Managed	Mix
10/06/00	First Source Loan Obligations Trust	First Source	640.5	Static	Mix
10/18/00	Fleet Commercial Loan Master LLC 2000-1	Fleet	200.0	MT	Mix
12/20/00	ACAS Business Loan Trust 2000-1	American Capital	153.9	Static	MML
12/28/00	Ark CLO 2000-1 Ltd.	Patriarch	1,306.5	Static	Mix[2]
2/14/01	First Source Loan Obligations Insured Trust	First Source	265.2	Static	Mix
10/25/01	Denali Capital CLO I, Ltd.	DC Funding	400.0	Managed	Mix
10/26/01	Ark II CLO 2001-1 Ltd.	Patriarch	665.5	Static	Mix[2]
12/19/01	MCG Commercial Loan Trust 2001-1	MCG Capital Corp.	353.6	Static	MML
3/13/02	ACAS Business Loan Trust 2002-1	American Capital	147.3	Static	MML
5/16/02	Capital Source Commercial Loan Trust 2002-1	CapitalSource	275.3	Static	MML
7/11/02	Mariner CDO 2002, Ltd.	Antares	410.5	Managed	Mix
7/22/02	Denali Capital CLO II, Ltd.	DC Funding	340.5	Managed	Mix
7/29/02	Fleet Commercial Loan Master LLC 2000-2	Fleet	100.0	MT	Mix
8/05/02	ACAS Business Loan Trust 2002-2	American Capital	210.5	Static	MML
8/29/02	GSC Partners Gemini Fund Ltd.	GSC Partners	692.6	Managed	MML[3]
10/25/02	Capital Source Commercial Loan Trust 2002-2	CapitalSource	325.5	Static	MML
4/14/03	Capital Source Commercial Loan Trust 2003-1	CapitalSource	450.1	Static	MML
5/21/03	ACAS Business Loan Trust 2003-1	American Capital	308.1	Static	MML
11/25/03	Capital Source Commercial Loan Trust 2003-2	CapitalSource	500.0	Static	MML
12/17/03	Foxe Basin CLO, Ltd.	RBC Capital	381.4	Managed	Mix
12/19/03	ACAS Business Loan Trust 2003-2	American Capital	396.9	Static	MML
4/01/04	Bernard National Loan Investors Ltd.	Bernard Capital	157.0	Managed	MML
6/22/04	Capital Source Commercial Loan Trust 2004-1	CapitalSource	875.0	Static	MML
6/22/04	Denali Capital CLO III, Ltd.	DC Funding	407.4	Managed	Mix
7/14/04	CoLTS Trust 2004-1	Wachovia Bank, N.A.	262.5	Static	Mix
			13,767.1		

American Capital: American Capital Strategies Ltd.; Antares: Antares Asset Management; Bernard Capital: Bernard Capital Funding LLC; CapitalSource: CapitalSource Finance LLC; CLO: Collateralized loan obligation; DC Funding: DC Funding Partners LLC; First Source: First Source Financial Inc.; Fleet: Fleet National Bank, MA; MML - Middle market; MT: Master trust; Patriarch: Patriarch Partners LLC; RBC Capital: RBC Capital Partners.
1. Antares Capital manages loans; Mass Mutual manages bonds.
2. Distressed senior secured loans.
3. Pool will start out as primarily middle-market loans but based on reinvestment criteria is expected to evolve into a more traditional CLO.
Source: Bloomberg L.P. and Wachovia Securities.

weight borrower revenue when estimating default probability penalizes smaller MM loans including traditional bank loans and may force banks to hold greater amounts of capital against these loans, reducing their profitability.

In conjunction with analyzing the effect of Basel, most large banks have explored the effect of mark-to-market (MTM) accounting on their MM loan portfolios. Certain banks have gone so far as to integrate MTM in their loan approval and compensation decisions. Although unlikely to influence banks away from the use of their balance sheets to generate ancillary income, these events will place the profitability of traditional bank loans under greater scrutiny.

We anticipate implementation of Basel and MTM applications to track relationship profitability will result in nominal spread widening for traditional bank loans.

S&P was the first rating agency to publish a methodology allowing use of its proprietary credit scoring model CreditModel™ to evaluate MM loans for inclusion in CLOs. As the volume of historical loan data increases, the predictive power of these models should improve and expand application to smaller MM loans (i.e., $5 million–$25 million EBITDA).

We anticipate Fitch and Moody's to outline conditions under which their credit scoring models may be used to evaluate MM loans for inclusion in CLOs. Continued development of these models should open the door for inclusion of smaller MM loans in traditional CLOs and support use of revolving periods in MM CLOs.

Historically tight credit spreads have compelled broadly syndicated loan managers to structure nominal buckets for MM loans in traditional CLOs. Consistent with the current application of agency credit scoring models, loan managers are focused on MM loans with $25 million–$50 million of EBITDA. Lack of balance-sheet and trade-or-business issues will continue to restrict smaller loan managers from underwriting MM loans, but we fully expect loan managers with multiple CLOs under management will explore underwriting MM loans.

Continued development of credit scoring models will propel the trend of including MM loan buckets in traditional CLOs. Increased liquidity driven by CLO appetite will further compress credit spreads, primarily in the $25 million–$50 million EBITDA portion of the market.

MM CLOs have continued to evolve with structures now including pro rata amortization of principal and money market tranches. Seasoned issuers with substantial historical data will allow the market to continue to evolve, including the application of many structural features employed by traditional CLOs.

The strong historical performance of MM CLOs and continual structural improvements will continue to position them as the ideal funding vehicle for MM loans. Future structural enhancements will likely include longer reinvestment periods and the ability to include unfunded cash flow revolvers. Recent entrants to the MM sector lack the balance sheet typical of most banks and should result in greater issuance volume of MM CLOs.

These trends are opening the MM sector to many new participants, but it does not alleviate the prerequisite of lenders to have infrastructures designed to manage relatively illiquid credits and the need for strong credit underwriting standards. Tight loan spreads in the broadly syndicated loan market and enticing yield relating to MM loans will likely draw participants lacking the necessary credit tools or infrastructure. We believe these ill-prepared participants in the MM sector will represent the largest portion of losses experienced in the sector.

These current trends will further enhance transparency and liquidity in the MM sector, but we anticipate the market will "tier" lenders by performance. Investors would be wise to evaluate issuers of CLOs including MM loans to determine if their motivation, infrastructure, skills and credit process appropriately address the challenges associated with these loans. Substantial use of the capital markets (i.e., MM CLOs) to fund MM loan activity should ensure the sector continues to be attractively priced from a risk/reward standpoint, although the illiquidity premium associated with these loans will continue to slowly erode.

Chapter 4

Synthetic CDOs:
An Investor's Guide

INTRODUCTION

In the rapidly changing world of collateralized debt securities (CDOs), the synthetic CDO (SCDO) market is perhaps the most dynamic and has generated great interest from issuers and investors alike. Starting as a convenient tool for banks to hedge unwanted risk in their loan portfolios or to obtain regulatory capital relief, SCDOs have become a common fixture in the arbitrage market. In 2002 and 2003, more than half of the deals transacted in the United States and Europe were synthetic, up from just above 25% in 2000.

A confluence of three events led to the creation and rapid expansion of the SCDO market. First, the creation of a super-senior tranche significantly reduced the cost of liabilities in SCDOs and permitted these securities to thrive even when the economics of a cash-based transaction were unattractive. Second, increased attention from the rating agencies has given investors confidence that the risk they are taking is commensurate with the premium they receive, opening the door for many additional investors. Finally, the development and standardization of credit default swap (CDS) technology, including documentation, has allowed disparate market participants to communicate more efficiently, acquire collateral[1] faster and hedge more efficiently where appropriate.

Given their advantages, the rapid rise of SCDOs should not be surprising. Compared with cash-based CDOs, SCDOs are straightforward and efficient structures. Generally, there is no fixed/floating interest rate mismatch or maturity mismatch between assets and liabilities. Currency mismatches are handled seamlessly without the need for explicit

---

1. We will take some liberties with the use of the term *collateral*, as CDS contracts are not collateral in the true sense of the term. Although SCDO purists will undoubtedly find the term *reference portfolio* preferable, we often find that term to be awkward and distracting for the reader.

currency hedges. And there are other advantages as well: quick and easy ramp-up of collateral, greater collateral diversity, payment of fees over time and generally greater structural flexibility. In fact, synthetic CDO transactions can be tailored around the needs of a single investor.

The first half of this chapter is devoted to a brief history of the synthetic market and an overview of basic SCDO structure. Afterward, we identify and discuss recent developments and trends in the SCDO market, such as the incorporation of coverage and quality tests, changes to credit derivatives definitions and the rise of single-tranche CDOs. Finally, we review several investment considerations. Where appropriate, we will compare synthetic with cash-based CDOs, with an eye on the relative advantages of SCDO structures.

GROWTH AND EVOLUTION OF THE SCDO MARKET

SCDOs originated in the late 1990s as a way for banks to transfer the credit risk of their loan portfolios without removing the loans from their balance sheet. In doing so, a bank could lower its regulatory capital requirement on these assets from 100% to 20%.[2] Transactions motivated by regulatory capital relief or risk management are termed balance-sheet CDOs (as opposed to arbitrage CDOs, which are discussed later). BISTRO 1997-1, issued in December 1997, was the first bank balance-sheet transaction that closely resembled the synthetic structures of today.[3] As the market has evolved, banks have applied this technology

Exhibit 1: Key Events that Shaped the CDO Market

First Synthetic Balance Sheet CDOs	Russian Default Crisis and LTCM Stress CDS Market	Standard ISDA Definitions	First Arbitrage SCDOs	First Structured-Finance SCDOs	Conseco Restructuring	First Managed SCDOs	Rise of Single-Tranche SCDOs	Revised ISDA Definitions
1997	1998	1999	2000	2001		2002		2003

CDOs: Collateralized debt obligations; CDS: Credit default swaps; ISDA: International Swaps and Derivatives Association; LTCM: Long-Term Capital Management; SCDOs: Synthetic collateralized debt obligations.
Source: Wachovia Securities.

2. Under Basel I, banks must hold 8% regulatory capital against the par of assets that are 100% risk weighted. Most regulators will lower this regulatory capital requirement to 1.6% (20% of the 8%), where risk is transferred via a default swap as long as the swap counterparty is an Organization for Economic Cooperation and Development (OECD) institution. If the risk is transferred in a credit-linked note (CLN) format and the collateral for those notes is very high quality, such as Treasurys, the risk weighting could be even lower.
3. Before BISTRO 1997-1, there were a limited number of SCDOs that were issued without a super-senior tranche and were created purely to decrease regulatory capital charges on the balance sheets of the sponsoring banks. Examples include Triangle Funding Ltd. and SBC Glacier Finance Ltd.

to other assets that carry high-risk weightings, the most notable of which are asset-backed securities.

Since the late 1990s, the SCDO market has expanded beyond its European roots as a balance-sheet management tool (key milestones are highlighted in Exhibit 1). SCDOs are now issued regularly in the United States, Japan and Hong Kong. In fact, based on the combined European and U.S. numbers for 2002 and 2003, more CDOs have been issued in synthetic form than cash form (Exhibit 2).[4]

Exhibit 2: Synthetics Make Up the Majority of CDO Issuance by Number of Transactions

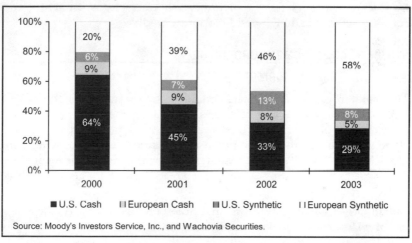

Source: Moody's Investors Service, Inc., and Wachovia Securities.

The purpose of synthetic execution has also evolved. Many SCDOs are now executed for arbitrage purposes (transactions designed to exploit inefficiencies in the debt markets). Starting as highly negotiated first-to-default baskets, arbitrage-motivated SCDOs evolved first into static-pool, tranched structures and then into managed tranched structures that incorporate many cash-based CDO features. Arbitrage SCDOs are usually smaller than their balance-sheet counterparts and are $500 million–$1 billion in notional. Typically, balance-sheet-motivated SCDOs carry a large notional amount at $1 billion–$10 billion and reference investment-grade assets.

4. U.S. and European market only; excluding market value CDOs but including European single-tranche synthetic CDOs.

Early arbitrage SCDOs were purely synthetic. In other words, transaction assets and liabilities were unfunded and governed solely by a swap confirmation.[5] Oftentimes, there were only a few participants in a transaction. Starting in 2001, many arbitrage-motivated SCDOs evolved into broadly syndicated structures issued in both funded and unfunded forms.[6] That short-lived trend reversed itself in 2002 with the rise of single-tranche (bespoke) CDOs that are typically sold to a single investor.

As of 2004, the SCDO market is diversified and dynamic, with a growing list of transaction types. Balance-sheet SCDOs reference structured-finance assets and corporate investment-grade credits. Synthetic arbitrage transactions reference structured-finance assets, investment-grade corporate credits and high-yield corporate credits.[7]

SYNTHETIC CDOS FROM THE GROUND UP

First Came Credit Default Swaps...

The standardization of CDS has enabled the expansion of the SCDO market beyond its use as a balance-sheet management tool. In fact, the development of arbitrage SCDOs was predicated on the expansion and standardization of the single-name CDS market, which provides the major means for SCDO sponsors to source/hedge their exposure. Therefore, understanding a simple CDS is critical to understanding SCDOs.

Initially, the CDS market was a small interbank market used to transfer credit risk. Lenders looked to distribute the credit risk of large-loan positions to other banks without selling the loans and possibly jeopardizing bank-client relationships. Each CDS contract was highly negotiated and designed to transfer primarily default risk. From this foundation, CDS contracts become standardized and are now traded by bank portfo-

5. In an unfunded transaction, no proceeds are exchanged at the outset of the deal. The protection buyer pays premiums until maturity or a credit event. In the case of a credit event, the protection seller will make a payment to the buyer.
6. Funded portions are issued in a credit-linked note (CLN) format. The performance of a CLN is tied directly to the performance of the reference pool through a CDS. Proceeds from the CLNs are invested in high-quality assets until liquidated to pay for losses in the reference pool or returned to the investor. The high-quality assets generally provide the LIBOR portion of the CLN coupon from interest generated by the high-quality assets, and the margin owed above this is covered by the premium paid by the sponsor.
7. Through 2003, no pure synthetic high-yield CDO transactions have closed. However, high-yield debt represents a significant portion of the reference pool of several SCDO transactions.

lio managers, insurance companies and arbitrageurs (e.g., hedge funds and CDOs) to hedge existing credit exposure or to accept new exposure to corporate credit risk. According to the British Bankers' Association (BBA) and the International Swaps and Derivatives Association (ISDA), the credit derivatives market grew from $180 billion notional in 1997[8] to an estimated $3.6 trillion notional in 2003.[9] The dramatic growth of the market may be attributed to a combination of the following:

- Standardized ISDA documentation, which created market conventions and industrywide benchmarks, including counterparty posting requirements

- Structured product offerings (i.e., SCDOs) with embedded CDS

- Increased focus and guidance from regulators

- Educated investors who profit from pricing/technical inefficiencies

A CDS is a contract between a protection buyer and a protection seller. Under this agreement, the protection buyer pays a premium to the protection seller in return for payment if a credit event (typically bankruptcy, failure to pay or restructuring) occurs with respect to the reference entity.[10] Usually, protection payment can be triggered by a default on any borrowed money — even on the most subordinate debt.[11]

For example, suppose a protection buyer (e.g., a bank) purchases $10 million of ABC Corp. five-year default protection[12] and agrees to pay 100 bps per annum to the protection seller (e.g., an investor/SCDO). In this case, the protection buyer pays $25,000 quarterly ($100,000 annually) to the protection seller until a credit event occurs or five years pass and the agreement expires. If a credit event occurs in the five-year period, the protection buyer delivers $10 million in face value of ABC Corp. debt (though likely worth less than the $10 million due to the credit event) to the protection seller in return for $10 million. This is known as *physical settlement*.

---

8. *BBA Credit Derivatives Report 2001/2002*, British Bankers' Association, 2002.
9. International Swaps and Derivatives Association news release, April 1, 2004.
10. *Credit events* are defined by the ISDA as bankruptcy, failure to pay, restructuring, obligation acceleration, obligation default or repudiation/moratorium, although other events can be negotiated between the related parties to the swap.
11. *Borrowed money* is defined by the ISDA as any obligation that is related to funds that the reference entity has borrowed, including, but not limited to, loans, bonds, letters of credit and deposits. This term is broader than bonds and loans but more narrow than payment, which includes any obligation for repayment.
12. Five-year default swaps are the market benchmark for CDS contracts, although we are starting to see other maturities trade, particularly shorter maturities.

Alternatively, the contract can use *cash settlement* following a credit event, which requires a payment from the protection seller to the protection buyer equal to the difference between the initial price (usually par) and the current price of the debt based on the valuation procedure indicated in the CDS contract.[13] Using the same example of ABC Corp., if the value of the defaulted debt is determined to be $6 million (the recovery), then the protection seller will pay the protection buyer $4 million (par minus recovery).[14] The payments for physical settlement and cash settlement are shown in Exhibit 3.

Exhibit 3: Credit Default Swap Payment Mechanics

| Initially | Protection Buyer (Short ABC Corp.) | No exchange of cash! | Protection Seller (Long ABC Corp.) |

Until a Credit Event Occurs or Maturity — Protection Buyer (Short ABC Corp.) — 100 bps per annum on $10 million notional paid quarterly on an Act/360 day count → Protection Seller (Long ABC Corp.)

Physical Settlement (Standard)

$10 million face value of ABC Corp. debt (worth $6 million)

$10 million cash

or
Cash Settlement

$4 million cash

If Credit Event Occurs — Protection Buyer (Short ABC Corp.) / Protection Seller (Long ABC Corp.)

Source: Wachovia Securities.

Buying protection is similar to shorting a cash instrument, and selling protection is similar to going long a cash instrument, but CDS and cash bonds are *not* identical investments. Direct investment in fixed-rate corporate debt contains interest-rate and funding risk, whereas a CDS investment does not. Interest-rate risk is absent from a CDS investment because there is no initial cash outlay and funding risk is mitigated

---

13. In contrast to physically settled CDS contracts, payments in cash-settled CDS contracts are tied generally to a specific obligation as indicated in the swap confirmation. Physically settled CDS contracts may reference a specific obligation to clarify the reference entity or the seniority of the deliverable obligation, but any pari passu obligation may be delivered.

14. In certain instances, the loss payment may be assigned a priori (regardless of the realized recovery) and the cost of protection is adjusted appropriately.

because there is no need to borrow. In contrast, when an investor borrows money to fund an investment, funding risk is created. If the investor's funding cost increases, the spread between the investment and the investor's cost of funds decreases, lowering the economic benefit of the investment while the risk remains unchanged.[15] Therefore, the unfunded nature of a CDS creates a pure credit risk position.

...Then Came Synthetic CDOs

In its simplest form, a SCDO is the application of a CDS to a pool of reference credits. For example, the pool of reference credits could be tied to loans or to a group of structured-finance securities that reside on the sponsor's balance sheet (a synthetic balance-sheet transaction). Or, the pool of reference credits could be tied to a defined group of corporations (typically an arbitrage transaction).

In a synthetic balance-sheet transaction, the sponsor is a buyer of protection and the investors are the sellers of protection. If certain predefined credit events occur on any of the reference entities, then the sellers of protection must make the buyer whole. For this protection, the sponsor pays a premium based on the notional amount of the pool.[16] If no credit

Exhibit 4: Unfunded SCDO: No SPV and No Proceeds Exchanged

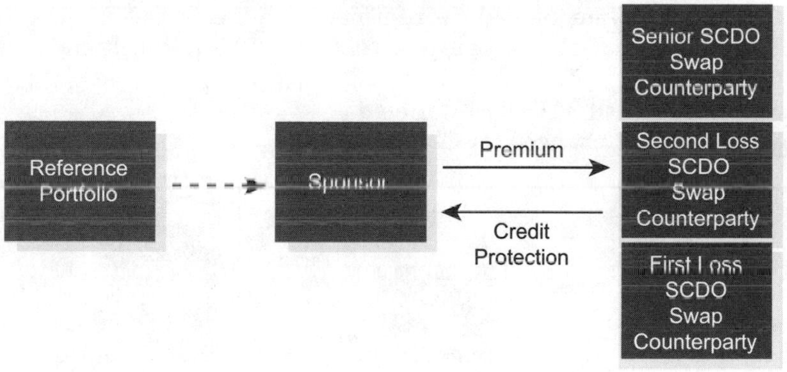

SCDO: Synthetic collateralized debt obligation; SPV: Special-purpose vehicle.
Source: Wachovia Securities.

15. Ignoring any collateral posting requirements that may be required due to the counterparty's credit risk. We describe comparable cash-based transactions in more detail in Appendix A.
16. The notional amount of a pool is also known as the face amount and represents the contractual size of the pool on which all calculations of premium and recovery will be based.

events occur, the only cash transferred throughout the course of the deal would be the premium paid by the protection buyer. If a credit event occurs, the seller of protection pays a settlement amount to the buyer of protection. At this point, CDO technology can be layered in to allow investors to participate at different risk levels (Exhibit 4). CAST 1999-1 is an example of this type of transaction. Synthetic arbitrage transactions behave similarly except that the portfolio of reference credits typically is assembled with securitization as the primary goal, and often the reference credits do not reside on the balance sheet of the sponsor.

Synthetic CDOs can be funded or unfunded. In they are unfunded transactions, the sponsor (protection buyer) must rely on the swap counterparty's (investor's or protection seller's) ability to make the required loss payments during the course of the deal because no cash is exchanged at the outset. The terms of payment are specified in the CDS confirmation. Therefore, the investor must be able to execute a CDS, which excludes many pension plans, CDOs and other fund managers. In addition, counterparties (investors) may be required to post collateral based on how the sponsor views their credit risk. Collateral posting requirements are not generally one-for-one but are based on the credit quality of the investor/swap counterparty. To expand the investor base and remove counterparty credit risk, sponsors incorporated credit-linked notes (CLNs), which are funded instruments, into the SCDO framework. Under this format, a special-purpose vehicle (SPV) is normally created to

**Exhibit 5: Funded SCDO: SPV Added
and Proceeds Exchanged for CLNs**

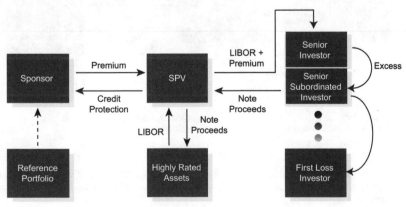

CLNs: Credit-linked notes; SCDO: Synthetic collateralized debt obligation; SPV: Special-purpose vehicle.
Source: Wachovia Securities.

provide a bankruptcy-remote depository for the high-quality assets (Exhibit 5). An example of this type of transaction is Biltmore 2002-2.

Most current SCDO transactions are actually a hybrid of the funded and unfunded structures shown in Exhibit 5. A single, highly rated investor (typically a monoline insurance company) will invest in the most senior tranche in unfunded form (CDS), whereas the rest of the liability structure is purchased by various investors in funded (CLN) or unfunded form. The unfunded, senior-most tranche is known as the "super-senior" tranche to reflect its position above the AAA rated tranche.

The super-senior tranche paved the way for the broad-scale application of SCDO technology to bank balance sheets and later to arbitrage transactions backed by investment-grade assets. In the late 1990s, banks were eager to shed much of their investment-grade bank loan risk because those loans were often extended for relationship reasons and generated low returns. In addition, loan assets carry a 100% risk weighting, which means that a bank is charged an 8% regulatory capital charge. Early SCDOs permitted banks to reap the benefits of regulatory capital relief, but they had to bear the cost of funding provided by transactions with traditional tranching (i.e., without a super-senior tranche). Often, those

Exhibit 6: Partially Funded SCDO: Super Senior Added

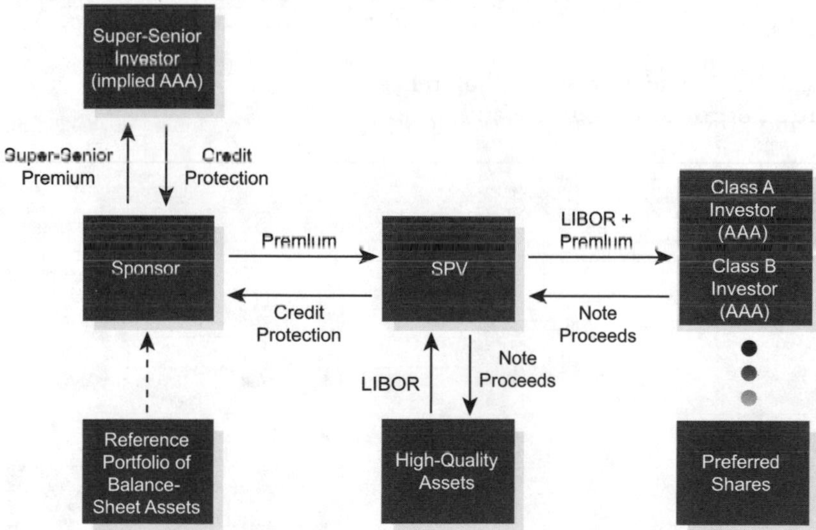

SCDO: Synthetic collateralized debt obligation; SPV: Special-purpose vehicle.
Source: Wachovia Securities.

transactions were not economically attractive. The super-senior tranche dramatically improves SCDO economics and thus facilitates efficient regulatory capital relief.

Senior to the AAA tranche, the super-senior frequently accounts for 85% or more of the capital structure (assuming an investment-grade pool of assets) and carries a low spread (e.g., 8 bps–15 bps)—much lower than the spreads commanded by AAA tranches—which reduces the weighted average cost considerably. A typical balance-sheet SCDO in today's market is similar to that seen in Exhibit 6.

The credit protection premium is passed from the sponsor to the super-senior investor and to the SCDO. The portion passed to the SCDO is partitioned among the SCDO investors according to the size of their investment and the amount of risk they have taken. When a credit event occurs on a reference entity, high-quality assets are liquidated in an amount equal to the payment obligation on the CDS, and the proceeds are then passed to the sponsor. Losses are applied to the investors in reverse order of priority, though sometimes the realization of the loss is postponed until the end of the transaction, allowing noteholders to earn interest on the entire outstanding amount of their investment.

The structure described in Exhibit 6 is typical, but variations are common. In some transactions, the super-senior investor is a counterparty of the SPV and the entire premium is passed from the sponsor

Exhibit 7: Arbitrage SCDO: Reference to a Portfolio of Credit Default Swaps

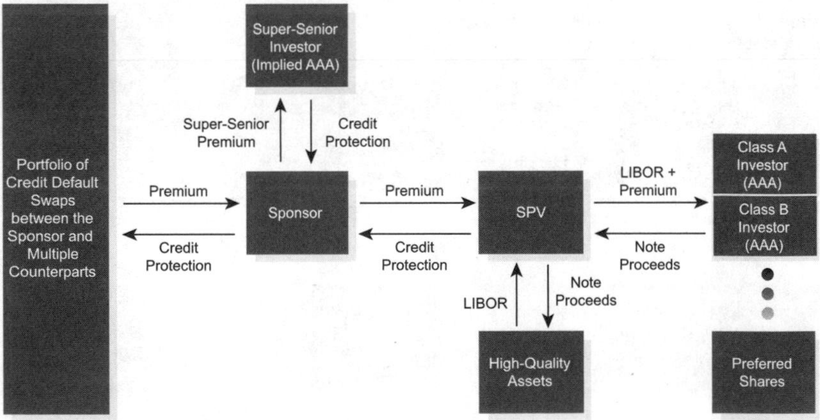

SCDO: Synthetic collateralized debt obligation; SPV: Special-purpose vehicle.
Source: Wachovia Securities.

to the SPV where it is then partitioned. In other transactions, a portion of the Class A, B or C notes may be unfunded or partially funded. One of the benefits of an SCDO is the versatility afforded to investors and structurers.

The transactions described in Exhibits 5 and 6 are typical of a balance-sheet-motivated transaction where the sponsor collects interest and fees from cash assets held on its balance sheet. Based on this structure, an arbitrage transaction can be constructed easily if the sponsor selectively enters CDS contracts with the market (Exhibit 7). In this case, preferred shareholders benefit from any premium remaining after payment to the super-senior counterparty and the rated notes.

Settlement Mechanics: Physical or Cash

A CDS may be settled physically or in cash. Although SCDOs may employ either method, cash settlement is more common. Certain managed SCDO transactions employ physical settlement, but even in this subset of the SCDO market, physical settled SCDOs remain a minority. For cash settled transactions, a 2003 study by Fitch Ratings[17] indicates that as many as 12 different valuation methodologies have been employed in transactions Fitch has rated. All of the methodologies involve a bidding process whereby the reference asset is valued by CDS dealers. However, some methods specify multiple valuation rounds and multiple bids, whereas others permit just one round and two bids, of which one could be a party involved in the transaction.

The risk of moral hazard is higher when only a few bids are required, especially if the sponsor provides one of the bids. Therefore, investors should seek transactions with multiple valuation bids. As of 2003, the market standard was at least five nonaffiliated bids for CDS on corporate names and at least three for CDS linked to structured-finance securities. Fewer bids are to be expected for structured-finance securities because fewer banks are equipped to value these instruments.

As mentioned previously, physical settlement is used in some managed SCDOs where a "hands-on" approach is to be expected. It is also more straightforward because complicated valuation processes are avoided. However, concerns persist in the market over the specific assets that are eligible for delivery and the portfolio manager's ability to work through problem credits is critical. Investors benefit when a manager has the flexibility to maximize recoveries. Therefore, investors should consider

17. Shin Yukawa, Jill Zelter and Michael Gerity, "Credit Events in Global Synthetic CDOs: 2000-2003," Fitch Ratings (May 12, 2003).

whether the portfolio manager has the expertise and the resources to devote to a work-out security (this was highlighted in the original). There are also practical complications with physical delivery when used in an SCDO. For example, the defaulted security must be funded and is likely not paying interest, which imposes a cash drag on the structure.

A COMPARISON WITH CASH CDOS

Although SCDOs use tranching technology similar to that employed by traditional cash-based CDOs, in many respects the structures are very different. Cash-based transactions tend to be long-dated arbitrage transactions that use a variety of assets, including high-yield bonds, leveraged loans or structured products as collateral. In contrast, SCDOs tend to have shorter maturities (five years), are balance-sheet or arbitrage motivated and are referenced to investment-grade corporate obligations or structured-finance securities. In this section, the general characteristics of an SCDO are compared with those of a typical cash-based CDO. Exhibit 8 compares the characteristics of the typical cash CDO versus that of the typical SCDO.

Life Cycle

The life cycle of an SCDO may look different from a traditional CDO. For instance, SCDOs referenced to investment-grade corporate credits take a short time to ramp up due to a developed and liquid CDS market. Furthermore, the "collateral" will remain outstanding until maturity, which is usually in bullet form. Amortization does not exist because CDS contracts *reference* a particular entity but not a specific security. The termination date of the contract is freely negotiable, therefore structurers are free to arrange for simultaneous maturity of all contracts (Exhibit 9).

If the portfolio consists of contracts referenced to structured securities and the transaction is managed, there is little difference between SCDOs and cash-based CDOs because the CDS is tied to specific securities instead of reference credits: The ramp-up period is followed by a revolving period and an amortization period. A typical ramp-up period for structured-finance SCDOs is six months to one year. The revolving period is generally 3–5 years, potentially leaving a 25-year amortization period. As in traditional cash-based CDOs, managed synthetic transactions are subject to early termination of the revolving period and acceleration of payment (through the capture of excess spread) if the collateral pool does not perform well.

Exhibit 8: Comparison of a Typical Cash CDO to a Typical Synthetic CDO

Characteristic	Typical Cash CDO	Typical Synthetic CDO
Collateral Pool	• High-yield corporate bonds • ABS • Leveraged loans • CMBS/REITs • Trust preferred securities • Emerging market debt	• Credit default swap linked to a pool of balance-sheet assets (loans, senior or mezzanine structured finance) or to a reference pool of corporate credits (usually investment grade)
Size	• $200 million–$600 million, generally	• $1 billion plus
Collateral Quality	• Investment grade or below investment grade and even distressed collateral	• Primarily investment grade
Diversity	• Diversity score of 10 (SF CDOs) to 60 (corporates)	• Similar to cash CDOs but generally higher due to the larger size of the transactions
Management	• Typically managed	• Typically static, though there is a growing managed market
Moral Hazard	• Possible through the purchase or sale of collateral designed to benefit one class of investors over others.	• Generally no due to the static nature of these transactions
Payment Frequency	• Quarterly or semiannually	• Quarterly
Legal Final	• Generally 12 years for transactions tied to corporate credits but as long as 30 years for transactions tied to ABS	• For balance-sheet or arbitrage transactions linked to corporates, 4–6 years • For structured-finance deals, 10–30 years
Expected Maturities	• Generally 7–12 years for transactions tied to corporate credits depending on the payment priority of the investment	• For arbitrage and balance-sheet transactions linked to corporates, 3–5 years • For structured-finance deals, approximately eight years for senior debt and 15 years for subordinate debt
Ramp-Up Period	• 0–6 months	• Generally, immediate to one month although arbitrage SF SCDOs may have periods as long as a year
Prepayment Risk	• Yes	• Generally, no
Reinvestment Risk	• Yes, for transactions with reinvestment periods	• Generally, no due to the static nature of these transactions
Interest Rate Risk	• Managed with swaps and other derivatives	• In unfunded form, there is no interest rate risk • For CLNs, floating-rate assets and liabilities create a natural hedge
Equity Leverage	• 8–12 times due to a generally lower-quality collateral pool	• Frequently 30 times but as much as 100 times for transactions linked to IG corporate credits and highly rated structured-finance securities

ABS: Asset-backed securities; CDO: Collateralized debt obligation; CLN: Credit linked note; CMBS: Commercial mortgage-backed securities; IG: Investment grade; REIT: Real estate investment trust; SCDO: Synthetic CDO; SF: Structured finance.
Source: Wachovia Securities.

Trading

Like cash-based balance-sheet CDOs, balance-sheet SCDOs typically are not permitted to trade reference entities in or out of the reference pool on a discretionary basis for regulatory reasons. Limited substitution can take place, however, and both the old and new reference entities are exchanged at a par notional. In contrast, managed arbitrage SCDOs permit trading, although the mechanism is different than that used in a cash-based arbitrage CDO.

Exhibit 9: Life Cycles of SCDOs Illustrated

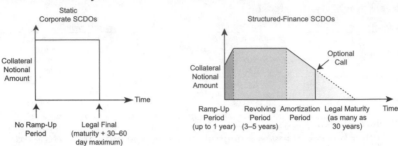

SCDOs: Synthetic collateralized debt obligations.
Source: Wachovia Securities.

A position in the reference pool of a managed SCDO can be removed by either terminating the CDS or buying protection to hedge the position (as opposed to an outright sale in a cash-based transaction). If the position is terminated, an early-termination payment will be made by the SCDO if there is a loss (the CDS spread has widened) or the SCDO will receive cash if there is a gain (the CDS spread has tightened). If an offsetting position is taken after the credit has deteriorated, and the CDS spread has widened, the excess spread on the transaction will be negatively affected because the SCDO will pay more in premium on the new CDS than it receives on the original CDS. However, if the credit has improved then the SCDO can use the same technique to lock in a spread premium on the credit and enter a new contract on another credit.

Rating agencies and noteholders typically favor purchasing protection to offset a CDS if the credit has deteriorated (the spread has widened) because cash flow to equity is reduced and the collateral balance is maintained. This prevents cash from "leaking" to equity holders despite significant losses in the reference pool. To mitigate excessive spread deterioration, investors and rating agencies impose a minimum spread test to ensure that sufficient interest is available to pay rated noteholder interest. When using offsetting trades, it is advisable to select CDS contracts that have identical terms. However, this is not always possible, therefore the rating agencies frequently limit the number of offsetting trades that are permitted.

Market standards regarding the amount of trading that is permitted have not emerged as of January 2004. Many managed transactions limit trades to approximately five per year. These transactions are known as "lightly" managed, and typically the trades are used to shed credit risk positions. "Fully" managed transactions permit all of the trading freedoms normally found in a cash-based structure: credit-risk and credit-improved trading and a bucket for discretionary trading (usually 10%). Investors seem to favor lightly managed trading because it permits defensive trading of the portfolio without the cost of a completely managed portfolio.

Some fully managed SCDOs permit portfolio managers to adopt a net short position in a credit (e.g., Jazz CDO B.V. I and II). This allows managers to capitalize on a negative view of a particular credit or to take a relative credit view between competitors by going short one and long the other but maintaining a neutral stance on the industry. To the extent that the portfolio manager is successful in these strategies, equity holders and noteholders will benefit from this added flexibility. To our knowledge, there have been no cash-based transactions with this feature as of 2003.

Coverage and Quality Tests

Synthetic transactions typically do not have overcollateralization (OC) tests but benefit from additional subordination. However, for transactions with OC tests, the senior-most tranche (the super-senior tranche) may be excluded from the OC calculation, which differs from the typical cash OC test. In these synthetic transactions, the OC ratio is calculated as

$$\text{Class X OC Ratio} = \frac{\text{Cash Collateral Account Balance}}{\text{Notional Amount of Class X Notes and Notes Senior excluding the Super Senior}}$$

The OC test is breached if the cash collateral account declines to a level where the OC ratio falls below a certain threshold. Regardless of the method used, credit events and trading losses can result in a breach of the OC test as cash collateral is depleted to cover losses incurred. If the OC test is breached, excess spread is directed away from junior tranches and equity and allocated to a cash account where it is held to pay future losses. Like cash-based CDOs, quality tests such as the diversity and weighted average rating factor tests are used to maintain portfolio quality during the ramp-up period and revolving (replenishment) periods.

CREDIT EVENTS AND DEFAULTS

Corporate Credit Events: Focus on Restructuring

Credit events define the risks that are transferred from the buyer to the seller of protection in a CDS and, theoretically, can be negotiated between the buyer and seller of protection to cover a multitude or only a

few risks. However, in 1999, the ISDA introduced a standard set of credit derivatives definitions, including credit event definitions, that are now
market standard for use in SCDOs referenced to corporate credits
(Exhibit 10). These definitions may be modified in any given transaction,
but they have been successful in creating a common language used by all
market participants. Since 1999, the ISDA has issued several supple-
ments to the definitions that address weaknesses revealed by various
credit events that occurred between 1999 and 2002. In 2003, the ISDA
introduced another version, which incorporates all of these changes.
However, the ISDA definitions were not developed with structured
products in mind, and application to that market requires some adjustment to the definitions and an understanding of the context in which
they are used, which we discuss later in this section.

Exhibit 10: Standard Set of Credit Event Definitions*

Credit Event	Layman's Description
Bankruptcy	The dissolution or insolvency of a reference entity, the inability to pay debts or the shift of control to a secured party, custodian or receiver
Failure to Pay	The failure of the reference entity to make payments due on any obligation before expiration of any applicable grace period
Restructuring	The reference entity or governmental authority changes an obligation by reducing the interest rate or the principal amount; postponing the payment of interest or principal; lowering the payment priority of the obligation; or changing the currency to one that is not permitted
Obligation Acceleration	An obligation of the reference entity becomes due and payable before it would otherwise have been due and payable as a result of a default or other similar condition or event other than a failure to pay
Obligation Default	An obligation of the reference entity becomes capable of being declared due and payable before it would otherwise have been due and payable as a result of a default or other similar condition or event other than a failure to pay
Repudiation/Moratorium	The validity of an obligation is rejected either by the reference entity or a governmental authority; this event is mostly applicable to sovereign credits

*Paraphrased from the *2003 ISDA Credit Derivatives Definitions.*
Source: Wachovia Securities.

Historically, ISDA credit event definitions have favored protection buyers (i.e., banks that were hedging risk) and captured a broader spectrum
of risks than what most investors and rating agencies would consider
"default." In the past, this was not an issue because the CDS transactions

were negotiated between two sophisticated parties that were aware of the risks involved. However, as the SCDO market has evolved and particularly as arbitrage SCDOs have emerged over the past few years, the additional risk transference has become a concern.

Restructuring drew significant attention in October 2000 when Conseco Finance Corp. extended the maturity of its loans, which the market viewed as a positive credit event. Nonetheless, protection buyers triggered on this credit event and delivered longer-dated bonds, which were trading cheaply, in exchange for par from the sellers of protection. This event underscored the risk of the cheapest-to-deliver option. The following March, Moody's published a report discussing its concerns over the 1999 credit event definitions, including the restructuring credit event.[18]

The rating agency's main concern was maintaining consistency between losses that would result from a credit event in an SCDO with the agency's definition of default for a cash asset. This consistency is important to appropriately size credit enhancement for rated tranches of SCDOs. Restructuring and obligation acceleration were particularly troubling to Moody's because these fell short of their definitions of default and were deemed "soft" credit events—events that capture credit deterioration short of a default and hence make a CDS riskier than a cash position. These contrast with "hard" credit events that fit within the agency's view of default, including bankruptcy and failure to pay.

The SCDO market in the United States responded to the rating agency concerns by altering credit events to include only bankruptcy, failure to pay and a more limited form of restructuring known as modified restructuring. However, regulators and the CDS market in Europe were not able to come to terms with modified restructuring. Hence, the European deals included bankruptcy, failure to pay and the original restructuring, which became known as full restructuring. For transactions based on full restructuring, the rating agencies simply increased their default assumptions for the incremental risk from full restructuring or required that tighter language be incorporated into the definition.

As mentioned previously, the ISDA published the *2003 ISDA Credit Derivatives Definitions*, which took effect on June 20, 2003. That set of definitions addresses many of the market concerns with the 1999 definitions. In the new definitions, two delivery options for the restructuring

---

18. Jeffrey S. Tolk, "Understanding the Risks in Credit Default Swaps," Moody's Investors Service (March 16, 2001).

event have been created. The first, called Restructuring Maturity Limitation and Fully Transferable Obligation, or more commonly *modified restructuring*, is currently the market standard for U.S. participants and is more restrictive than the second option, called Modified Restructuring Maturity Limitation and Conditionally Transferable Obligation, or more commonly *modified, modified restructuring*.[19] Modified, modified restructuring is typically used among European participants. In both instances, the credit event language tightens the scope of the restructuring credit event to avoid future problems, but one of the risks inherent in a synthetic transaction is documentation risk, and so it remains to be seen if some unforeseen event will reveal further weakness that might necessitate more change. We highlight pertinent differences between each of the restructuring definitions in Exhibit 11.

Exhibit 11: Differences between the Three Types of Restructuring

	Full Restructuring	Modified, Modified Restructuring	Modified Restructuring
Maturity Limitation of the Deliverable Obligation	Cannot exceed maturity limitation specified in the confirmation, usually 30 years	Cannot exceed the restructuring date plus 60 months if the delivered obligation is a bond or a loan, or 30 months if it is not a bond or a loan	Cannot be longer than the earlier of the restructuring date plus 30 months or the latest maturity of any restructured bond or loan, and in no instance can it exceed the scheduled termination date date of the contract plus 30 months
Transferability of the Deliverable Obligation	Must meet the reference obligation characteristics specified in the confirmation	Can be conditionally transferable with consent required as long as consent cannot be unreasonably withheld or delayed	Must be fully transferable without consent of the obligor
Eligible Transferee	Not applicable	Most financial institutions	Financial institutions that pass a minimum asset test

Source: Wachovia Securities.

Cheapest-to-Deliver Option

If a reference entity is in default, all pari passu debt should trade at roughly the same level, but this is not always the case. Some credit events capture risk beyond that of pure default, such as restructuring and obligation acceleration. These events are called soft credit events. In these cases, the market may not view default as imminent, and the value

---

19. For clarification, the option called "Restructuring Maturity Limitation and . . ." in the ISDA definitions is known as modified restructuring by the market. Meanwhile, "Modified Restructuring Maturity Limitation and . . ." is normally called modified, modified restructuring (note *modified* twice). This may cause confusion for new participants.

of pari passu debt may still carry a time value factor. When credit events occur, the protection buyer has a cheapest-to-deliver option, which means the buyer can deliver to the seller a longer maturity instrument that will frequently be cheaper. In other CDS contracts, this is not the case. For example, in structured-finance SCDOs, the CDS typically references a specific issuance, which eliminates the cheapest-to-deliver option.

The restructuring definition that is used can affect the value of the cheapest-to-deliver option inherent in a CDS. This option is worth the most under full restructuring (the broadest language) and worth the least under modified restructuring (the most narrow language; Exhibit 12). We advise SCDO investors to inspect thoroughly the definitions being used to understand the protection they are "selling." This is especially true for secondary market investments because older transactions might include older ISDA language.

Exhibit 12: Restructuring Language Affects the Cheapest-to-Deliver Option

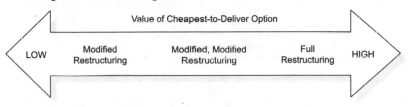

Source: Wachovia Securities.

Structured Product Credit Events: Unique Definitions Apply

Referencing structured-finance transactions in SCDOs created a new set of challenges for the synthetic market. The ISDA definitions were created with corporate credits in mind and are difficult to apply directly to structured product transactions. Regardless, many early transactions include the same credit events that were used for corporate transactions even though events such as bankruptcy are not readily applicable (CDOs are issued from bankruptcy-remote SPVs and are therefore not tied to the performance of a sponsor). Obligation acceleration is another event that is difficult to apply to structured products because it could be a positive development depending on the part of the capital structure affected. For instance, a CDO accelerating principal repayment to the senior noteholders because of a coverage test breach could actually lead to an upgrade for those noteholders even though the underlying reference credits might be performing poorly. In fact, of the six credit events that are commonly used in corporate CDS contracts, only failure to pay applies directly to structured product securities. To fully capture the default risk of structured products, the SCDO market has developed other credit events. Two of the most common, principal write-down and rating downgrade, are summarized in Exhibit 13.

**Exhibit 13: Standard Set of Credit Event Definitions
Found in Structured Finance SCDOs**

Credit Event	Layman's Description
Failure to Pay	The failure of the reference entity to make payments due on any obligation before the expiration of any applicable grace period; this would not include a tranche that PIKs according to its terms
Principal Write-Down (Loss Event)	Whenever any amount of principal with respect to any reference obligation is permanently reduced due to the allocation of losses, write-offs, charge-offs, defaults or liquidations; this is not a standard ISDA definition and therefore could be defined in a variety of ways
Rating Downgrade	The assignment of a below CCC rating in combination with the postponement of interest for two or more periods; this is not a standard ISDA definition and therefore could be defined in a variety of ways

ISDA: International Swaps and Derivatives Association; PIK: Payment in kind.
Source: Wachovia Securities.

Another difference in a structured-finance SCDO is that the credit events reference specific bonds rather than a transaction or an issuer, for example, Ford Credit Auto Owner Trust 2003-A A2B instead of Ford Motor Credit Co. This particular bond would have to be impaired as defined by the applicable credit event definitions before protection payments would be made by the seller. Impairment to classes below this class would not trigger a credit event nor would impairment to the corporate credit of Ford Motor Co. or Ford Motor Credit Co.

Today, market participants can generally expect to find 2–3 (but possibly more) credit events specified in any given SCDO (Exhibit 14).

Historical Credit Event Experience: Bankruptcy Dominates

So what credit events are most likely to occur? By and large, most credit events fall under the bankruptcy category. In a May 2003 study of 112 credit events triggered on 28 reference entities across 115 CDOs (some CDOs had no credit events) in the United States and Europe, Fitch

Exhibit 14: Typical Credit Events in Corporate and Structured-Finance CDOs

	Reference Entities Tied to	
Credit Event	**Corporate Debt**	**Structured-Finance Assets**
Bankruptcy	Standard	Not Standard
Failure to Pay	Standard	Standard
Restructuring*	Standard	Not Standard
Obligation Acceleration	Not Standard	Not Standard
Obligation Default	Not Standard	Not Standard
Repudiation/Moratorium	Not Standard	Not Standard
Write-Down (Loss Event)	Not Standard	Standard
Rating Downgrade	Not Standard	Occasionally

*Any of full restructuring, modified restructuring or modified, modified restructuring.
Source: Wachovia Securities.

found that 84.6% were triggered by bankruptcy, 9.9% by failure to pay, 3.3% by restructuring and 2.2% by repudiation/moratorium (Exhibit 15).[20] Evidently, there were no credit events linked to obligation acceleration or obligation default. Because the study only examined synthetic transactions that referenced corporate credits (and not structured-

Exhibit 15: Bankruptcy Dominates Credit Event Experience

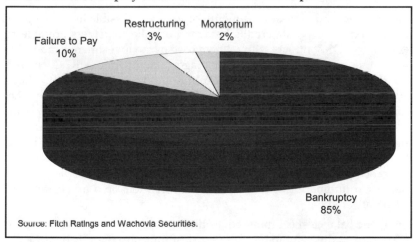

Failure to Pay 10%
Restructuring 3%
Moratorium 2%
Bankruptcy 85%
Source: Fitch Ratings and Wachovia Securities.

20. Shin Yukawa, Jill Zelter and Michael Gerity, "Credit Events in Global Synthetic CDOs: 2000-2003," Fitch Ratings (May 12, 2003).

finance securities), credit events due to write-down (loss) or rating downgrade were not recorded.

INVESTORS GAIN FROM SYNTHETIC CDOS

There are several benefits to the issuer and the investor when implementing an SCDO instead of a cash CDO, including

- Ease of execution
- Greater spread on the assets (CDS)
- Higher diversity
- Lack of prepayment risk in SCDOs linked to corporate credits
- Shorter average lives
- Bullet maturities
- Low cost of liabilities
- High-quality assets

Ease of Execution

Compared with cash-based CDOs, SCDOs are significantly easier to execute because they generally require shorter ramp-up periods, do not require balance-sheet capacity and have streamlined documentation (if fully synthetic).

Shorter ramp-up periods (one month or less) are possible in transactions referenced to corporate credits because portfolio managers are able to enter into CDS contracts with relative ease in the investment-grade CDS market. For example, a portfolio manager may include ABC Corp. as a reference entity in a five-year SCDO although ABC Corp. may only have 10-year debt outstanding. In other words, the investment-grade CDS market is not dependent on specific cash assets. Therefore, SCDO collateral aggregation is not dependent on the forward calendar of issuance or the availability of outstanding debt instruments in the way a cash-based transaction is dependent. Theoretically, the sponsor could declare a reference pool overnight and hedge later as it sees fit. This is possible because a number of dealers make active markets on a broad range of corporate credits.

Synthetic balance-sheet transactions and arbitrage transactions based on corporate credits tend to have the shortest ramp-up periods because the reference obligations are already on the balance sheet or exposure is readily sourced in the CDS market. In contrast, arbitrage structured-finance SCDOs tend to have longer ramp-up periods (up to a year) as issuers arrange hedges by purchasing cash assets.

For those issuers that do not already have assets on the balance sheet or for those with limited balance-sheet availability, corporate arbitrage SCDOs have the added benefit of not requiring any balance sheet to ramp up because CDS are unfunded instruments.

Finally, pure synthetic transactions benefit from simple documentation compared with funded CDOs. If executed in an unfunded form, the only documentation necessary is a swap confirmation. Participants in unfunded structures generally employ their own legal counsel to ensure that all of the risks are appropriately analyzed.

Greater Spread

Compared with a cash position, CDS often offer wider spreads from a credit protection seller's point of view. This is known as positive basis. For example, the five-year default protection on ABC Corp. may trade at 100 bps, whereas the asset-swapped spread on the five-year cash bond is LIBOR plus 95 bps (Appendix A). The positive basis in this case would be (100 bps – 95 bps) = 5 bps. There are several reasons for a positive basis:

- **Clarity of legal language.** As discussed earlier, protection sellers are frequently selling protection on more than just *default* in the classical sense and demand a premium for potential contractual or definitional problems.

- **Liquidity.** Some CDS may not be as liquid as the corresponding cash assets. Therefore, investors may demand additional spread to compensate for this risk. For example, below-investment-grade CDS are frequently less liquid than their cash (and investment-grade) brethren, therefore protection sellers demand a higher premium.

- **Anonymity.** Banks looking to reduce loan exposure without affecting client relationships often purchase credit protection "anonymously" through the CDS market, therefore protection spreads can increase when a new loan is syndicated.

- **Technical influences.** 1) Position limits and risk constraints may force dealers to reduce credit exposure through the purchase of protection. Loan or bond trading desks with excess inventory will sometimes purchase protection in the CDS market rather than sell bonds into a weak or thin cash market. 2) Convertible bond arbitrage funds purchase convertible bonds and credit protection simultaneously to create a cheap equity option, therefore CDS spreads can widen after a new convertible issue hits the market.

- **Optionality.** Physically settled CDS contracts provide a cheapest-to-deliver option to the protection buyer, which is paid for through a wider spread.

However, at times there is a negative basis. This generally occurs when several buyers of protection come to market. For example, if several large SCDOs are ramping "collateral" on identical reference credits, they could drive the spread (protection premium) tighter and possibly through comparable spread levels found in the cash market.

Higher Diversity

Due to the large scale of most SCDO transactions ($1 billion–$10 billion), a large number of credits can be referenced. Historically, an arbitrage SCDO of $1 billion notional would reference 100 separate corporate entities but could reference many more. Meanwhile, synthetic balance-sheet transactions could reference as many as 300 or more corporate entities. On the other hand, cash-based arbitrage transactions are usually significantly smaller ($300 million–$600 million) and contain 60–100 separate corporate obligations.

Lack of Prepayment Risk for Corporate SCDOs

The portfolio manager, if there is one, and investors benefit from the fact that CDS generally do not prepay. For SCDOs linked to corporate credits, CDS are usually not associated with a specific debt obligation. Therefore, if an entity prepays any of its loans (e.g., renegotiates new terms or terms out in the bond market), the CDS will not be affected. Therefore, the portfolio manager will need to be concerned only with managing overall credit exposure but not collateral maturities. Likewise, static corporate-referenced SCDO investors will be similarly unaffected by prepayment.

For SCDOs linked to structured products, there is some prepayment risk, which is dependent on the prepayment of the reference obligations. The super-senior holder bears most of the prepayment risk in these transactions due to its dominant position in the capital structure.

Bullet Maturities

Due to the contractual nature of CDS, SCDOs linked to corporate credits offer the attractive benefit of bullet maturities. In conjunction with the lack of prepayment risk, debt and equity investors benefit from bullet maturities, which allow them to plan their investment efficiently. This can be attractive to buy-and-hold investors who have low liquidity requirements and place a high priority on keeping funds invested. Unlike a traditional CDO, all collateral and debt mature simultaneously, and the repayment of noteholders will occur on a single day.[21] Furthermore, the maturity for many corporate SCDO transactions is 3–5 years (legal final may extend to six years), which is considerably shorter than what is typically available in the cash market.

Despite a certain amount of prepayment risk, the funded notes of SCDOs linked to structured-finance securities will likely be paid in bullet form as well. Many structured-finance SCDOs incorporate cleanup calls that unwind a transaction when the economics become unattractive. When the call is exercised, all rated investors will be paid simultaneously.

Lower Cost of Liabilities

Equity investors benefit considerably from the lower cost of liabilities afforded by synthetic structures. The super-senior tranche typically demands only a fraction of the spread that a traditional AAA CDO investor would require. Because the super-senior tranche represents so much of the capital structure—frequently 85% or more—the overall cost of liabilities for the SCDO is reduced dramatically. The "freed" excess cash is passed to the preferred shareholders. Debt holders may also benefit if provisions are made to trap excess cash when credit events occur and losses are realized. Super-senior investors (primarily monoline insurance companies) are willing to accept a low premium because of the considerable structural support provided them (the AAA investors are subordinate to the super senior) and the convenience of making their investment in unfunded form.

Transaction cost is driven down even further by generally lower structuring, administrative and trustee fees. For example, a portfolio manager may earn 50 bps per annum to manage a $300 million pool of collateral ($1.5 million per annum), whereas an equivalent fee for an SCDO manager requires only 15 bps per annum on a $1 billion collateral pool. The same principal can be applied to administrative and trustee fees.

In addition, structuring and placement fees in SCDOs are generally paid over the life of the transaction instead of up-front as is typical for cash-based CDOs. This typically leads to higher leverage, which benefits

21. It is possible that a portion of the payment could be withheld for a short period (approximately one quarter if static and up to one year for managed deals) if a credit event occurs to one of the reference entities in the collateral pool just before maturity.

equity holders, and more collateral at closing, which benefits noteholders.

High-Quality Assets

The low cost of liabilities found in SCDOs typically allows these transactions to reference higher-quality collateral (where the arbitrage is thinner) than collateral that is used to collateralize cash CDOs. This provides an additional diversification tool for investors who currently have exposure to cash-based CDOs and the credits that usually support them. On the corporate side, synthetic transactions reference assets that are typically rated BBB on average, whereas cash-based CDO collateral is usually rated in the B and BB range. Structured-finance SCDOs are usually referenced to pools of highly rated, often AAA, senior securities compared with cash-structured-finance CDOs, which are collateralized by assets that are rated BBB on average and are usually subordinate or mezzanine. Investors need to be aware that the higher-quality collateral also results in greater leverage and more sensitivity to event risk.

SINGLE-TRANCHE (BESPOKE) TRANSACTIONS

A niche of the SCDO market is worthy of special consideration. Commonly called single-tranche or bespoke CDOs, these transactions are private in nature and are often highly customized. In these transactions, the investor (protection seller) designs an SCDO around his or her credit views and risk tolerance: he or she selects the reference credits (spread, quality) and defines the level of risk to be accepted (e.g., AA). For example, an investor may choose 100 credits with an average rating of BBB and total notional value of $1 billion and indicate a desire for a $20 million exposure to this pool at an A level of risk. In return, the premium received is adjusted to suit the risk.

Single-Tranche Structure

Conceptually, a single-tranche CDO structure is similar to that of conventional synthetic CDOs with one significant difference — only one tranche is issued. A single-tranche CDO effectively represents the sale of credit protection[22] to the swap counterparty (i.e., an investment bank) on a slice of reference pool risk. The attachment and detachment points of

---

22. The person who sells protection accepts a contingent liability (agrees to pay for losses in the reference pool) in return for a coupon to be paid periodically by the protection buyer (receiver of loss payments).

the tranche define the slice of risk sold.[23] The rest of the risk (what otherwise would constitute the tranches above and below the tranche) is not issued. Exhibit 16 depicts a generic single-tranche CDO structure.

Exhibit 16: Generic Single-Tranche Structure

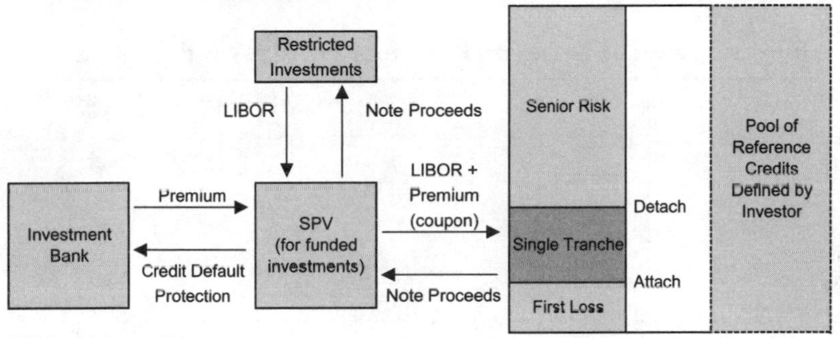

SPV: Special-purpose vehicle.
Source: Wachovia Securities.

The mechanics are straightforward. The investor chooses a pool of reference credits—generally names that are traded in the CDS market, although nonstandard assets may also be chosen—and indicates the amount and risk level of exposure. The investment bank then creates a customized tranche that meets the investor's criteria. The investor (protection seller) generally buys the tranche at par, and the proceeds are used to purchase restricted investments (usually investments rated AAA/Aaa) having the same notional as the single tranche issued.[24] In return, the investor receives a coupon equal to the interest generated by the restricted investments (LIBOR) plus the protection premium paid by the investment bank. If the aggregate reference pool losses exceed the amount of subordination (the amount of "unissued" tranches below the attachment point), then the restricted investments are liquidated dollar for dollar to compensate the investment bank, the protection buyer. Consequently, the principal balance of the single-tranche CDO investment may deteriorate over time. If defaults (and losses) continue, additional restricted investments are liquidated and the investor suffers

23. For the traditional CDO investor, the attachment point defines the percentage of the capital structure below the tranche, and the detachment point represents the starting point (attachment point) of the tranche immediately above in the capital structure. The difference between the two represents the size of the tranche.
24. Single-tranche CDOs are also available in unfunded form.

greater principal loss. Ultimately, the loss is capped at the amount of restricted investments posted (the detachment point). Concurrent with the liquidation of restricted investments, the "interest" paid to the investor is also adjusted downward in proportion to the principal reduction. In other words, losses are realized immediately.[25] These concepts are shown in Exhibit 17.

Exhibit 17: Effect of Losses on Return of Principal and Coupon

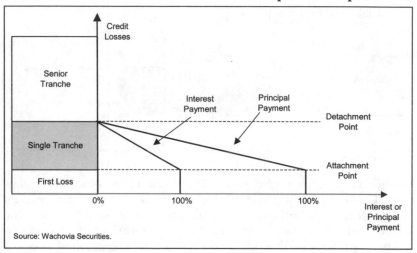

Source: Wachovia Securities.

Advantages of the Single-Tranche CDOs

Investors realize several benefits when investing in single-tranche SCDOs, including the following:

- **Credit selection and management.** Single-tranche CDOs are designed to meet the specific needs of individual investors; thus, unlike a conventional CDO investor who might be required to negotiate the characteristics of the transaction with other participants, the investor selects the reference portfolio and other features without interference from other investors. Investors can even elect to lightly manage their pools by replacing a small number of reference obligors per year. The ability to lightly trade the reference portfolio eliminates the so-called manager risk that exists in some multi-tranche managed CDOs, that is, the possibility that the manager

---

25. Structures that do not reduce the coupon upon loss can be created for investors who need the certainty of coupon and are willing to incur slightly greater principal loss.

could effect trades that are not necessarily aligned with the long-term good health of the tranche the investor bought. Single-tranche CDOs, like SCDOs in general, frequently offer significant diversification advantages. Single-tranche transactions typically reference a high-grade portfolio of 100–125 credits compared with a cash CDO, which normally includes 60–100 credits. Therefore, relative to the size of an investment, single-tranche transactions offer significant diversification.

- **Risk selection.** Single-tranche transactions allow investors to create investments with specified risk/return profiles through the selection of appropriate attachment and detachment points. Once features such as the number of reference obligors, reference obligor ratings, concentration levels and diversity are established, the attachment and detachment points are adjusted in conjunction with the rating agencies' requirements to determine the single-tranche rating.

- **Higher spread.** Single-tranche CDO spreads are often higher than those offered by similarly rated conventional cash flow CDOs because single-tranche spreads depend heavily on the reference pool chosen, the risk level chosen, the number of agency ratings assigned and the size of the investment—all of which can be modified to improve yield. However, single-tranche spreads can be relatively volatile because they tend to track the premium offered in the CDS market, even allowing single-tranche spreads to fall below conventional CDO spread levels for any given reference pool. In contrast, the asset spreads and liability spreads in the traditional cash-based CDO market are not as closely tied.

- **Ease of execution.** Single-tranche transactions are not dependent on a ramp-up of cash assets or the distribution of a full CDO capital structure and therefore can be executed in as little as 2–4 weeks. In addition to investment customization, these transactions are characterized by relatively quick closing times.

A single-tranche CDO investment also has the popular features of a fully banked synthetic CDO—bullet maturity (typically 3–5 years), no interest rate risk, no reinvestment risk and simple documentation that permits transaction execution within two weeks. In short, a single-tranche CDO investment is virtually identical to a fully banked synthetic CDO but has greater flexibility and additional benefits.

A Word of Caution: Portfolio Selection

The flexibility afforded by single-tranche CDOs can work against an inexperienced investor who may lack the knowledge to assess the risk of the reference portfolio (i.e., the true credit quality and default correlation of the reference obligors). Once the domain of the collateral manager, the selection of reference obligors is now the responsibility of the investor[26]; hence, there is a need to carry out more in-depth portfolio analysis. There are two important considerations for investors when selecting a reference pool: the credit quality of the reference pool and the default correlation among the reference obligors. Each of these will have a profound effect on the performance of the CDO investment, and each falls squarely on the investor. Good credit quality is an obvious desire and needs no explanation. However, one cannot always assume that a high (or low) default correlation is beneficial. In fact, for some investors, high default correlation is good, whereas for others it is bad. Therefore, single-tranche CDO investors should keep the following concepts in mind while choosing a reference portfolio:

- Default correlation is particularly important to the senior tranches. In fact, it could be argued that a clear understanding of the reference pool default correlation characteristics is more important than a clear understanding of the aggregate credit quality of the reference pool for these tranches. Furthermore, default correlation, and particularly low default correlation, becomes even more important to the senior tranches as the quality of the reference pool improves.

- The importance of default correlation decreases for investments lower in the capital structure and reaches a minimum for mezzanine tranches. For these tranches, good credit selection is paramount.

- At the bottom of the capital structure, default correlation again becomes important. However, for these investors, high default correlation is a beneficial reference portfolio characteristic that should be fostered. This desire stands in stark contrast to the desires of senior tranches referencing the same pool.

These concepts are shown graphically in Exhibit 18.

Investment Bank Hedging Strategy

On the other side of the single-tranche CDO trade, the protection buyer (i.e., the investment bank) will "delta hedge" its position through the sale of protection on individual names in the reference portfolio. The initial amount of protection sold for each name is determined by matching the sensitivity of the change in price (value) of the single tranche to the

---

26. The investor may hire a collateral manager to select and trade the reference portfolio for a fee of 50 bps–100 bps per annum based on the notional amount of the single-tranche investment.

Exhibit 18: Relative Importance of Asset Correlation and Credit Quality to the Performance of Single-Tranche CDO Investments (BBB reference pool)

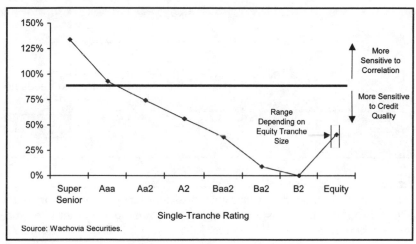

Source: Wachovia Securities.

change in price (value) of the single-name CDS. For example, if a 10 bps spread widening of Ford Motor Co. changes the mark-to-market value of a $10 million[27] CDS tied to Ford by a negative $50,000 (from the perspective of the investment bank as a potential protection seller) and changes the value of the single tranche by a positive $4,000 (from the perspective of the investment bank as a protection buyer), then the appropriate amount of Ford protection for the investment bank to sell is 8% (4,000/50,000) of $10 million, or $800,000 worth of Ford protection. As spreads change and reference entities default, the size of the hedge will change and, as a result, the investment bank will periodically alter the amount of single-name protection held through market purchases and sales. Therefore, a complete schematic of a single-tranche CDO transaction is similar to that shown in Exhibit 19.

The CDS market generally does not trade in increments of $800,000 notional. For this reason, banks generally desire fairly large correlation books (which are created from the sale of several single-tranche transactions) and will hedge the transactions in aggregate, allowing for finer control of the hedge.

27. Assume that the equivalent "fully banked" structure was tied to 100 CDS contracts of $10 million each.

Exhibit 19: Investment Bank Hedging Strategy

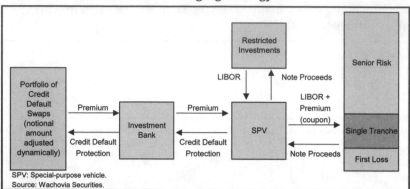

SPV: Special-purpose vehicle.
Source: Wachovia Securities.

INVESTOR'S GUIDE TO SYNTHETIC CDOS

There are a myriad of investment considerations in connection with CDO investments in general, and SCDOs are no different. Yet the emphasis may be different when looking at a synthetic transaction, and we suggest the following considerations be included in an investor's due diligence process in addition to their typical CDO due diligence process:

- Reference portfolio: quality and correlation are key

- Portfolio management: static, lightly or fully

- Credit event definitions: capturing the essence of default

- Loss calculation: methods differ but multiple bids are best

- Settlement procedures: now or later

- Discrete defaults: avoid continuous default assumptions

- Bifurcated risk: considering the high-quality assets

Reference Portfolio: Quality and Correlation are Key

We urge investors to pay particular attention to the portfolio of reference credits. Due to the high leverage of investment-grade SCDOs, just a handful of credit events can have significant implications for the performance of the investment. If the transaction is static and motivated by arbitrage reasons, investors should determine how the portfolio was constructed, including the parties involved and their interests, and carefully consider each name in the portfolio. For senior-tranche investors and equity investors, we also urge careful consideration of the default correlation within the reference pool. High default correlation could be devastating to senior investors while beneficial for equity investors (see A Word of Caution: Portfolio Selection).

Portfolio Management: Static, Lightly or Fully

Investors should consider whether the transaction is static, lightly managed or fully managed. This will guide the due diligence process. For static transactions, the focus is the portfolio of reference entities, whereas more emphasis is given to the manager in managed trans-actions. Unique to synthetic transactions is the concept of lightly managed transactions. In a compromise of sorts, equity investors and the super-senior investor have agreed to allow the portfolio manager to engage in a limited number of trades per year; usually these are credit-risk trades. Super-senior investors generally favor static transactions because it is easier to quantify the risk associated with their investment, whereas equity owners frequently prefer giving the portfolio manager discretion to remove credits that appear to be deteriorating. Finally, port-folio managers should have experience in CDS documentation and established trading relationships with a broad range of CDS brokers, which demonstrates their market access.

Credit Event Definitions: Capturing the Essence of Default

Much discussion has been devoted to the nuances of what constitutes a credit event and, unfortunately, some of these issues still need resolu-tion. The CDS market has attempted to react as unforeseen events have occurred (e.g., Conseco, Inc., Railtrack and National Power PLC), but there is still considerable discussion surrounding the definition of restructuring and guarantees.

Investors should study the credit event definitions. Broadly defined definitions will increase the risk to the protection seller, whereas narrowly defined definitions do not. For example, the CDS in an SCDO may specify full restructuring, modified restructuring or modified, modified restructuring or some variant of any of these as a credit event. Investors should understand these differences. The interests of various participating parties drive the definition of a credit event, and investors should be aware that the interest of the other parties might conflict with their own. In general, the rating agencies favor terms that simulate the default of a cash investment because their rating methodologies are based on cash-based default and recovery data. However, investors should be sensitive to the differences between a default in the cash market and a credit event in the credit default swap market.

Loss Calculation: Methods Differ but Multiple Bids Are Best

On the occurrence of a credit event, there is tremendous variation in the methods of loss calculation. As mentioned earlier, some methods specify multiple valuation rounds and multiple bids, whereas others permit as little as one round and two bids—of which one could be a party involved in the transaction. We recommend that investors require valuation methods that incorporate at least five nonaffiliated bids for CDS on corporate names and three for CDS linked to structured-finance securities. Furthermore, time constraints should be considered. If fewer than three bids are used to value the defaulted reference obligation or strict time constraints are applied to the pricing process, valuations could be depressed, which could increase the loss incurred by the investor.

Write-Down: Now or Later

When a credit event is cash settled, some SCDOs write down the principal of the equity and notes in reverse order of seniority as credit events occur and are settled, whereas other SCDOs wait until the end of the transaction. If write-down is postponed until the end of the transaction, SCDO debt that may be principally impaired will continue to receive interest on the full notional amount of the investment. Conversely, if the notes are written down immediately, impaired noteholders will receive only a portion of their expected interest payment.

Discrete Defaults: Avoid Continuous Default Assumptions

Investment-grade SCDOs are susceptible to event risk within the pool of reference assets, just like their cash counterparts. The highly leveraged nature of investment-grade CDOs (commonly, the equity tranche consists of less than 3.5% of the entire liability structure) increases the impact of losses on equity holders and junior note holders. By historical standards, a 2%–3% cumulative default rate that would significantly impair the equity of an investment-grade CDO is high for a five-year period, but in a pool of 100 names this equates to a small number of names experiencing problems. For instance, one default in a pool of 100 names is significantly below the historical average, whereas two defaults are significantly above it. Increasing diversity can mitigate much of the default "lumpiness," but we recommend that investors also identify and evaluate the weakest credits in the collateral pool. In large part, the performance of their investment will depend on those securities. Implicitly, therefore, we also recommend that investors measure defaults in terms of the number of defaults and not default rates (e.g., a 0.5% default rate is not possible in a pool of 100 equally weighted credits), which tends to underestimate the possibility of large losses and overestimate the stability of returns.

Other events can also adversely affect equity and note holders. Many would argue that the historical default numbers used to structure many corporate investment-grade CDOs did not anticipate the relatively high incidence of accounting fraud that rocked the investment-grade market in 2001 and 2002. Investment-grade corporate CDOs created in the late 1990s were not structured with this added stress in mind, and the sudden demise of previously investment-grade credits in this manner does not allow the portfolio manager or deal structure to react effectively.

Bifurcated Risk: Considering the High-Quality Assets

Investors who purchase CLNs depend not only on the creditworthiness of the reference entities but also on the performance of the high-quality assets that support their position. Frequently, the proceeds of the CLNs are invested in a government investment certificate (GIC), but sometimes highly rated ABS or Treasurys are also used. Regardless, the CLN's performance depends on the performance of those high-quality assets as well as the performance of the reference pool. The insolvency of the GIC provider or a default in any of the high-quality holdings would adversely affect the deal's ability to pay principal and interest when due. Although many market participants may consider default by any of these entities a remote possibility, we suggest investors consider the merits of the high-quality collateral and perform due diligence on the GIC provider, if any.

CONCLUSION

The structured products market and the credit derivatives market have merged to create SCDOs, a product that is attractive to investors and issuers alike. Investors find SCDOs appealing for a variety of reasons, including cleaner, more efficient structures that typically feature bullet payments, the ability to source credit risk on a wider variety of credits and greater structural flexibility. Issuers are also attracted by the structural simplicity of SCDOs as well as the way in which these structures eliminate currency and interest rate mismatches. In addition, SCDOs can be executed in a shorter time frame and, in the case of corporate-related credits, offer practically nonexistent ramp-up periods.

The learning curve for investors who currently participate in the cash CDO market should be relatively short because SCDO structures bear similarity to the cash market and many cash CDO concepts are transferable. Other concepts such as ISDA documentation and CDS mechanics have been presented here to provide investors with the basic tools to understand those areas that are different from the cash CDO market.

In the form of SCDOs, the CDO market continues to prove its structural flexibility. Emerging from its humble beginnings as a tool for banks to obtain regulatory capital relief, SCDOs have become a dominant fixture in the greater CDO market. Today, the SCDO market includes arbitrage transactions tied to corporate credits and structured-finance securities (e.g., ABS, CMBS and RMBS) as well as balance-sheet transactions. This variety provides a myriad of investment opportunities tailored to a particular risk appetite and credit exposure that often can be difficult to source in the cash market. Given the flexibility of the SCDO product, market participants should expect continued evolution and expansion of this market.

APPENDIX A: REPLICATING A CREDIT DEFAULT SWAP IN THE CASH MARKET

Selling protection (long the credit risk) on ABC Corp. can be replicated in the cash market as follows:

- The long position funds at LIBOR – 5 bps to finance the purchase of ABC Corp. bonds in the open market

- The long position enters into an interest rate swap on the ABC bonds to LIBOR + 95 bps

- Net long position = (LIBOR + 95 bps) – (LIBOR – 5 bps) = 100 bps

Exhibit 20: Long Position in the Cash Market

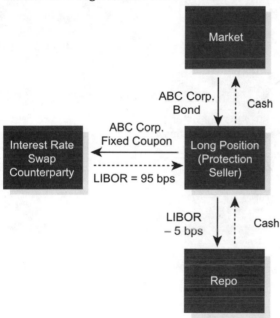

Source: Wachovia Securities.

Buying protection (short the credit risk) on ABC Corp. can be replicated in the cash market as follows:

- The short position borrows ABC Corp. bonds in the repo market and earns the repo rate (LIBOR – 5 bps) on the pledged cash

- The short position sells ABC Corp. bonds in the market (LIBOR + 95 bps)
- Net short position = (LIBOR – 5 bps) – (LIBOR + 95 bps) = –100 bps

Exhibit 21: Short in the Cash Market

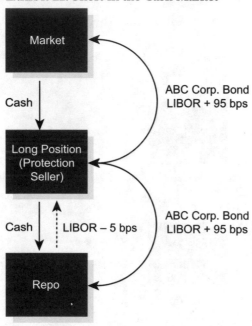

Source: Wachovia Securities.

Structural Innovations

Chapter 5

APEX Cash Flow CDOs: Enhancement through Fundamental Structural Change

EXECUTIVE SUMMARY

The recent credit downturn has exposed certain weaknesses in tradition-al cash flow collateralized debt obligation (CDO) structures. Corporate defaults, compounded by lower recoveries, certainly are two of the major causes behind rating volatility, but another factor—a misalign-ment of the respective interests of CDO collateral managers (CMs) and equity holders with the debt holders—may be a more significant reason for the increased downgrades.

Using credit derivative technology, Wachovia Securities (WS) has developed the APEX structure to balance the risk/reward dynamic between the equity holders and debt holders by encouraging CMs to focus more on the credit of their investments rather than the structural nuances of the CDO. Along the way, we show that both equity holders and debt holders will benefit from this paradigm shift.

INTRODUCTION

Rating volatility has been a topic of concern in the CDO market over the past few years as CDO downgrades have steadily increased. Although much of the focus has been on the collateralized bond obligation (CBO) sector, other CDO sectors have also experienced negative rating actions. Clearly, corporate defaults combined with lower recoveries are two of the major causes but we contend, and the rating agencies in recent months have concurred, that the complete answer is not so simple. In fact, the credit downturn has highlighted certain weaknesses in tradi-tional cash flow CDO structures, such as the misalignment of CM and equity holder interests with debt holder interests, which are possibly even more important.[1]

1. Yvonne Fu and Gus Harris, "U.S. High-Yield CBOs: Analyzing the Performance of a Beleaguered CDO Category," Jan. 21, 2003, Moody's Investors Service, Inc.

Improving the traditional CDO structure requires balancing the risk/reward dynamic for the note and equity holders. Structural changes are needed that encourage CMs to focus more on the credit of their investments rather than on the structural nuances of the CDO. In recent months, the rating agencies have suggested several structural changes designed to improve the rating stability of CDO debt, and we have noted a broad-based market enthusiasm for some of these improvements. Most notably, these include supplemental overcollateralization (OC) tests, CCC haircuts and discounted purchase price haircuts (Appendix A).

Although we view these innovations for traditional cash flow (CF) CDOs as positive, we believe there are more fundamental structural changes that could be made that would mitigate the natural tension between equity holder interests and note holder interests. The key is to match the distribution of cash to the performance of the underlying collateral pool. The supplemental tests cited above accomplish the goal of diverting residual cash flows sooner to protect the note holders, but a more comprehensive solution exists that can be implemented through the use of credit derivative technology. WS has engineered such a solution and calls it APEX. The APEX structure retains the most attractive features of a traditional CF CDO[2] but balances investor interests, enhances investor returns and encourages the CM to focus on credit decisions — not structure.

To introduce the reader to the APEX structure, we will

- Describe the basic mechanics of APEX and how these differ from a traditional CF CDO.

- Explain why we believe the APEX structure provides a framework for CMs within which they are freed to focus on credit rather than structural nuances.

- Illustrate both the subjective and quantifiable rewards and risks to note and equity holders vis-à-vis a traditional CDO.

Although APEX may initially look complicated to an investor, we believe the benefits outweigh the incremental education required for a new investor to understand this product. Exhibit 1 shows a sample capital structure for an APEX transaction that we will reference throughout this chapter (see the modeling assumptions in Appendix B). To date, four transactions have been completed that are similar to it (see Appendix C).

---

2. APEX builds on traditional CDO technology and therefore uses the same rating agency methodology. APEX transactions have been rated by all three rating agencies.

Exhibit 1: Sample APEX Structure

Class	% of Liabilities	WAL	Ratings Moody's/S&P	Spreads
Class A Notes	82.70%	7.40	Aaa/AAA	L + 55
Class B Notes	1.10%	11.14	Aa2/AA	L + 100
Class C Notes	10.70%	11.25	Baa2/BBB	L + 275
Preferred Shares	5.60%	4.25*	NA	NA

*Modified duration.
Source: Wachovia Securities.

APEX SWAP OVERVIEW

Introduction to the APEX Structure

APEX was initially conceived as a securitization vehicle for leveraged loans that addressed certain note holder concerns with traditional CDO structures. Since that time, the APEX structure has been applied to loan portfolios with a small bond allocation, but there is no reason that the technology could not be used for other asset classes as well. APEX is similar to a traditional cash flow CDO but uses credit derivative technology to help maintain a target level of collateral throughout the life of the CDO. The driving force of the APEX structure is the APEX swap, which reimburses the transaction for principal losses on defaulted assets or on the sale of credit risk securities.

The APEX swap is a combination of three swaps (the APEX credit swap, the APEX income swap and the APEX balance swap) that are necessary to simplify the documentation process. However, it is easier to understand the mechanics of the APEX swap by thinking of the three combined as one swap, which we will refer to as the APEX swap. The swap counterparty will be called the APEX swap counterparty (ASC). At the end of this section, we show how the three swaps interact.

The CM draws on the APEX swap after a default or a credit risk sale has occurred and will repay the ASC from excess spread that would otherwise be distributed to the subordinate notes, the CM (as a subordinate management fee) and equity. This is a revolving structure, so when draws are repaid that amount will become available again. The revolving nature of the APEX swap amplifies the amount of credit enhancement available. The APEX swap is available for the life of the transaction.

Credit Protection

To understand the need for credit protection in the form of a swap, first consider a traditional CDO structure as a backdrop. In a traditional

CDO, excess cash is "leaked" to equity investors despite losses in the collateral pool. This continues until one of the coverage tests is tripped, causing a diversion of cash to pay down the notes. However, by the time a coverage test is breached, significant deterioration in the collateral pool has already occurred.

Instead, what if excess cash is trapped at the first dollar of loss and then reinvested in additional collateral? A CDO with this feature would effectively have zero OC cushion, and excess spread would immediately be used to create additional enhancement for the notes.

APEX incorporates credit derivatives technology to effectively create such a CDO.[3] However, instead of simply trapping excess spread (which may not be enough to reimburse the collateral pool fully), the APEX swap forwards principal losses from credit risk or defaulted securities. Therefore, the CM has the proceeds from the sale or liquidation and the funds from the APEX swap to reinvest in new collateral.[4] The loss amount that is forwarded will be the difference between the initial amount paid for the security and the amount received when it is sold or liquidated. The same amount will be repaid to the swap counterparty starting with the next distribution date[5] via excess spread that usually flows through the waterfall and is released to the equity holders.

If the CM decides not to liquidate a defaulted security, the APEX swap forwards the difference between the initial amount paid for the security and the market value. Then, at quarterly intervals,[6] the defaulted security is revalued and any additional principal losses are forwarded to the transaction at that time. This process continues until the defaulted asset is sold or deemed worthless. Therefore, the APEX swap makes the CM whole for the principal loss and helps the pool to stay fully funded.

For example, if a security initially purchased for $10 million defaults and the market value of the defaulted security is $8 million, then the APEX swap will advance $2 million to the CM for reinvestment during

---

3. In an APEX CDO, as in a traditional CDO, the CM has discretion in categorizing a security as a credit risk and, therefore, par deterioration could take place without tapping the swap.

4. During the amortization period, proceeds that are forwarded by the APEX swap will be added to principal collections and used to amortize the notes rather than used for reinvestment.

5. If sales premiums become available from either the sale of a security above its purchase price or from post-marking recoveries (the liquidation amount that exceeds the initial marking of the security at default) on defaulted obligations, these amounts will be applied to any outstanding APEX credit swap balance on the next day.

6. Some earlier APEX transactions have a six-month interval.

the reinvestment period or to pay down the notes after the reinvestment period. Three months later, if the defaulted security trades to $6 million, the APEX swap will advance another $2 million. If there is no change in the value of the defaulted security or if the value rises, no payments are exchanged. This process will repeat every three months as long as the CM holds the defaulted security.

The APEX swap must be collateralized for protection of the APEX swap counterparty. To accomplish this internally in the APEX structure, the amount of proceeds that are received from issuing the Class C notes is set aside and invested in restricted investments that are high-quality (Aaa/AAA) securities with floating-rate coupons. The ASC has a first priority lien on the restricted investments, and the Class C notes have a second priority lien.

Provisions for Payments to the Class C Notes

The protection and credit enhancement provided to the Class A and Class B notes from the APEX swap are apparent. However, benefits to the Class C notes are less obvious. To better understand the risks to the Class C note cash flows, we separately examine the LIBOR interest, the spread interest and the principal.

LIBOR Interest

The LIBOR interest component for the Class C notes is paid by the ASC for the life of the transaction. In return, the ASC receives the interest generated by the restricted investments, absorbing any excess or shortfall.

Spread Interest

The spread for the Class C notes is paid from excess cash flowing through the waterfall. In addition, during the first five years, the ASC advances to the CDO an amount equal to the Class C note spread. In return, the ASC is repaid the spread component farther down in the waterfall. This advance is also collateralized by the restricted investments. At the end of the reinvestment period, the ASC stops advancing the Class C note spread but the CDO stops paying the APEX swap fee,[7] which increases available excess spread and helps pay the Class C note spread.

---

7. The APEX swap fee is a payment to the ASC for up-front deal expenses, including underwriting and structuring fees, that takes place over the first five years of the transaction.

Principal

At the end of the transaction or when the CDO is called, the Class C notes will be repaid from the restricted investments and the collateral pool. However, the Class A and Class B notes have a senior claim on the collateral and the ASC has a senior claim on the restricted investments. For example, assuming there is $48 million of restricted investments and $10 million is due to the ASC at the time the deal terminates, the Class C notes would receive $38 million of restricted investments and the balance due would be taken from any remaining proceeds from the collateral pool after retiring the senior notes. Given the principal replenishing features of the APEX swap, the collateral pool at termination should be of higher quality than might typically be found in a similar but traditional CDO. We discuss this further under Benefits to the Note Holders.

Financing Deal Expenses over Time

Finally, the ASC pays closing expenses on the closing date, including underwriting and structuring fees as well as other up-front fees such as rating agency, legal and accounting fees. In contrast, many CDOs pay for these expenses from the proceeds of the liabilities issued, which reduces the amount of proceeds available to be invested in collateral. This generally requires the CM to purchase the collateral at a cheaper price and/or issue additional preferred shares to cover these expenses. Closing fees and expenses can be substantial, as much as 2% of the deal.

The Three APEX Swaps

It can be confusing to look at the APEX swaps individually and therefore, until now, we discuss them in aggregate as the APEX swap. In reality, three swaps are required to simplify documentation[8] and accomplish all of the tasks cited above. Therefore, the grouping of function under each swap might not seem complementary (Exhibit 2). However, most important is the substance of what the swaps accomplish in aggregate, not what each does independently.

The cash flow payments for each swap are as follows (not necessarily in the priority of payment):

APEX Credit Swap

- **Principal Losses:** The ASC pays for any principal losses resulting from the sale of credit risk obligations or defaulted obligations.

---

8. APEX swaps use standardized ISDA documentation.

Exhibit 2: The Three APEX Swaps

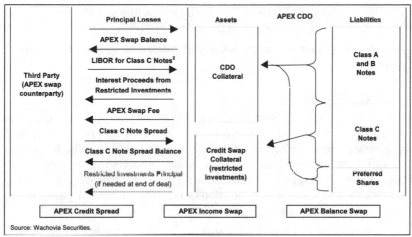

| Third Party (APEX swap counterparty) | Principal Losses → APEX Swap Balance ← LIBOR for Class C Notes[2] → Interest Proceeds from Restricted Investments ← APEX Swap Fee ← Class C Note Spread → Class C Note Spread Balance ← Restricted Investments Principal (if needed at end of deal) ← | Assets | APEX CDO | Liabilities |

APEX Credit Spread | APEX Income Swap | APEX Balance Swap

Source: Wachovia Securities.

- **APEX Swap Fee:** The CDO pays the APEX swap fee to the ASC during the first five years but starting on the second distribution date.

- **Class C Note Spread Balance:** The CDO pays the Class C note spread balance to the ASC.[9]

APEX Income Swap

- **LIBOR for the Class C Notes:** The ASC pays LIBOR on the Class C notes.

- **Interest Proceeds from Restricted Investments:** The ASC receives all of the interest proceeds from the restricted investments.[10]

APEX Balance Swap

- **Class C Note Spread:** The ASC pays the spread on the Class C notes during the first five years.

- **APEX Swap Balance:** The CDO pays an amount equal to the APEX swap balance.[11]

9. The Class C note spread balance represents the Class C note rated spread paid by the ASC.
10. Provided an APEX swap payment default has not occurred.
11. The APEX swap balance represents the amount of principal losses paid into the transaction by the ASC that have not been paid back to the ASC.

And on the final distribution date:

- The restricted investments are liquidated and used to reimburse the ASC and then used to retire the Class C notes.[12]

We can now blend the APEX swap payments into the payment waterfalls.

THE APEX WATERFALLS

The cash flow waterfalls will clarify many of the concepts introduced in our explanation of the APEX structure. In addition, this section will help an investor better understand the priority of payments and how it affects the different classes of notes. In the waterfall in Exhibit 3, we include 1) expenses, 2) senior and subordinate fees, 3) interest for each of the three classes of notes, 4) distributions to the equity and 5) payments to and from the APEX swaps.[13]

Like a traditional CDO, interest and principal collections are separated and passed down the corresponding waterfall on each distribution date. Unlike a traditional CDO, 1) there are several APEX-specific payments and 2) the principal and interest waterfalls are combined before payment to the Class C notes where there is also 3) an additional entry point for cash received from the ASC.

The interest waterfall is used to pay fees (including the APEX swap fee for the first five years), to pay Class A and Class B note interest, to cure any coverage test breeches and finally to pay any outstanding APEX swap balance to the ASC. The principal waterfall reinforces the interest waterfall before proceeds are either reinvested or used to pay down the notes. If the Class B notes have been paid, then the remaining principal would repay any outstanding APEX swap balance before combining with excess cash from the interest waterfall.

After the interest and principal waterfalls are combined, the ASC injects the Class C note spread (for the first five years) and the LIBOR component for the Class C note holders (for the life of the deal) into the combined waterfall. This mechanism ensures that there will always be

---

12. Restricted investments may be liquidated before the final distribution date if the ASC defaults.

13. This is an abbreviated waterfall that is intended to convey the approximate order of payments in an APEX transaction. We have given an overview of the elements that we believe are most relevant to understanding the structure. The waterfall of any specific transaction may differ from what is presented here. For complete details, we recommend the reader consult an offering memorandum for one of the previously issued APEX transactions.

Exhibit 3: Sample APEX Waterfall

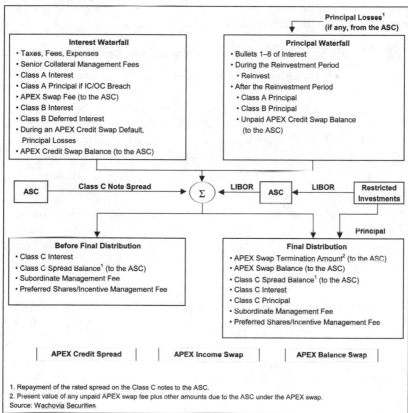

1. Repayment of the rated spread on the Class C notes to the ASC.
2. Present value of any unpaid APEX swap fee plus other amounts due to the ASC under the APEX swap.
Source: Wachovia Securities

sufficient interest proceeds to pay the LIBOR component on the Class C notes and, during the first five years, the Class C spread as well. Without this mechanism, the Class C notes would be susceptible to PIKing, under moderately high default scenarios.

Before the final distribution date, the Class C interest is paid and any remaining amounts from the collateral interest are used to pay the Class C spread balance (the amount that was just forwarded by the ASC), the subordinate management fee, and the incentive management fee and the preferred shares.

On the final distribution date, restricted investments are liquidated and combined with cash from the interest and principal waterfalls. This combined amount will be used to pay any monies owed to the ASC and then will be used to retire the Class C notes. Any remaining money will be used to pay the subordinate management fee, the incentive management fee and the preferred shareholders.

COMPARISON OF APEX STRUCTURES AND TRADITIONAL STRUCTURES

Thus far, we have focused on describing the APEX swap and the cash flow waterfalls as we believe these two elements are critical to understanding the APEX structure and are also the two that differentiate APEX from more traditional CF CDOs. Now we will focus on the similarities between APEX and other CDOs. In this section, we will review the general aspects of a CDO structure to illustrate the similarities (and a few differences).

Rating Methodology

APEX and traditional structures rely on the same rating agency methodology and, in fact, APEX transactions have been rated by all three major rating agencies (Moody's Investors Service, Inc., Standard & Poor's Corp. and Fitch Ratings).

Life Cycle

Both have three life stages including a ramp-up period, a reinvestment period and an amortization period. The weighted average life of the notes is comparable and the legal final for both is generally 12 years.

Exhibit 4: CDO Life Cycle

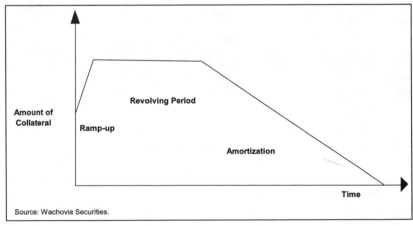

Source: Wachovia Securities.

As is common in a traditional CDO at closing, at least 50% of the collateral is warehoused and the first interest period is typically long (approximately six months) to allow the CM to complete the purchase of collateral (the ramp-up period). The effective date is the date at which all collateral has been purchased and defines the end of the ramp-up period.

The next stage in the lifespan of a transaction is the reinvestment period, which begins on the effective date and typically lasts five years. As in a traditional transaction, the principal proceeds received during this period are reinvested in additional collateral.

Finally, assuming no performance trigger has been breached, the pool will start to amortize after five years. As collateral either defaults, matures or is prepaid, principal proceeds will flow through the principal waterfall to pay off the senior-most notes. As usual, although natural amortization could ultimately completely pay down the transaction, we believe it is highly likely that the rising weighted average cost of liabilities will lead to an optional call well before the 12-year legal maturity date.

Coverage Tests and the Threshold Utilization Test

The manner in which the Class A OC test is calculated differs slightly from that of a traditional CDO, although the interest coverage test is the same. The undrawn portion of the APEX swap, measured as the amount of the APEX swap limit (the maximum amount that can be drawn on the swap) over the APEX swap balance (the amount drawn on the swap) is added to the principal collateral value[14] in the OC test numerator. The OC test is calculated as follows:

$$\text{Class A OC Test} = \frac{\text{Principal Collateral Value} + \text{APEX Swap Limit} - \text{APEX Swap Balance}}{\text{Class A Notes}}$$

As in traditional transactions, if the OC or IC test fails and remains out of compliance, then any remaining interest proceeds after the Class A note interest is paid will be used to pay the Class A note principal until the test is brought back into compliance. Therefore, tranches junior to the Class A may defer interest during this period. If a coverage test breach occurs within the first five years, the Class C notes will be unaffected because interest for these holders is forwarded by the APEX swap. After

---

14. Principal collateral value is loosely defined as the par amount of performing collateral plus principal proceeds plus the market value of defaulted securities.

the fifth year, the ASC no longer forwards the spread component of the coupon, and the Class C notes may defer some interest. Generally, OC tests for the Class B and Class C notes are not included in APEX transactions as a result of the excess cash diversion feature of the APEX swap.

Unique to the APEX structure is the threshold utilization test. This test is simply the ratio of the APEX swap balance (the amount drawn on the swap) over the APEX swap limit (the maximum amount that can be drawn on the swap). Historically, this ratio has been set at 50%–60%. Breaching the threshold utilization test will lead to the termination of the reinvestment period, although the APEX swap will continue to advance on losses in the collateral pool until the threshold utilization test ratio equals one.

Portfolio Profile Test and Quality Tests

CDOs include portfolio profile and quality tests to help ensure that portfolio diversity and quality are maintained by the CM during the life of the transaction. If any of these tests are breached, rather than resulting in a diversion of cash flow, the CM's trading abilities will be limited to only those trades that will maintain or improve the tests that are out of compliance. The types of tests and the relevant parameters for those tests are similar in APEX and a traditional CDO.

INVESTOR ANALYSES: BALANCING DEBT AND EQUITY INTERESTS

The point of improving the CDO structure is not to overly enhance the note holders completely at the risk of the equity holders; rather, it is to balance these interests. Now that we have conveyed the general mechanics of the APEX structure, we can explain in more detail how APEX improves on other, more traditional structures to achieve this equilibrium.

For the remainder of this chapter, we refer to the two structures shown in Exhibit 5. The first is a traditional CDO that is reflective of a marketable transaction circa the writing of this chapter. The second was introduced earlier and is an APEX CDO from the same period. Both transactions have the same collateral assumptions and comparable structural assumptions (Appendix B). To permit a true comparison between the structures, both structures finance underwriting, structuring and closing expenses over the first five years (although few traditional CDOs finance these fees).

Exhibit 5: Comparison of an APEX Structure to a Comparable Traditional Structure

	Sample APEX Structure					Traditional Cash Flow CLO			
Class	% of Liabilities	WAL	Ratings Moody's/S&P	Spreads (LIBOR +)	Class	% of Liabilities	WAL	Ratings Moody's/S&P	Spreads (LIBOR +)
Class A	82.7%	7.40	Aaa/AAA	55	Class A	75.8%	6.94	Aaa/AAA	55
Class B	1.1%	11.14	Aa2/AA	100	Class B	4.0%	9.34	Aa2/AA	100
Class C	10.7%	11.25	Baa2/BBB	275	Class C	4.3%	9.81	A2/A	160
PS	5.6%	4.25*	NA	NA	Class D	5.5%	10.54	Baa2/BBB	275
					Class E	3.6%	11.40	Ba2/BB	750
					PS	6.9%	3.81*	NA	NA

*Modified duration.
Source: Wachovia Securities.

BENEFITS TO THE NOTE HOLDERS

Note holders of traditional CDOs have struggled over the past few years with the discovery of structural weaknesses inherent to CDOs that have led to increased rating volatility. The two primary concerns are 1) leakage of excess spread to the equity holders early in a transaction and 2) manipulative management tactics used to maintain distributions to the equity holders. The general feeling has been that note holders, particularly those in the subordinate classes, are bearing more risk than is appropriate. To illustrate the benefits of an APEX CDO for note holders, we will explore three aspects of traditional CDOs that have contributed to note holder angst and the manner in which APEX mitigates those concerns.

Matching of Losses and Diversion of Excess Spread

The APEX structure provides better matching of losses with diversion of excess spread than a traditional CDO structure. In a traditional CDO, the level of the OC trigger is meant to protect investors but does not necessarily address collateral deterioration quickly enough or with enough vigor. The problem is that the OC test is typically set well below the initial OC level, creating a cushion that allows erosion of the collateral pool to happen before any diversion of excess spread occurs. This makes the subordinate and mezzanine investors particularly vulnerable to rating downgrades and principal defaults.

Using our traditional collateralized loan obligation (CLO) model, we have found that in certain moderately high default scenarios (6.65% constant annual default with 75% recoveries), equity investors receive significant distributions early in the transaction (Exhibit 6) yet the risk to note holders increases due to 5% in par deterioration. In fact, in this example, the Class E note holders did not receive full repayment of principal and, although other debt holders did not lose principal, their security was jeopardized early in the transaction.

Exhibit 6: Equity Distributions in a Traditional Structure (6.65% constant annual defaults)

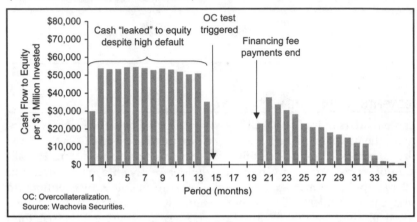

APEX protects note holders in this situation through the use of credit derivative technology. Principal losses are immediately replenished in an APEX transaction and later repaid from the excess cash flow stream starting with the next payment date. Incorporating this technology is similar to setting a supplementary OC test at the initial OC value. In this way, the equity holder bears the cost of deterioration at the time of a loss, not after losses have eroded substantial value. The cash flows to equity investors under a similar default and recovery scenario look like this in an APEX structure. Note that APEX equity cash flow is reduced significantly early in the transaction but is more robust late in the transaction (Exhibit 7).

Incentive to Game the OC Test Removed

Some of the features of traditional CDOs that were designed to increase CM flexibility simultaneously create competing interests that the manager must balance: those of the equity investors (of which the manager is frequently one) and the note holders. This introduces a level of subjectivity on the part of the CMs that can often lead to trading practices that are detrimental to the note holders.

One such case in a traditional CDO is the temptation for a CM, who is close to triggering an OC test, to hold credit risk securities. In this case, a

Exhibit 7: Equity Distributions in an APEX Structure (6.65% constant annual defaults)

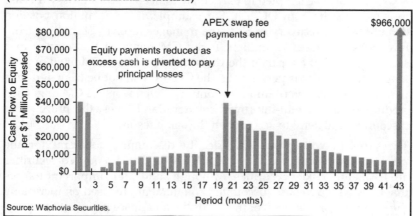

Source: Wachovia Securities.

CM can either sell the security in a credit risk sale or hold it, betting that the credit will improve. If the CM sells the credit, the proceeds will be only a fraction of the original investment and the loss will cause a violation of the OC test, which would divert cash away from equity holders. In this situation, the CM may be motivated to hold the credit in the hope that it improves (and carry it at par) even though, in the CM's judgment, the value of the credit will likely deteriorate further.

The temptation to apply this strategy increases in a deteriorating credit environment (as we have seen over the past few years). Under these circumstances, there may be several other problem credits in a portfolio, and credit risk sales or defaults may prevent equity investors from *ever* getting another payment. If several credit risk securities are held to avoid tripping the OC tests, the risk of the note holders (as measured by the mark-to-market of the collateral pool) could rise significantly.

We believe the APEX structure, due to its replenishing nature, encourages the CM to make more appropriate credit decisions. If the OC test is close to being triggered, it is likely that there are draws on the APEX swap and that equity flows are already being diverted. Therefore, equity holder and note holder interests are aligned in a desire to minimize losses. After all, if the CM truly believes that the credit is at risk, the longer the CM waits, the larger the loss may become and the longer the excess spread will be diverted from the equity holders to repay the swap counterparty. Thus, APEX encourages the manager to focus on credit rather than on managing to specific tests and preempts this moral hazard that is present in a traditional CF CDO.

Deep Discount Buying Not as Likely under the APEX Structure

A CM may also be tempted to participate in deep discount, risky trading to avoid breaching an OC test. For example, if a $10 million position defaults with a recovery of 80%, the manager receives $8 million from recoveries and loses $2 million. If the CM reinvests this money in a security selling at 80, par in the transaction will be maintained and, as long as the security is performing, the OC test will not be triggered thus permitting equity distributions to continue. Even worse, a CM might sell credit-neutral or credit-improved collateral and invest the proceeds in discounted collateral to accomplish the same result.

The problem with purchasing deeply discounted collateral for the purpose of maintaining the OC test levels is that discounted securities are frequently riskier securities. Although subtle, it is important to note that CMs who purchase discounted collateral are focused on increasing the volatility (or riskiness) of the portfolio, and hence payment to equity, rather than on minimizing losses.

We believe the APEX structure discourages use of this strategy.[15] First, the overriding mitigant to this practice is that the temptation to manage to the OC trigger is removed by the fact that equity cash flows are diverted as each loss is realized — not after they build up. Therefore, to resume payments to equity holders, the CM is motivated to minimize losses (not increase volatility) even when close to triggering an OC test. Second, regardless of whether the CM executes a credit risk sale or liquidates a defaulted security, the CM will have the same proceeds that were originally used to purchase the liquidated position. If a $10 million position defaults with a recovery of 40%, the manager receives $4 million from recoveries and $6 million from the APEX swap (assuming the security was purchased at par). By advancing the full amount of the loss to the CM, the manager will have the resources to purchase quality collateral. For these two reasons, APEX discourages the purchase of riskier, discounted collateral.

Rating Agency Suggestions

The rating agencies are well aware of these CM behavioral issues and have suggested corrective features to improve the stability of CDO

---

15. The APEX structure does not completely eliminate the motivation for deep discount trading because the CM is not required to tap the APEX swap for principal losses if the par of the collateral is greater than the required par amount (but would be required to tap it if below it). Therefore, there is a possibility that a manager could engage in deep discount trading to build a cushion that allows some flexibility in having to tap the APEX swap in the future.

credit ratings. Some improvements include haircutting techniques that will incorporate market value pricing for CCC and below rated securities and supplemental OC tests. The justification for these changes is that the market often trades securities as effectively defaulted where there is a high probability that the bond will default. Obviously, for purposes of the OC test, carrying a deeply discounted bond at par is questionable. Although in some respects duplicative, some of these features are being incorporated into APEX-structured CDOs (Appendix A).

BENEFITS TO THE EQUITY HOLDERS

There are two structural differences between APEX CDOs and traditional CDOs that benefit the equity holder and together they lead to higher expected returns over a wide range of default scenarios:

- Higher leverage
- Collateral preservation

Higher Leverage

The APEX swap reduces risk to the note holders because equity cash flows are trapped upon collateral default, which maintains enhancement for the notes. Because the rating agencies assign ratings based on the expected losses of the notes (Moody's) or the probability of default on the notes (S&P), there is a general migration of the CDO liabilities up the capital structure in APEX. For example, the Ba2/BB rated note in the traditional CDO has been eliminated and the amount of equity has been reduced from 6.9% to 5.6%.[16] As a result, a traditional deal that was 14.5x leveraged is now an 18.0x leveraged APEX transaction and each dollar of equity will receive relatively more excess spread.

The APEX equity holder also benefits from a lower cost of funds. The weighted average cost of capital has fallen considerably, from LIBOR plus 95 bps to LIBOR plus 76 bps in our example. This also permits more excess spread per equity dollar invested. Therefore, it is clear that equity investors benefit from higher leverage as long as the collateral pool is performing well.

Collateral Preservation

Collateral preservation through the forced reinvestment of excess cash upon principal losses also permits equity investors a higher internal rate of return (IRR) over relatively high annual default rates (Exhibit 8).

---

16. Compared with the traditional CDO, the A rated notes have also been eliminated.

Although it may be easy to understand why APEX equity performs better than traditional equity at low default rates (due to higher leverage), it is not as clear why APEX equity performs better at relatively high default rates (~7%) where increased leverage would seem to be detrimental. In fact, it seems counterintuitive. To understand the benefit of the APEX structure under these conditions, one has to look at the marginal use of cash.

Exhibit 8: Equity Returns in Traditional and APEX CLOs

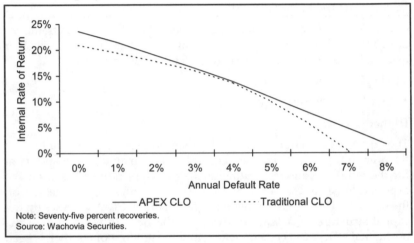

Note: Seventy-five percent recoveries.
Source: Wachovia Securities.

In a collateral pool that is not performing well, excess cash and money collected upon recovery from defaulted collateral can be used for one of two uses: to pay down the senior notes (as in a traditional CDO) or to purchase additional collateral (as in an APEX CDO). In the first case, the traditional CDO is retiring a liability that is earning LIBOR plus 55 bps and, in the second case, the APEX CDO is investing in new collateral earning LIBOR plus 330 bps. The difference, which is 275 bps, is the marginal benefit to the APEX CDO for investing in new collateral. Of course, this is only a benefit if the new collateral performs reasonably well. Given an assumed recovery rate (say 75%), we can solve for the default rate at which the equity holder should be indifferent to paying down senior notes or reinvesting in new collateral. Mathematically, the relationship between the marginal benefit and the default rate looks like the following:

$$\text{Marginal Benefit} = \text{Default Rate} \times (1 - \text{Recovery Rate})$$

or

$$0.0275 = \text{Default Rate} \times (1 - 0.75)$$

or

$$\text{Default Rate} = 11\%[17]$$

Therefore, provided the recovery rate is 75%, a CDO generates more excess cash by investing recoveries in additional collateral up to the point where the annual default rate reaches 11%. In APEX, the additional collateral purchased with excess cash directly benefits the equity investors late in the life of the CDO in the form of principal payments (Exhibit 9). Beyond this default rate, traditional CDO equity would outperform APEX equity, though one would have to ask whether sustained default rates at or above 11% are reasonable.

Exhibit 9: Equity Distributions in APEX and Traditional CLOs (6.65% constant annual defaults)

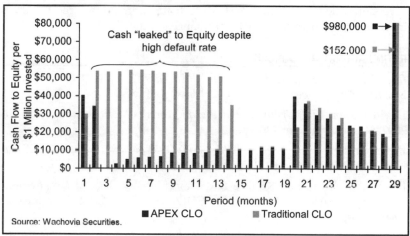

Source: Wachovia Securities.

Therefore, even though APEX equity flows may be temporarily reduced or eliminated when credit risk securities are sold or defaulted securities are liquidated, the IRR to equity holders is actually higher over a wide range of constant annual default scenarios. Not only are the note holders better protected in this structure by building in more appropriate incen-

17. The true crossover default rate may differ due to factors such as length of default lockout, call timing and other modeling assumptions.

tives to improve the CM's trading activity, but the equity holder also benefits from higher expected returns. In this way, the APEX structure balances note holder and equity holder interests.

CONCLUSION

Rating volatility has been a topic of concern in the CDO market over the past few years, as CDO downgrades have steadily increased. Corporate defaults and lower recoveries are two of the major causes, but the complete answer is not so simple. As we have shown, the credit downturn has served to highlight certain weaknesses in traditional cash flow CDO structures, such as the mismatch of equity distributions and collateral performance, and the misalignment of CM/equity holder and debt holder interests.

As the marketplace struggles for an appropriate response to these issues, we believe the key to improving the traditional CDO structure lay in balancing the risk/reward dynamic for the note and equity holders. The APEX structure does just this by matching collateral losses and equity diversions and encouraging the CMs to focus more on the credit of their investments than on the structural nuances of the CDO.

RATING AGENCY RESOURCES

Danielle Nazarian, *Structural Features Aimed at Enhancing CDO Ratings Stability: An Overview*, July 11, 2002, Moody's Investors Service, Inc.

David Tesher, *CDO Spotlight: Par-Building Trades Merit Scrutiny*, July 15, 2002, Standard & Poor's Corp.

David Tesher, *Balancing Debtholder and Equityholder Interests in CDOs*, Nov. 13, 2002, Standard & Poor's Corp.

Henry Albulescu, Nik Khakee and David Tesher, *Beyond Defaults and Recoveries: Structural Provisions in CDOs*, Nov. 13, 2002, Standard & Poor's Corp.

Henry Albulescu, Nik Khakee and David Tesher, *New Structural Enhancements for Cash Flow CDOs: Building on the Existing Foundation*, Nov. 13, 2002, Standard & Poor's Corp.

APPENDIX A: HAIRCUTS AND SUPPLEMENTAL REINVESTMENT TESTS

The following is a description of commonly used collateral haircutting techniques and supplemental reinvestment tests that have appeared in recent transactions:

- **Supplemental OC test.** This test is calculated in the same manner as the traditional OC tests, but the trigger is set at a higher level and therefore redirects equity cash flows at an earlier stage. Triggering this test redirects excess spread to purchase additional collateral rather than to delever the transaction by paying principal to the note holders.

- **CCC haircuts.** For the purposes of calculating the OC tests, assets rated CCC and below in excess of a specified percentage will be carried at the lower of their market value and applicable recovery rate. This adjusts the OC tests for credit migration that might occur to collateral.

- **Discount purchase haircuts.** Assets purchased below a certain percentage, for instance, 75%, will be carried at their purchase price, until such time as the market value of such asset exceeds another percentage, for instance, 90%, at which time it will be carried at par. These parameters provide protection against misguided deep discount trading that might be engaged in by the manager to maintain equity distributions. Technically, a CM cannot purchase credit risk securities, but this parameter provides some level of insurance against the abuse of the usually vague definition.[18]

---

18. Typically, a credit risk security is defined as a security that, in the CM's reasonable business judgment, has a significant risk of declining credit quality and, with a lapse of time, becoming a defaulted obligation.

APPENDIX B: MODELING ASSUMPTIONS

Unless otherwise indicated, these assumptions apply to the traditional structure and the APEX structure.

Collateral Assumptions

Collateral Feature	Covenant Level	Marketing Level
Floating-Rate Securities	Minimum of 100%	100.0%
Initial Purchase Price	Maximum of 100	100
Reinvestment Purchase Price	Maximum of 100	100
Diversity Score	Minimum of 45	NA
Weighted Average Ratings Factor	Maximum of 2300	NA
Weighted Average Spread	Minimum of 3.00%	3.30%
Reinvestment Spread	Minimum of 3.00%	3.30%
Moody's Weighted Average Recovery Rate	Minimum of 43.75%	NA
S&P Weighted Average Recovery Rate	Minimum of 53.25%	NA

Collateral Ramp-up	
Closing	60%
30 Days after Closing	10%
60 Days after Closing	10%
90 Days after Closing	10%
120 Days after Closing	10%
Total	100%

Structural Features	
Tenor	12 years
Reinvestment Period	5 years
Payment Frequency	Quarterly (6-month first period)
Administration Fees	4.5 bps
Trustee Fees	4.0 bps
APEX/Financing Fee	60 bps on $377 million annually*
Senior Management Fee	12.5 bps
Junior Management Fee	30.0 bps
Subordinate Management Fee	25% of excess cash after equity achieves 15% IRR
Prepayment Rate	20%
Default Rate	2.0% (unless otherwise indicated)
Default Lockout	0.5 years
Default Timing	End of period
Recovery Rate	75%
Call Date	7.5 years
Principal Reserve Fund	$1 million

Traditional Interest Coverage (IC) Tests	IC at Close	Minimum IC Ratio
Class A/B IC Test	187%	120%
Class C/D IC Test	173%	115%
Class E IC Test	153%	110%

Traditional Overcollateralization (OC) Tests	OC at Close	Minimum OC Ratio
Class A/B OC Test	125%	111%
Class C Note OC Test	119%	108%
Class D Note OC Test	111%	106%
Class E OC Test	107%	102%

APEX Interest Coverage Test	IC at Close	Minimum IC Ratio
Class A IC Test	163.2%	110.0%

APEX Overcollateralization Test	OC at Close	Minimum OC Ratio
Class A OC Test	120.7%	113.0%

APEX Threshold Utilization Test (TUT)	TUT at Close	Maximum Ratio
Class A OC Test	0.0%	60.0%

IRR: Internal rate of return.
*Beginning on the second distribution date and lasting for 4.5 years.
Source: Wachovia Securities.

APPENDIX C: PRIOR APEX TRANSACTIONS

Deal	APEX (IDM) CDO I, LTD.
Manager	Institutional Debt Management[1]
Closing Date	9/26/00

Class	Size ($million)	Original WAL (years)	Ratings (Moody's/S&P)	Coupon
A	687.00	7.00	Aaa/AAA	3ML + 41
B	33.00	10.30	A3/—	3ML + 130
C	78.30	8.70	Baa3/—	3ML + 275
PS	38.70			
Total	837.00			

Deal	CARLYLE HIGH YIELD PARTNERS IV, LTD.
Manager	Carlyle Investment Management, L.L.C.
Closing Date	4/17/02

Class	Size ($million)	Original WAL (years)	Ratings (Moody's/S&P)	Coupon
A-1	215.30	7.45	Aaa/AAA	3ML + 44
A-2[2]	130.00	7.45	Aaa/AAA	3ML + 44
A-3[3]	20.00	7.45	Aaa/AAA	3ML + 44
B	11.70	11.12	A3/A-	7.59%
C-1	24.50	11.33	Baa1/BBB+	3ML + 250
C-2	22.00	11.33	Baa1/BBB+	3ML + 228
PS	26.00			
Total	449.50			

Deal	1888 FUND, LTD.
Manager	Guggenheim Investment Management, LLC
Closing Date	12/20/02

Class	Size ($million)	Original WAL (years)	Ratings (Moody's/S&P)	Coupon
A-1	290.00	7.44	Aaa/AAA	3ML + 55
A-2[4]	75.00	7.44	Aaa/AAA	3ML + 55
B	10.00	11.07	A1/A+	3ML + 160
C	47.00	11.32	Baa2/BBB	3ML + 275
PS	26.00			
Total	448.00			

Deal	APEX (TRIMARAN) CDO I, LTD.
Manager	Trimaran Advisors, L.L.C.
Closing Date	6/27/01

Class	Size ($million)	Original WAL (years)	Ratings (Moody's/Fitch)	Coupon
A-1[2]	150.00	7.91	AAA/AAA	3ML + 50
A-2	250.00	7.91	AAA/AAA	3ML + 50
B-1	17.70	12.05	BBB-/BBB-	3ML + 400
B-2	29.80	12.05	BBB-/BBB-	3ML + 400
PS	13.30			
Total	460.80			

1. Owned by the MassMutual Financial Group.
2. Delayed settle.
3. Revolving.
4. Delayed funding.
Source: Wachovia Securities.

Chapter 6

The CDO Framework for Hedge Fund–Linked Principal-Protected Securities*

ABSTRACT

Principal-protected securities linked to hedge funds are a popular investment vehicle. The principal amount of these securities is guaranteed at maturity by a financial institution. The financial institution covers its exposure under the guarantee by using either a static or dynamic hedging methodology. The dynamic hedging is based on Constant Proportion Portfolio Insurance (CPPI) technology pioneered by André Perold of Harvard and, simultaneously, Fischer Black and Robert Jones of Goldman Sachs in 1986. In this chapter, we provide a framework for structuring principal-protected securities transactions based on collateralized debt obligation (CDO) technology. The CDO framework obviates the need for a financial institution to guarantee the principal amount of the securities, enhances the economic efficiency of the securities, provides structural transparency and broadens market participation in the securities. We believe the framework described in this chapter would be valuable for fixed-income CDO professionals and equity derivative professionals in creating principal-protected structured products transactions.

I. INTRODUCTION

The use of leverage to enhance the return on investments in alternative assets is becoming prevalent in the structured products market. The leverage is structured in a variety of forms, such as secured loans, total return swaps, call options or CDOs. CDOs are recognized as the most efficient form of leverage, and their application continues to grow. Several CDO transactions for hedge fund and private equity portfolios have been consummated.

*This chapter, written by Shanker Merchant, appeared in the *Journal of Alternative Investments*, Winter 2003 issue.

Principal-protected securities (the "protected securities") linked to hedge funds are an example of a structured product. In these transactions, a financial institution guarantees the return of principal at maturity of the securities, and the return on principal is linked to the performance of hedge funds. The financial institution uses a static or dynamic hedging methodology to guarantee return of principal, and employs leverage to generate return on principal. In this chapter, we provide a CDO framework for a transaction in which a financial institution does not take on such a direct role in the transaction. The benefits of this type of framework are twofold.

Structural Transparency

Traditional structures of protected securities transactions are by and large opaque and involve a high guarantee fee. As a result, these securities are less attractive to institutional investors. The CDO framework 1) provides an open platform for the transaction, 2) obviates the need for the guarantee and 3) facilitates a stand-alone rating on the securities, which would be more appealing to institutional investors.

Broader Market Participation

Only a few financial institutions are active in providing guarantees and leverage for protected securities transactions. Each of these institutions has its rules and restrictions for participating in such transactions. As a result, there is no market standard for the terms or the structure of the transaction. The lack of a choice in selecting a financial institution for the guarantee and leverage components of a transaction and the lack of a market standard have inhibited the growth of the market, reduced the cost efficiency of the transaction and contributed to the illiquidity of the securities. The CDO framework provides more of a market standard structure for the transaction, the most efficient source for leverage and the broadest possible range of leverage providers.

The fixed-income groups of banks focus on the development of CDO structures and their applications, whereas the equity derivative groups focus on the development of protected securities transactions for hedge funds. These two groups seldom have reason to communicate with each other because they are not under the same management. As a result, fixed-income professionals have not applied the protected securities structures to CDO transactions and, likewise, equity derivative professionals have not applied CDO structures to protected securities transactions. This chapter should not only enable structured product professionals in the fixed-income and equity derivative groups to integrate their product development efforts for protected securities transactions but also help fixed-income professionals in structuring protected securities transactions for other classes of assets.

The remainder of this chapter is organized as follows: Section II outlines the general framework for CDO transactions, Section III describes the static hedging structure for protected securities transactions, Section IV establishes the CDO framework for the static hedging structure, Section V provides a description of the dynamic hedging methodology for protected securities and Section VI establishes the CDO framework for the dynamic hedging structure.

II. THE CDO FRAMEWORK

A CDO is a source of nonrecourse financing for a broad range of assets based on static cash flow, market value or synthetic structures, depending on the characteristics of the assets. A hedge fund CDO is structured as a market value transaction. The framework of a CDO consists of two components: debt and equity. Debt comprises more than one class of investment-grade senior/subordinated liabilities, which acts as a source of leverage for the equity.

A hedge fund CDO transaction is structured and referred to as a collateralized fund obligation (CFO), which involves raising capital in the form of debt and equity, managing the deployment of the capital in hedge funds and administering the distribution of the capital. Each of these aspects of the transaction is described in the following paragraphs.

Raising the Capital

A bankruptcy-remote special-purpose entity (the "Fund") is established in a jurisdiction conducive to the legal and tax considerations of the transaction. The Fund generally issues several classes of investment-grade debt in a senior/subordinated structure along with a single class of equity (which could be structured as protected securities).

Managing the Capital

The proceeds from the issuance of debt and equity are invested in a portfolio of hedge funds, which is managed in accordance with the investment guidelines of the Fund and the terms and conditions of the debt. The level of a class of debt outstanding at any time during the life of the Fund is subject to compliance with the overcollateralization ratio (the "OC Ratio") for that class of debt.

- **OC Ratio.** The OC Ratio for a class of debt is defined as the ratio of (x) the value of the assets of the Fund and (y) the sum of 1) the outstanding amount of that class of debt, 2) the aggregate outstanding amount of all other classes of debt senior to this class and 3) all applicable accrued and unpaid administration expenses and interest costs of the Fund. The OC Ratio for each class of debt is set forth at the inception of the transaction (by the rating agencies or the provider of the debt).

The performance of the Fund determines the aggregate level of debt outstanding at any time during the life of the Fund. If the performance is too weak to support the aggregate level of the debt outstanding, the Fund must be deleveraged. Subsequent to deleveraging, if the performance is strong enough to support an additional level of debt, the Fund will be releveraged. The leverage (i.e., the level of debt outstanding at any time) is therefore managed dynamically during the life of the Fund.

- **Deleveraging of the Fund.** If the Fund fails to comply with the OC Ratio with respect to a class of debt at any time during the life of the Fund, the Fund is deleveraged by 1) liquidating a certain amount of the hedge fund assets of the Fund and 2) applying the proceeds from such liquidation to either reduce the debt outstanding by such amount or invest in cash equivalent assets that will become assets of the Fund, until the resulting OC Ratio meets or exceeds its target.

- **Releveraging of the Fund.** In the event that the OC Ratio exceeds its target for a class of debt subsequent to a deleveraging event, the Fund is releveraged by either allocating the cash equivalent assets, if any, of the Fund to the hedge fund assets or issuing an additional amount of the most senior class of the debt and deploying the proceeds thereof to bring the OC Ratio down to its target.

Administering the Capital

All CDO transactions are subject to a prespecified priority of payments (also referred to as a waterfall) on all liabilities of the Fund. The payment priorities are generally as follows:

- **On a payment date before the maturity of the Fund.** First, to the payment of all accrued and unpaid fees and expenses in connection with the administration of the Fund; second, to the payment of accrued and unpaid interest expenses on all classes of debt in the sequential order of their senior/subordinated designations; third, to the retirement of debt in full or in part, as applicable, in the event of a deleveraging of the Fund; fourth, to the payment of accrued and unpaid management fees due to the Fund; and fifth, to the payment of the required distribution (if any) on the equity interests in the Fund.

- **On the maturity date or the early termination date of the Fund.**
  First, to the payment of all accrued and unpaid fees and expenses in connection with the administration of the Fund; second, to the payment in full of the interest and principal outstanding on each class of debt in the sequential order of their senior/subordinated designations; third, to the payment of the accrued and unpaid management fee of the Fund; fourth, to the payment of the performance fee (if any); and fifth, to the payment of all remaining proceeds to the holders of the equity interests in the Fund.

III. STATIC HEDGING STRUCTURE

The structure of a protected securities transaction based on static hedging consists of two independent components: 1) the hedge component required for the return of principal at maturity of the securities and 2) the leverage component required to generate the expected return on the securities. Each of these components is described in the following paragraphs.

Hedge Component

At the inception of the transaction, a significant portion (D_0) of the proceeds (P) from the issuance of the protected securities (assuming the issuance at par with no transaction cost) is invested in "riskless assets" (e.g., zero-coupon U.S. Treasurys) to fully and permanently hedge the principal payment obligation at the maturity of the securities. This initial hedge placed in the transaction is not altered or managed at any time during the life of the transaction, hence the name static hedging. The value (D_t) of the riskless assets at any time (t) in the investment horizon depends on the yield $(Y_{(m-t)})$ on these assets for the remaining maturity $(m - t)$, which can be expressed as follows:

$$D_t = P \times (1 + Y_{(m-t)}/2)^{[-2 \times (m-t)]}$$

(Eqn. 1)

The value of the riskless assets grows with the passage of time and becomes equal to the par amount (P) at the maturity of the protected securities.

Leverage Component

The remaining portion $(P - D_0)$ of the proceeds (the investable amount) from the issuance of the protected securities together with a certain fixed amount of additional proceeds (the fixed leverage amount) provided by a financial institution is invested in a hedge fund or a fund of such hedge funds (the "Fund") to generate an enhanced return on the securities. Initially, the fixed leverage amount (L_{f0}), together with the investable amount, is deployed in the hedge fund assets (H_0) of the Fund.

$$H_0 = (P - D_0) + L_{f0}$$

(Eqn. 2)

Thereafter, the fixed leverage amount may decrease or increase depending on the performance of the Fund. The leverage is critical to generating the return on the protected securities, and is described in the following paragraphs.

Description of the Leverage

The Fund can employ a variety of structures to leverage the investable amount. One of the commonly used structures is the barrier call option structure. Under this structure, the Fund issues a call option (the option) at a premium equal to the investable amount, and a strike price equal to the sum of the fixed leveraged amount (L_{f0}) and the accrued interest thereon at a periodic interest rate (i). The strike price (S_t) at any time (t) during the investment horizon can be expressed by the following equation (which is subject to change depending on the terms of the option):

$$S_t = L_{f0} \times (1 + i)^t$$

(Eqn. 3)

The strike price represents essentially the aggregate level of leverage for the Fund. Therefore, the investment in hedge fund assets is affected by the strike price, in addition to being affected by the performance of the Fund. The maximum investment in hedge fund assets (H_t) at any time (t) during the investment horizon is governed by the following equation (wherein each term except the leverage factor is expressed as a percentage of the par amount of the protected securities):

(Hedge Fund Assets)$_{max}$ = (Leverage Factor) × (Value of the Option)

= (Leverage Factor × (Portfolio Value – Strike Price)

$$(H_t)_{max} = (F) \times (V_t - S_t)$$

(Eqn. 4)

The leverage factor is a constant multiplier established at the inception of the transaction and depends on the volatility and liquidity of the hedge fund assets.

In the event that the allocation to hedge fund assets at any time (t) determined by this formula is greater than the funds available therefor, the Fund employs a variable leverage amount (L_{vt}) to support the increased allocation. Currently, the market practice is to limit the variable leverage amount to 50% of the par amount of the protected securities. The fixed leverage amount and the variable leverage amount are managed dynamically during the investment horizon, subject to the terms of the leverage.

In the event of a decline in its performance, the Fund is subject to deleverage, which is accomplished by liquidating the hedge fund assets and allocating the proceeds to cash equivalent assets, or to reduce the leverage by such amount to comply with the terms of the leverage. In the event of a subsequent rise in its performance, the Fund is releveraged by increasing allocation to hedge fund assets through the deployment of the cash equivalent assets of the Fund, and then the variable leverage amount.

Example of Static Hedging

The value of the option at any time during the investment horizon determines the net asset value of the Fund, which, in turn, determines the return on the protected securities. The following example is designed to show 1) changes in the value of the option due to changes in the value of the Fund and 2) the allocation of the assets of the Fund between the hedge fund assets and the riskless assets due to deleverage and releverage resulting from decreases and increases in the value of the Fund, under certain assumptions specified herein.

IV. CDO FRAMEWORK WITH STATIC HEDGING

The CDO framework for a protected securities transaction based on the static hedging methodology, as described previously, is formulated by establishing two separate bankruptcy-proof special-purpose entities, with the first entity (the "Company") engaged in the hedge component of the transaction and the second entity (the "Fund") in the leverage component of the transaction. Each of these two aspects of the framework is described in the following paragraphs.

At the Company Level

- **Raising the capital.** The Company would issue protected securities at par with a zero coupon and principal (P) payable at maturity, and link the return on the protected securities with the performance of the Fund. It would invest a certain amount of the proceeds from the issuance of the securities in the riskless assets, and the remaining

Exhibit 1: Valuation of Protected Securities under Static Hedging

Assumptions	($million)
Par Amount of Protected Securities	100.00
Value of Riskless Assets	75.00
Return on Riskless Assets (per annum)	5.00%
Leverage Factor	4.00
Fixed Leverage Amount	75.00
Cost of Leverage (per annum)	2.50%

		Performance (at year-end)		
		Year 1	Year 2	Year 3
	Initially	Increases	Decreases	Increases
($million)	T = 0	10%	10%	10%
Value of the Fund	100.00	110.00	96.19	103.48
Strike Price of Option	75.00	76.88	78.80	80.77
Value of the Option	25.00	33.13	17.39	22.71
Allocation to Hedge Fund Assets	100.00	132.50	69.56	90.84
Allocation to Riskless Assets	0.00	0.00	26.63	12.64
Variable Leverage Amount	0.00	22.50	0.00	0.00
Value of Riskless Assets	75.00	78.75	82.69	86.82
Value of Protected Securities	100.00	111.88	100.08	109.53

Notes:
1. The short-term interest rate on riskless assets equals 1.25% per annum.
2. Certain simplifying assumptions are made in the exhibit for illustration purposes.
Source: Wachovia Securities.

Exhibit 2: Behavior of Allocation of Hedge Fund Assets

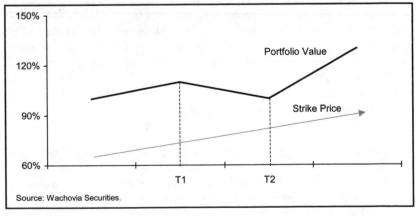

Source: Wachovia Securities.

Exhibit 3: Transaction Structure under Static Hedging

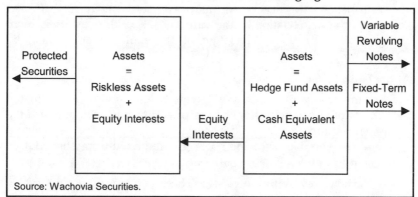

Source: Wachovia Securities.

amount in the equity interests (E_0) issued by the Fund. The performance of the equity interests will therefore be the source of return on the protected securities.

*   **Managing the capital.** At the inception of the transaction, the Company would invest in the riskless assets an amount of the issuance proceeds necessary to fully and permanently defease the payment obligations on the protected securities. Thereafter, during the transaction, the investment in the riskless assets does not change regardless of the performance of its equity interests in the Fund.

At the maturity of the transaction, the Company will 1) liquidate the investment in the riskless assets and 2) redeem the equity interests and distribute the proceeds to the holders of the protected securities, subject to the payment priorities of the Company with regard to the distribution of such proceeds.

The annualized return (R_t) on the protected securities at any time (t) during the transaction depends on 1) the market value of the riskless assets (D_t) of the Company and 2) the value of the equity interests (E_t) in the Fund held by the Company. This return expressed in terms of bond equivalent yield (%) is provided in the following equation:

$$R_t = 2 \times [\{ (D_t - A_t + E_t)/P\}^{(1/2t)} - 1],$$

(Eqn. 5)

where A_t is the accrued and unpaid fees and expenses, if any, of the Company.

In a rising interest rate environment, the return on the protected securities at any time before maturity may be adversely affected unless the depreciation in the value of the riskless assets is more than offset by the appreciation of the equity interests held by the Company.

At the Fund Level

- **Raising the capital.** The Fund would issue senior/subordinated classes of debt and a single class of equity interests, and use the issuance proceeds to invest in hedge fund assets. The debt would comprise variable revolving notes (L_v) and fixed-term notes (L_f), as described in the following paragraphs.

  - **Variable revolving notes (L_v).** These notes represent a variable credit facility with a LIBOR-indexed interest rate thereon, and payable on a revolving basis until the maturity of the notes (the same as the maturity of the protected securities). The par amount of the credit facility (L_{vt}) outstanding at any time (t) during the transaction is subject to the terms of these notes and compliance with the OC Ratio for such notes.

  - **Fixed-term notes (L_f).** These notes represent one or more classes of senior/subordinated investment-grade notes with LIBOR-indexed current coupons, and fixed-term maturities equal to those of the protected securities. The aggregate par amount of such notes is based on the leverage desired in the transaction, and the amount outstanding (L_{ft}) at any time (t) during the transaction depends on compliance with the OC Ratio for such notes.

  - **Equity interests (E).** The equity interests represent the residual interest in the Fund payable to the Company only on liquidation of the assets of the Fund after the payment of liabilities of the Fund on or before its maturity.

- **Managing the capital.** The outstanding par amount of each class of debt at any time during the transaction is subject to compliance with the OC Ratio for the respective class of the debt. The assets of the Fund are therefore managed dynamically to ensure compliance at all times during the life of the Fund. The OC Ratios for the variable revolving notes and the fixed-term notes at any time (t) during the transaction are provided in Eqn. 6.

Variable Revolving Notes: $(V_t) / (L_{vt} + A_t) \geq X$

Fixed-Term Notes: $(V_t) / (L_{vt} + L_{ft} + A_t) \geq Y$

Where:

V_t is the sum of the values of 1) the hedge fund assets (H_t) and 2) the cash equivalent assets (C_t). That is, $V_t = H_t + C_t$.

A_t is the aggregate amount of accrued and unpaid fees and expenses, including interest costs, of the fund.

X and Y are the OC Ratios set forth at the inception of the transaction for each class of the notes.

(Eqn. 6)

If the Fund fails to comply with the OC Ratios, it will be deleveraged. If the Fund exceeds the OC Ratios, it will be releveraged or leveraged further. The leveraging, deleveraging and releveraging of the Fund will be managed in accordance with the OC Ratios, as described in Section II herein.

The annualized return (r_t) at any time (t) on the equity interests (E_0) issued by the Fund depends on the value of the equity interest (E_t) at such time, which, in turn, depends on the market value of the hedge fund assets (H_t) of the Fund and the aggregate amount of all liabilities of the Fund at such time. This return expressed in terms of bond equivalent yields (%) is provided in Eqn. 7:

$r_t = 2 \times \{E_t / E_0)^{(1/2t)} - 1\}$, where:

$E_t = \{ (H_t + C_t) - (L_{ft} + L_{vt} + A_t) \}$

(Eqn. 7)

The return on the protected securities will be less than the return on the riskless assets in the event that the value of the equity interests (E_t) depreciates below its initial value (E_0).

V. DYNAMIC HEDGING STRUCTURE

The structure of a protected securities transaction based on dynamic hedging consists of two independent components: 1) the hedge component required for the return of principal at maturity of the securities and 2) the leverage component required to generate the expected return on the securities. Both of these components are the same as described in the static hedging structure. However, unlike the static hedging, 1) the hedge is managed dynamically during the life of the transaction rather than being placed fully and permanently at the inception of the transaction, and 2) there is no explicit fixed leverage amount to enhance the return on the securities.

The proceeds from the issuance of the protected securities are initially allocated between hedge fund assets and riskless assets according to an asset allocation formula, as described in the following paragraphs. Thereafter, depending on the performance of the assets, adjustments are made periodically to existing allocations whereby assets are reallocated between hedge fund assets and the riskless assets, in accordance with the formula. This formula-based adjustment to allocations to hedge fund assets and riskless assets from time to time throughout the term of the transaction hedges the obligation under the protected securities, hence the name dynamic hedging. The most widely recognized form of dynamic hedging is portfolio insurance, which has its origins in portfolio insurance theories based on option pricing models.

Portfolio Insurance

The value of a portfolio can be protected (i.e., insured) from declining below a certain level through investment in a put option. The cost of an option on a portfolio is less than the aggregate cost of options on assets constituting the portfolio. Therefore, the option at the portfolio level is more cost-effective in protecting the value of the portfolio, if such an option is available or can be replicated. But if the portfolio consists of non-exchange-traded securities, such as interests in hedge funds, the option at the portfolio level is not available and is difficult or noneconomic to replicate. The unavailability, cost-ineffectiveness and illiquidity of such an option gave rise to the development of an alternative form of put-option-like portfolio insurance called Constant Proportion Portfolio Insurance (CPPI), pioneered by André Perold of Harvard and, simultaneously, by Fischer Black and Robert Jones of Goldman Sachs in 1986. The main advantage of CPPI is that it is extremely simple to understand, easy to implement and does not require the use of an option.

Constant Proportion Portfolio Insurance

The objective is to maximize the return on the protected securities while preserving the return of principal at the maturity of the securities. The return on the securities is maximized by allocating the maximum possible amount to hedge fund assets at the inception and at all times during the life of the transaction. Simultaneously, the return of principal is preserved by ensuring that if the hedge fund assets were liquidated and the proceeds from such liquidation were invested into the riskless assets, it would result in an amount equal to the principal amount of the protected securities at maturity. The CPPI formula for the allocation of assets between hedge fund assets and riskless assets is designed to accomplish this objective.

The maximum amount of capital allocation to hedge fund assets at any time during the transaction is governed by the following equation (wherein each term, except the leverage factor, is expressed as a percentage of the principal amount of the protected securities):

$$(\text{Hedge Fund Assets})_{max} = (\text{Leverage Factor}) \times (\text{Portfolio Value} - \text{Defeasance Value})$$

$$(H_t)_{max} = (F) \times (V_t - D_t)$$

$$= (F) \times (E_t)$$

(Eqn. 8)

where:

- **Leverage factor (F)** is a constant multiplier, which depends on the volatility and liquidity of the hedge fund assets.

- **Portfolio value (V$_t$)** is the net asset value of the portfolio after deduction of all accrued and unpaid fees and expenses and the outstanding liabilities associated with the transaction.

- **Defeasance value (D$_t$)** is the value of the riskless assets required to defease the par amount of the protected securities at maturity. The defeasance value is therefore a function of the interest rate for the time remaining before the maturity of the protected securities.

- **Equity value (E$_t$)** is the buffer amount necessary to realize the defeasance value required to defease in full the protected securities against losses (if any) in the event of liquidation of the hedge fund assets in the portfolio.

The equity value determines the level of allocation to hedge fund assets at any time during the transaction. The allocation of the assets in the portfolio is adjusted as a result of increases and decreases in the equity value. For example:

- If the equity value increases, allocation to hedge fund assets in the portfolio may be increased through an explicit leverage provided by a financial institution (the variable revolving amount, as in the case of the static hedging structure). The equity value may grow due to an appreciation in the portfolio value, a rise in the interest rate (which will have the effect of reducing the defeasance value) or a combination thereof.

- If the equity value decreases, allocation to hedge fund assets in the portfolio may have to be liquidated in accordance with the formula, and the proceeds from such a liquidation are then invested in riskless assets to satisfy the formula. The equity value may decrease due to a depreciation in the portfolio value, a decline in the interest rate (which will have the effect of increasing the defeasance value) or a combination thereof.

Example of Dynamic Hedging

The equity value at any time during the investment horizon determines the return on the protected securities. The following example is designed to show changes in the equity value due to changes in the portfolio value. The example also shows the allocation of the assets of the portfolio between the hedge fund assets and riskless assets due to deleverage and releverage resulting from decreases and increases in the portfolio value, under certain assumptions specified herein.

Exhibit 4: Valuation of Protected Securities under Dynamic Hedging

Assumptions	($million)
Par Amount of Protected Securities	100.00
Defeasance Value	75.00
Return on Riskless Assets (per annum)	5.00%
Leverage Factor	4.00
Cost of Leverage (per annum)	2.50%

		Performance (at year-end)		
		Year 1	Year 2	Year 3
	Initially	Increases	Decreases	Increases
($million)	T = 0	10%	10%	10%
Portfolio Value	100.00	110.00	97.13	103.39
Defeasance Value	75.00	78.75	82.69	86.82
Equity Value	25.00	31.25	14.44	16.57
Allocation to Hedge Fund Assets	100.00	125.00	57.75	66.28
Allocation to Riskless Assets	0.00	0.00	39.38	37.11
Variable Leverage Amount	0.00	15.00	0.00	0.00

Notes:
1. The short-term interest rate on riskless assets equals 1.25% per annum.
2. Certain simplifying assumptions are made in the exhibit for illustration purposes.
Source: Wachovia Securities.

VI. CDO FRAMEWORK WITH DYNAMIC HEDGING

The CPPI formula for a protected securities transaction is rewritten in the following equation in a slightly modified form by separating the riskless assets as part of the assets of the portfolio, as follows.

$$(H_t)_{max} = (F) \times [V_t - (D_t - d_t)]$$

where:

V_t = The value of the hedge fund assets together with all other assets except the riskless assets

D_t = As defined earlier, the value of the riskless assets required to defease the principal amount (P) of the protected securities

d_t = The value of the riskless assets in the portfolio with a principal amount (p); this represents the defeased principal amount (p) of the protected securities

$(D_t - d_t)$ = The value of the riskless assets required to defease the remaining principal amount (P - p) of the protected securities

(Eqn. 9)

Alternatively, the formula can be expressed as follows:

$$(H_t)_{max} / (F) = V_t - (D_t - d_t)$$

Equity   = Assets – Liabilities

OC Ratio   = $(V_t) / (D_t - d_t)$

(Eqn. 10)

This characterization of the CPPI formula in terms of assets and liabilities clearly shows that the CDO framework can be used to formulate the structure of a protected securities transaction with $(D_t - d_t)$ as the implicit CDO liability (leverage) in the structure. This implicit leverage can be supplemented with an explicit CDO leverage to further enhance the return on the protected securities.

The CDO framework for a protected securities transaction based on the dynamic hedging methodology, as described previously, is similar to the framework described for the static hedging methodology. It is also formulated by establishing two separate bankruptcy-proof special-purpose entities, with the first entity (the Company) engaged in the hedge component of the transaction, and the second entity (the Fund) in

Exhibit 5: Transaction Structure under Dynamic Hedging

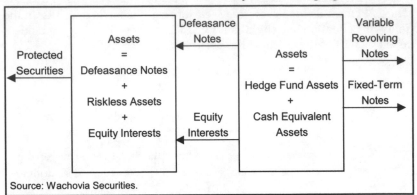

Source: Wachovia Securities.

the leverage component of the transaction. Each of these two aspects of the framework is described in the following paragraphs.

At the Company Level

- **Raising the capital.** The Company would issue protected securities at par with a zero coupon and principal (P) payable at maturity, and link the return on the protected securities with the performance of the Fund. The Company would use the issuance proceeds to invest in 1) the defeasance notes with a put option thereon issued by the Fund, 2) the equity interests issued by the Fund and 3) riskless assets, if any, with a maturity equal to that of the protected securities. The defeasance notes are zero-coupon notes with principal and maturity equal to those of the protected securities, as more fully described in the following paragraphs.

- **Managing the capital.** At the inception of the transaction, the Company would allocate the issuance proceeds among the defeasance notes, riskless assets and equity interests subject to the following considerations:

  — **Par amount allocation.** The par amount of the protected securities (P) will equal the sum of 1) the outstanding par amount of the defeasance notes (D_t) and 2) the par amount of the riskless assets (d_t), if any. That is,

  $$P = \text{Par} (D_t) + \text{Par} (d_t)$$

  (Eqn. 11)

  — **Value allocation.** The proceeds from the issuance of the protected securities will equal the sum of 1) the value of the outstanding defeasance notes, 2) the value of the riskless assets, if any, and 3) the value of the equity interests.

$$P = D_t + d_t + E_t$$

(Eqn. 12)

At any time during the transaction, the par amount of the protected securities will equal the sum of the par amounts of the defeasance notes and the riskless assets, if any. At the maturity of the transaction, the Company would receive the proceeds from 1) the redemption of the defeasance notes and the equity interests and 2) the liquidation of the riskless assets. It would distribute the proceeds to holders of the protected securities, subject to the payment priorities with regard to the distribution of such proceeds.

In the event of noncompliance by the Fund with the OC Ratio for the defeasance notes, the Company will exercise the put option, in full or in part, depending on the level of such noncompliance, and invest the proceeds therefrom in riskless assets. Subsequently, if the OC Ratio for the defeasance notes improves, the Company would liquidate the riskless assets, in full or in part, depending on the level of the improvement, and reinvest the proceeds from such liquidation in the defeasance notes.

The annualized return (R_t) on the protected securities at any time (t) during the investment horizon of the transaction depends on the value of the assets of the Company, which comprises the defeasance notes (D_t), the riskless assets (d_t) and the equity interests (E_t). The return expressed in terms of bond equivalent yield (%) is provided in Equation 13.

$$R_t = 2 \times [\{ (D_t - A_t + E_t + d_t) / P \}^{(1/2t)} - 1],$$

(Eqn. 13)

where A_t is the aggregate amount of accrued and unpaid fees and expenses of the Company.

At the Fund Level

- **Raising the capital.** The Fund would issue senior/subordinated classes of debt and a single class of equity interests and use the issuance proceeds to invest in hedge fund assets. The debt would comprise defeasance notes, variable revolving notes (L_v) and fixed-term notes (L_f), in an increasing order of subordination. That is, the fixed-term notes would be subordinated to both the defeasance and revolving notes, and the revolving notes would be subordinated to the defeasance notes. Each of these components of the debt is described in the following paragraphs:

— **Defeasance notes (D_t).** These are zero-coupon notes with an aggregate par amount equal to P, maturity equal to those of the protected securities and an issue price (D_0) equal to the market value of the zero-coupon Treasurys of the same maturity. The market value (D_t) of defeasance notes at any time (t) before its maturity is the present value of the riskless assets discounted at the zero-coupon Treasury yield for the remaining maturity of the notes. Furthermore, the holder of the notes (i.e., the Company) has the option to

  • Put some or all of the defeasance notes back to the Fund at a strike price equal to the market value of the defeasance note, and

  • Reacquire the defeasance notes, subject to the compliance by the Fund with the OC Ratio for the notes.

  The defeasance notes function essentially as a repo facility provided to the Fund by the Company on a marked-to-market basis. The notes are marked-to-market using the zero-coupon Treasury yield for their remaining maturity.

— **Variable revolving notes (L_{vt}).** These notes represent a variable credit facility with a LIBOR-indexed interest rate thereon and payable on a revolving basis until the maturity of the protected securities. The par amount of such notes (L_{vt}) outstanding at any time (t) during the transaction is subject to compliance with the OC Ratio for the notes.

— **Fixed-term notes (L_{ft}).** These notes represent a subordinated class of debt with a LIBOR-indexed coupon and a fixed-term maturity equal to those of the protected securities. The initial par amount of such notes is based on the leverage desired in the transaction, and the amount outstanding thereafter (L_{ft}) at any time (t) during the transaction depends on the compliance with the OC Ratio for such notes.

— **Equity interests (E_t).** The equity interests represent the residual interest in the Fund payable to the Company only upon liquidation of the assets of the Fund after payment of all liabilities of the Fund on or before maturity.

• **Managing the capital.** The proceeds from the issuance of the defeasance notes, variable revolving notes, fixed-term notes and the equity interests by the Fund are invested in hedge fund assets. These assets are managed dynamically pursuant to the OC requirements for each class of the liabilities, as provided in Equation 14:

Defeasance Notes	$(V_t) / (D_t + A_t)$	$\geq X$
Variable Revolving Notes	$(V_t) / (D_t + L_{vt} + A_t)$	$\geq Y$
Fixed-Term Notes	$(V_t) / (D_t + L_{vt} + L_{ft} + A_t)$	$\geq Z$

(Eqn. 14)

Each of the terms in the OC Ratios has the same meaning as ascribed to them under Section IV, except that A_t represents the accrued and unpaid fees and expenses as well as the interest costs of the Fund. The OC Ratios X, Y and Z are set forth at the inception of the transaction for each class of the notes. If the Fund fails to comply with the OC Ratios, it will be deleveraged. If the Fund exceeds the OC Ratios, it will be releveraged or leveraged further. The leveraging, deleveraging and releveraging of the Fund is managed in accordance with the OC Ratios as described in Section II.

The annualized return (r_t) at any time (t) on the equity interests (E_0) issued by the Fund depends on the value of the equity interest (E_t) at such time, which, in turn, depends on 1) the market value of the hedge fund assets (H_t) of the Fund and 2) the aggregate amount of all liabilities of the Fund at such time. This return expressed in terms of bond equivalent yields (%) is provided in Eqn. 15:

$$r_t = 2 \times \{ (E_t / E_0)^{(1 / \tau t)} - 1 \}, \text{ where:}$$

$$E_t = \{ (H_t + C_t) - (D_t + L_{tf} + L_{tv} + A_t) \}$$

(Eqn. 15)

The return on the protected securities will be less than the return on the riskless assets in the event that the value of the equity interests (E_t) depreciates below its initial value (E_0).

Chapter 7

CPORTS^{SM}:
A Tailor-Made CDO Investment

EXECUTIVE SUMMARY

Single-tranche CDOs have become popular with traditional and new structured finance investors. A significant part of the appeal is due to the flexibility these notes offer: The investor plays a major role in choosing the reference obligor pool and in selecting the level of credit risk exposure desired. Thus, the investor becomes the de facto architect of the investment instrument.

In this chapter, we focus on three aspects of these investments. We explain the basic features of single-tranche CDOs, compare the characteristics of single-tranche CDOs against those of more conventional CDO tranches and explore the relative importance that asset correlation and reference pool credit quality play in the performance of a given single tranche.

More specifically, this study shows that for super-senior investments, correlation is more important than credit quality (a dominance that is exacerbated when the quality of the reference pool improves). Also, we show that the relative importance of correlation decreases in relation to credit quality as the rating of the single tranche moves down. The influence of correlation reaches a minimum (a situation known as "correlation neutral") when the rating of the single tranche is roughly three notches below the rating of the reference pool. At that point, the performance of the single tranche is determined almost exclusively by the credit quality of the reference pool. Finally, the influence of correlation tends to increase (relative to the credit quality of the pool) at the level of a single tranche having "equity-like" risk features. That said, this influence, which is not as pronounced as the influence observed at the super-senior level, is beneficial rather than detrimental to the performance of the single tranche.

INTRODUCTION

In the ever-evolving CDO market, single-tranche CDOs have become common in the structured products arena. The reason for their broad acceptance is simple: These transactions are designed around a specific investor's credit views and risk tolerance. Typically, an investor will request a desired level of risk exposure (e.g., AAA, AA or A) to a chosen pool of credits in return for coupon payments.[1] The coupon depends on the credits selected and the level of risk chosen. For example, an investor may choose 100 reference credits and indicate a desire for a $20 million exposure to this pool at an "A" level of risk in return for coupon payments of LIBOR plus a spread.

CPORTS[SM] (customized portfolio tranched securities) is Wachovia Securities'[2] proprietary single-tranche CDO offering and constitutes one of the recent innovations in the CDO market. In this chapter, we discuss the general structure of CPORTS, highlight its advantages relative to conventional synthetic or cash flow CDO transactions, and assess the relative importance of reference credit quality and reference credit correlation to investment performance with the help of several examples.

THE CPORTS STRUCTURE

Conceptually, the CPORTS structure is similar to that of conventional synthetic CDOs with one significant difference—only one tranche is issued. A CPORTS investment effectively represents the sale of credit protection[3] to the swap counterparty (i.e., Wachovia Securities) on a slice of reference pool risk. The slice of risk sold is defined by the attachment and detachment points of the tranche.[4] The rest of the risk (what otherwise would constitute the tranches above and below the CPORTS tranche) is not issued. Exhibit 1 depicts a generic CPORTS structure.

---

1. For funded investments, market convention is to call payments to the investor *coupons,* whereas for unfunded investments, the convention is to call the payments premiums. Throughout this chapter, we use the term *coupon* although single-tranche CDO investments can be made in unfunded form.
2. Throughout this chapter, we will use "Wachovia Securities" to refer to Wachovia Bank, N.A., as the swap counterparty and Wachovia Capital Markets, LLC, as the arranger. Please see the disclosure on the last page of the book.
3. The person who sells protection accepts a contingent liability (agrees to pay for losses in the reference pool) in return for a coupon to be paid periodically by the protection buyer (receiver of loss payments).
4. For the traditional CDO investor, the attachment point and the detachment point define the size of the tranche and represent the percentage of the capital structure below and above the tranche, respectively.

Exhibit 1: Generic CPORTS Structure

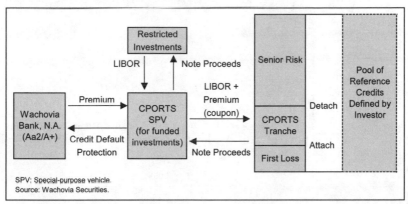

SPV: Special-purpose vehicle.
Source: Wachovia Securities.

The mechanics are straightforward. The investor chooses a pool of reference credits—generally names that are traded in the credit default swap (CDS) market although nonstandard assets may also be chosen—and indicates the amount and risk level of exposure. Wachovia Securities then creates a customized CPORTS tranche that meets the specified criteria. The investor (protection seller) generally buys the CPORTS tranche at par and the proceeds are used to purchase restricted investments (usually investments rated AAA/Aaa) having the same notional as the single tranche issued.[5] In return, the investor receives a coupon equal to the interest generated by the restricted investments (LIBOR) plus the protection premium paid by Wachovia Securities. If the aggregate reference pool losses exceed the amount of CPORTS subordination (the amount of "unissued" tranches below the attachment point), then the restricted investments are liquidated dollar for dollar to compensate Wachovia Securities, the protection buyer. Consequently, the principal balance of the CPORTS investment may deteriorate over time. If defaults (and losses) continue, additional restricted investments are liquidated and the CPORTS investor suffers greater principal loss. Ultimately, the loss is capped at the amount of restricted investments posted (the detachment point). Concurrent with the liquidation of restricted investments, the "interest" paid to the investor is also adjusted downward in proportion to the principal reduction. In other words, losses are realized immediately.[6] These concepts are shown in Exhibit 2.

5. CPORTS investments are also available in unfunded form.
6. Structures that do not reduce the coupon upon loss can also be created for investors who need the certainty of coupon and are willing to incur slightly greater (accelerated) principal loss.

Exhibit 2: Effect of Losses on Return of Principal Coupon

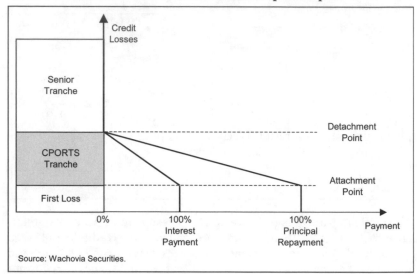

Source: Wachovia Securities.

In general, although this is not a requirement per se, CPORTS investments reference high-grade portfolios of 100–150 corporate credits. This compares favorably with cash CDOs, which frequently include only 60–100 credits. Therefore, CPORTS offers significant diversification advantages.

HEDGING STRATEGY

Questions have been raised regarding Wachovia Securities' strategy of hedging the protection that it purchases (by virtue of selling a CPORTS security).[7] Although this should not be a concern for investors as it is unrelated to Wachovia Securities' obligation to pay the CPORTS coupon as promised, we describe briefly the framework that is used.

On the other side of the CPORTS trade, the protection buyer (Wachovia Securities) will delta hedge its position through the sale of protection on individual names in the reference portfolio. The initial amount of protection sold for each name is determined by matching the sensitivity of the change in price (value) of the CPORTS tranche to the change in

7. In other words, if the reference assets are not currently on balance sheet (and therefore are not opportune targets for the purchase of protection) and no assets default, then Wachovia Securities has the obligation of paying a quarterly coupon without any return.

price (value) of the single-name credit default swap. For example, if a 10 bps spread widening of Ford Motor Co. changes the mark-to-market value of a $10 million[8] CDS tied to Ford by a negative $50,000 (from the perspective of Wachovia Securities as a potential protection seller) and changes the value of the CPORTS tranche by a positive $4,000 (from the perspective of Wachovia Securities as a protection buyer), then the appropriate amount of Ford protection for Wachovia Securities to sell is 8% (4,000/50,000) of $10 million, or $800,000 worth of Ford protection. As spreads change and reference entities default, the size of the hedge will change and, as a result, Wachovia Securities will periodically alter the amount of single name protection held through market purchases and sales. Therefore, a complete schematic of a CPORTS transaction is similar to that shown in Exhibit 3.

Exhibit 3: Investment Bank Hedging Strategy

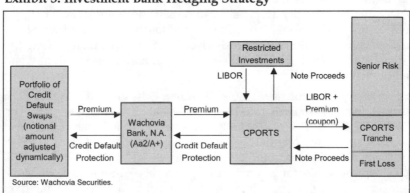

Source: Wachovia Securities.

Readers will note that the CDS market generally does not trade in increments of $800,000 notional. For this reason, banks generally desire fairly large correlation books (which are created from the sale of several single-tranche transactions) and will hedge the transactions in aggregate, allowing for finer control of the hedge. A more detailed discussion of hedging strategies is beyond the scope of this chapter.

ADVANTAGES OF THE CPORTS STRUCTURE

CPORTS tranches are designed to meet the specific needs of individual investors; thus, the investor selects the reference portfolio as well as the

---

8. Assume that the equivalent "fully banked" structure was tied to 100 CDS contracts of $10 million each.

size and risk level of the investment. Investors can even elect to lightly manage their pools by replacing a small number of reference obligors per year. Features such as reference obligor ratings, the number of obligors, concentration levels and diversity, in conjunction with the rating agencies' requirements, then determine the coupon of the CPORTS tranche, the attachment point (the level of subordination) and the detachment point. Therefore, unlike a conventional CDO investor, which might be required to negotiate the characteristics of the transaction with other participants, the CPORTS investor can tailor the note to meet specific needs while making few sacrifices. The ability to lightly trade the reference portfolio also eliminates the so-called manager risk that exists in some multitranche managed CDOs, that is, the possibility that the manager could effect trades that are not necessarily aligned with the long-term good health of the tranche the investor bought. A CPORTS investment also has the popular features of a fully banked synthetic CDO—bullet maturity (typically 3–5 years), no interest rate risk, no reinvestment risk and simple documentation that permits transaction execution within two weeks. In short, a CPORTS investment is virtually identical to a fully banked synthetic CDO but has greater flexibility and additional benefits.

Spreads available for new CPORTS transactions are often higher than those offered by similarly rated conventional cash flow CDOs. However, new issue CPORTS spreads can be relatively volatile because they tend to track closely the premium offered in the credit default swap market, occasionally allowing CPORTS spreads to fall below conventional CDO spread levels for any given reference pool. In contrast, the asset spreads and liability spreads in the traditional cash-based CDO market are not as closely tied. That said, CPORTS spreads could be altered significantly for a particular transaction by selectively choosing the reference pool, the risk level, the number of agency ratings and the size of the investment (tranche).

Of course, this flexibility can work against an inexperienced investor who may lack the knowledge to assess correctly the risk profile of the reference portfolio (i.e., the true credit quality and default correlation of the reference obligors). This flexibility also puts an extra burden on the investor, who must monitor the pool and decide which assets to substitute, if substitution is permitted.

We discuss herein the relative importance of two key performance drivers of CPORTS investments—the credit quality of the reference pool and asset (default) correlation among the reference obligors. Control of these parameters (credit quality and correlation) falls squarely on the investor.

PORTFOLIO SELECTION: QUALITY VERSUS CORRELATION

The CPORTS investor, as the main architect of the CPORTS instrument, faces more challenges and responsibilities compared with the conventional CDO investor. Once the domain of the collateral manager, the selection of reference obligors is now the responsibility of the investor[9]; hence, there is a need to carry out more in-depth portfolio analysis. The effects of default probability and default correlation in the pool of reference obligations — arguably the two most important factors that drive the performance of a CPORTS tranche — are investigated below. Specifically, we address these questions:

- Which factor is more important to the performance of a CPORTS investment: asset (default) correlation or quality of the reference pool (probability of default)?

- Does the relative importance of these two factors change depending on the subordination level of the CPORTS investment?

In short, the answers to these questions are "it depends" and "yes," respectively. We arrived at these conclusions after investigating the sensitivity of the expected return of principal to 1) a unit change in the credit quality of the reference obligors and 2) a unit change to the level of default correlation between the obligors as described more fully below.

METHODOLOGY

We investigated seven CPORTS investments, each with different attachment points and detachment points, backed by a hypothetical pool of reference credits. Both the structures and the reference pool are typical, therefore our findings should be relevant to all CPORTS investors.

The sensitivity analysis consisted of four steps. First, we selected a simplified but representative pool of reference obligors. Second, we established attachment and detachment points for seven hypothetical CPORTS investments using conventional rating methodologies. Next, we employed a Monte Carlo method to simulate reference obligor performance and determine the expected return of principal for each CPORTS investment. Finally, we evaluated the change in the expected return of principal for each tranche due to changes in credit quality and asset correlation. Readers familiar with Monte Carlo methods and who

---

9. The investor may hire a collateral manager to select and trade the reference portfolio for a fee of 50 bps–100 bps per annum based on the notional amount of the CPORTS investment.

do not wish to review our methodology may wish to skip directly to the sensitivity analysis.

Pool of Reference Obligors

The reference portfolio consisted of 100 equally weighted obligors with ratings divided evenly among five credit quality bins: A2, A3, Baa1, Baa2 and Baa3 (20 obligors in each rating bucket). The weighted average rating factor (WARF) of the pool was 306 (Baa1/Baa2) and it had a Moody's diversity score of 50. For purposes of the Monte Carlo simulator, the asset correlation between obligors was assumed to be 25%. Although these characteristics are typical of a reference pool backing a CPORTS investment (or any other single-tranche investment), they are by no means exclusive and investors may wish to deviate from them to improve yield or lower risk. For example, an investor may choose fewer reference obligors, lower credit quality obligors or a lower diversity reference pool to improve the yield on their CPORTS investment.

Attachment and Detachment Points

Moody's Investors Service, Inc.'s multibinomial CDO rating methodology[10] was used to assign attachment and detachment points to seven CPORTS tranches based on the risk characteristics of the reference portfolio. The tranches represented investments at the super-senior, Aaa, Aa2, A2, Baa2, Ba2 and equity levels (Moody's rating methodology was not needed for the super-senior or equity level because these tranches are generally not rated). Except for the super-senior tranche and the equity tranche, the size of each CPORTS tranche was held constant at 3% of the capital structure to improve comparability. The super-senior tranche consisted of the top 88.5% of the capital structure and the equity tranche consisted of the bottom 2%. The size of the equity tranche was reduced from 3% to 2% to accentuate the importance of correlation to this tranche and because equity holdings tend to be smaller as a percentage of the overall structure for transactions backed by investment-grade credits. Each tranche is shown in Exhibit 4.

Although the Moody's rating methodology was used to establish the attachment and detachment points of each CPORTS investment, a Monte Carlo method was employed to calculate the expected return of principal as a function of the basic assumptions regarding credit quality and asset correlation within the reference pool. For this study, we used the

10. See *Moody's Approach to Rating Synthetic CDOs*, July 29, 2003. Either Standard & Poor's Corp.'s or Fitch Ratings' methodology could have been used as well. The main objective was simply to divide the reference pool risk into reasonably appropriate tranches.

Exhibit 4: Hypothetical CPORTS Investments at Various Risk Levels

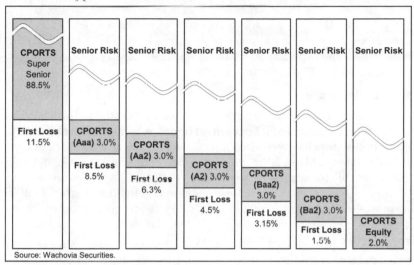

Source: Wachovia Securities.

expected return of principal as the metric by which return sensitivity was evaluated.

Monte Carlo Simulator

A single period reduced-form Monte Carlo simulation was used to evaluate the default behavior of obligors within the reference pool. Conceptually, each scenario was generated assuming that the asset values followed a standard normal distribution and defaulted if the asset value fell below a threshold, which was determined by the default probability of the asset. Cholesky decomposition was used to create multivariate normal random numbers having the desired asset correlation. As a base case, asset correlation between obligors in the reference pool was assumed to be 25% and Moody's idealized default rates for corporate bonds were used as the probability of default. The number of simulations ranged from 20,000 to 100,000 depending on the CPORTS tranche. For the super-senior, Aaa and Aa2 tranches, 100,000 simulations were run, 50,000 simulations were run for the A2 and Baa2 tranches, and 20,000 simulations were run for the remaining tranches. For those readers who desire a deeper theoretical discussion of Monte Carlo models, we suggest the article, "A Comparison of Stochastic Default Rate Models," by Christopher C. Finger for further reading.[11]

11. Finger, Christopher C., "A Comparison of Stochastic Default Rate Models," *Risk Metrics*, November 2000.

After each simulation, principal losses in the reference pool were passed through the CPORTS structure and CPORTS investment losses, if any, were recorded. The average loss was calculated for each CPORTS tranche as the arithmetic average of principal losses experienced in each simulation. The expected return of principal was then simply calculated as the initial CPORTS investment minus the average principal loss.

Sensitivity Analysis

The relative importance of credit quality and asset (default) correlation on the performance of a CPORTS investment as measured by the expected return of principal was studied by adjusting the probability of default for all reference obligors up and down one rating notch, and adjusting the level of correlation between the obligors by a commensurate amount.[12] Therefore, nine cases were evaluated for each CPORTS tranche—three levels of default probability (base, up and down) times three levels of asset correlation (base, up and down).

It is worth noting that the assumptions used to evaluate the expected principal loss are different than those used to create the CPORTS structures (i.e., assign attachment points and detachment points), which were based on rating agency methods and assumptions. For this study, we evaluated the CPORTS tranches ex post facto using Monte Carlo methods and the corresponding Monte Carlo assumptions (obligor ratings and asset correlation), which might or might not have corresponded exactly to the rating agency assumptions. In other words, no changes were made to the CPORTS structures as a result of adjustments to the reference pool assumptions discussed earlier. The sensitivity analysis assumptions were meant to capture more realistically the investor's view of quality and asset correlation of the reference pool.

For each of the nine cases, the expected return of principal for each CPORTS tranche was determined using the Monte Carlo simulator. For example, the expected return of principal for the Aaa CPORTS investment in the base case (reference pool with WARF of 306 and an asset correlation among reference obligors of 25%) is 99.5% (Exhibit 5).[13] If the

---

12. For example, if the original portfolio WARF is 306 and, after adjusting the reference obligor ratings down one notch, the new WARF is 470, which represents a 54% increase, then the asset correlation was also adjusted upward by 54% to 38.4% (from 25%).

13. Some readers may note that the expected loss for this tranche seems to be higher than what Moody's would indicate for an Aaa rated tranche. The difference in expected loss is due to the differences between the assumptions used for the Monte Carlo simulations and Moody's rating assumptions.

Exhibit 5: Expected Return of Principal for an Aaa CPORTS Tranche

		Asset Correlation		
		16.2%	25.0%	38.4%
	198	100.0%	99.8%	99.5%
WARF	306	99.9%	99.5%	98.8%
	470	99.4%	98.5%	97.2%

WARF: Weighted average rating factor.
Source: Wachovia Securities.

asset correlation is instead 38.4%, then the expected return of principal is only 98.8%.[14]

We are concerned, however, with the relative change in the expected return of principal rather than the absolute change. To this end, it is useful to evaluate the expected return of principal relative to the base case (therefore, the base case change is 0% by definition). Thus, Exhibit 6 shows the same data as Exhibit 5 but on a relative basis. For example, we determined that a 54% increase in WARF (from 306 to 470) leads to a 1.00% reduction in expected principal return, whereas a 54% increase in correlation (from 25.0% to 38.4%) leads to a 0.76% reduction in expected return of principal. As a result, we conclude that the Aaa rated CPORTS investment is approximately 76% (0.76%/1.00%) as sensitive to a change in asset correlation as to a change in credit quality.

Exhibit 6: Change in Expected Return of Principal for an Aaa CPORTS Tranche

		Asset Correlation		
		-35%	0.00%	54%
	-35%	0.45%	0.32%	-0. 06%
WARF	0%	0.35%	0.00%	-0.76%
	54%	-0. 10%	-1.00%	-2.33%

WARF: Weighted average rating factor.
Source: Wachovia Securities.

Conversely, if the credit quality improves such that the new WARF is 198 (representing a 35% reduction), then the expected return of principal rises 0.32%. This is slightly less than the 0.35% improvement we would expect from a reduction in asset correlation of 35% (from 25% to 16.2%). From this, we conclude that the Aaa rated CPORTS investment is approximately 109% (0.35%/0.32%) as sensitive to a change in asset

---

14. Results for the other CPORTS tranches may be found in Appendix A.

correlation as a change in credit quality. In fact, the true relative sensitivity is somewhere between 76% and 109% and, for the purposes of this study, we simply average the values and state that the Aaa rated CPORTS investment is 0.93 times as sensitive to a change in asset correlation as to a change in credit quality.

RESULTS

The sensitivity analysis detailed in the previous section was repeated for each of the seven CPORTS tranches and the results are plotted in Exhibit 7. The numerical data are included in Appendix A.

Exhibit 7: Relative Importance of Asset Correlation to Default Probability to the Performance of Various CPORTS Tranches

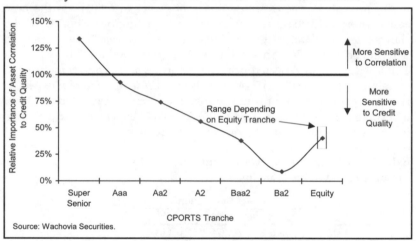

Source: Wachovia Securities.

For a super-senior investor, we see from Exhibit 7 that a percent change in the default correlation is more important than a percent change in the credit quality of the reference obligations (as measured by WARF). In fact, a 1% change in default correlation has the same effect on the super senior's expected loss as a 1.33% change in credit quality. At the Aaa level, a percent change in credit quality is approximately equivalent to a 0.92% change in default correlation. The relative importance of default correlation gradually decreases down to the Ba2 tranche. The Ba2 CPORTS holder is effectively indifferent to asset correlation among obligors in the reference pool. In other words, the expected performance is driven only by the quality of the reference obligors (i.e., the Ba2 investor is correlation neutral). However, at the equity level, asset (default) correlation again exerts an influence but in a beneficial way — decreasing the expected loss as default correlation increases. This may not be obvious from Exhibit 7 because the relative importance of the correlation has been plotted in terms of the absolute value (disregarding the sign).

To explore the sensitivity of the trends shown in Exhibit 7 for CPORTS investments backed by reference pools of higher or lower credit quality, we conducted a similar analysis for two additional reference pools. A reference pool with Moody's WARF of 86[15] and 1005 were both investigated. New capital structures for the CPORTS investments were created per Moody's rating methodology, and the Monte Carlo simulator was again used to calculate the expected return of principal for each tranche subject to variations in the credit quality and asset correlation of the reference pools. The results for all three reference portfolios are shown in Exhibit 8. For the reference pool with WARF = 86, it was not possible to create meaningful[16] Ba2 or B2 tranches and therefore data for those tranches are absent. Similarly, it was not possible to create a meaningful B2 tranche for the reference pool with WARF = 306.

Exhibit 8: Relative Importance of Asset Correlation and Default Probability to Various CPORTS Tranches and Reference Pools

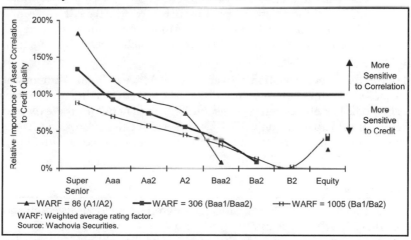

15. A WARF of 86 is high and probably cannot be duplicated in the market. However, for purposes of the study, it will provide insight into the behavior or CPORTS investments with high-quality reference pools.
16. The subordination below these tranches was so low that the tranche became almost indistinguishable from equity.

Four observations may be gleaned from Exhibit 8. First, the general trends that we found for CPORTS investments backed by a Baa1/Baa2 pool of reference obligors held also for reference pools rated higher and lower. The super-senior investor tends to be most sensitive to a percent change in the default correlation, and the most subordinate debt holder is the least sensitive. At the equity level, default correlation again exerts an influence but in a beneficial way.

Second, the higher the credit quality of the reference pool, the more important asset (and default) correlation is to the performance of the senior notes and the super-senior tranches. For example, the change to the expected return of principal for a super-senior investor is 1.8 times greater for a percent change in correlation than a percent change in credit quality when the reference pool WARF is 86 (A1/A2). This value, 1.8, falls to 0.9 when the credit quality of the reference pool falls to WARF = 1005 (Baa1/Baa2). This trend holds for the Aaa tranche, the Aa2 tranche and the A2 tranche as well.

Third, the point where positive correlation becomes beneficial to investors moves higher in the capital structure (as measured by rating) as the credit quality of the reference pool increases. For example, a CPORTS investor at the B2 level of risk is essentially indifferent to asset correlation when the WARF of the reference pool is 1005, but when the credit quality of the reference pool is increased to a WARF of 86, the point of indifference rises to Baa2. Furthermore, the point of indifference seems to be consistently about three rating notches below the average rating of the reference pool.

Fourth, the asset correlation between the reference obligors is important to equity investors but not as important as the credit quality of the reference pool. For all reference pools studied, the change to the expected return of principal was only 0.25–0.50 as sensitive to a change in correlation as a change in credit quality. In other words, for equity investors, credit selection still reigns supreme.

FINAL REMARKS

Single-tranche (CPORTS) investors are offered tremendous freedom and flexibility. But those features come with a price. Because the investor plays a major role in selecting the reference pool of obligors, the burden of making appropriate decisions falls more on the investor's shoulder. Reference obligor correlation and credit quality (default probability) are the two primary drivers that determine the CPORTS' performance. Our study explored the relative importance of these factors under several conditions. The findings (described more fully in the body of this chapter) should serve as useful guidelines for CPORTS investors interested in choosing reference pools that could adequately meet their risk appetite and needs.

APPENDIX A: CHANGE IN EXPECTED RETURN OF PRINCIPAL FOR VARIOUS CPORTS TRANCHES AS A RESULT OF CHANGES TO CREDIT QUALITY AND ASSET CORRELATION IN THE CASE WHERE THE AVERAGE RATING OF THE REFERENCE POOL IS BAA1/BAA2

		Expected Return of Principal			Change in Expected Return of Principal		
Super Senior		Correlation			Correlation		
					16.20%	25.00%	38.40%
	198	100.00%	100.00%	99.98%	0.01%	0.01%	-0.01%
WARF	306	100.00%	99.99%	99.95%	0.01%	0.00%	-0.04%
	470	99.99%	99.96%	99.87%	0.00%	-0.03%	-0.12%
Aaa		Correlation			Correlation		
		16.20%	25.00%	38.40%	16.20%	25.00%	38.40%
	198	99.97%	99.84%	99.46%	0.45%	0.32%	-0.06%
WARF	306	99.87%	99.52%	98.76%	0.35%	0.00%	-0.76%
	470	99.42%	98.53%	97.20%	-0.10%	-1.00%	-2.33%
Aa2		Correlation			Correlation		
		16.20%	25.00%	38.40%	16.20%	25.00%	38.40%
	198	99.89%	99.60%	99.01%	1.00%	0.71%	0.11%
WARF	306	99.56%	98.90%	97.90%	0.67%	0.00%	-1.02%
	470	98.38%	97.04%	95.56%	-0.53%	-1.89%	-3.38%
A2		Correlation			Correlation		
		16.20%	25.00%	38.40%	16.20%	25.00%	38.40%
	198	99.66%	99.14%	98.38%	1.88%	1.34%	0.56%
WARF	306	98.83%	97.83%	96.68%	1.02%	0.00%	-1.17%
	470	96.28%	94.63%	93.23%	-1.59%	-3.27%	-4.70%
Baa2		Correlation			Correlation		
		16.20%	25.00%	38.40%	16.20%	25.00%	38.40%
	198	99.07%	98.30%	97.44%	3.11%	2.31%	1.42%
WARF	306	97.29%	96.07%	95.01%	1.27%	0.00%	-1.11%
	470	92.63%	91.10%	90.22%	-3.58%	-5.18%	-6.09%
Ba2		Correlation			Correlation		
		16.20%	25.00%	38.40%	16.20%	25.00%	38.40%
	198	96.26%	95.37%	94.82%	6.03%	5.05%	4.44%
WARF	306	91.56%	90.79%	90.69%	0.85%	0.00%	-0.10%
	470	82.19%	82.42%	83.67%	-9.47%	-9.22%	-7.84%
Equity		Correlation			Correlation		
		16.20%	25.00%	38.40%	16.20%	25.00%	38.40%
	198	76.61%	79.03%	82.78%	11.73%	15.27%	20.73%
WARF	306	64.48%	68.56%	74.34%	-5.96%	0.00%	8.42%
	470	48.71%	54.87%	62.88%	-28.96%	-19.97%	-8.29%

WARF: Weighted average rating factor.
Source: Wachovia Securities.

Chapter 8

A Marriage of Convenience: Money Market Tranches and CDO Structures

EXECUTIVE SUMMARY

Tight credit markets and the resultant narrowing of the funding gap have made it difficult for conventional CDO structures to deliver attractive equity returns. To deal with this situation, bankers have devised an alternative structure that replaces the senior AAA tranche (or at least a significant portion of it) with a money market tranche. Despite the additional cost associated with the short-term funding (remarketing agent fees and put counterparty fees), the overall funding cost is normally reduced to a point at which the equity returns become attractive. In this chapter, we discuss the general structure of CDOs that include money market tranches, the mechanisms used to "roll over" such tranches and the key factors that investors should consider when evaluating this type of investment.

INTRODUCTION

It has been said that necessity is the mother of all invention, and there are many examples to support this view. For instance, nations situated near the desert have developed creative farming systems to deal with the lack of water and arable land. On the other hand, those located below sea level have constructed ingenious dams to protect themselves from sudden water "attacks." The same holds true for more mundane matters. For example, the Earl of Sandwich was once in a hurry, could not afford to wait for a full formal meal and came up with the idea of the "two pieces of bread with something in between" that bears his name.[1]

This distinguished tradition of innovation has influenced the financial services industry as well, and continues to do so; investment bankers,

---

1. North Carolina (where Wachovia's headquarters is located) has a rich tradition of ingenuity that includes, among others, the Wright brothers, Caleb Bradham and Allen Gant.

who years ago conceived the CDO (something that only works when there is sufficient "arbitrage"),[2] once again found themselves faced with the challenge of developing alternative strategies to remain competitive in the market. At present, portfolio asset spreads have compressed to the point at which a CDO is difficult to structure. To overcome this obstacle, bankers have risen to the occasion and have delivered a creative solution: the money market tranche that replaces the conventional AAA senior piece. The main advantage of this innovation is that it permits the creation of stable structures with attractive equity returns.

In this chapter, we discuss the general structure of CDOs that employ this new strategy, some of the key features of money market tranches and the main factors investors should pay attention to when considering this type of investment proposition.

CDOS WITH MONEY MARKET TRANCHES: GENERAL STRUCTURE

Conceptually, CDOs with money market tranches are similar to traditional CDOs except that the conventional senior (AAA) class is replaced by a money market tranche in addition to a "junior" AAA tranche. Strictly speaking, the so-called money market tranche actually consists of two or three money market tranches with staggered maturities.[3] The rationale for this partition is to facilitate the remarketing process (discussed later in further detail). Exhibit 1 shows a typical configuration. The interest and principal waterfalls are similar to those of standard CDOs except that they include provisions to pay the remarketing agent and put counterparty fees (discussed later) at or near the top of the interest waterfall. Also, cash diversion tests (interest-only [I/C] and overcollateralization [O/C] tests) and trading restrictions are similar to those found in traditional transactions.

The money market tranches serve three purposes. First, and most important, they reduce the average cost of funding for the CDO, which in turn increases the amount of cash available to distribute to equity holders.

---

2. Actually, this so-called arbitrage should more accurately be referred to as the funding gap. That is, the difference between the cost of funding of the assets and the liabilities. Arbitrage, strictly speaking, refers to a risk-free situation, hardly the CDO standard conditions.

3. Some CDOs have been structured with a combination of money market tranches (a maturity of less than 397 calendar days and thus eligible under Rule 2a-7 under the Investment Company Act of 1940) and medium-term notes (MTNs) having two-, three-, four- or five-year maturities, for example. Although the MTNs do not meet the definition of money market securities, these CDOs are referred to, in common parlance, as CDOs with money market tranches.

Even with the additional fees associated with the put counterparty and the remarketing agent, the all-in cost typically falls short of the term issuance. For example, at the time of this writing, a reduction in the overall funding cost of 10 bps–20 bps would be common. Second, the added subordination afforded to the money market tranches serves to mitigate the credit risk exposure of these securities (and that of the put counterparty). And third, the "junior" AAA tranche offers a yield higher than standard senior (AAA) tranches, making them an attractive target for resecuritizations or repackagings. Therefore, in today's market environment, this construct has a powerful appeal.

Exhibit 1: Comparison between a Traditional CDO and a CDO with a Money Market Tranche

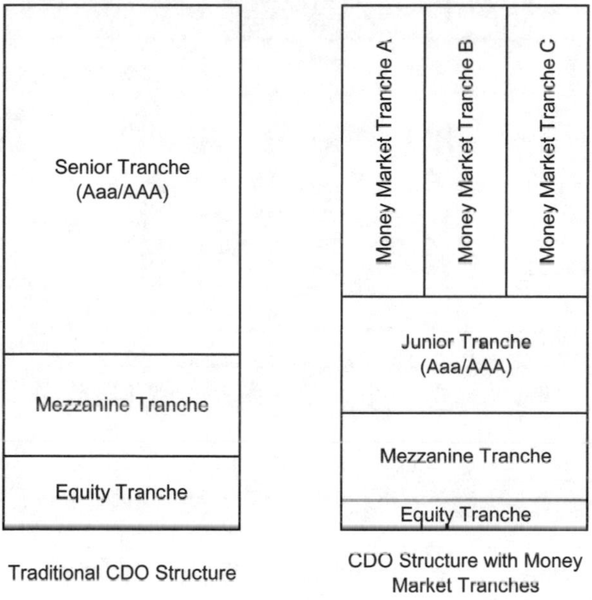

Traditional CDO Structure

CDO Structure with Money Market Tranches

Source: Wachovia Securities.

The need for cheap funding cannot be overemphasized. Tight collateral spreads have pushed the CDO arbitrage to near extinction in several segments of the market. For example, speculative-grade bond yields are at three-year lows and are near six-year lows.[4] Yields on Aaa/AAA asset-backed securities (ABS; which are frequently used as collateral in

4. Citigroup B/BB High-Yield Corporate Index.

many CDOs of ABS) are also at or near historic tights (Exhibit 2).[5] At the same time, the spreads on AAA CDO liabilities have not suffered an equivalent compression. The combined effects of these factors (plus a rosier credit outlook) have been a reduction in the expected returns of CDO equity. On the other hand, for a transaction that is 50 (or more) times leveraged (such as CDOs with a highly rated collateral pool), a minor reduction in the funding cost can translate into a major increase in the expected equity return. Thus, the funding benefits of incorporating money market tranches have made them a regular feature under the current market circumstances. This situation has been evidenced by the growing issuance of money market tranches (Exhibit 2).

**Exhibit 2: CDOs with Money Market Tranche Issuance,
AAA ABS Yields and B/BB Corporate Yields**

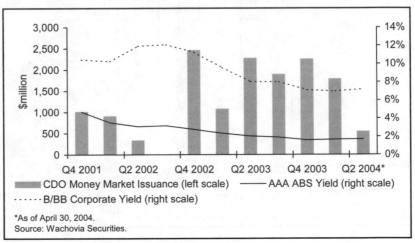

*As of April 30, 2004.
Source: Wachovia Securities.

The first CDO transaction to access the money market directly was Blue Heron Funding I, which closed in October 2001.[6] After a gradual increase, CDO money market issuance surged in Q4 2002 as collateral

5. Bear Stearns Aggregate AAA ABS Index.
6. In fairness, it must be recognized that before 2001 other structured finance vehicles had already issued money market instruments. However, these vehicles were not CDOs. For instance, in 1995 Citibank started its Dakota program, a CP-like program supported by credit card receivables and allowed to issue notes with maturities of 390 days or less. Later, other institutions started similar programs (e.g., the Emerald Notes program by MBNA). Source: Moody's Investors Service, Inc.

spreads tightened and has remained robust ever since. To date, at least 25 transactions have employed money market tranches as a source of funding, and the list is growing daily (Exhibit 3).

Exhibit 3: Sample of CDOs with Money Market Tranches

No.	Closing Date	Transaction	Portfolio Manager	Liquidity/ Put Provider	Money Market Notional (US$)	Total Deal Notional (US$)
1	10/18/01	Blue Heron Funding I	WestLB AG	WestLB AG	910,000,000	1,000,500,000
2	11/21/01	Putnam Structured Products CDO 2001-1*	Putnam	AIG	106,000,000	300,000,000
3	3/22/02	Blue Heron Funding II	WestLB AG	WestLB AG	910,000,000	1,000,000,000
4	6/20/02	G-Force CDO 2002-1	GMAC	AIG	178,000,000	508,000,000
5	6/20/02	G-Star 2002-1	GMAC	AIG	162,200,000	311,800,000
6	10/29/02	Blue Heron Funding III	WestLB AG	WestLB AG	910,000,000	1,000,000,000
7	11/01/02	G Star 2002 2	GMAC	AIG	220,000,000	397,500,000
8	12/16/02	Putnam Structured Products CDO 2002-1	Putnam	AIG	880,000,000	1,880,000,000
9	12/17/02	Blue Heron Funding IV	WestLB AG	WestLB AG	455,000,000	499,044,000
10	2/26/03	Blue Heron Funding V	WestLB AG	WestLB AG	910,000,000	1,000,000,000
11	2/26/03	North Lake CDO I	Deerfield	AIG	174,000,000	303,500,000
12	5/21/03	Blue Heron Funding VI	WestLB AG	WestLB AG	1,138,750,000	1,234,936,000
13	5/30/03	Blue Heron Funding VII	WestLB AG	WestLB AG	1,138,750,000	1,233,451,000
14	7/14/03	Grenadier Funding Ltd.	ACA	Citibank, N.A.	1,320,000,000	1,500,000,000
15	7/30/03	Grand Central CDO 2003	Vanderbilt Capital	AIG	182,500,000	300,000,000
16	9/09/03	Newcastle CDO III Ltd.**	Newcastle	AIG	395,000,000	500,000,000
17	10/02/03	Davis Square Funding, Ltd.	TCW	AIG	192,000,000	1,000,000,000
18	10/08/03	Putnam Structured Products CDO 2003-1	Putnam	B of A	369,000,000	501,000,000
19	11/07/03	Orchid CDO	ST Asset Mgmt.	AIG	175,000,000	238,125,000
20	11/30/03	TIAA Real Estate CDO 2003-1**	TIAA	AIG	222,000,000	300,000,000
21	12/12/03	Blue Bell Funding, Ltd.	GMAC	Citibank, N.A.	1,112,500,000	1,250,000,000
22	12/12/03	Commodore CDO II	Fisher Francis	AIG	186,000,000	300,000,000
23	1/30/04	Millstone	Church Tavern	Citibank, N.A.	880,000,000	1,000,000,000
24	2/18/04	Blue Heron IX	WestLB AG	WestLB AG	910,000,000	1,000,000,000
25	5/04/04	Davis Square Funding II, Ltd.	TCW	Wachovia	548,000,000	1,191,000,000
Total					14,584,700,000	19,808,856,000

ACA: ACA Management LLC; AIG: AIG Financial Products Corp.; B of A: Bank of America N.A.; Church Tavern: Church Tavern Advisors; Deerfield: Deerfield Capital Management LLC; Fisher Francis: Fisher Francis Trees & Watts; GMAC: GMAC Institutional Advisors LLC; Newcastle: Newcastle Investment Corp.; Putnam: Putnam Advisory Co.; ST Asset Mgmt.; ST Asset Management Pte: TIAA: TIAA Advisory Services LLC: Wachovia: Wachovia Bank, N.A.
*$105 million of pari passu AAA term notes issued.
**CMBS and REITs.
Source: Wachovia Securities

MONEY MARKET SECURITIES

The term *money market securities* normally refers to short-term debt instruments with maturities ranging from one day to less than one year. They are typically issued by highly rated institutions, providing them with an efficient means of borrowing and lending for short periods. In general, these are liquid and safe instruments (i.e., a low probability of default). In addition, certain money market securities are unique in that they are eligible for inclusion in money market funds. These funds are attractive for investors who otherwise, due to the minimum denomination requirements, might be precluded from gaining access to this market segment.[7] Also, these funds offer the extra benefits of diversification plus professional management.

The eligibility criteria governing the purchase of money market instruments by funds are specified by Rule 2a-7 under the Investment Company Act of 1940. These rules take into account ratings, remaining maturity, currency denomination, secondary market liquidity, guarantees of interest and principal repayment and other factors. Specifically, although the term *money market securities* is generally understood to refer to securities with maturities of less than one year, the funds are allowed to purchase instruments with a remaining maturity of 397 calendar days or less. Exhibit 4 lists some common money market instruments.

Exhibit 4: Some Common Money Market Instruments

Instrument	Characteristics
Banker's Acceptances	Issued in connection with foreign trade transactions; actively traded in the secondary market; secured instruments (lien on goods if the bank issuing the instrument runs into trouble)
Certificates of Deposit	Issued by banks; typically in denominations of $100,000–$1,000,000; can be negotiable or nonnegotiable
Treasury Bills	Issued by the U.S. government; highly liquid
Commercial Paper	Normally issued by highly rated corporations or SPVs supported by highly rated ABS; matures in 270 days or less; unsecured debt
Repurchase Agreements (Repos)	Technically a security; works similarly to a collateralized loan; a dealer sells a security and agrees to buy it back in the future at an agreed upon higher price
Bond Anticipation Notes (BANs), Tax Anticipation Notes (TANs), Revenue Anticipation Notes (RANs), etc.	Instruments issued by U.S. municipalities

SPVs: Special-purpose vehicles.
Source: Wachovia Securities.

Countless investors have embraced money market securities and, about 30 years after the advent of the money market fund, these instruments have become a regular feature of the capital markets landscape.

---

7. In the 30 years since they have been introduced, money market funds have grown to almost $1.4 trillion in total debt outstanding. Source: www.federalreserve.org.

Therefore, it should not be surprising that CDO issuers, keen on tapping the deep pool of money market investors, have begun to structure CDO debt that meets money market fund criteria.

MECHANICS OF CDOS WITH MONEY MARKET TRANCHES

At the root of the money market CDO, there is a "fundamental incompatibility" that needs to be resolved: the short-term nature of the money market tranches and the much longer tenor of the assets and remaining liabilities that make up the rest of the structure. Simply stated, there is a need for a mechanism to "roll over" the money market tranches in such a way that they can mimic the behavior of a longer maturity liability.

At present, there are three mechanisms to deal with this situation: a) the extendable note structure, b) the note with a hard put and c) the commercial paper approach. We discuss them below in detail.

The Extendable Note Structure

In this case, the holders of the money market notes benefit from a remarketing agreement between the CDO issuer and a remarketing agent. Under the remarketing agreement, the remarketing agent periodically solicits bids (spread over LIBOR) for the notes and, if the bids are satisfactory (below the maximum remarketing spread), pays the existing holder with the principal proceeds received from the new note holder (interest on the note is paid through the CDO waterfall). The interest rate for the following period is adjusted according to demand and, in all likelihood, will vary from period to period. More precisely, the interest rate is set, by way of a Dutch auction, at the point where the remarketing agent can just meet demand, with the notes on hand. The notes are always (re)sold at par.[8]

Consider the following example. Suppose $200 million in money market notes are reoffered by the remarketing agent. In principle, two situations could occur.

Successful remarketing. Assume investor interest reaches $300 million. The remarketing agent will sort the bids (spread over LIBOR) from low to high until enough bids are logged to sell the $200 million of notes. The

8. In a Dutch auction (also known as a Vickrey auction), investors are invited to submit sealed, independent bids. The bids are then matched to the items to be sold and the marginal bid (in this case, the lowest rate needed to sell the notes) is selected as the sales price and all items are sold to the winning bidders at that price. This auction is appealing to investors because bidders are ensured that they will not pay an "excessive" price relative to other winners.

interest rate will be the lowest bid that "clears" all of the notes, without exceeding the maximum remarketing spread (Exhibit 5). Typically, this process occurs every six months, but it can occur more or less frequently depending on the specific transaction and the particular tranche.[9]

Exhibit 5: Successful Remarketing of Money Market CDO Paper

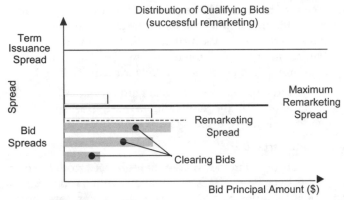

Source: Wachovia Securities.

The downside for investors, of course, is that they must actively bid for the money market notes periodically and may not be able to renew their investment at the spreads they find attractive (assuming they want to "roll over" the notes). In any case, this is what happens when everything operates smoothly.

Unsuccessful remarketing. If the underlying CDO portfolio is perceived to be performing poorly, the put counterpart is having troubles or if money market spreads "blow out," the remarketing agent may not be able to generate sufficient interest in the notes at a rate that is below the maximum remarketing spread to pay off existing holders (Exhibit 6).

If this occurs, the existing note holders will likely be forced to hold their investment for another six-month period, albeit at the maximum remarketing spread. If, after the additional period (normally, but not necessarily, a six-month period), the remarketing agent is still unable to place the notes, the put counterparty is obligated to either 1) purchase the notes at

9. CDOs are often structured with multiple money market tranches to "distribute the maturity dates" of the notes through time, making it easier for the remarketing agent to resell the notes.

Exhibit 6: Unsuccessful Remarketing of Money Market CDO Paper

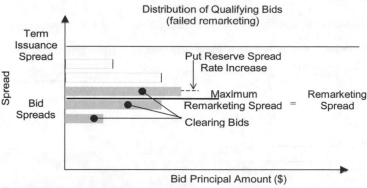

Source: Wachovia Securities.

par (by virtue of the put agreement)[10] and the interest rate remains at the maximum remarketing spread or 2) deposit the appropriate amount into a reserve account to cover the difference between the clearing spread over LIBOR and the maximum remarketing spread.[11]

Remarketing process: step by step. This entire process is best described schematically with the help of the diagram shown in Exhibit 7.

A) The money market notes are issued initially at a nominal spread over LIBOR.

B) Suppose the notes are remarketed after six months and a clearing bid is determined. In this case, the clearing bid is below the maximum remarketing spread (successful remarketing). The notes are then reissued and another six months pass uneventfully.

C) After an additional six months, the clearing bid turns out to be higher than the maximum remarketing spread permitted by the transaction (unsuccessful remarketing). Thus, the spread is set at the maximum

10. Put agreements are usually provided by a bank, an insurance company or some financial services organization with the balance sheet to accommodate such an agreement. Some of the major players in this market include Citibank, WestLB and AIG Financial. Collectively, these three entities provided put options for more than $14 billion in CDO money market tranches from 2001 to 2004. For their participation, the put counterparties all received roughly the same fee. A typical CDO money market tranche will price in a 20 bps put premium, which goes directly to the put provider.
11. In certain transactions, there is a put reserve account, which is funded at close and can be tapped into at the option of the put counterparty.

Exhibit 7: Remarketing Process for Money Market CDO Paper

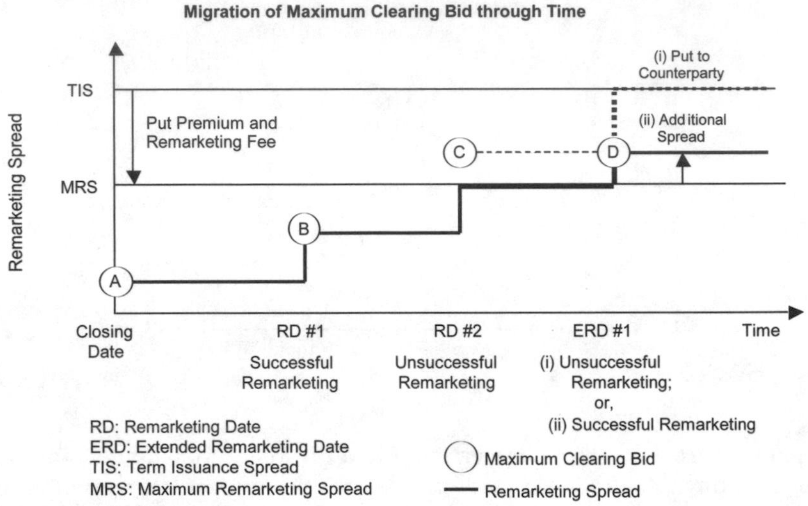

Migration of Maximum Clearing Bid through Time

Source: Wachovia Securities.

remarketing spread and the current note holders are required to retain the notes for six additional months (at a below market rate).

D) After the next period, the remarketing agent will again attempt to reissue new notes below the maximum remarketing spread.[12] If the notes are successfully remarketed, the process continues as before but, if not, the put counterparty is called on to either i) purchase the notes at par (plus accrued and unpaid interest, if any) or ii) infuse sufficient cash to pay for any additional spread required by investors that is above the maximum remarketing rate.[13]

If the put counterparty declines to infuse cash and instead opts to purchase the money market notes at par (event D(i), unsuccessful remarketing) then the remarketing agreement and put agreement might be terminated (in some transactions) and the spread is set to the maximum remarketing spread (approximately the spread that would have been assigned the notes had they originally sold in the term market). This spread becomes the new maximum remarketing spread.

12. At its discretion, the remarketing agent may attempt to resell the notes during the six-month period.
13. See footnote 11.

If the put counterparty chooses to infuse cash (event D(ii), successful remarketing), the total spread on the money market notes will exceed the maximum remarketing spread for the following six months. In this case, all of the reissued notes are placed and the remarketing is considered a success and the "clock" is reset.

Partial remarketing. However, there is an additional possibility that needs to be considered. What if there are too few bids to clear all of the remarketed notes at any spread level? For example, what if $300 million of notes are remarketed but only $200 million of interest is shown? Under these conditions, a portion of reissued notes is sold to new investors at the remarketing spread to "retire" a portion of the existing notes, whereas the remaining investors are asked to hold their investment for another six months (to the extended remarketing date). In this case, the process outlined earlier is applied independently to each group. In this way, investors are able to make the investments they desire and the put counterparty is compelled to take fewer bonds.

Some final thoughts. As mentioned earlier, the issuer can extend the investment holding period by as much as six months without consent from the note holders. It is true that the note holders will, in all likelihood, receive a higher spread (the maximum remarketing spread) for this inconvenience but, nonetheless, they might end up being unwilling participants. Standard & Poor's Corp. (S&P), for example, has taken an especially harsh view of the potential for extension and directed rated money market funds to consider extendable CDO money market securities "illiquid."[14] Typically, 10% allocation limits are placed on the amount of illiquid securities that a money market manager can buy and still maintain its S&P rating. As a result, money market CDO notes fashioned in the extendable note manner generally trade wide compared with other varieties. On the other hand, put providers like this structure because it gives them considerable time to find additional investors either in the money markets or the term markets, and potentially avoid the obligation to purchase the notes.

Notes with a Hard Put

Under *hard put* arrangements, investors are not compelled to hold their notes for another period if they do not want to.[15] In this case, unwanted

14. "Standard & Poor's Clarifies and Amends 10% Limited Liquidity Basket for Rated Money Funds," Press Release, Oct. 3, 2003.
15. Provided the put counterparty does not default. This is, however, an unlikely event. Put providers are required to maintain a high investment-grade rating or post collateral.

and unsuccessfully remarketed notes are put to the put counterparty immediately. Otherwise, the rules governing CDOs issuing money market notes with hard puts are similar to the rules governing extendable notes: The remarketing agent solicits bids before the remarketing date, ranks the bids in order from lowest to highest (up to the maximum remarketing spread) and allocates the notes accordingly. Also, should some of the remarketed notes fail to clear below the maximum remarketing spread, the put counterparty may choose to infuse additional cash, just as in the extendable note procedure. In summary, the key difference between notes with hard puts and notes that are extendable is the inability of the issuer to force note holders to retain their investment for another interest accrual period. Investors obviously benefit from this feature but, all other things equal, they receive a lower spread for such notes. Investors are expected to give a concession of a few basis points in exchange for this feature.

Commercial Paper (CP) Notes

In some CDO structures, the vehicle issues debt directly into the CP market. These notes are issued at a discount and generally mature within a year. In this case, unlike the previous two cases, the original notes are actually retired and new notes are issued. However, as with other methods, investors have the benefit of a put agreement should the SPV fail to issue (roll) new CP at interest rates comparable with term-funded interest rates that could have been achieved at the time of deal closing. As with the notes structured with hard puts, investors should expect to give a concession of a few basis points in exchange for this feature.

RELATIVE VALUE

In terms of relative value, three factors are worth mentioning.

Better Spread

Money market paper issued by CDOs normally offers more attractive spreads than similar securities. However, these instruments are, in general, less liquid than more traditional money market instruments such as bank notes, bank CP and asset-backed conduit CP. Nevertheless, they could be enticing for money market managers even if they are forced to include them in the illiquid buckets of their funds. For example, traditional money market paper currently yields LIBOR minus 5 bps–7 bps.[16] In contrast, CDO money market paper is currently issued with a coupon of LIBOR flat to 10 bps–15 bps. Another factor affecting the liquidity is

16. CP is generally issued at a discount.

the size of the issuance. Big money market funds, in general, do not buy money market instruments unless they meet a certain minimum size.

Double Protection

That said, an additional benefit of money market paper issued by CDOs (in contrast to more conventional money market instruments) is the "double protection" afforded to these instruments. Consider CP issued by a bank, for example; it constitutes an unsecured obligation of that institution. There is nothing to protect investors should the bank become insolvent. Money market paper issued by CDOs, on the other hand, enjoys structural protections (e.g., subordination and cash diversion tests) plus the advantages of having a put counterparty.[17]

Additional Due Diligence

Also, the existence of a put counterparty brings an additional level of care in terms of due diligence (i.e., in addition to the oversight that the rating agencies bring to the transaction). Finally, although in theory the investor might suffer if the remarketing effort fails, in practice, such an event is unlikely due to the negative implications that this could have to the reputation of the remarketing agent.

ADDITIONAL CONSIDERATIONS

As with any private, highly structured investments there are a number of important technical considerations for potential investors. We highlight some of them below.

Remarketing Agreement

Investors should note that the remarketing agreement can, at least in theory, be cancelled at any time by the remarketing agent. If this occurs, the issuer may have difficulty appointing a replacement and investors will be required to hold their investment until the put date, which could be a year from the most recent (re)investment date. Therefore, investors should look for transactions with strong sponsorship from the remarketing agent.

Put Agreement

If the put counterparty defaults, investors will be forced to hold their investment until a successful remarketing or the maturity of the notes.

---

17. In addition, because the rating agencies normally force the bankers to run all of the analyses assuming that the money market tranches are rolled over at the maximum remarketing spread, to the extent that these tranches are rolled over at a lower rate, this situation will provide the investors with some "extra cushion."

Furthermore, the money market notes will no longer be eligible for purchase by money market funds under Rule 2a-7 of the Investment Company Act of 1940, as they will become long-dated bonds with stated maturity equal to the maturity of the transaction. Likewise, any downgrade or default of the put counterparty will likely result in a downgrade of the short-term rating of the money market tranches. Also, the quality of the put counterparty has a major effect on the liquidity of the notes.

Credit Risk versus Liquidity Risk

There are two important factors that all investors must consider: credit risk and liquidity risk. CDOs with money market tranches are designed to cope with each independently.[18] Although it may seem that a liquidity facility might also provide credit support, some money market put agreements have triggers built into the structure that terminate the put agreement should the transaction run into credit difficulties. Hence, those puts are designed as liquidity facilities only. In those cases, investors must rely on the structural support of the CDO to mitigate credit deterioration in the underlying collateral pool.

Other put agreements in CDOs with money market tranches are structured to take credit risk. Thus, these investors are taking substantially less risk (relatively speaking) because they are secured by both the CDO structure and the put counterparty, often a large commercial bank or insurance company rated A/A or higher.[19] Therefore, investors must consider carefully the triggers by which the put agreement can be terminated to determine whether they have this additional protection. Of course, investors should be prepared to pay a premium for this feature.

Remarketing Considerations

Certain investors may plan to roll their investment from one period to another for an undetermined length of time. However, there is the potential risk that such investors might be precluded from doing this if they do not submit a sufficiently aggressive bid.

Equity Returns

Equity investors should pay particular attention to the remarketing procedures of the money market notes as small changes in the spread offered on those securities will have an important effect on the excess

---

18. *Credit risk* is the risk that the collateral, due to defaults, may not produce sufficient cash flows to pay all money due. *Liquidity risk* is the risk that an investor might not be able to sell or unwind his or her position within a reasonable time at a reasonable price.
19. We assume this to be the case in our discussion of Mechanics of CDOs with Money Market Tranches.

cash available for equity holders. This is a direct result of the high leverage that is characteristic of many CDOs with money market tranches (e.g., those supported by investment-grade collateral pools).

CONCLUSION

Money market tranches issued by CDOs serve a dual purpose. First, by reducing the CDO funding cost they make it possible to structure transactions with enticing (and often more stable) equity returns even when the funding gap is tight. Second, they provide money market funds with an attractive (albeit less liquid) investment compared with other traditional instruments. That said, in addition to examining the collateral pool, investors should pay close attention to the transaction's structural complexities, namely, the remarketing agreement, the strength of the sponsor and the put agreement provisions. These three factors together have a paramount influence on a money market instrument's performance.

Most scientific and professional disciplines sooner or later face the same problem: the need to bring together, under the same umbrella, two apparently disconnected elements of their universe. It is a natural consequence of mankind's search for unity and beauty. Physicists, for example (notwithstanding Brian Greene's optimistic claims), are still struggling to develop the so-called Unified Field Theory, a theory that could bind together the physics of small things (quantum mechanics) and the physics of large objects (Einstein's general relativity theory). Economists, on the other hand, simply gave up on their efforts and learned to live with the schizophrenic duality of microeconomics and macroeconomics. CDO practitioners, however, have been more successful. They have managed to create a vehicle—the CDO with money market tranches—that brings together instruments with short and long maturities at the same time. In doing so, they have created a stable marriage between two groups of investors who otherwise would never interact: money market funds and traditional CDO bond holders. Let us celebrate CDO ingenuity!

Chapter 9

An Introduction to
Synthetic CDO-Squared

OVERVIEW

Chapters 5 and 8 gave the reader an overview of synthetic collateralized debt obligations (CDOs) and single-tranche synthetic CDOs referencing corporate credits (CPORTS). This chapter will build on that information to discuss synthetic CDOs that reference as their underlying a combination of asset-backed securities (ABS) and CPORTS (commonly referred to as synthetic CDO-squared or SCDO², although in this chapter, we will use the Wachovia brand-name Calibre to describe these products). In its most common form, Calibre references a portfolio typically consisting of 50%–85% high-quality ABS (often AAA), with the remainder of the portfolio in CPORTS (typically rated BBB to AAA). The schematic in Exhibit 1 gives an overview.

The structure is similar to CPORTS and other synthetics in that the issuer is a special-purpose vehicle (SPV; often Cayman) that enters into a default swap with Wachovia Bank, N.A., and issues notes to investors to collateralize that swap. The issuer then invests the proceeds from the note issuance in eligible investments, typically an AAA guaranteed investment contract or possibly high-quality assets supported by a total return swap. Under the default swap, the issuer writes protection on a reference portfolio consisting of ABS assets and CPORTS in exchange for a premium. The premium is combined with the interest on the eligible investments to pay the coupon on the notes, however, in the event that aggregate losses in the reference portfolio exceed the first loss, some of the eligible investments must be redeemed or sold at par, with the proceeds used to pay Wachovia under the default swap. This will result in a write-down of the note principal because there will no longer be sufficient eligible investments to support the full note notional.

There are several structural features that make the Calibre structure potentially attractive to investors. One key feature is that Calibre typically has a soft bullet maturity of 5–7 years, even though the structure

Exhibit 1: Calibre Schematic

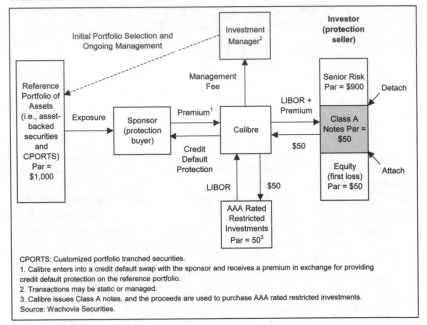

CPORTS: Customized portfolio tranched securities.
1. Calibre enters into a credit default swap with the sponsor and receives a premium in exchange for providing credit default protection on the reference portfolio.
2. Transactions may be static or managed.
3. Calibre issues Class A notes, and the proceeds are used to purchase AAA rated restricted investments.
Source: Wachovia Securities.

references ABS assets with maturities that can often exceed this by many years. In these structures, Wachovia wears the tail-risk on any ABS assets in the pool that have not matured before the maturity of the Calibre transaction (this is one reason the structure typically references very high-quality ABS). A second key point is that although these structures can be static or managed, they are typically 100% ramped at closing in either case, so there is no ramp-up risk to the investors, and the portfolio is available for inspection before the closing of the transaction.

But perhaps the most compelling reason for the increasing popularity of this product with investors is the credit environment we have entered in 2004. We have seen a dramatic tightening in corporate credit spreads and in the spreads of virtually all structured-finance asset classes, reflecting improved investor sentiment that we are entering a period of relative stability with respect to corporate defaults and downgrades. This has led investors to seek increased yield in more highly structured (and more highly leveraged) investments such as Calibre.

Clearly, however, the significant yield pickup in this new asset class is not free—these structures come with certain inherent risks. The most obvious, of course, is the increased structural complexity of these investments, and investors should carefully investigate the structures to ensure they understand the nuances of the structural mechanics and the protection provided by subordination on subordination. In addition, investors should be aware that some of this increased spread comes from increased leverage. In a positive credit environment, increased leverage provides increased returns in the form of higher yields. But in a negative credit environment, the loss curve is "flatter," meaning that in the event the investment experiences principal losses, there is a higher probability of larger principal losses.

To address these two points, this chapter will first seek to show the effect of the increased leverage by comparing a Calibre note with a CPORTS note that would achieve the same rating. We will then try to help investors understand some of the nuances of the structure by addressing three questions frequently asked by investors considering the Calibre product:

- Why include several different CPORTS in the portfolio? Is this any different from simply having one large CPORTS with an identical portfolio?

- How does overlap between the various CPORTS portfolios within the Calibre structure affect the risk of the investment? Is the investor always better off with lower overlap to improve pool diversification?

- What are some of the trade-offs between a lower CPORTS attachment with a higher Calibre attachment versus a higher CPORTS attachment with a lower Calibre attachment?

METHODOLOGY

In this chapter, we seek to address the previous questions by creating a number of examples and using Monte Carlo simulation techniques (with 200,000 paths) to derive loss distributions for different investments.* To keep the examples simple, we have made several simplifying assumptions. First, we assume that all corporate assets are rated BBB with a five-year default probability of 2.50% and a recovery given default fixed at 33.3%. We have then created eight corporate portfolios. Each portfolio consists of 80 names, with 317 corporate names used between the eight portfolios and an average overlap between the portfolios of 12 names

---

*We have used estimated rating as the constant across which to base our comparisons, and these estimated ratings are calculated using a "first dollar of loss" approach. Different conclusions might be reached if estimated ratings were based on an "expected loss" approach.

(or 15%). These eight portfolios were used to create eight CPORTS tranches, each with 5.20% subordination and a tranche thickness of 3.00%; each of the tranches was structured to have the equivalent of an implied A rating. Finally, we created a Calibre structure that had a reference portfolio consisting of 76% AAA ABS assets and 24% CPORTS (each of the eight CPORTS created is 3.00% of the Calibre reference portfolio). The Calibre has a 3.00% tranche thickness with subordination of 1.90% to achieve an estimated A rating. This structure is what we used as the basis for the comparisons that follow, and is often referred to as the "base" Calibre structure.

CALIBRE VERSUS CPORTS

To show the increased leverage that comes from investing in a Calibre structure, we have chosen to compare our base A rated Calibre note with an A rated CPORTS note. We have chosen to compare Calibre with CPORTS for the ease of exposition, but qualitatively, the Calibre structure is also leveraging up the ABS component in a similar fashion. The A rated CPORTS with which we are comparing the base Calibre is one of the eight CPORTS tranches included in the base Calibre. Exhibit 2 shows the loss distributions for the Calibre investment and the CPORTS investment.

Exhibit 2: CPORTS versus Calibre Loss Distributions

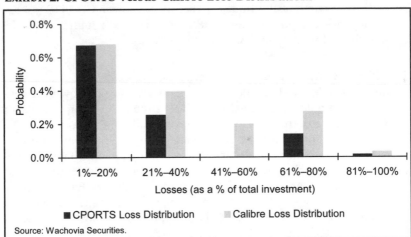

Source: Wachovia Securities.

It is clear that the Calibre loss distribution has a noticeably fatter tail than the CPORTS loss distribution, which is to be expected given the higher leverage within the Calibre structure. The distributions also do not appear smooth and, in fact, the CPORTS shows no probability of loss between 41% and 60%. This is a result of the fixed recovery assumption that results in discrete losses in the two structures.

WHY USE MULTIPLE CPORTS IN THE CALIBRE REFERENCE PORTFOLIO?

A common question we receive from investors considering an invest-ment in Calibre is why we create multiple CPORTS tranches in the reference portfolio; is this not the same as a single CPORTS tranche that has a reference portfolio equal to the sum of the various CPORTS refer-ence portfolios?

Qualitatively, we can show the difference with a simple example. Consider a Calibre transaction (Calibre A) that has three CPORTS (CPORTS A1, A2, and A3) and an ABS portfolio and compare this to a Calibre (Calibre B) that references a single large CPORTS (CPORTS B) and the same ABS portfolio. Assume each of CPORTS A1, A2 and A3 has three names, with an attachment point of 11% and a tranche thickness of 11%, and that CPORTS B contains all nine credits and has subordination equal to the sum of the subordination of CPORTS A1, A2 and A3 and principal equal to the sum of the principal amounts of CPORTS A1, A2 and A3. Now assume that one name defaults in CPORTS A1 with a recovery of zero. In this case, CPORTS A1 would experience a loss of principal equal to the tranche thickness of 11%, and this loss would decrease Calibre A's subordination. However, CPORTS B would experi-ence no loss, although its subordination would be entirely eroded. As a result, Calibre B would have no loss of subordination. Next, assume a second default occurs in CPORTS A1 and that CPORTS's principal has already been wiped out, so there is no additional loss of subordination to Calibre A. But CPORTS B now has a loss equal to the full notional of that credit, which is also the full notional of CPORTS B, and Calibre B loses subordination equal to three times the subordination lost by Calibre A on the first default. However, if the second default had been in CPORTS A2 rather than A1 again, the results would have been different for Calibre A but unchanged for Calibre B.

Of course, this is a simplistic example to illustrate the point that when we have multiple CPORTS, the losses are path dependent, whereas this is not the case with a single larger CPORTS. Moreover, to maintain the same rating on the Calibre notes, CPORTS B would have subordination that would not necessarily equal the sum of the subordination of CPORTS A1, A2 and A3.

To show a more realistic example, we have taken the same base Calibre structure used in the previous example and combined the CPORTS into a single large CPORTS, with subordination of the large CPORTS determined such that the Calibre tranche maintained its A rating with the same subordination at the Calibre level. The aggregate subordination of the eight CPORTS was $416 million, whereas the subordination on the single large CPORTS was only $290 million. Exhibit 3 shows the respective loss distributions that resulted.

Exhibit 3: Single versus Multiple CPORTS

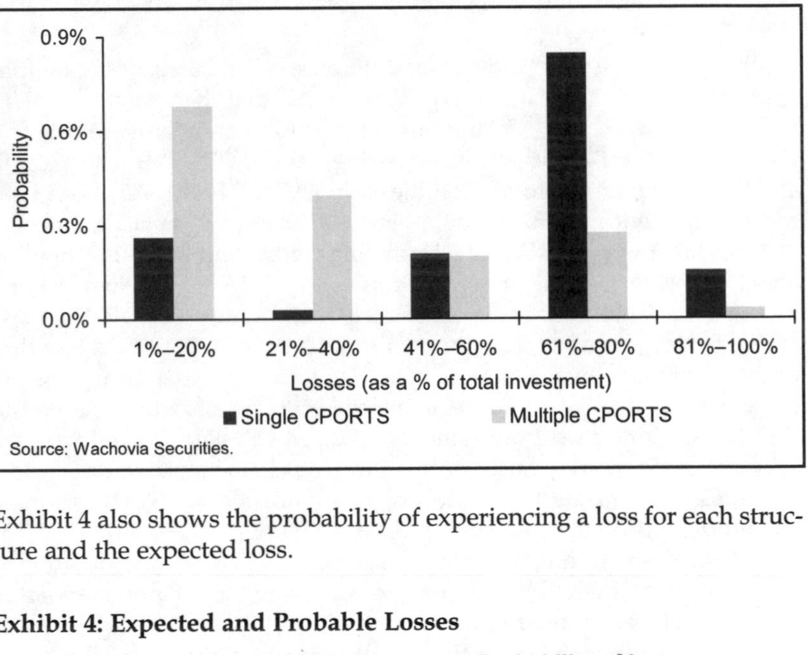

Source: Wachovia Securities.

Exhibit 4 also shows the probability of experiencing a loss for each structure and the expected loss.

Exhibit 4: Expected and Probable Losses

	Expected Loss	Probability of Loss
Single CPORTS	0.903%	1.497%
Multiple CPORTS	0.473%	1.582%

Source: Wachovia Securities.

Because we are using a "first dollar of loss" approach to rate the structures, it is not surprising that the probability of experiencing a loss is roughly the same. However, from Exhibits 2 and 4, it is clear that the severity of loss is significantly greater for the structure with a single CPORTS. This is because once losses begin to eat into the Calibre tranche, every subsequent default will result in an additional loss to the Calibre tranche in the single CPORTS structure. However, in the multiple CPORTS structure, there may be some defaults that do not result in a loss to the Calibre tranche either because they occur in a CPORTS portfolio that still has some remaining subordination or they occur in a CPORTS portfolio that has lost all of its principal already.

THE IMPACT OF OVERLAP

Another common question from investors is what impact overlap in the CPORTS portfolios has on their investment. A common assumption is that less overlap between the CPORTS reference portfolios is always desirable because this increases diversification in the Calibre reference portfolio. However, if we think about a traditional CDO (as opposed to a Calibre structure), we see that increased correlation (i.e., less diversification) within the asset portfolio is a positive for equity investors and a negative for senior investors (see Chapters 8 and 11 for more details on this topic). In this case, overlap between the CPORTS portfolios increases the correlation between the CPORTS, which are the assets in the Calibre portfolio. Hence, overlap between the CPORTS portfolios can be a positive for equity and lower mezzanine investors in the Calibre structure, whereas it is generally a negative for the most senior investors in the Calibre capital structure.

To give a quantitative example of this behavior, we have used the same base Calibre structure with eight portfolios used in the two previous

Exhibit 5: Impact of Overlap—0.00%–1.90% Tranche

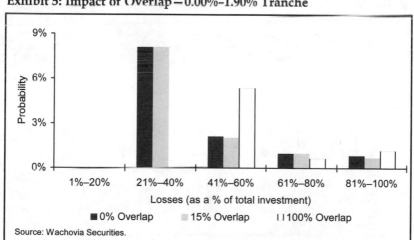

Source: Wachovia Securities.

examples. The average overlap between those portfolios is 12 names (or 15%), which is not atypical for this type of structure. We ran the loss distributions for four tranches encompassing the entire Calibre capital structure. These were an equity tranche (0.00%–1.90%), the same A tranche we have been using previously (1.90%–4.90%), a senior mezzanine tranche equal to the next 5% of losses above the A tranche (4.90%–9.90%), and a super-senior tranche encompassing the remainder

Exhibit 6: Impact of Overlap—1.90%–4.90% Tranche

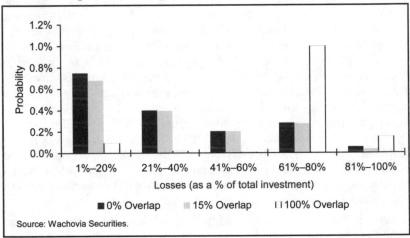

Source: Wachovia Securities.

Exhibit 7: Impact of Overlap—4.90%–9.90% Tranche

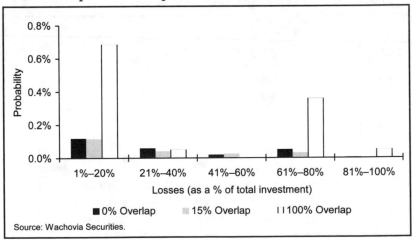

Source: Wachovia Securities.

Exhibit 8: Impact of Overlap — 9.90%–100.00% Tranche

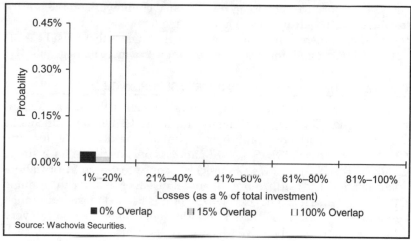

Source: Wachovia Securities.

of the portfolio (9.90% to 100.0%). Exhibits 5–8 show the loss distribution for each of these four tranches under each of the three overlap scenarios.

Exhibit 9 also gives the expected loss for each of these tranches under each overlap scenario.

Exhibit 9: Expected Losses under Each Overlap Scenario

	0% Overlap	15% Overlap	100% Overlap
Below A	4.872%	4.731%	3.692%
A	0.507%	0.473%	0.911%
5% Above A	0.078%	0.060%	0.415%
Super Senior	0.001%	0.000%	0.020%

Source: Wachovia Securities.

From these results, it is clear that, as expected, reduced overlap is not always better, all else equal, for all tranches. When losses occur for a tranche, they are generally more severe in the highest overlap scenario, but for the lower tranches, the likelihood of any loss is also decreased. In particular, the more senior tranches have lower expected losses with lower overlap between the CPORTS portfolios, whereas the most junior tranche has considerably lower expected losses with 100% overlap. The difference is least significant for the mezzanine tranches, and when looking within the range of 0%–15% overlap, the difference is negligible at almost all levels in the capital structure, implying that overlap does not have a tremendous impact for moderate amounts of overlap. This would suggest that for investors doing fundamental credit work on the portfolio, there may be advantages to having a moderate amount of overlap in the portfolios, thereby reducing the number of names that must be evaluated and monitored from 640 in our example to a more manageable 317.

CALIBRE SUBORDINATION VERSUS CPORTS SUBORDINATION

A third common question from investors is whether there is an advantage to higher CPORTS attachments and lower Calibre attachments or vice versa. Intuitively, Calibre subordination is available for any CPORTS, whereas CPORTS subordination is only available for a single CPORTS. Based on this, we can quickly deduce that each $1 of Calibre subordination is "worth more" than $1 of subordination in a single CPORTS because it can be used wherever it is needed most, but it must certainly be "worth less" than $1 of additional subordination in every CPORTS. Indeed, when we decreased the subordination of each CPORTS in our base case example by $10 million, or 1.00%, the amount of Calibre subordination required to maintain the estimated A rating was $42 million, or 4.20%, an increase of $23 million over the base Calibre structure.

To investigate this further, we analyzed the trade-off between Calibre subordination and CPORTS subordination by comparing this new A

**Exhibit 10: Lower CPORTS Subordination
versus Higher CPORTS Subordination**

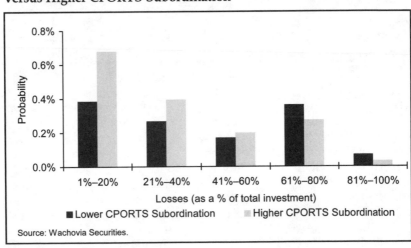

Source: Wachovia Securities.

Calibre note with our base case A Calibre note. Exhibit 10 shows the results.

The expected loss and probability of loss for each of the two structures are shown in Exhibit 11.

Exhibit 11: Expected and Probable Losses

	Expected Loss	Probability of Loss
Lower Subordination	0.577%	1.257%
Higher Subordination	0.473%	1.582%

Source: Wachovia Securities.

The results indicate that the structure with lower subordination on the CPORTS side and higher subordination on the Calibre side has a slightly lower probability of incurring losses (although because we are comparing structures on a "first dollar of loss" basis as discussed earlier, this difference should be viewed as a result of the simulation process and not significant), but it has a fatter tail in those scenarios when a loss occurs, resulting in a higher expected loss for this structure. This is, of course, the behavior that one would expect from a position that has higher leverage. Because the structure with a lower CPORTS attachment has more leverage and a slightly higher expected loss, the investor should be able to receive a slightly higher coupon for the lower attachment CPORTS structure, making this a potentially attractive alternative for an investor who is focused on maximizing returns for a given likelihood of experiencing a loss.

SUMMARY

The subordination on subordination and leverage on leverage provided in the Calibre structure add an extra level of complexity for the investor, as well as an extra level of flexibility in determining what type of customizations the investor would like to see in the transactions. The reward for investors willing and able to do the extra work is a relatively high yield compared with similarly rated investments in a market where investor perceptions of a low-risk credit environment have dramatically decreased the yields available in traditional investments. In an attempt to help investors get a head start on analyzing this product, we have addressed a number of commonly asked questions. The results generally confirm our intuition and should help investors make decisions regarding the trade-offs between pricing and structural features including CPORTS attachment points, Calibre attachment points and portfolio overlap. Specifically:

- The decision to invest in a CPORTS structure or a Calibre structure is, in part, a function of the amount of leverage an investor wishes to take. The Calibre structure, because it is generally more leveraged, can give investors slightly higher yields for a similar rating compared with CPORTS, but the trade-off, of course, is a fatter tail on the loss distribution—if losses occur, the more leveraged investment would have a higher expected loss severity.

- Combining all of the underlying CPORTS tranches into a single large CPORTS should increase the expected loss slightly given the same rating on the Calibre investment. However, for investors seeking additional simplicity in the structure, this trade-off might be worthwhile.

- The amount of overlap in the portfolios may well be a red herring for most investors unless either 1) they are investing at the very bottom or very top of the Calibre capital structure or 2) they are looking at a transaction with an excessive amount of overlap.

- Investors with a positive outlook for the credit markets may choose to take advantage of the additional leverage embedded in the Calibre structure to get enhanced yields through lower attachments on the CPORTS tranches.

Analytics and Relative Value

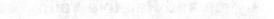

Chapter 10

CDOs and Correlation:
Are Your Ventures in One Bottom Trusted?

"My ventures are not in one bottom trusted,
Nor to one place; now is my whole estate"
William Shakespeare, *The Merchant of Venice*, Act I, Scene I

EXECUTIVE SUMMARY

This chapter addresses correlation within the context of a collateralized debt obligation (CDO) portfolio. This topic is critically important for an investor wishing to assess the degree of diversification of a pool of CDO holdings. Basic concepts are introduced with simple examples and a general method to estimate correlation is presented. An example based on a typical collateralized loan obligation (CLO) structure shows that senior tranches can exhibit a fairly low to moderate degree of correlation even when there is a significant "degree of overlap" at the underlying collateral level. Correlation, however, is much higher among mezzanine-level tranches; this fact emphasizes the importance of monitoring correlation when building a portfolio of BBB/Baa tranches. Finally, the example also shows the danger of estimating the correlation between two CDO tranches using some simple (albeit misguided) concepts, such as the "degree of similarity" or "percentage of overlap" with respect to the underlying collateral pools.

INTRODUCTION

Long before Harry Markowitz (who won the Nobel Prize in Economics in 1990) articulated the benefits of portfolio diversification, Shakespeare had hinted that there were advantages in not putting all of one's eggs in the same basket. This is clear in the opening conversation between Antonio and Salarino in *The Merchant of Venice*. In it, Antonio explains to Salarino why "...my merchandise makes me not sad." He has distributed his merchandise across many ships ("my ventures are not in one bottom trusted..."), and thus he sleeps well at night.

Many factors must be considered when building a diversified and balanced portfolio. Four hundred years after the Antonio-Salarino interchange, correlation (which is probably the most difficult factor to measure and the one that drives diversification) still remains a chief concern for investors. From a theoretical point of view, correlation is straightforward: It is a well-defined mathematical concept that refers to the degree to which "two things move together" (to put it in layman's terms). In practice, however, correlation is frequently difficult to observe and therefore hard to measure.

CDO investors, who normally hold not one but many CDO positions, are often concerned about the correlation between their CDO tranches and the effect that it could have on the risk profile of their portfolios; all things being equal, positively correlated holdings lead to riskier portfolios. However, correlation between CDO tranches is difficult to measure because the correlation that matters (the correlation between the *default behavior* of two tranches) is driven not by one but two factors: 1) the default correlation of the underlying CDO assets (as defaults are ultimately what determine the performance of a CDO tranche) and 2) the structure of each CDO. Worse, correlation can be time-dependent (it is not a number that one measures once, puts in a model and then forgets), and sometimes different data sets yield contradictory results.

Moreover, there are many misconceptions regarding correlation and, unfortunately, the term is often used in a loose manner to convey concepts or ideas that are not quite related to the original (and correct) meaning. This chapter attempts to address some of these issues, namely what is correlation (intuitively and mathematically), what is its relevance within the context of a CDO portfolio and how one can estimate it. Key points are illustrated with several examples. With respect to CDO tranches, correlation estimates are presented based on a typical CDO structure and collateral overlap. Interestingly enough, simulations show that the correlation between the default behavior of two senior CDO tranches is fairly low even if there is a considerable asset overlap at the underlying collateral pool level.

CORRELATION: WHAT IS IT, ANYWAY?

Intuitively, correlation refers to the extent to which two quantitative variables move together (e.g., the degree to which unemployment in New York and unemployment in New Jersey move together or the degree to which beer consumption in Canada and the United States move together). One cannot talk, however, about correlation between New York and New Jersey—there has to be a measurable variable in the statement, otherwise the statement does not make sense. For instance, one cannot say that CBO A and CBO B are correlated. On the other hand, the statement: *the IRR of the senior tranche of CBO A and the IRR of the senior tranche of CBO B seem to be uncorrelated* does make sense because its validity can be investigated—whether the statement is true is a different story.

Mathematically, the correlation between two variables, X and Y, is defined as follows:

$$\rho = \frac{E[(X - \mu_x)(Y - \mu_y)]}{\sigma_x \sigma_y}$$

(Eqn. 1)

where,

ρ (pronounced "rho") represents the correlation;

μ_x is the expected value of X;

μ_y is the expected value of Y;

σ_x is the standard deviation of X;

σ_y is the standard deviation of Y; and

E represents the *expected value* operator.

In terms of a discrete number of observations (N), the correlation can be estimated as

$$\rho = \frac{N\Sigma(x_i y_i) - \Sigma x_i \Sigma y_i}{\sqrt{(N\Sigma x_i^2 - (\Sigma x_i)^2)(N\Sigma y_i^2 - (\Sigma y_i)^2)}}$$

(Eqn. 2)

It follows from this definition that ρ (the correlation coefficient or simply the correlation) can only take values between -1 and 1. A positive number close to 1 indicates that the two variables (X and Y) move together at the same time and in the same direction to a high degree. Alternatively, a ρ close to -1 indicates that X and Y move in the opposite direction to a large degree. And a ρ close to 0 refers to two variables that are independent from each other. In other words, knowing something about the behavior of X provides little insight into the behavior of Y.

EXAMPLES

Exhibits 1–3 illustrate the concepts mentioned above. The example in Exhibit 1 corresponds to two variables that have a high positive correlation. Exhibit 2 shows two variables with a strong negative correlation.

And Exhibit 3 corresponds to two variables that are almost totally uncorrelated (ρ close to 0), that is, the two variables have almost "nothing to do with each other."

Exhibit 1: Positively Correlated Variables

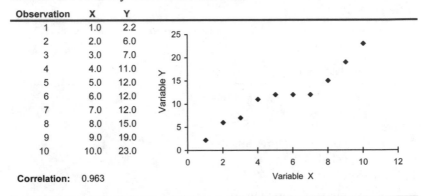

Observation	X	Y
1	1.0	2.2
2	2.0	6.0
3	3.0	7.0
4	4.0	11.0
5	5.0	12.0
6	6.0	12.0
7	7.0	12.0
8	8.0	15.0
9	9.0	19.0
10	10.0	23.0

Correlation: 0.963

Source: Wachovia Securities.

Exhibit 2: Negatively Correlated Variables

Observation	X	Y
1	1.0	10.0
2	2.0	9.0
3	3.0	8.0
4	4.0	6.0
5	5.0	7.0
6	6.0	5.0
7	7.0	4.0
8	8.0	1.0
9	9.0	1.0
10	10.0	0.0

Correlation: -0.979

Source: Wachovia Securities.

Exhibit 3: Two Uncorrelated Variables

Observation	X	Y
1	1.0	9.0
2	2.0	10.0
3	3.0	4.0
4	4.0	0.0
5	5.0	1.0
6	6.0	6.0
7	7.0	6.0
8	8.0	6.0
9	9.0	8.0
10	10.0	8.0

Correlation: 0.056

Source: Wachovia Securities.

TWO TRICKY ISSUES

There are two widespread misconceptions regarding correlation. First, correlation does not allow one to establish a cause-effect relationship. That is, a high correlation between X and Y does not imply that Y causes X or X causes Y. In short, X *might* or *might not* be the cause of Y—correlation says nothing about this. In fact, Y and X might not be linked at all and still exhibit a high correlation simply due to a coincidence. For instance, consider Exhibit 4, which shows some interesting data: Chile's GNP and the amount of glass recycled in the United States from 1985 to 1994. A visual inspection indicates a high correlation between these variables. The actual computation of ρ is even more convincing, $\rho = 0.993$. However, concluding from this situation that the increase in glass recycled in the United States *caused* economic growth in Chile would be far-fetched. (Or, for that matter, concluding that the increase in Chile's GNP motivated Americans to recycle.) Examples of variables exhibiting high correlation without having a cause-effect relationship, or actually, without having any link at all abound.

That said, there are instances where some cause-effect relationships may exist, but it is far from obvious, and correlation, unfortunately, does not clarify the issue. A case in point is a recent study by a University of Texas economics professor. His research focused on the relationship between physical appearance and teaching ability. The results showed that good-looking professors received significantly higher teaching evaluation scores than their less fortunate (i.e., uglier) colleagues. In short, good looks and teaching effectiveness exhibited a high correlation. But, do good looks actually cause someone to be a better teacher? This is not

Exhibit 4: Chilean GNP and Glass Recycled in the United States

Year	Chilean GNP (US$ billion)	Glass Recycled in the United States (000 tons/year)
1985	16.1	132.0
1986	17.3	130.0
1987	18.9	140.0
1988	20.3	155.0
1989	22.6	164.0
1990	23.5	178.0
1991	25.2	198.0
1992	28.1	212.0
1993	30.3	229.0
1994	31.4	241.0
Correlation:	0.993	

Source: World Bank, SAEFL, November 2001.

clear and further elaboration on the implications of these findings is certainly beyond the scope of this chapter.[1]

Second, correlation and conditional probability (the likelihood that event X could happen given that event Y has already happened) are different concepts and should not be confused. Let variables X and Y indicate whether assets X and Y have defaulted; a 1 indicates that the asset has defaulted and a 0 means it has performed (not defaulted). Exhibit 5 shows several observations of X and Y. Using Equation 2 from above, the default correlation between X and Y is determined to be 0.763. The probability that Y might default given that asset X has already defaulted, however, is 0.666 (of the three cases in which X defaulted, Y defaulted only twice). And the probability that X might default given that Y already defaulted is 1 (whenever Y defaulted so did X). Clearly, the two concepts (as well as the "numerical values" associated with them) are different.[2]

1. Varian, Hal R., "Economic Scene," *The New York Times,* page C2. Aug. 28, 2003.
2. Mathematically, the relationship between correlation and conditional probability can be described as

$$\rho_{X,Y} = \frac{P(X \mid Y)P(Y) - P(X)P(Y)}{\sqrt{P(X)P(Y)(1 - P(X))(1 - P(Y))}}$$

where P(X) and P(Y) represent the probability of X defaulting and Y defaulting, respectively, and P(X|Y) represents the probability that X will default given that Y has defaulted (i.e., the conditional probability of X defaulting). The default correlation between X and Y, and the probability that X will default given that Y has defaulted are clearly not equivalent.

Exhibit 5: Default Behavior of X and Y

Observation	X	Y
1	1	0
2	0	0
3	0	0
4	1	1
5	0	0
6	0	0
7	1	1
8	0	0
9	0	0
10	0	0

Note: 1 = default, 0 = perform.
Source: Wachovia Securities.

CORRELATION AND CDOS: WHAT CORRELATION IS AND WHY IT MATTERS

Back to CDOs. In the context of CDOs, *correlation* matters because most CDO investors hold not one but many positions. Hence, it is critical to quantify the correlation between two tranches or, more precisely, the correlation between two measurable variables associated with any two tranches. This is a particularly important consideration for managers who are assembling a portfolio of CDOs to be used as collateral in a CDO of CDOs transaction.

Suppose an investor has N holdings and must estimate the correlation between any two assets, covering all the possibilities. This information is summarized in the so-called correlation matrix — a square and symmetric array of numbers with 1's along the diagonal and $\rho_{i,j}$ (the correlation between asset i and asset j) in the i, j position. All in all, an N × N correlation matrix involves estimating $N(N-1)/2$ different correlation coefficients — by no means an easy task.

Having said that, correlation has to be studied in relation to a measurable characteristic and several choices are possible when looking at CDO tranches. One possibility is to look at the default correlation between two tranches. For that purpose, one might define a default indicator (1 or 0) signifying default or no default, as in the preceding example, and examine the correlation between the indicator variable of one CDO tranche and the indicator variable of the other.

Alternatively, one could explore the correlation between the internal rate of return (IRR) associated with each tranche, or perhaps the loss experienced by them, where loss is defined as the present value (PV) of the cash flows received by the tranche under consideration compared with the initial investment.

Other variables, less relevant in the context of CDO performance, but perhaps useful in the context of a different analysis could be duration, "PIKability," time until return of principal or stability (measured as the standard deviation of some performance variable).

This study explores the correlation between the senior and mezzanine tranches of two CDOs (actually, CLOs in this case) with respect to three different variables: 1) a default indicator (1 or 0), 2) IRR and 3) loss. Both CLOs have structurally identical tranche sizes, triggers and waterfall, but they differ in the actual asset composition of the collateral pool (to be discussed later).

A GENERAL FRAMEWORK FOR ANALYZING CORRELATION BETWEEN CDO TRANCHES

It is useful to look at CDO correlation with the help of a simple example. Exhibit 6 depicts a CLO structure with three tranches: senior, mezzanine and equity. The collateral consists of 100 homogeneous loans (B1/B2, WARF = 2,400) each having a 1% par value, an eight-year bullet maturity profile and a probability of default, p, equal to 22%. Complete modeling assumptions may be found in Appendix A.

Exhibit 6: Typical CLO Structure

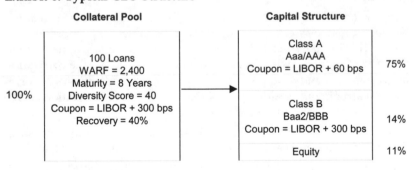

Source: Wachovia Securities.

For a given capital structure, the default of a CDO tranche depends on the number of defaults in the collateral pool, the timing of those defaults and the recovery rate of the defaulted assets. To simplify the CDO correlation analysis, however, defaults are assumed to occur evenly through time (between year 0 and year 4) and the recovery rate is assumed to be constant (40%). With these simplifying assumptions and the help of a cash flow model, it is possible to determine the value of 1) the tranche default indicator variable, 2) the IRR and 3) the loss for each tranche in the CDO and for any number of defaults in the collateral pool. Appendix B shows this table. The table covers all of the possible default scenarios (namely: 0, 1, 2, . . . up to 100 defaults). Notice that whenever there is a loss, no matter how small, the default indicator is 1.

Clearly, the correlation between any two tranches is driven by two elements: 1) the structural characteristics of the CLO (i.e., waterfall, capital structure, tranche size and triggers) and 2) the default correlation at the level of the underlying pool. The table shown in Appendix B captures the first element. The second element will be determined by the composition of the underlying pools.

Thus, before proceeding, it is necessary to make some assumptions regarding the asset composition of the two collateral pools supporting the CDO transactions and the degree of default correlation between their respective assets. To this end, a well-accepted practice among CDO analysts is to look at the entire universe of assets and classify the assets into different groups (determined by industrial sector, geographical area or other features). In this framework, one needs to specify a value for the default correlation between two assets that belong to the same group ("intra" correlation) or different groups ("inter" correlation).

Default Correlation between Assets in the Collateral Pool

Default correlation values are not directly observable and, therefore, are difficult to estimate. Market participants have been forced to rely, so far, on a mix of indirect methods (using other variables as a proxy for correlation), ad hoc assumptions and, frankly, intuition to estimate these values. Furthermore, the data available are sparse and sometimes contradictory. Not surprising, the correct default correlation coefficient between any two assets is still a question searching for a definitive answer.

The rating agencies, due to the role they play as market moderators, have been the first to publish default correlation assumptions and discuss the manner in which those assumptions contribute to their overall rating approach. Moody's Investors Service, Inc., for example, has circumvent-ed the correlation issue by virtue of its diversity score. Behind the diversity score, however, is the assumption that the default correlation between two assets that belong to different groups ("industries") is 0, whereas the default correlation between two assets in the same group is approximately 17% (though this has never been stated formally by Moody's).

Fitch Ratings, on the other hand, has estimated the default correlation between two obligors by using asset correlation as a starting point. Once the asset correlation has been established (this can be done using equity prices as a proxy) the default correlation is estimated using the following expression,

$$\text{Corr } (X_i, X_j) = \frac{p_{ij} - p_i \, p_j}{\sqrt{p_i(1- p_i) \, p_j (1- p_j)}}$$

(Eqn. 3)

This process is explained in more detail in Fitch's report *Default Correlation and Its Effect on Portfolios of Credit Risk.*[3] In summary, Fitch assumes for the intra-industry asset correlation values between 17% and 43% and for the inter-industry asset correlation values between 0% and 35%. This results in default correlation values in the 5% to 18% range for obligors within the same industry and values between 3% and 14% for obligors in different industries (after making some simplifying assumptions regarding the homogeneity of a hypothetical pool of assets), depending on the average probability of default of the collateral pool.

Standard and Poor's Corp. (S&P) derives, similarly to Fitch, default correlation values from asset correlation assumptions: 30% for intra-industry asset correlation and 0% for inter-industry correlation. This results in default correlation values in the 6% to 19% range for obligors in the same group and 0% for obligors in different groups (again, after making the simplifications described above). In both the Fitch and S&P approaches, the default correlation depends also on the quality of the assets (higher correlation for lower-quality assets), whereas in the case of Moody's it is independent of the quality of the assets. Exhibit 7 summarizes this information.

A discussion of the merits of each approach is beyond the scope of this chapter. For the case under study, it suffices to say that it was assumed that the inter-industry asset correlation was 3%, whereas the intra-industry asset correlation was 30%. For a homogeneous pool with a probability of default of 22%, this corresponds to default correlation values of 1% and 17%, respectively.

3. *Default Correlation and Its Effect on Portfolios of Credit Risk*, Fitch Ratings, Feb. 20, 2003.

Exhibit 7: Implied Rating Agency Default Correlation Assumptions

Average Probability of Default	Implied Inter-Industry Default Correlation (Average)			Implied Intra-Industry Default Correlation (Average)		
	Moody's	S&P	Fitch	Moody's	S&P	Fitch
1%	0.00%	0.00%	3.20%	17.00%	6.30%	5.30%
2%	0.00%	0.00%	4.90%	17.00%	7.80%	8.30%
3%	0.00%	0.00%	5.60%	17.00%	9.20%	9.20%
4%	0.00%	0.00%	8.60%	17.00%	9.60%	10.20%
5%	0.00%	0.00%	9.20%	17.00%	10.60%	11.00%
10%	0.00%	0.00%	9.00%	17.00%	13.70%	13.70%
15%	0.00%	0.00%	11.70%	17.00%	15.20%	16.10%
20%	0.00%	0.00%	13.10%	17.00%	16.40%	17.60%
30%	0.00%	0.00%	14.50%	17.00%	18.70%	18.90%

Source: Fitch Ratings, Moody's Investors Service, Inc., and Standard and Poor's Corp.

Composition of the Collateral Pools

Having made assumptions regarding default correlation, one needs to make an assumption regarding the composition of the collateral pools of both CLOs. Based on an internal study of 13 high-yield CBOs and seven leveraged loan CLOs issued in 1998–2001, it was observed that 1) the CBOs exhibited, on average, a 23% obligor overlap (in other words, based on notional amount outstanding, 23% of the assets were identical), whereas the CLOs exhibited a 34% obligor overlap, and 2) in terms of industry overlap (i.e., the same industries but not necessarily the same obligors), these figures were 87% and 89%, for CBOs and CLOs, respectively. As one would expect, transactions ramped in the same time span or those having the same portfolio manager tended to show a higher degree of overlap.

To capture a realistic situation while keeping the model simple, 100 equal size obligors were assigned to each portfolio. However, only 30 obligors were identical in both pools (i.e., the two pools have 30% obligor overlap). In addition, a total of 30 possible industries were considered though only 25 industries were represented in any particular collateral pool. Furthermore, 80% of the industries (20 industries) found in one collateral pool are also found in the other (i.e., the two pools have 80% industry overlap). These assumptions are summarized in Exhibit 8.

Monte Carlo Simulation

With capital structures and collateral pools in place, several Monte Carlo simulations were run. Each simulation was started with a different seed and consisted of 8,000,000 possible default scenarios. The need for such a large number of scenarios was dictated by the desire to capture a significant number of defaults at the senior tranche level—not a

Exhibit 8: Obligor and Industry Overlap Assumptions

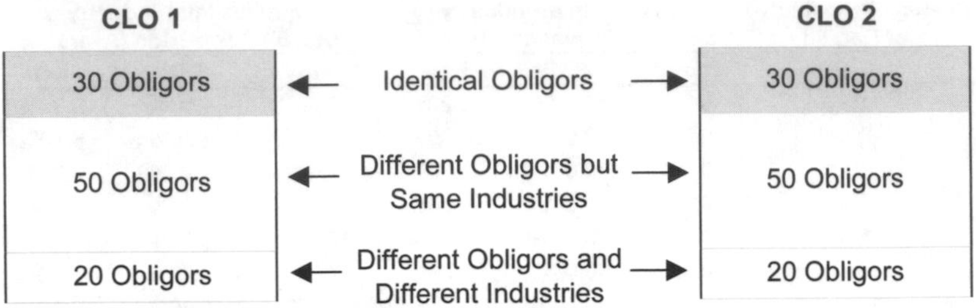

CLO 1		CLO 2
30 Obligors	← Identical Obligors →	30 Obligors
50 Obligors	← Different Obligors but → Same Industries	50 Obligors
20 Obligors	← Different Obligors and → Different Industries	20 Obligors

Source: Wachovia Securities.

likely event in the case of an Aaa/AAA tranche, thus the need to run 8,000,000 cases.

Each scenario was characterized by a given number of defaults, which, with the help of the table in Appendix B, allowed the determination of the corresponding value of 1) the tranche default indicator, 2) the tranche IRR and 3) the tranche loss. In total, 12 time series of 8,000,000 data points were constructed for each simulation (three variables, two tranches and two CLOs) and a total of eight simulations were performed. The correlations were computed from these time series using Equation 2 and taking the average over the eight simulations.

The Monte Carlo method was employed to generate the default scenarios, and correlation was handled at the asset level assuming asset correlation values of 30% (intra) and 3% (inter). This corresponded, as stated before, to default correlation values of 17% (intra) and 1% (inter) for a pool with a 22% default probability. The scenarios were generated assuming that the asset values followed a normal distribution (defaulting when the asset value falls below a given threshold level determined by the default probability of the asset). Then, the so-called Cholesky decomposition method was used to create a multivariate normal having the desired asset correlations.

Exhibit 9: Correlation Estimates for Default Indicator, Internal Rate of Return and Loss

	Correlation Estimates of Senior Tranches	Correlation Estimates of Mezzanine Tranches
Default Indicator	[14%+/- 1%]	[46%+/- 0%]
Internal Rate of Return	[18%+/- 1%]	[51%+/- 0%]
Loss	[18%+/- 1%]	[56%+/- 0%]

Source: Wachovia Securities.

RESULTS

As expected, correlation (for default, IRR and loss) at the senior level was low compared with the correlation exhibited at the mezzanine level. Also expected was the fact that the correlation values for the IRR and loss (whether at the senior or mezzanine level) were higher than the correlation exhibited by the default indicator. This can be explained by noticing that the IRR and loss are gradual functions of the number of defaults, whereas the default indicator is a step-function (1 or 0).

The default correlation for the senior tranches seems low in absolute value (14%). However, if one considers the two senior tranches to be assets within the same industry, this value (14%), while lower than Moody's assumption (17%), is somewhat higher than the estimates given by Fitch or S&P for highly rated assets (Exhibit 7). That said, the important fact is that the correlation between the behavior of the senior pieces — whether measured by the default indicator, IRR or loss — is within the range of what one would consider low or moderately low. This is good news for senior tranche CDO investors because it shows that a fair degree of diversification can be achieved by holding several senior CDO tranches.

At the mezzanine level, however, correlation was much higher. That stresses the importance of looking at the composition of the collateral pools when building a portfolio of mezzanine (typically, BBB/Baa) investments. The values observed are much higher than the values attributed by the rating agencies to assets within the same "industry" and having a default probability of 10%–30%, a range that is normally associated with mezzanine assets (Exhibit 7). Therefore, investors assembling a portfolio of mezzanine positions must be more mindful of the composition of the underlying pools. In fact, by monitoring the composition of the underlying pools the investors could have a better grasp of the degree of diversification achieved by their BBB/Baa portfolio. The framework provided here could be an important tool to help such investors build a reasonably diversified portfolio of mezzanine positions.

CONCLUSIONS AND FUTURE WORK

The framework outlined in this chapter is useful in assessing the correlation within a portfolio of CDO holdings if one knows the composition of the collateral pools or can make some reasonable assumptions regarding their composition (i.e., obligor concentrations and overlap). In the context of a CDO of CDOs, this approach could help the manager monitor the degree of diversification of his holdings and guide future acquisitions.

That said, some simplifying assumptions were made. For example, the recovery values for the defaulted assets were assumed to be constant and the timing of the defaults was not stochastic (default timings were evenly distributed overtime). Only the number of defaults in a given scenario was treated probabilistically (using the Monte Carlo). While considerable computation expediency was achieved with these assumptions and several simulations indicated that such assumptions did not have any material effect on the correlations estimates, this topic could be explored further. In any event, these two assumptions are conservative in the sense that, if anything, they tend to increase the correlation. Also, one must keep in my mind that the assumptions made in terms of portfolio composition and overlap can have an important impact on the correlations of the tranches. However, this is a subject that warrants a separate study. The choice made here was based on a realistic ("typical") situation.

Finally, two important facts remain: 1) correlation at the senior tranche level is not high even when the underlying pools have considerable similarities and 2) mezzanine investors must be mindful of the correlation of their holdings. A final warning: This study shows that "estimating" the correlation using a proxy such as "the degree of overlap" between two pools (30% in the example) is both dangerous and misleading because it can lead to overestimating the default correlation at the senior tranche level (30% > 14%) and underestimating the default correlation at the mezzanine level (30% < 46%).

APPENDIX A : CDO MODELING ASSMPTIONS

Collateral Features

Floating-Rate Securities	100%
Reinvestment	None
Weighted Average Spread	3.00%
Percentage Ramped at Close	100%
Prepayment Rate	0%
Recovery Rate	40%
Diversity	40
WARF	2,400
WAL (Bullet)	8 Years

Structural Assumptions

Tenor	8 Years
Payment Frequency	Semiannually
Administration Fees	None
Trustee Fees	None
Management Fees	None
Interest Rate Environment	Flat at 4%; No Hedges

Interest-Coverage Triggers

Class A Interest-Coverage Test	125%
Class B Interest-Coverage Test	100%

Overcollateralization Triggers

Class A Note Overcollateralization Test	118%
Class B Note Overcollateralization Test	107%

Source: Wachovia Securities.

APPENDIX B

Number	Default*		IRR		Loss	
of Defaults	Senior	Mezzanine	Senior	Mezzanine	Senior	Mezzanine
0	0	0	4.6%	7.0%	.0%	.0%
1	0	0	4.6%	7.0%	.0%	.0%
2	0	0	4.6%	7.0%	.0%	.0%
.	.	.	.	.	.	.
.	.	.	.	.	.	.
33	0	0	4.6%	7.0%	.0%	.0%
34	0	0	4.6%	7.0%	.0%	.0%
35	0	1	4.6%	6.6%	.0%	3.0%
36	0	1	4.6%	6.0%	.0%	6.3%
37	0	1	4.6%	5.4%	.0%	9.6%
38	0	1	4.6%	4.8%	.0%	13.0%
39	0	1	4.6%	4.1%	.0%	16.3%
40	0	1	4.6%	3.5%	.0%	19.7%
41	0	1	4.6%	2.8%	.0%	23.1%
42	0	1	4.6%	2.1%	.0%	26.5%
43	0	1	4.6%	1.3%	.0%	29.8%
44	0	1	4.6%	0.5%	.0%	33.1%
45	0	1	4.6%	-0.4%	.0%	37.1%
46	0	1	4.6%	-1.4%	.0%	41.1%
47	0	1	4.6%	-2.6%	.0%	45.0%
48	0	1	4.6%	-3.9%	.0%	48.9%
49	0	1	4.6%	-5.3%	.0%	52.9%
50	0	1	4.6%	-6.6%	.0%	57.0%
51	0	1	4.6%	-8.3%	.0%	60.9%
52	0	1	4.6%	-10.4%	.0%	64.8%
53	0	1	4.6%	-13.0%	.0%	68.7%
54	0	1	4.6%	-16.2%	.0%	72.6%
55	0	1	4.6%	-20.1%	.0%	76.5%
56	0	1	4.6%	-24.5%	.0%	80.6%
57	0	1	4.6%	-33.3%	.0%	84.6%
58	1	1	4.6%	-98.0%	.3%	87.0%
59	1	1	4.4%	-98.0%	1.2%	87.0%
60	1	1	4.2%	-98.0%	2.1%	87.0%
61	1	1	4.0%	-98.0%	3.0%	87.0%
62	1	1	3.9%	-98.0%	3.8%	87.0%
63	1	1	3.7%	-98.0%	4.7%	87.0%
64	1	1	3.5%	-100.0%	5.5%	87.5%
65	1	1	3.3%	-100.0%	6.1%	88.8%

APPENDIX B (CONTINUED)

Number	Default*		IRR		Loss	
of Defaults	Senior	Mezzanine	Senior	Mezzanine	Senior	Mezzanine
66	1	1	3.2%	-100.0%	6.7%	90.0%
67	1	1	3.0%	-100.0%	7.6%	90.1%
68	1	1	2.7%	-100.0%	8.4%	90.1%
69	1	1	2.5%	-100.0%	9.3%	90.1%
70	1	1	2.3%	-100.0%	10.1%	90.1%
71	1	1	2.1%	-100.0%	10.9%	90.1%
72	1	1	1.9%	-100.0%	11.7%	90.1%
73	1	1	1.6%	-100.0%	12.5%	90.1%
74	1	1	1.4%	-100.0%	13.3%	00.1%
75	1	1	1.1%	-100.0%	14.1%	90.1%
76	1	1	.9%	-100.0%	14.9%	90.1%
77	1	1	.6%	-100.0%	15.7%	90.1%
78	1	1	.3%	-100.0%	16.5%	90.1%
79	1	1	.1%	-100.0%	17.3%	90.1%
80	1	1	-0.2%	-100.0%	18.1%	90.1%
81	1	1	-0.5%	-100.0%	18.9%	90.1%
82	1	1	-0.9%	-100.0%	19.7%	90.1%
83	1	1	-1.2%	-100.0%	20.5%	90.1%
84	1	1	-1.5%	-100.0%	21.3%	90.1%
85	1	1	-1.9%	-100.0%	22.1%	90.1%
86	1	1	-2.3%	-100.0%	22.9%	90.7%
87	1	1	-2.6%	-100.0%	23.6%	91.7%
88	1	1	-3.0%	-100.0%	24.2%	92.6%
89	1	1	-3.4%	-100.0%	25.0%	93.2%
90	1	1	-3.9%	-100.0%	25.9%	93.2%
91	1	1	-4.4%	-100.0%	26.8%	93.2%
92	1	1	-5.0%	-100.0%	27.7%	93.2%
93	1	1	-5.5%	-100.0%	28.5%	93.2%
94	1	1	-6.2%	-100.0%	29.4%	93.2%
95	1	1	-6.8%	-100.0%	30.3%	93.2%
96	1	1	-7.6%	-100.0%	31.2%	93.2%
97	1	1	-8.4%	-100.0%	32.1%	93.2%
98	1	1	-9.3%	-100.0%	32.9%	93.2%
99	1	1	-10.3%	-100.0%	33.8%	93.2%
100	1	1	-11.5%	-100.0%	34.7%	93.2%

IRR: Internal rate of return.
*1 = default; 0 = perform.
Source: Wachovia Securities.

Chapter 11

CDO Recovery Rates: Looking into the Future

EXECUTIVE SUMMARY

Assumptions commonly used in the marketplace may systematically underestimate recovery rates for certain CDO securities and overestimate recovery rates for others. Given a default has occurred, we believe CDO recovery is dependent on whether the tranche is senior most in the capital structure but otherwise not tied to rating (or position in the capital structure) as currently assumed by many market participants. This chapter reviews and analyzes the rating agencies' structured-finance recovery rate assumptions, provides our recovery rate expectations, which differ considerably, and identifies those classes of CDO securities that we believe hold relative value. Though the focus of this chapter is on CDO securities in particular, the general conclusions herein may extend to several other structured-finance asset classes as well.

INTRODUCTION

Rating agencies, investment banks and even investors seem content to use simple estimates of recovery based on lookup tables instead of recovery rate distributions when evaluating current or prospective CDO holdings. In part, this is due to a lack of historical recovery rate data and in part this stems from a desire to keep the structuring models and/or valuation models simple. Unfortunately, the result is an inadequate (or at least incomplete) understanding of the importance of recovery assumptions in the creation of structured-finance (resecuritization) CDO capital structures and the nature of CDO returns themselves. We believe assumptions commonly used in the marketplace systematically underestimate recovery rates for certain CDO securities and overestimate recovery rates for others. As a proxy for current market thinking on CDO recovery rates, and more generally structured product recovery rates, we present rating agency (Moody's Investors Service, Inc., Standard & Poor's Corp. [S&P] and Fitch Ratings) recovery rate assumptions.

This chapter presents historical structured product recovery rate data as well as rating agency assumptions. However, because historical recovery rate data for structured products are scarce, we supplement our study with simulated recovery rates from a simple recovery rate model. Based on our analysis of historical data and our recovery rate model, we contrast our recovery rate expectations with rating agency assumptions and identify particular classes of CDO securities that hold relative value.

Our focus is CDO recovery rates in particular, but we believe the conclusions extend to other structured-finance asset classes with sequential pay structures because the rating agencies assume the factors that drive CDO recovery performance and the recovery performance of other structured products are the same. Only Moody's distinguishes between CDOs and other structured-finance asset classes, but even then its approach is similar. Therefore, while discussing the agency approaches we will broaden our view to include all structured products.

RATING AGENCY RECOVERY RATE ASSUMPTIONS
FOR STRUCTURED PRODUCTS

For current market thinking, we look to each of the three nationally recognized rating agencies — Moody's, S&P and Fitch — for their views of structured product recovery rates. In general, the agencies consider the current rating of the security and one or more other factors when assigning estimated recovery rates. These factors include the type of structured-finance security (ABS, CMBS, etc.), the relative rating of the security and the tranche being rated, and the absolute rating of the tranche being rated. We comment on each approach relative to our findings but do not hold out one as better than any other. Readers familiar with rating agency recovery assumptions may wish to skip to the S&P Recovery Rate Study.

It is important to establish two definitions to facilitate our discussion before delving into rating agency assumptions with respect to structured product recovery rates. *Structured-finance collateral* refers to the collateralized debt obligations (CDOs), commercial mortgage-backed securities (CMBS), residential mortgage-backed securities (RMBS) and similar products that support a CDO transaction (i.e., the first level of collateral) and the *underlying collateral* refers to the bonds, loans and leases that support the CDOs, CMBS, RMBS and similar products (Exhibit 1).

Exhibit 1: Definitions Relating to Collateral Level

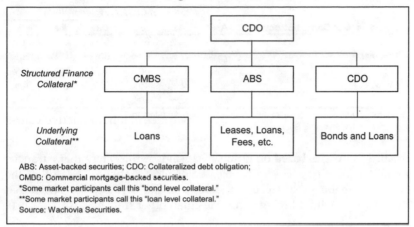

ABS: Asset-backed securities; CDO: Collateralized debt obligation;
CMBS: Commercial mortgage-backed securities.
*Some market participants call this "bond level collateral."
**Some market participants call this "loan level collateral."
Source: Wachovia Securities.

Moody's Recovery Rate Assumptions

Moody's divides structured-finance collateral into five categories depending on the nature of the underlying collateral (i.e., diversified securities, residential securities, undiversified securities, high-diversity CDOs and low-diversity CDOs), and each category is assigned a recovery rate matrix. The matrices depend on the rating of the security and the size of the security as a percentage of the particular structure. As the rating improves and the size increases, the assumed recovery rate rises. For example, high-diversity Aaa rated CDOs are assumed to have a recovery rate 15%–20% higher than high-diversity A2 rated CDOs (Exhibit 2).

Higher recovery rates are also assumed for larger tranches.[1] For example, an Aa2 rated tranche that constitutes 15% of the liability structure will command a 70% recovery rate, whereas an Aa2 rated tranche that constitutes only 7% of the liability structure will receive a 55% recovery rate. This makes sense conceptually because, once impaired, a thick tranche can withstand more defaults than a thin tranche. Each of the five matrices works similarly though the recovery rates are different.

In general, we like the Moody's approach because it incorporates tranche size, which we believe to be a significant factor. However, as we will show later, we see no evidence to support adjustments to structured-

---

1. This is in contrast to Moody's corporate recovery rate assumptions, which are dependent on the type of security (bond or loan) and the rating being sought.

Exhibit 2: Moody's Recovery Rates for High-Diversity CDOs

Tranche as % of Capital Structure	Rating of Collateral Securities*					
	Aaa	Aa	A	Baa	Ba	B
> 70%	85%	80%	65%	55%	45%	30%
≤ 70%, >10%	75%	70%	60%	50%	40%	25%
≤ 10%, >5%	65%	55%	50%	40%	30%	20%
≤ 5%, >2%	55%	45%	40%	35%	25%	10%
≤ 2%	45%	35%	30%	25%	10%	5%

*Each rating represents a group of ratings category (e.g., Aa refers to Aa1, Aa2 or Aa3).
Source: Moody's Investors Service, Inc.

finance recoveries based on rating. That said, to the extent that a tranche rated Aaa also happens to be the senior-most tranche (as is often the case), we believe the recovery rates for the senior-most structured product will exhibit higher recoveries than other tranches.

S&P Recovery Rate Assumptions

S&P also has a progressive recovery rate system but its adjustments are based on slightly different factors. Like Moody's, higher-rated securities receive higher recovery rates but in lieu of capital structure percentage, S&P looks to the desired rating of the liability being rated. In this case, assumed recovery rates are reduced as the desired rating increases (thus increasing the modeling stress for higher-rated tranches). In other words, S&P assumes lower recovery rates in AAA default environments than in AA or A environments. For example, if the desired rating of a tranche backed by junior BBB collateral is AAA the recovery rate is 30%, whereas the assumed recovery rate of the same BBB collateral for an A rated tranche is 40%. Lastly, S&P distinguishes between senior and junior structured-finance securities.

Unlike the Moody's approach, S&P does not incorporate tranche size, which we believe to be a significant factor. S&P does, however, make a distinction between senior and junior structured-finance securities, which we believe is appropriate. We see no evidence to support recovery rate adjustments based on the structured-finance collateral rating. Finally, adjustments to recovery rates based on the target rating of the liability being evaluated are simply part of the S&P methodology, and we accept that for what it is.

Fitch Recovery Rate Assumptions

The recovery rate methodology imposed by Fitch is also dependent on the position of the structured-finance collateral within the capital structure and the relative rating of the collateral to the desired rating of the

Exhibit 3: S&P Recovery Rates for Structured-Finance Securities*

Rating of Collateral Securities**	Rating of Secured Note**						
	AAA	AA	A	BBB	BB	B	CCC
Senior Structured-Finance Security							
AAA	80%	85%	90%	90%	90%	90%	90%
AA	70%	75%	85%	90%	90%	90%	90%
A	60%	65%	75%	85%	90%	90%	90%
BBB	50%	55%	65%	75%	85%	85%	85%
Junior Structured-Finance Security							
AA	55%	65%	75%	80%	80%	80%	80%
A	40%	45%	55%	65%	80%	80%	80%
BBB	30%	35%	40%	45%	50%	60%	70%
BB	15%	15%	15%	25%	35%	40%	50%
B	3%	5%	5%	10%	10%	20%	25%
CCC	0%	0%	0%	0%	3%	5%	5%

*Excluding project finance, future flows, synthetics, CDO repacks of ABS or CDOs, guaranteed ABS, distressed debt CDOs, synthetic CDOs, emerging market CDOs and market value CDOs. For these securities, S&P must review the structure before assigning recoveries.
**Each rating represents a group of ratings category (e.g., AA refers to AA+, AA or AA-).
Source: Standard & Poor's Corp.

note (similar to S&P). However, distinctions are made when the desired rating of the secured note is equal to or less than the collateral rating, one rating category above the collateral rating and two or more rating categories above the collateral rating. For example, the recovery rate is assumed to be 20% if the desired liability rating is AA and the collateral pool average rating is subordinate investment grade (e.g., BBB). Had the collateral pool been rated A, a recovery rate of 30% would be assumed for a desired tranche rating of AA. Unlike Moody's, but like S&P, Fitch does not distinguish between types of structured products.

Exhibit 4: Fitch Recovery Rates for Structured-Finance Securities

Collateral Securities Type	Stress Case Equal to or Less than Collateral Rating	Stress Case with One Rating Category Greater than Collateral Rating	Stress Case with Two or More Rating Categories Greater than Collateral Rating
REITs—Senior Unsecured	60%	50%	50%
Senior Investment-Grade Tranches	60%	60%	60%
Subordinate Investment-Grade Tranches	40%	30%	20%
Non-Investment-Grade Tranches	10%	5%	0%

Source: Fitch Ratings.

Fitch incorporates position within the capital structure as a factor in assigning recovery rates though it does not make a distinction between asset classes. We believe a distinction is appropriate between the senior-most tranches and all others but see no need to distinguish within junior tranches. Instead, we would prefer that Fitch incorporate tranche size, which we believe to be a significant factor. Finally, like S&P, Fitch makes adjustments to recovery rates based on the target rating of the liability being evaluated and we accept this without comment.

S&P RECOVERY RATE STUDY

Due to the relative youth of the structured-finance market, there is little published recovery rate data for structured-finance securities. In fact, we are aware of just one study, which was published by S&P in September 2002 (the latest yearly report published by S&P).[2] The S&P study divided the structured product market into RMBS, CMBS and other asset-backed securities (ABS). Two time periods were analyzed: the first period, from market inception to June 2002, included 114 default occurrences, whereas the second period, from July 2001 to June 2002, included 64 default occurrences. By and large, recovery rates appear high (60%–100%) for all but B rated RMBS, A rated CMBS and select tranches of ABS (Exhibit 5).

Exhibit 5: S&P Recovery Rate Findings

Rating of Collateral Securities	RMBS		CMBS		ABS*	
	7/01/01–6/30/02	1978–6/30/02	7/01/01–6/30/02	1985–6/30/02	7/01/01–6/30/02	1985–6/30/02
AAA		96%				93%	93%
AA	91%	75%		89%		
A	93%	66%		0%	71%	38%
BBB	83%	67%			37%	37%
BB	94%	67%	97%	97%	65%	46%
B	75%	36%	98%	79%	100%	60%

*Consists of subprime auto, credit cards, CDOs, franchise loans, manufactured housing, synthetic securities and nonperforming loans.
Source: Standard & Poor's Corp.

For the purposes of the S&P study, a security is defaulted if it misses an interest payment or experiences "a loss at the transaction level that has fully eroded the credit protection for the credit class in question and caused it to experience principal loss." Therefore, unlike a corporation, the tranche itself defaults—not the entire structure. A mezzanine tranche could be assigned a rating of D and find its way into the study,

2. Hu, Pollsen, Chun and Coyne. "Recoveries of Defaulted U.S. Structured Finance Securities: Inception to June 30, 2002," Standard & Poor's Corp., September 2002.

whereas the senior tranche of the same transaction is not considered defaulted because it has not missed an interest payment or experienced a principal loss.

In general, S&P concludes that recovery prospects for structured products seem favorable though the agency (and we) have reason to believe recovery rates could be overstated in this study. In some cases, projected cash flows are used to estimate the recovery amount and these flows may not be realized (e.g., the study assumes that principal balances that have not been written down will be paid).

S&P also concludes that, with the exception of RMBS recoveries, the data does not seem to support a relationship between recovery rates and the original credit rating (all three agencies assume this relationship exists in their rating methodology for repackagings). We will return to this point later, but for now suffice to say that we believe the senior-most tranche will experience high recovery. Otherwise, we agree that there is no correlation between original rating and recovery (unless original rating happens to be correlated with tranche size).

RECOVERY RATE SIMULATION

Recovery rate data for structured products remain extremely scarce and subject to a great deal of interpretation. Therefore, we endeavored to simulate the recovery rate experience of structured-finance securities to create more data. Although the particular structured product we chose to simulate is a CDO, we believe our approach and the results will apply generally to structured products that have sequential pay structures. The remainder of this section is divided as follows:

- Select a collateral portfolio
- Simulate defaults in the collateral pool
- Create a liability structure
- Record tranche losses and analyze results

Selection of a Collateral Portfolio

To facilitate the duplication of our results, we chose the sample portfolio that is available in S&P's CDO Evaluator product,[3] which should be familiar to most market participants. In addition, CDO Evaluator has a Monte Carlo simulator that will be used to simulate portfolio defaults.

3. A description of the CDO Evaluator product can be found in "CDO Evaluator Applies Correlation and Monte Carlo Simulation to Determine Portfolio Quality" by Sten Bergman at Standard & Poor's Corp.

The key statistics of the collateral portfolio are summarized in Exhibit 6 and the complete portfolio is described in Appendix A.

Exhibit 6: Portfolio Summary

No. of Entries	66
No. of Obligors	53
Total Principal Balance	$310,800,000.00
Performing	$290,800,000.00
Defaulted	$0.00
Cash Balance	$20,000,000.00
Weighted Average Purchase Price ($)	100.00
Weighted Average Maturity (years)	7.574
Weighted Average Rating	BB
Weighted Average Performing Coupon	8.00%
Recovery Rate	30.0%

Source: Standard & Poor's Corp. and Wachovia Securities.

Simulate Defaults in the Collateral Pool

Fifteen thousand default scenarios are quickly generated using the S&P CDO Evaluator program,[4] and a cumulative default rate distribution can be created along with a cumulative default probability table (Exhibit 7).

In Exhibit 7, we see that there is a fairly wide distribution of default outcomes and a noticeable probability of high defaults well above the average. This fat tail is due to the positive default correlation imposed on the assets during the simulation. Positive default correlation indicates that when one security defaults, another positively correlated to it is also likely to default. Nonetheless, a CDO liability structure can now be constructed based on the probability of various levels of default.

Create a Liability Structure

We have designed a CDO structure around the sample collateral pool (Exhibit 8). This is a sequential pay structure whereby the principal proceeds are first applied to pay down the Class A notes, then the Class B notes and so on. We assume that collateral does not revolve (i.e., it is static) though our results do not depend on this assumption. Other market participants may develop slightly different structures due to factors such as the cushion between the break-even default rate and the

---

4. Select "Quick Run" and "Save Simulation Results" under the "Run Portfolio…" button.

Exhibit 7: Default Distribution

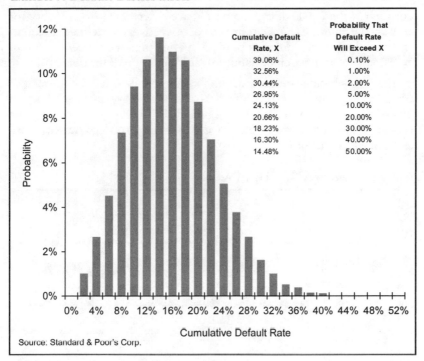

Cumulative Default Rate, X	Probability That Default Rate Will Exceed X
39.06%	0.10%
32.56%	1.00%
30.44%	2.00%
26.95%	5.00%
24.13%	10.00%
20.66%	20.00%
18.23%	30.00%
16.30%	40.00%
14.48%	50.00%

Source: Standard & Poor's Corp.

scenario default rates (SDRs), the amount of accrued interest, transaction fees, management fees, overcollateralization (OC) test cushions and cash trapping features. Small variations in structure are not material to our conclusions regarding recovery rates, therefore we do not elaborate on our method for generating the structure.

Exhibit 8: Capital Structure

Class	Par Amount ($million)	% of Liabilities	Rating	Spreads
Class A	243.0	75.5%	AAA	L + 60
Class B	20.9	6.5%	A	L + 175
Class C	12.9	4.0%	BBB	L + 300
Class D	11.3	3.5%	BB	L + 800
Equity	33.8	10.5%	NA	NA

Source: Wachovia Securities.

Record Tranche Losses and Analysis of Results

For each of the 15,000 default scenarios, we determined the recovery for all tranches in our CDO. For our purposes, recovery is defined as collateral principal minus defaults plus recoveries plus the present value of excess spread minus senior liabilities (see Appendix B for details).

In effect, this became our data set and we simply counted the number of occurrences of default for each tranche and the recovery of each tranche given the fact that a default had occurred. In Exhibit 9, we present the probability of various levels of recovery for each tranche in our structure as realized by this process.

Exhibit 9: Recovery Rate Distributions

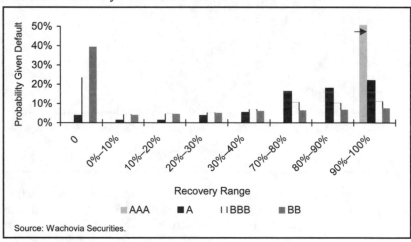

Source: Wachovia Securities.

Several interesting features should be noted:

- For the Class A notes (AAA), the probability of recovering 90%–100% of value is 100%. The lowest realized recovery was 95%, and the average was 99%.

- The recovery rate distribution of the Class B notes (A) is skewed to the right, which indicates a bias toward high recovery rates. In fact, the average recovery rate given default for the Class B notes is approximately 67% and there is little chance that the Class B notes will be zeroed out (i.e., receive no return of principal).

- The recovery rate distribution of the Class C notes is broadly distributed with a significant chance of being zeroed out (24%), but otherwise there is a slight bias toward high recovery rates. The average recovery rate given default over our scenarios for the Class C notes is approximately 45%.

- Given default, the recovery rate distribution of the Class D notes has an even more significant chance of being zeroed out (39%) and a fairly constant probability distribution across all other recovery rates. The average recovery rate given default for the Class D notes over our scenarios is approximately 33%.

Based on Exhibit 9, it might be tempting to conclude that higher-rated tranches will have higher recovery rates and that junior tranches have a higher probability of being zeroed out. In our example, the average recovery rates fall continuously as we move down the capital structure from 99% to 67% to 45% and, finally, 33% for the Class A, B, C and D notes, respectively. Furthermore, it appears that the probability of being zeroed out is higher for junior tranches than for senior tranches.

Both of these conclusions are misleading because expected recoveries will change if the capital structure is adjusted. For example, if we move $13 million of the Class B notes to the Class C tranche, the recovery rate distributions for these two tranches change dramatically (this effectively makes the Class B notes stronger by increasing subordination). The new structure is shown in Exhibit 10. Now, given default, the probability of the Class B notes (rated AA) being zeroed out has increased dramatically (Exhibit 11). Originally around 4%, the probability of being zeroed out now represents a significant 26% and, as a result, the expected recovery rate has fallen from 67% to 47%.

The recovery distribution for the Class C notes (rated BBB+) has also changed significantly. A zero recovery is relatively unlikely and there is a noticeable skew toward high recovery (much like the Class B notes previously). The average recovery is now 67% versus 45% previously. Therefore, we cannot conclude that higher-rated tranches will recover

Exhibit 10: New Capital Structure

Class	Par Amount ($million)	% of Liabilities	Rating	Spreads
Class A	243.0	75.5%	AAA	L + 60
Class B	7.9	2.5%	AA	L + 100
Class C	25.9	8.0%	BBB+	L + 300
Class D	11.3	3.5%	BB	L + 800
Equity	33.8	10.5%	NA	NA

Source: Wachovia Securities.

Exhibit 11: New Recovery Rate Distribution

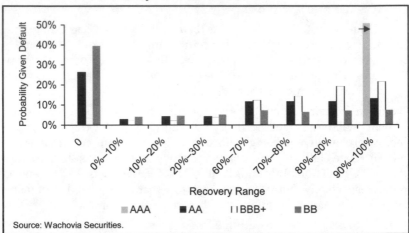

Source: Wachovia Securities.

more than junior tranches nor can we conclude that the probability of being zeroed out is higher for junior tranches.

For a junior tranche, a much better predictor of recovery is the size of the tranche rather than its position in the capital structure. For example, a tranche that is large (represents 10% or more of the capital structure) may be expected to have a relatively high recovery rate and little probability of being zeroed out, whereas a small (5% or less of the capital structure) tranche has a high probability of large losses and zero recovery given default. This makes intuitive sense if one considers a tranche composed of a single $1 note. In this example, if the $310.8 million collateral pool were to perform so badly as to cause a default in the $1 tranche, there is a high probability that the entire $1 will be lost and the tranche will be zeroed out. In other words, it is unlikely that the $310.8 million collateral pool will have a final cash value within any one dollar range. Conversely, if a tranche is thick, the probability of being zeroed out is low.

Recovery rates for senior notes (the Class A notes) are different and deserve special attention for two reasons. First, as we have seen above, high recovery rates are associated with large tranches and the Class A tranche is typically the largest. Second, the probability of being zeroed out is proportionate to the probability of the tranche above defaulting and, because there is no tranche above the Class A notes, this is zero. As a result, unlike the recovery rate distributions of other tranches, the Class A tranche recoveries are concentrated. Based on our simulation, the recovery rates for the Class A notes were remarkably high (about 99%) despite rather conservative assumptions. In fact, even if we assign no value to excess spread and assume zero recovery value on defaulted collateral, the average recovery rate is approximately 95%. This is significantly higher than the 60%–90% recovery rate currently assigned by the rating agencies.

CONCLUSION

Much effort is devoted to analyzing the default behavior of collateral destined for resecuritization in CDOs but relatively little is given to recovery rates. As a result, there is an inadequate (or at least incomplete) understanding of the importance of recovery assumptions in the creation of CDO capital structures and the nature of CDO returns. CDO recovery rates are dependent on whether the tranche is senior most in the capital structure, but otherwise they are not closely tied to position in the capital structure (or original rating). For non-senior tranches, recovery rate simulations point to the relative size of the tranche as a better indicator of average recovery for the tranche. As a result, we believe the agencies and other market participants may underestimate the recoveries of senior tranches but possibly overestimate the recoveries for highly rated but thin non-senior tranches. Other structured-finance securities with sequential pay structures likely behave similarly.

Although an investor should always consider the quality of the collateral pool when estimating the recovery of any particular structured-finance security because the quality of the pool will skew actual recoveries either higher or lower, we offer these suggestions all else being equal:

* There is some historical evidence and strong simulation-based evidence that recovery rates assigned to the senior-most tranches of structures may be underestimated. Agencies currently assume a 60%–90% recovery, whereas observed data would indicate a more appropriate value would be 95% and simulation-based results indicate an even higher recovery rate (99%). Based on this conclusion, we believe there is relative value in senior-most structured-finance securities and, in particular, transactions based on senior-most structured-finance securities.

* Recovery rates for non-senior tranches depend on the thickness of the tranche or, more precisely, the rating (probability of default) of the tranche relative to the rating of the tranche above it — not on the tranche rating alone. Should a thin non-senior tranche default, there is a relatively high probability that recovery could be zero. This

depresses the average expected recovery rate for this tranche to levels that are below estimates assumed by the agencies (and possibly by the market). For example, when given a choice between a thin original issuance AA security and a thick AA security that has been downgraded from AAA, an investor should strongly consider choosing the downgraded AAA security for the simple reason that there is less volatility in the recovery rate should the security default.[5] Therefore, we believe there is relative value in thick tranches relative to thin tranches all else being equal.

Finally, comparing S&P's structured-finance recovery rate study and simulated recovery rate data to the estimates used by the agencies, we conclude that simple estimates of recovery based on lookup tables are crude and do not accurately capture the distribution of recoveries for non-senior tranches. We appreciate the need and desire to keep methodologies simple and easy to use but wonder if the price of simplicity is too high. Rating agencies, as well as investors, may wish to reconsider their approach to structured product recovery rates.

5. On the other hand, there is some indication that once downgraded, a security is prone to further downgrades (i.e., rating migration momentum).

BIBLIOGRAPHY

Anderberg, Coyne and D'Erchia. "U.S. Cash Flow CDO Transactions 2002 Performance Review: Another Painful Year for Bond Deals," Standard and Poor's Corp., February 2003.

Bergman, Sten. "CDO Evaluator Applies Correlation and Monte Carlo Simulation to Determine Portfolio Quality," Standard & Poor's Corp., November 2001.

Carosielli, Hrvatin, Katz and Schiavetta. "Rating Criteria for Cash Flow ABS/MBS CDOs," Fitch ICBA, Duff & Phelps, November 2000.

"Global Cash Flow and Synthetic CDO Criteria," Standard and Poor's Corp., March 2002.

Gluck and Remeza, "Moody's Approach to Rating Multisector CDOs," Moody's Investors Service, Inc., September 2000.

Hamilton, David. "Default & Recovery Rates of Corporate Bond Issuers," Moody's Investors Service, Inc., February 2003.

Hu, Pollsen, Chun and Coyne. "Recoveries of Defaulted U.S. Structured Finance Securities: Inception to June 30, 2002," Standard & Poor's Corp., September 2002.

Keisman, David. "Trends in Recovery Analysis," Standard & Poor's Corp., March 2003.

Verde and Mancuso. "High Yield Defaults 2002," Fitch Ratings, February 2003.

APPENDIX A: S&P CDO EVALUATOR SAMPLE PORTFOLIO

Obligor ID	Asset Type	S&P Credit Rating	Weighted Average Maturity	Current Balance ($)	Current Coupon (annualized)	Current Market Price ($)	Country Code	Sovereign Foreign Currency Rating	Region Code	Industry Local Regional Global
C00	Cash			20,000,000		100.00	USA	AAA	101	Global
C01	Chemicals and Plastics	AA+	5/01/09	10,750,000	8.00%	100.00	USA	AAA	101	Global
C02	Financial Intermediaries	B+	7/15/06	500,000	8.00%	100.00	USA	AAA	101	Regional
C03	Sovereign		4/01/08	3,500,000	8.00%	100.00	Mexico	BBB-	1	
C03	Sovereign		1/14/12	8,000,000	8.00%	100.00	Mexico	BBB-	1	
C04	Telecommunications	BBB-	10/01/08	500,000	8.00%	100.00	USA	AAA	101	Global
C05	Sovereign		8/28/07	4,250,000	8.00%	100.00	Morocco	BB	11	
C05	Sovereign		1/01/09	8,000,000	8.00%	100.00	Morocco	BB	11	
C06	Sovereign		7/23/12	6,500,000	8.00%	100.00	Panama	BB	2	
C07	Telecommunications	BB-	8/20/12	500,000	8.00%	100.00	USA	AAA	101	Global
C08	Financial Intermediaries	BB	4/01/09	1,250,000	8.00%	100.00	Venezuela	B	3	Regional
C09	Utilities	BB	5/15/12	2,000,000	8.00%	100.00	Philippines	BB+	8	Regional
C09	Utilities	BB	4/15/09	4,250,000	8.00%	100.00	Philippines	BB+	8	Regional
C11	Publishing	B	4/01/08	250,000	8.00%	100.00	USA	AAA	101	Local
C11	Publishing	B	5/15/11	1,500,000	8.00%	100.00	USA	AAA	101	Local
C12	Financial Intermediaries	BB	12/01/09	5,700,000	8.00%	100.00	Poland	BBB+	15	Regional
C13	Sovereign		3/25/09	1,000,000	8.00%	100.00	Uruguay	B	4	
C13	Sovereign		6/22/10	4,250,000	8.00%	100.00	Uruguay	B	4	
C13	Sovereign		1/20/12	6,500,000	8.00%	100.00	Uruguay	B	4	
C14	Sovereign		3/31/10	1,000,000	8.00%	100.00	Russia	BB-	14	
C15	Food Service	BB	9/01/07	500,000	8.00%	100.00	USA	AAA	101	Regional
C16	Sovereign		4/25/12	5,700,000	8.00%	100.00	South Africa	BBB-	12	
C17	Rail Industries	BB-	6/15/09	1,400,000	8.00%	100.00	Mexico	BBB-	1	Regional
C17	Rail Industries	BB-	6/15/07	1,600,000	8.00%	100.00	Mexico	BBB-	1	Regional
C18	Leisure Goods/Activities/Movies	BBB+	3/15/06	1,750,000	8.00%	100.00	USA	AAA	101	Local
C19	Financial Intermediaries	BBB	12/10/08	4,250,000	8.00%	100.00	Poland	BBB+	15	Regional
C20	Utilities	BB-	9/01/04	9,000,000	8.00%	100.00	Dominican Republic	BB-	2	Regional
C21	Sovereign		6/15/10	7,000,000	8.00%	100.00	Turkey	B-	16	
C22	Conglomerates	BBB-	2/15/11	1,000,000	8.00%	100.00	Luxembourg	AAA	102	Global
C23	Sovereign		3/15/07	3,500,000	8.00%	100.00	Ukraine	B	14	
C24	Sovereign		3/31/07	1,650,000	8.00%	100.00	Venezuela	B	3	
C24	Sovereign		12/18/07	12,000,000	8.00%	100.00	Venezuela	B	3	
C25	Electronics/Electrical	B-	5/15/07	300,000	8.00%	100.00	Turkey	B-	16	Global
C26	Sovereign		8/28/07	2,700,000	8.00%	100.00	Vietnam	BB-	8	
C27	Telecommunications	BB-	12/15/06	1,250,000	8.00%	100.00	China	BBB	7	Global
C28	Clothing/Textiles	B+	1/15/06	15,000,000	8.00%	100.00	USA	AAA	101	Regional
C29	Conglomerates	B+	4/01/10	15,000,000	8.00%	100.00	USA	AAA	101	Global
C31	Drugs	B+	4/09/11	15,000,000	8.00%	100.00	USA	AAA	101	Global
C32	Telecommunications	AA+	11/01/07	500,000	8.00%	100.00	USA	AAA	101	Global
C32	Telecommunications	AA+	9/15/10	8,000,000	8.00%	100.00	USA	AAA	101	Global
C33	Sovereign		3/04/10	14,500,000	8.00%	100.00	Algeria	B+	11	
C33	Sovereign		8/28/07	4,500,000	8.00%	100.00	Algeria	B+	11	
C34	Radio and Television	BB-	8/01/07	9,000,000	8.00%	100.00	Greece	A	15	Regional
C35	Sovereign		7/11/11	5,000,000	8.00%	100.00	Egypt	BB+	11	
C38	Financial Intermediaries	A	4/25/12	5,000,000	8.00%	100.00	Tunisia	BBB	11	Regional
C39	Aerospace and Defense	BB-	5/01/11	1,000,000	8.00%	100.00	USA	AAA	101	Regional
C40	Sovereign		1/11/12	700,000	8.00%	100.00	Brazil	B+	4	
C40	Sovereign		4/15/12	12,000,000	8.00%	100.00	Brazil	B+	4	
C41	Containers and Glass Products	BB	10/15/10	500,000	8.00%	100.00	USA	AAA	101	Regional
C42	Building and Development	B+	7/15/05	750,000	8.00%	100.00	USA	AAA	101	Local
C43	Sovereign		7/28/11	5,000,000	8.00%	100.00	Bulgaria	BB-	16	
C44	Telecommunications	BB	2/15/11	3,000,000	8.00%	100.00	USA	AAA	101	Global
C45	Telecommunications	BB+	11/15/10	9,000,000	8.00%	100.00	Philippines	BB+	8	Global
C46	Telecommunications	BB	1/15/06	2,700,000	8.00%	100.00	Chile	A-	4	Global
C47	Financial Intermediaries	BB	4/01/10	3,000,000	8.00%	100.00	South Korea	A-	8	Regional
C48	Sovereign		4/09/11	5,000,000	8.00%	100.00	Colombia	BB	3	
C48	Sovereign		1/23/12	8,000,000	8.00%	100.00	Colombia	BB	3	
C49	Financial Intermediaries	B	4/15/08	2,000,000	8.00%	100.00	USA	AAA	101	Regional
C50	Sovereign		8/28/07	3,000,000	8.00%	100.00	Croatia	BBB-	16	
C51	Retailers (except food and drug)	BB+	9/15/07	10,500,000	8.00%	100.00	USA	AAA	101	Local
C52	Nonferrous Metals/Minerals	CCC-	12/15/06	750,000	8.00%	100.00	USA	AAA	101	Global
C53	Sovereign		5/15/11	600,000	8.00%	100.00	Jamaica	B+	2	
C54	Utilities	B+	7/15/04	2,000,000	8.00%	100.00	Mexico	BBB-	1	Regional
C54	Utilities	B+	12/01/06	2,000,000	8.00%	100.00	Mexico	BBB-	1	Regional
C55	Financial Intermediaries	BB	3/01/10	2,000,000	8.00%	100.00	South Korea	A-	8	Regional
C57	Sovereign		12/13/05	2,000,000	8.00%	100.00	Pakistan	B-	5	

Source: Standard & Poor's Corp.

APPENDIX B: RECOVERY CALCULATIONS

For each of the 15,000 default scenarios, we determined the recovery for all tranches in our CDO. For our purposes, recovery is defined as collateral principal minus defaults plus recoveries plus the present value of excess spread minus senior liabilities.

Because we are primarily concerned with situations where the transaction is having difficulty (resulting in default on the liabilities), we assume that excess spread is trapped and applied to payment of principal. To simplify our analysis, we assume the present value of excess spread is $16 million[6] and remains constant regardless of default timing or the tranche being analyzed. While this assumption would clearly change the constant annual default rate at which a particular tranche PIKs or breaks, it will not greatly affect the shape of the recovery rate distribution. Therefore, although somewhat simplistic, this assumption should not alter our general conclusions. It will, however, have a small effect on the magnitude of the expected recovery rate of each class.

In addition, we do not consider the present value of the recovery itself. All payments are considered return of principal on a dollar-for-dollar basis regardless of when the payment occurs. We believe this is consistent with recovery rate studies and rating agencies' assumptions with respect to recovery rates. Investors may wish to discount the recovery at some rate to account for the time value of money. Incidentally, this will likely introduce a correlation between recovery rate (on a present value basis) and rating because junior tranches will be discounted at a higher rate and for a longer period.

Using the capital structure shown in Exhibit 8, for example, a 25% cumulative default rate and $16 million in excess spread will result in total cash of $272.4 million generated by our collateral pool. This is enough to pay off the Class A notes, the Class B notes and 66% of the Class C notes. The Class C and Class D notes and equity, however, do not receive any return of principal. Therefore, the recovery rate is 66% for the Class C notes and 0% for the Class D notes. Each of the recovery values is stored and another scenario is analyzed and, after all 15,000 default scenarios have been analyzed, we can simply count the number of occurrences of default for each tranche and the recovery of each tranche given the fact that a default had occurred.

6. This value is deliberately underestimated for the senior tranches to induce more defaults within our liability structure and achieve greater clarity around the distribution of recovery rates. A significantly larger amount (~$25 million or more) will generally be available to the senior tranche, whereas a much smaller amount (~$6 million or less) could be available to the most subordinate tranche.

Sources of Cash			Uses of Cash			Recovery
Collateral Pool Par	310.8		Class A	(243.0)		**100%**
Cumulative Defaults (25%)	(77.7)		Remainder		29.4	
Collateral Principal		233.1	Class B	(20.9)		**100%**
			Remainder		8.5	
Recoveries from Defaults (30%)	23.3		Class C	(12.9)		**66%**
Subtotal		256.4	Remainder		0.0	
			Class D	(11.3)		**0%**
Present Value of Excess Spread	16.0		Remainder		0.0	
Total Cash Available		272.4	Equity	(33.8)		**0%**
			Remainder		0.0	

Source: Wachovia Securities.

Chapter 12

Valuation of Cash Flow CDOs— Introducing the Wachovia Securities Methodology

A collateralized debt obligation (CDO) is a series of tranches for which cash flows are derived from a portfolio of collateral assets. The collateral of a cash flow CDO consists of assets with future cash flows that would be predictable in the absence of default, such as corporate and asset-backed bonds and loans.[1] The challenge of CDO valuation is therefore to model the default behavior of the underlying assets.

Wachovia Securities (WS) has developed a valuation model whereby the default behavior of the collateral depends on four basic assumptions: 1) the *default probability* of individual assets in the portfolio together with the timing of the possible default, 2) the *default correlation* between assets, 3) the *recovery rate* of defaulted principal and the *time lag* from default to recovery and 4) the *reinvestment strategy* for the principal proceeds, that is, the credit quality and other characteristics of assets purchased to replace those that have dropped out of the portfolio.[2]

The basic difference between our model and simplified rating agency models, for example, Moody's Investors Service, Inc.'s binomial expansion technique (BET), is that we do not homogenize collateral cash flows. Each asset is treated according to its individual cash flow and default characteristics. Because the number of possible combinations of defaulting asset cash flows is too large to be enumerated, we use Monte Carlo simulation to generate the defaults and hence the tranche cash flows.

Although we try to use the best available data for default assumptions, we realize that all behavioral assumptions concerning future defaults are somewhat arbitrary and inaccurate. The utility of valuation models is not

---

1. A later version will handle market value CDOs backed by equities, hedge funds or other non-fixed-income assets. The distinguishing feature of market value CDOs is that their collateral pool and tranche balances must be readjusted when the market value of the collateral falls below specified trigger levels.
2. The required reinvestment credit rating and other characteristics are usually specified in the offering document.

so much the accuracy for individual securities but rather the comparison of relative values of different securities on a consistent basis.

DEFAULT ASSUMPTIONS

We begin with the default probability of an individual asset. We model asset default using an exponential time-to-default distribution. This approach has the advantage of modeling the timing of defaults, not just whether they occur.

Exhibit 1: Default Probability Distribution

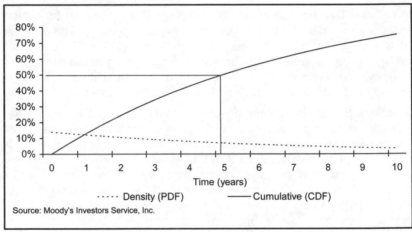

Source: Moody's Investors Service, Inc.

Exhibit 1 depicts the probability density function (PDF) of an exponential distribution for times to default. The area under this curve is the cumulative probability that default will occur before some specified time (five years in the exhibit). Exhibit 1 also shows the cumulative distribution function (CDF), which is the integral of the density.[3]

The distribution shown in Exhibit 1 represents a Caa2 rated bond with a five-year remaining term and a cumulative default probability of 48.75%, as presented in Moody's idealized cumulative default table (Exhibit 3). If a vertical line is drawn above the five-year term and then a horizontal line where it intersects the CDF curve, the cumulative default probability can be read off the vertical axis.

---

3. The exponential density is $f(t) = \lambda \exp(-\lambda t)$ for intensity parameter $\lambda > 0$ and the CDF is $F(T) = \mathrm{Pr\,ob}\{t <= T\} = \int_0^T f(t)dt = \int_0^T \lambda \exp(-\lambda t)dt = 1 - \exp(-\lambda T)$.

The time-to-default distribution varies from one asset to another depending on its default characteristics. For rating-driven default models, these distributions are a family of exponential curves, where the parameters that govern the shape of each default curve are chosen to match cumulative default probabilities provided by Moody's or other sources. Exhibit 2 shows a family of such curves labeled by their current Moody's rating.

Exhibit 2: Default Probability versus Moody's Rating

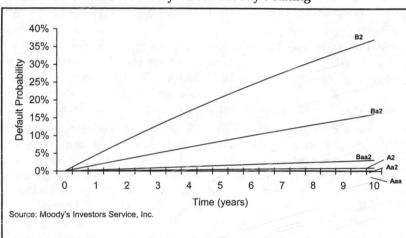

Source: Moody's Investors Service, Inc.

The parameters of this distribution are inferred from a cumulative default history provided by Moody's or from expected default frequencies provided by KMV. We provide a fragment of Moody's idealized cumulative default rate table.[4]

It is not enough to specify the likelihood of default for each individual asset. We must also specify the likelihood that groups of assets will default together because the correlation of asset defaults has a significant effect on the risk of the deal tranches.

Of the four assumptions listed above, default correlation is the most difficult to understand and measure. One reason is that default correlation is a misnomer: Corporate defaults are too infrequent to obtain accurate correlation statistics. Instead, we use correlations of equity

---

4. As cited in Tabe (2002).

Exhibit 3: Moody's Idealized Cumulative Default Probabilities

Horizon*	1	2	3	4	5	6	7	8	9	10
Aaa	0.0001%	0.0002%	0.0007%	0.0018%	0.0029%	0.0040%	0.0052%	0.0066%	0.0082%	0.0100%
Aa2	0.0014%	0.0080%	0.0260%	0.0470%	0.0680%	0.0890%	0.1110%	0.1350%	0.1640%	0.2000%
A2	0.0109%	0.0700%	0.2220%	0.3450%	0.4670%	0.5830%	0.7100%	0.8290%	0.9820%	1.2000%
Baa2	0.1700%	0.4700%	0.8300%	1.2000%	1.5800%	1.9700%	2.4100%	2.8500%	3.2400%	3.6000%
Ba2	1.5600%	3.4700%	5.1800%	6.8000%	8.4100%	9.7700%	10.7000%	11.6600%	12.6500%	13.5000%
B2	7.1600%	11.6700%	15.5500%	18.1300%	20.7100%	22.6500%	24.0100%	25.1500%	26.2200%	27.2000%
Caa2	26.0000%	32.5000%	39.0000%	43.8800%	48.7500%	52.0000%	55.2500%	58.5000%	61.7500%	65.0000%

*Years.
Source: Moody's Investors Service, Inc.

prices, total asset value or annualized returns as a proxy for default correlation.[5]

Internally, our model accepts default correlations between arbitrary pairs of collateral assets. In practice, default correlation data is often available only between groups of assets classified by country and industry sectors. In our numerical examples, we assume that all assets are domestic and specify constant intra- and intersector correlations.

The values of senior tranches in a CDO deal are sensitive to default correlation. To see why, consider an idealized portfolio consisting of a large number of assets with identical cash flows but different issuers and assume that each asset has a 25% probability of default. Suppose the senior tranche is unaffected by a default of up to 50% of the collateral assets. If the assets were uncorrelated, approximately 25% of the assets would default for each scenario and the likelihood of generating scenarios with more than 50% of the assets defaulting would be negligible.

At the other extreme, if the assets were 100% correlated, then either none or all of them will default for any given scenario, and the probability of generating scenarios where all assets default is now 25%. The second case will obviously have more impact on the cash flows of the senior tranche. Junior tranches with lower default thresholds will also be affected by increased default correlation, but not to the same extent.

Exhibit 4 illustrates this phenomenon under more realistic assumptions for an actual CBO deal. The expected loss of the most senior tranche increases dramatically when the correlation level is increased by 10%, whereas the impact on the more junior tranches is more limited. Increasing the overall default probability by 10% tends to have less impact on senior tranches and greater impact on junior tranches than the corresponding increase in default correlation.

---

5. KMV points out that equity price correlations are poor proxies for default correlation and recommend the use of total asset value correlations.

Exhibit 4: Sensitivity of Expected Losses to Correlation for a Generic CBO Deal

Tranche	Rating	Base Case Exp. Loss	110% Correlation Exp. Loss	110% Correlation Change	110% Default Prob. Exp. Loss	110% Default Prob. Change
A	Aaa	0.0159%	0.0397%	249.7%	0.0348%	218.9%
B	Baa2	3.5796%	4.0637%	113.5%	4.2699%	119.3%
C	Ba2	14.3530%	15.1771%	105.7%	17.7966%	123.4%

Source: Wachovia Securities.

The histograms in Exhibits 5 and 6 illustrate the effect of correlation on the distribution of defaults per scenario. The horizontal axis measures the number of defaults, which can range from zero to the total number of assets in the portfolio. Increasing the correlation by 50% has the effect of increasing the likelihood that very few or very many defaults per scenario will occur, which explains why the distribution in Exhibit 6 has fatter tails.

We handle the recovery rate for defaulted principal in two different ways: deterministically and probabilistically. The deterministic method uses a constant recovery rate for each defaulted asset based on the asset's seniority.[6] We can stress the recovery rate by using Moody's lowest quartile rates or lowering recoveries by a multiple of the standard

Exhibit 5: Default Histogram with 100% of the Base Case Correlation Assumption

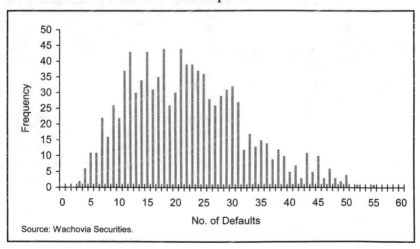

Source: Wachovia Securities.

6. For some data sets, recovery depends on the asset's current credit rating as well.

**Exhibit 6: Default Histogram with 150%
of the Base Case Correlation Assumption**

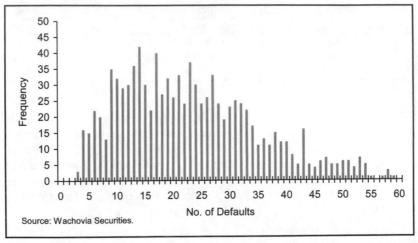

Source: Wachovia Securities.

deviation in Exhibit 7. Exhibit 8 shows an interval of one standard deviation bracketing the mean recovery rates for each priority.

Exhibit 7: Moody's Recovery Rates, 1970–2000[7]

Priority	Mean	Standard Deviation	Median	Q1	Q3
Senior/Secured Loan	64.0%	24.4%	72.0%	45.3%	85.0%
Senior/Unsecured Bond	46.9%	28.0%	44.0%	25.0%	66.8%
Subordinated Bond	31.6%	21.2%	28.5%	15.0%	44.1%

Source: Moody's Investors Service, Inc.

One reason to use random recovery rates is that the standard deviations
in Exhibit 7 are large compared to their means. In other words, the variation in observed recovery rates is so large that we really cannot assume
that they are constant. Another reason to use random recoveries is that
we can correlate them to the likelihood of default, so that bonds with
higher default probabilities will tend to have lower recovery rates.[8]

---

7. From Exhibit 35 in Hamilton, Gupton and Berthault (2001).
8. Defaults and recoveries are correlated through the state of the economy. In the
top (bottom) of the business cycle, default likelihood falls (rises) and recovery
rates increase (decline). See Hamilton and Carty (1999) and Hamilton, Gupton
and Berthault (2001) for the relation between default recovery and macroeconomic
variables.

Exhibit 8: Recovery Rates by Seniority

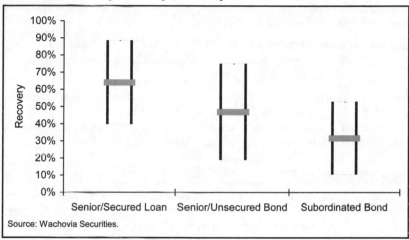

Source: Wachovia Securities.

Exhibit 9: Beta versus Empirical Distribution of Recovery Rates

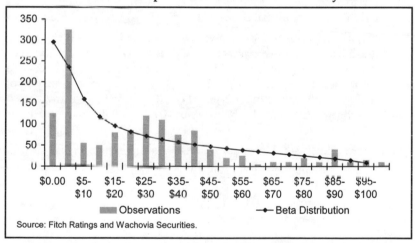

Source: Fitch Ratings and Wachovia Securities.

Random recovery rates are generated from a beta distribution, which traps recovery between 0% and 100%. We can parameterize the beta distribution by matching its mean and standard deviation to empirical recovery data. Exhibit 9 shows the fit to the recovery distribution in a Fitch study by Gordon (2001).

For assets trading well below par, market price is a more accurate guide to expected recovery when an asset is perceived to have a high probability of default. As pricing data becomes available, we will implement this by overriding the historical recovery model whenever the asset price falls below a user-specified level.

We do not yet have market data for the time lag from default to recovery of principal, so we arbitrarily used a six-month time horizon.

Finally, the credit quality and maturity range of the reinvestment vehicle(s) for defaulted principal are usually specified in advance, so this is not really an assumption. We used the average credit quality and maturity of the current collateral portfolio in our example because reinvestment data is not currently available in our database.

HOW THE MODEL WORKS

We use Monte Carlo simulation to generate a collection of random default scenarios, where a scenario is a list of defaulting assets together with the timing, recovery and default-to-recovery time lag of each asset.[9] For each scenario, we generate the future cash flows of each CDO tranche.[10] The present values of these scenario-dependent cash flows can be used to calculate value-at-risk (VaR) measures, for example, the expected loss at a 5% probability level.

The scenario-dependent cash flows are averaged to obtain a single default-adjusted cash flow for each tranche as shown in Exhibit 10.[11] The default-adjusted cash flow is used to calculate the default-adjusted yield for all tranches, the spread to the implied zero-coupon Treasury spot curve (ZS) and the discount margin (DM) for floating-rate tranches.[12] These results are compared to their default-free equivalents to obtain the cost of default in terms of a yield spread or differences in ZS or DM.

Perhaps the most useful summary statistic is the expected loss (EL) of each tranche. We define EL as the difference between the discounted

9. Only the asset defaults are random in our model. Future interest rates for floaters and prepayment speeds for mortgage-backed assets are presumed to be known in advance.
10. We currently use vendor software from INTEX to calculate the tranche cash flows.
11. Because the discount rates are identical for each scenario, the default-adjusted cash flows are just the weighted averages of the cash flows for each default scenario. This can be extended to variable discount rates by weighting the scenario cash flows according to their present values (Rose 1994).
12. We define ZS as the spread over the spot Treasury curve that equates the discounted present value of a cash flow to its market price plus accrued interest. The DM for floating-rate tranches is the corresponding spread over the forward curve for the index rate that determines the interest payments. When the interest payments depend on more than one index rate, we arbitrarily choose a primary index.

Exhibit 10: No-Default versus Default-Adjusted Cash Flows

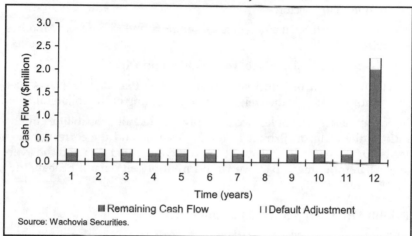

Source: Wachovia Securities.

present values of the default-free and default-adjusted cash flows divided by the former, where the default-free yield is used as the discount rate for both cash flows.[13] Intuitively, the EL is the average percentage loss in present value of a CDO tranche caused by defaults in the underlying collateral.

All of this is straightforward except for the default scenario generation, which we will explain in detail after examining the output of some sample calculations.

NUMERICAL EXAMPLES

Our examples for a generic high-yield CBO use the following assumptions:

- Default probabilities from Moody's matrix of idealized cumulative default experience as a function of rating and remaining term.[14]
- Default probabilities adjusted by Moody's multipliers to stress the senior tranches (Exhibit 11).

---

13. The point is that the same discount rate is used for both cash flows; the choice of default-free yield as the common discount rate is arbitrary.
14. We are currently augmenting Moody's historical default data with KMV's default frequencies, which are based on an option pricing model.

- Default correlation of 30% (20%) between assets in the same (different) industry sectors.[15]

- Recovery rate as function of asset seniority and rating from Moody's data.

- Six-month time lag to recover defaulted principal.

- Reinvestment of principal proceeds at B3 default rate (5.64% per annum), which is the weighted average rating of the collateral.

In our numerical examples, we multiply the default probabilities by the ratio of the factor in Exhibit 11 for the tranche and the corresponding factor for the collateral.[16] Thus, if the tranche is rated Aaa and the average collateral rating is Ba2, we would multiply all default probabilities by $1.50/1.07 = 1.402$.

Exhibit 11: Moody's Stress Multipliers

Rating	Multiplier	Rating	Multiplier
Aaa	1.50	Baa	1.15
Aa	1.40	Ba	1.07
A	1.31	B	1.00

Source: Moody's Investors Service, Inc.

We generate 1,000 equally weighted scenarios using these assumptions, which are then input to the cash flow generator. The average number of asset defaults per scenario is 17 out of 73 underlying assets, ranging from 0 to 51 defaults per scenario.[17]

Exhibit 12 lists the cash flow yield and zero-coupon spread ("zero spread" or ZS) or discount margin (DM) calculations for the tranches of our generic deal, where all tranches are priced at par. For fixed-rate tranches, we calculate the ZS as a spread to the implied spot Treasury curve that equates their present values to their full market prices. For floating-rate tranches, we calculate the DM as the spread to the forward curve for the index rate that drives the tranche interest payments.[18] In

---

15. The industry sectors are provided by Intex. We are adding KMV's asset value correlations to our database and will incorporate them in our CDO model shortly.
16. This is a standard procedure in the application of Moody's BET methodology.
17. This is for a stress multiplier of 1; the average number of defaults per scenarios would rise with greater multipliers.
18. When a tranche floats over several index rates, we arbitrarily pick a "primary" index.

this example, we used six-month LIBOR as the index and the LIBOR curve is flat.[19]

Exhibit 12: Summary Output for Generic High-Yield CBO Deal

Tranche	Rating	No-Default Yield	No-Default ZS/DM	Adjusted-Default Yield	Adjusted-Default ZS/DM	Change Yield	Change ZS/DM	Expected Loss
A	Aaa	2.26%	50.2 bps	2.26%	49.9 bps	0.36 bps	0.4 bps	0.0159%
B	Baa2	8.11%	427 bps	7.50%	358 bps	60.6 bps	68.4 bps	3.5796%
C	Ba2	10.89%	690 bps	8.53%	438 bps	236.0 bps	251.0 bps	14.3530%
EQ	NR	25.72%	2,244 bps	4.95%	111 bps	2,077.0 bps	2,132.0 bps	47.4270%

DM: Discount margin; ZS: Zero spread.
Source: Wachovia Securities' estimates.

PRACTICAL APPLICATIONS

The most significant use of our model is the search for relative value between tranches of different deals with the same or similar ratings. These relative values depend on both the quality of the underlying collateral and the details of the "waterfall" structure that define the tranche cash flows, so undervalued tranches may be found in deals with strong collateral and vice versa. Exhibit 13 compares the yield change and expected losses under identical pricing assumptions for tranches with the same rating from three different deals.

Exhibit 13: Yield Change and Expected Loss for Three CDO Deals

Rating	Deal No. 1 Yield Change	Deal No. 1 Expected Loss	Deal No. 2 Yield Change	Deal No. 2 Expected Loss	Deal No. 3 Yield Change	Deal No. 3 Expected Loss
Aaa	0.01 bps	0.0159%	0.23 bps	0.0123%	0.15 bps	0.0072%
Baa2	43.80 bps	3.5790%	69.80 bps	5.3575%	28.40 bps	2.1157%
Ba2	230.80 bps	14.3530%	203.00 bps	11.1624%	329.90 bps	15.5279%

Source: Wachovia Securities' estimates.

Exhibit 14 plots the default yield spread (the difference between the default free yield and the default-adjusted yield) versus the expected loss of a large number of Baa rated high-yield CBO tranches from different deals. Most of these tranches are outside Moody's expected loss range because collateral credit quality has apparently deteriorated since the tranches were rated. This functionality is the heart of the model. It enables the investor to compare the risk return trade-off among many CDO deals, based on real-time calculation of two metrics: default yield spread and expected loss. The scatter diagram in Exhibit 14 gives the portfolio manager useful insight for finding attractive relative values.

---

19. We will infer the forward LIBOR curve from market data later on.

Exhibit 14: Yield Spread versus Expected Loss for Baa Rated Tranches

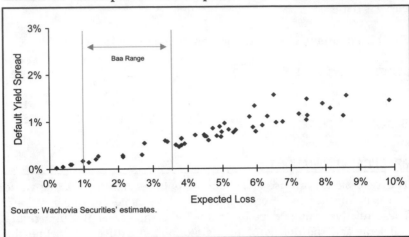

Source: Wachovia Securities' estimates.

Next, we perform value-at-risk (VaR) calculations using the entire distribution of simulated losses for each scenario (Exhibits 15 and 16). For each tranche, we sorted the scenarios in decreasing loss order to calculate the percentiles. In other words, the fifth percentile loss is the loss of the 50th worst scenario out of 1,000. In this case, we are 95% certain that there will be essentially no loss for Tranche A and that the losses for Tranches B and C will be no worse than 13.89% and 96.08%, respectively.

Exhibit 15: Loss Distribution

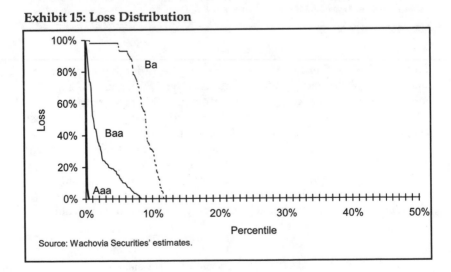

Source: Wachovia Securities' estimates.

Exhibit 16: Value-at-Risk: Loss at Various Percentiles

Tranche	1%	2.5%	5%	10%	25%	50%	Expected Loss
A	0.0012%	0.0010%	0.0009%	0.0007%	0.0004%	0.0002%	0.0159%
B	52.5914%	24.3307%	13.8883%	0.0002%	0.0000%	0.0000%	3.5796%
C	98.0779%	98.0779%	96.0807%	30.2254%	0.0000%	0.0000%	14.3530%

Source: Wachovia Securities' estimates.

Finally, Exhibits 17–19 show how the value of each tranche in the deal changes as we vary the default probability, correlation and recovery rate. Whenever we compare tranche values—either within or between deals—it is prudent to compare yields and spreads over a range of input parameters to make sure our conclusions are robust.

Exhibit 17: Sensitivity to Default Probability

Tranche	Default Probability 90%		Default Probability 110%		Change	
	Yield	Expected Loss	Yield	Expected Loss	Yield	Expected Loss
A	2.2802%	0.0094%	2.2543%	0.0348%	0.59 bps	0.0254%
B	7.6921%	2.4510%	7.3832%	4.2699%	30.89 bps	1.8189%
C	8.9941%	11.6200%	7.9504%	17.7970%	104.37 bps	6.1766%

Source: Wachovia Securities' estimates.

Exhibit 18: Sensitivity to Correlation

Tranche	Correlation 90%		Correlation 110%		Change	
	Yield	Expected Loss	Yield	Expected Loss	Yield	Expected Loss
A	2.2621%	0.0005%	2.2534%	0.0397%	0.87 bps	0.0392%
B	7.5903%	3.0585%	7.4203%	4.0637%	17.00 bps	1.1720%
C	8.7498%	13.1108%	8.8347%	15.1771%	36.51 bps	2.0663%

Source: Wachovia Securities' estimates.

Exhibit 19: Sensitivity to Severity = 100% Minus Recovery Rate

Tranche	Severity 90%		Severity 110%		Change	
	Yield	Expected Loss	Yield	Expected Loss	Yield	Expected Loss
A	2.2612%	0.0049%	2.2544%	0.0350%	0.68 bps	0.0301%
B	7.5844%	3.0978%	7.3371%	4.5523%	24.73 bps	1.4545%
C	8.9587%	11.8644%	8.2044%	16.2634%	75.43 bps	4.3990%

Source: Wachovia Securities' estimates.

SCENARIO GENERATION

We take a "copula" approach to scenario generation by sampling points from a multivariate normal distribution and then mapping the marginal distributions to exponential distributions that govern the time-to-default of each asset.[20] The reason we begin with normal distributions is that they roughly correspond to the distribution of asset returns that we want to correlate. Default scenario generation proceeds in four steps:

First, generate random numbers from a standard normal distribution for each asset and populate a matrix of standard normal deviates where the rows correspond to assets and the columns to scenarios. Thus, the matrix elements for the ith asset and n^{th} scenario are

$$x_i^n = \Phi^{-1}(u_i^n)$$

(Eqn. 1)

where Φ is the standard normal cumulative distribution function (CDF) and the u_i^n's are drawn from a uniform [0,1] distribution. The rows are normalized so that their means and standard deviations are exactly zero and one, respectively, and the correlation between distinct rows is exactly zero.[21] In other words, we force the random sample of normal variates to have the same first and second moments as the normal population.

Second, correlate these independent normal distributions to produce a multivariate normal distribution. Let L denote the positive-definite inter-asset correlation matrix, perform the Cholesky decomposition $\Lambda = LL^T$ and replace the original matrix rows x_i with linear combinations $y_i = L^T x_i$ so that the inter-row correlations exactly match the elements of the correlation matrix.[22]

Third, map the normal marginal distributions to exponential distributions that govern the time-to-default of each asset.[23] We solve the equation

20. See Li (2000) for more information about using normal copulas to simulate time-to-default.
21. We subtract the row mean from each matrix row, perform a Gram-Schmidt procedure to orthogonalize the rows and divide each row by its standard deviation. The number of columns must exceed the number of rows for this to work.
22. You can verify this by calculating the inner products
$(y_i, y_j) = (L^T x_i, L^T x_j) = (LL^T x_i, x_j) = (\Lambda x_i, x_j) = \Lambda_{ij}$ for rows i and j.
23. We treat asset default as a Poisson process, so that the time-to-default is exponentially distributed.

$$1 - \exp\left(-\int_0^T \lambda_i(t)dt \right) = \Phi(y_i^n)$$

(Eqn. 2)

for the time-to-default T_i^n where the left side is the exponential CDF with intensity $\lambda_i(t)$ and F is the standard normal CDF. Defaults after the deal maturity are ignored, whereas times to default prior within the deal life are rounded up to the next payment time.

The intensity is basically the ith asset's instantaneous probability of default. In our numerical examples, we use a constant intensity λ_i that equates the exponential CDF to the cumulative probability of default $F_i(T)$ for a remaining term of T years

$$\lambda_i = -\log(1 - F_i(T))/T$$

(Eqn. 3)

The cumulative default probability as a function of rating and remaining term can be derived either from the asset's current rating and remaining term or from an option-pricing model.[24] For default matrices that reflect expected loss, rather than the probability of default, consistency requires the parameter λ_i to be the right side of Eqn. 3 divided by the survival rate.

Fourth, we specify the recovery rate for defaulted principal, the time lag from default to recovery and the reinvestment strategy for every asset that defaults before the end of the deal. Our numerical examples use fixed recovery rates based on asset seniority and current rating, fixed time lag and assume that all recovered principal is reinvested in a "generic" asset for which the default probability is derived from the average rating and remaining term of the assets in the collateral pool. However, the model also provides for random recoveries and time lags using beta and rectangular distributions, respectively, fit to market data provided by the rating agencies.

For random recoveries, we generate a standard normal variate z_i^n and then correlate it to the normal variate x_i^n we used above to calculate the time-to-default. If η is the correlation between the default and recovery rates, then the random recovery rate R_i^n is given by

24. The constant default rate λ derived by applying Eqn. 3 to Moody's cumulative default matrix tends to drop as the remaining term T decreases, and we are concerned that we could be underestimating default risk for longer-maturity assets. This is why we provide the option of freezing T, for example, T = 1 year.

$$R_i^n = F_{re\,covery}^{-1}(\Phi(\sqrt{1-\eta^2}\,z_i^n + \eta x_i^n))$$

(Eqn. 4)

where the recovery distribution is a beta distribution with parameters chosen to match the observed mean and standard deviation of recovery rates for assets in each seniority class. The CDF of the beta distribution is

$$F(x) = \beta(x, a, b)/\beta(1; a, b) \quad \text{where} \quad \beta(x, a, b) = \int_0^x y^{a-1}(1-y)^{b-1}\, dy.$$

(Eqn. 5)

CONCLUSIONS

WS has developed a general-purpose model for the valuation of cash flow CDO tranches that allows the user to specify the four basic assumptions that govern the default behavior of the underlying collateral. This yields consistent valuation across tranches and deals. We also provide numerical techniques to accelerate the convergence of the simulations for senior CDO tranches.

APPENDIX: COMPUTATIONAL EFFICIENCY

Monte Carlo simulation is flexible but has the disadvantage of slow convergence in many applications. In practice, the convergence of Monte Carlo methods is often measured by running the same simulation over and over again with different random number seeds and noting the variance of the resulting sample means. Numerical techniques to improve Monte Carlo convergence are therefore known as "variance reduction" techniques.[25]

The most challenging numerical issue for CDO valuation is the accurate simulation of senior tranche values using a relatively small number of scenarios. This is difficult because only a small fraction of the scenarios have any effect on these tranches. In other words, the effective sample size is small because most of the scenarios just reproduce default-free tranche cash flows and contribute nothing to the accuracy of the simulation.

We enhanced the basic Monte Carlo method with techniques to produce sample paths abnormally rich in default-laden scenarios that provoke losses in the senior tranches. These techniques are versions of *importance sampling*, the notion that we need not generate the scenarios from the same probability distribution that governs the asset defaults. Instead, we generate scenarios from an alternative distribution designed for numerical efficiency and then weight the scenarios unequally so that the original distribution is preserved.

Importance sampling is conceptually simple. Suppose we want to approximate the expected value $E_P(f)$ of a function $f(x)$ where x is distributed according to probability distribution P. The standard method ("raw" simulation) is to randomly sample N independent values $x_1, ..., x_N$ from distribution P and average the resulting function values:

$$S_N = \tfrac{1}{N} \sum_{n=1}^{N} f(x_n) \approx E_P(f) = \int f(x) dP(x) = \int f(x) p(x) dx,$$

(Eqn. 6)

where $p(x)$ and $P(x)$ denote the density and CDF of distribution P. For an alternative distribution Q, the expected value is

$$E_P(f) = \int f(x) p(x) dx = \int f(x) \frac{p(x)}{q(x)} q(x) dx = E_Q(\tfrac{p}{q} f).$$

(Eqn. 7)

25. Chapter 4 of Fishman (1996) contains a detailed discussion of variance reduction techniques.

Importance sampling uses the approximation

$$\widetilde{S}_N = \sum_{n=1}^{N} w_n \, f(y_n) \approx E_P(f)$$

(Eqn. 8)

where the weights $w_n = p(y_n)/q(y_n)$ are density ratios normalized to sum to one and points $y_1, ..., y_N$ are randomly drawn from distribution Q. Importance sampling is effective if the distribution of unequally weighted sums $\widetilde{S}_N$ has significantly lower variance than the distribution of equally weighted sums S_N.

We tried two independent strategies to produce samples rich in scenarios containing enough defaults to affect the senior tranches. One is to artificially inflate the default probability for each asset and the other is to inflate the default correlations between assets.

To inflate default probabilities, modify the first step in scenario generation by sampling from a nonuniform distribution in Eqn. 1 for which mass is concentrated near zero. We choose the nonuniform distributions to effectively inflate the cumulative default function by some specified percentage. The required scenario weights are the reciprocals of products of the PDFs for the independent nonuniform distributions.

To inflate default correlations, multiply the off-diagonal elements of the original correlation matrix Λ by a factor $\gamma > 1$ to obtain an inflated correlation matrix Ω. In the second step above, use Ω to generate an alternative joint normal distribution.

The weighting factors are ratios of multivariate normal densities

$$w^n = p_\Lambda(y^n)/p_\Omega(y^n)$$

where points $\vec{y}^n = \left(y_1^n, ..., y_I^n\right)$ are drawn from the multivariate standard normal distribution with correlation matrix Ω.[26]

Exhibit 20 compares these importance sampling schemes against those of "raw" (equally weighted) simulation. We calculated the standard deviation of the expected loss of each tranche by reseeding the random number generator 100 times to simulate repeated sampling with 100 scenarios per sample.

---

26. The multivariate standard normal density function is

$$p_\Lambda(x_1, K, x_N) = \exp(-\tfrac{1}{2}\sum_{i,j=1}^{N} x_i \Lambda_{ij}^{-1} x_j)/\sqrt{(2\pi)^N \det(\Lambda)}$$

where Λ is the correlation matrix.

Exhibit 20: Standard Deviation of Simulated Expected Losses

Tranche	Raw	Correlation			Default Probability			Both Methods		
		5%	10%	20%	5%	10%	20%	5%	10%	20%
A	0.044%	0.038%	0.033%	0.046%	0.035%	0.031%	0.039%	0.036%	0.029%	0.033%
B	0.837%	0.810%	0.787%	1.056%	0.710%	0.700%	0.819%	0.747%	0.669%	0.783%
C	2.238%	2.367%	2.350%	2.732%	2.246%	2.289%	2.804%	2.271%	2.175%	2.332%

Source: Wachovia Securities' estimates.

For all three methods, simulation variance decreases as we inflate the default probability or correlation and then begins to increase. The reason is that convergence is accelerated as we generate more scenarios with enough defaults to affect the senior tranches, but begins to degrade when the scenario weights (density ratios) become concentrated on a small subset of scenarios. When many weights are close to zero, the reduction in effective sample size can actually make importance sampling less accurate than unweighted simulation.

The most effective variance reduction method appears to be inflation of both default probabilities and correlations by about 5%. The resulting improvement may not seem like much, but it is computationally less expensive than increasing the number of scenarios in the simulation.

REFERENCES

Fishman, George S. 1996. "Monte Carlo: Concepts, Algorithms, and Applications." Springer Series in Operations Research. Springer-Verlag.

Gordon, Brian D. 2001 (August). "An Empirical Study of CDO Asset Defaults and Recoveries." Fitch IBCA, Duff & Phelps.

Hamilton, David T., Greg Gupton and Alexandra Berthault. 2001 (February). "Default and Recovery Rates of Corporate Bond Issuers: 2000." Moody's Investors Service, Inc.

Hamilton David T., and Lea V. Carty, 1999 (June). "Debt Recoveries for Corporate Bankruptcies." Moody's Investors Service, Inc.

Li, David X. 2000. "Copula Approach to Default Simulation." CreditMetrics Group.

Rose, Michael E. 1994 (September). "The Effective Cash Flow Method." J. Fixed Income.

Tabe, Henry. 2002. "Moody's Approach to Rating ith-to-Default Basket Credit Linked Notes." Moody's Investors Service, Inc.

Chapter 13

CDO Equity Investing: A Fistful of Tips

EXECUTIVE SUMMARY

Investing in CDO equity can be a challenging, complex and even confusing endeavor. But it can also be immensely rewarding if done properly. In this chapter, we discuss a number of useful tips to properly assess the risks and rewards of potential CDO equity investments.

INTRODUCTION

When Michelangelo painted the Sistine Chapel, he was paid 3,000 ducats by his patron, the irascible Pope Julius II. That amount, quite significant at the time, was received over a four-year period and forced Michelangelo to make some difficult investment decisions. Initially, he deposited the money at 5% interest per year with his bank, Santa Maria Nuova Bank, in his native Florence. Later, unhappy with what he considered a paltry return, he ventured into the private equity arena and purchased a farm that his brothers would manage. The result was mixed.

It is unclear what the value of FIBOR (Florence Inter-Bank Offering Rate) was at that time, but it is reasonable to assume that Michelangelo was justified in looking for a better return. Unfortunately, at that time, the options were limited in terms of alternative investment vehicles. Even today, almost 500 years later, few investors would be thrilled with the prospect of earning a low risk return. Nowadays, investors have many more choices than Michelangelo had in his time, however, the complexity and variety of those choices make the task of selecting the right one daunting. Investing in CDO equity is one of these options.

A CDO equity investment requires a detailed analysis that takes into consideration both the qualitative factors (e.g., manager evaluation) and the quantitative factors, such as returns under different cash flow scenarios. This report focuses on the quantitative aspect of the investment decision. Specifically, we discuss certain metrics that should help investors assess the advantages and disadvantages of a potential CDO equity investment vis-à-vis other alternative assets or other CDO equity positions.

BACKGROUND

Traditionally, some investors (granted, naive investors) have focused on the equity internal rate of return (IRR) under a handful of simplistic, predefined credit default scenarios and interest rate movements to evaluate a potential CDO equity investment. Worse yet, often comparisons between two transactions are made based on a single base-case scenario, typically, a fairly optimistic view of the future that sometimes fails to materialize. There are two problems with this approach. First, the IRR may not be the most pertinent measure and, second, a limited set of scenarios can provide only a limited amount of information regarding the stability of the returns.

A better approach is to examine not only the equity IRR but also a number of other metrics (i.e., figures of merit) to assess the return characteristics of the equity. Further still, it is beneficial to look at these metrics in a probabilistic context when possible.

A VERSATILE MODEL IS IMPORTANT

Most CDO investors have access to a cash flow model: a detailed computer model that captures the unique features of the transaction under consideration (e.g., waterfall, hedge strategy, cash diversion tests) and determines the amount of cash available for the equity position under different scenarios.[1] What is lacking is the ability or desire to assign a probability of occurrence to each of these scenarios. Some investors endorse the view (simplistic but sometimes effective) of defining average, best-case and worst-case scenarios specified by some ad-hoc choice of default patterns and recovery rates. Then, each scenario is assigned a certain probability and an expected (average) value, corresponding to whatever measure is of concern, is estimated. On the other extreme is the idea of running a full-blown Monte Carlo (using whatever assumptions the investors deem acceptable) to estimate the expected value as the average across all scenarios. Somewhere in between fall binomial (or multinomial) inspired approaches in which the collateral pool is decomposed using an array of uncorrelated assets. Whatever the

1. For those who do not, most investment banks will run such analyses at the request of a potential investor.

approach taken, the key point is that the valuation measure should be characterized in terms of its expected value and distribution rather than a single number computed using the base case. Only then will a true picture of the investment risk-and-reward balance emerge.

ALTERNATIVE CDO EQUITY EVALUATION METRICS

Now that we have defined the modeling requirements, let us examine each of the different equity valuation measures, starting with the most obvious and commonly used measure, IRR. The following analyses can provide additional information regarding the characteristics (or personality) of a potential CDO equity position.

- **Equity IRR.** The equity IRR, useless when computed only for the so-called base-case scenario or for a handful of "representative" scenarios, can provide a much more accurate picture of risk if we compute it for many scenarios and assign a probability of occurrence to each—that is, if we determine the distribution of the IRR. In short, we must introduce a probabilistic dimension to this analysis.

    Once this is done, though most return distributions are not perfectly normal, one can get a good sense of the IRR stability by looking at its standard deviation. Furthermore, investors should explore how the E(IRR) changes if one varies certain key assumptions (e.g., recovery rates, collateral pool default probabilities, OC triggers).[2]

- **Payback period (PBP).** This is the amount of time required to recover the initial investment; in other words, the time it takes to achieve a 0% IRR. Again, this should be computed for different scenarios to estimate an average value and its possible dispersion (stability).

- **Probability of exceeding a risk-free return (P [IRR] > T).** This refers to the likelihood that the IRR could exceed the return of an AAA/Aaa bond (e.g., a Treasury bond) with a comparable maturity.

- **Cash flow interruption default rate (DIRate).** This refers to the minimum cumulative collateral default rate that causes the equity payments to be interrupted for the first time. Obviously, this depends on the default pattern assumed (e.g., constant default rate, front loaded, back loaded). A constant default rate (CDR) analysis is

---

2. E(IRR) denotes the expected value of the IRR, that is, the average value of the IRR across all possible scenarios, and weighted by the probability of the occurrence of those scenarios.

typically a good starting point because it serves to benchmark the equity against other choices. Also, the DIRate gives an idea of how tight the overcollateralization (OC) triggers are set. Clearly, a low DIRate suggests that the equity cash flow will likely be interrupted. In itself, this is not a bad thing because it can be mitigated by a big payment once the senior liabilities have been retired. However, for investors who are sensitive to current cash flow, a high DIRate is important. Furthermore, we suggest that DIRate is viewed in the context of the signature of the cash flows.

- **Cash flow signature.** This analysis, essentially examining the patterns exhibited by the equity cash flow distributions over time (for different scenarios), is more qualitative in nature. It is aimed at determining whether the cash flow patterns tend to be, for example, front loaded, back loaded or likely to suffer interruptions. Also, this analysis gives a clear indication of what the cash-on-cash returns look like over time. For instance, they could exhibit stable behavior, grow over time or fluctuate widely.

- **Sensitivity with respect to interest rate fluctuations.** The performance of CDO equity, specifically the E(IRR), is driven not only by defaults in the collateral but also by interest rate variations. More to the point—a bad hedge structure can put a heavy burden on the cash flows available to pay the liabilities. At the senior tranche level, this can be tolerable. At the equity level, this can be devastating. Hence, it is important to examine the stability of the IRR with respect to variations in the forward curve. If a minor variation in the forward curve (e.g., a parallel shift of 50 bps, up or down) reveals a major change in the IRR, the prudent thing to do is to reexamine the hedge structure—or perhaps look for a different investment.

CONCLUDING REMARKS

Investing in CDO equity can be taxing from a decision-making viewpoint but extremely rewarding from a total return perspective. We have attempted to provide investors with a set of tools that, when taken as a whole, could be useful in evaluating a potential CDO equity investment. We have purposely avoided including a numerical example, for there are no clear-cut, black-and-white rules. Rather than patronizing the reader with a group of easy (and probably useless) guidelines, we have preferred to outline the tools available to investors and let them make the decision. After all, a risk/reward trade-off that is acceptable to one investor might not fit well with another investor's risk appetite. In short, what is important is to know how to assess the risk. Once the relevant metrics have been identified and the risk has been measured, the decision to invest or not to invest becomes easier to make. And the more tools one has, the easier it is to assess the risk. Go ahead, invest in CDO equity — but don't make up your mind based on a single number!

Chapter 14

CDO Equity Investing, Part *Deux:* Alternative Thoughts on an Alternative Asset

EXECUTIVE SUMMARY

Recently, with the advent of new market participants, CDO equity investing has come under fresh scrutiny. Most of the attention has focused on two issues: the importance of historic return data and the alleged lack of correlation between CDO equity performance and other assets. We discuss these issues in some detail. Specifically, we argue that the relevance of historic data is a lot less than what most people assume and that there are a lot of misunderstandings behind the notion that CDOs, per se, manufacture portfolio diversification.

INTRODUCTION

Most people are encouraged to ask questions from an early age. In fact, "the more the better" seems to be the current trend, according to experts ranging from child psychologists to financial analysts to late-night-TV celebrities. Moreover, we are often told that there are no dumb questions and, for the most part, we agree. But at some point enough is enough: the unfortunate consequence of this well-intended policy has been (predictably) too many questions of dubious informative value. Specifically, when a question is based on an invalid premise, or tricks someone into accepting a strained proposition, the answer is often useless and irrelevant. At best, such questions distract people from more pertinent issues and concerns. At worst, they damage friendships, marriages or carpooling arrangements. That said, one of those useless and misguided questions is, "What have been the historical (or typical or average) returns of CDO equity?"[1] Another is, "What is the correlation between CDO equity returns and some 'market representative' index?"

---

1. The motivation behind this question is the desire to use the so-called historic data to estimate what future returns could be.

Granted, any reasonable CDO equity investor wants to have some indication of the future performance of a potential investment, or its relationship with other investments. In this context, the questions in the preceding paragraph seem reasonable, if not intelligent and prudent. Yet under the appearance of soundness lies something deceiving. Let us look at each question in turn.

What have been the historical returns of CDO equity?

The unfortunate truth, and incidentally, something everybody hates to hear, is that most CDOs are so dissimilar that any attempt to describe "average" returns would almost be of no use. Yet the question is often asked (and market pundits are eager to answer it in whatever manner suits their purpose).

To some extent, this situation is similar to that of a potential investor who asks a "What has been the average return of real estate investments?" The only honest answer is: It depends. Those who bought property in London's Kensington five years ago did well. The same holds true for those who bought a two-bedroom apartment in Paris' 7th arrondissement in 1999 and unloaded it last year. Quite a different experience had the misguided souls who purchased residential property in Los Angeles in 1989 and were forced to sell five years later. Or those who invested in luxury apartments in Hong Kong in 1997 (still 40% down as of today). This, of course, refers only to the residential market. There are also raw land investments, commercial properties (e.g., hotels and office buildings), parking lots or shopping malls, vacation properties, among others. All are different *animals* with different track records.

The variety within CDOs is nearly as wide as in real estate. Factors such as vintage, waterfall provisions, trading rules (static versus managed), the type of hedge arrangements, reinvestment provisions, the structure of the cash diversion tests, and most important, the type of assets and the type of manager, bring a tremendous level of variety to the CDO landscape. Dumping all of these varieties of CDOs in one basket and making sweeping statements regarding typical returns is worse than comparing apples and oranges. It is like unregulated *tutti-frutti.*

Beyond all of this, of course, remains the glaring problem that we still lack sufficient historical data (i.e., reliable, nonfabricated data) regarding CDO equity returns. But we leave that where it lies. This problem is not an indictment of the question itself.

What is the correlation between CDO equity returns and some "market representative" index?

The rationale for that question is the secret hope that for some reason CDOs can automatically manufacture portfolio diversification. Specifically, some investors have been led to focus on the "surprisingly" low correlation between CDO equity returns and some seemingly similar index. The reality is that CDO equity performance is driven strictly by the nature of the underlying assets, which may or may not be correlated to some index. Therefore, any absence of correlation between CDO equity and some index is driven by the lack of correlation between such an index and the underlying CDO assets, not by some magical CDO property that supposedly makes correlation disappear.

Broadly speaking, we will attempt to refocus investors' attention by demonstrating that each of the above questions is, in its own way, fundamentally flawed. In so doing, we hope to convince the reader of two important things. First, we will show that CDO equity investment is a high return—very high volatility game that should only be played by those with sturdy stomachs—a game in which past history offers little guidance and in which averages offer little enlightenment (or solace) in terms of future performance. Second, we will argue that CDO equity investors should approach this game in the same way that participants in the private equity market look at potential investments: one opportunity at a time and based on the individual merits of the investment proposition, while keeping an eye on their existing holdings.

CDO EQUITY: WHAT IS IT, ANYWAY?

Most readers are familiar with the typical CDO structure (Exhibit 1). The equity tranche is, of course, the "first loss" position. That is the short (and accurate) characterization. A more descriptive answer is that CDO equity is a nonrecourse, leveraged investment in a pool of corporate debt (or ABS or trust preferred securities or other CDO tranches). By nonrecourse, we mean an investment that does not require additional funding other than what is originally tendered—regardless of how poorly the investment performs. For instance, common stocks of corporations are among the most notable nonrecourse investments. The stockholder, as a partial owner of a potentially defaulting company, is not liable for money due to lenders, suppliers, tax collectors or employees of the company. This stands in contrast to an investment with recourse, such as the mortgage on a home.

Exhibit 1: Typical CDO Liability Structure

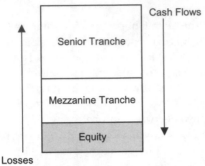

Source: Wachovia Securities.

By *leveraged,* we mean the investor borrowed money to purchase the investment, presumably at a lower interest rate than the expected return on the investment. This allows investors to increase the potential return on their investment. In essence, the leveraged investment can be good or terrible depending on the performance of the pool.

With respect to CDO equity as part of a broader portfolio, there are two primary reasons why it is important to understand the leveraged, nonrecourse features of this type of investment:

- As a leveraged investment in a pool of assets, the performance of CDO equity depends highly on the performance of those assets (i.e., it is highly correlated to the performance of those assets).

- As a nonrecourse investment, CDO equity's performance is not perfectly correlated with the performance of the assets. In other words, once the pool of assets deteriorates sufficiently, any further deterioration will not cause additional harm to the CDO equity investment.

Of course, there are other reasons CDO equity performance may not be perfectly correlated with the underlying assets. For instance, structural nuances such as reserve accounts or cash diversion tests will weaken the correlation. However, the effect of these factors on the correlation between underlying asset performance and CDO equity performance tends to be minor.

In what follows, we focus on the main characteristics of CDO equity returns, the importance of historical data and the relationship between the performance of CDO equity and the underlying assets as well as other market indexes.

METHODOLOGY

First, the facts: no reliable data exist for CDO equity returns. Considering that this market only took off in 1996 and that the average life of a CDO is between eight and 12 years, any CDO equity data one could obtain would only address performance over a brief period and would not encompass even one full investment cycle. Hence, one is forced to *simulate* CDO equity performance from collateral data.

Reliable data exist for defaults of corporate bonds (broken down by rating categories) and recovery values from 1970 until today. Unfortunately, no such data exist for leveraged bank loans for a comparable time frame, and fewer data exist for other asset classes. Thus, we will restrict ourselves to default and recovery data for corporate bonds for the period from 1983 to 2003, as reported by Moody's Investors Service, Inc.[2] Despite focusing on only one asset class (high-yield bonds), we will see that the conclusions have broader and more general implications.

The goal is to generate typical high-yield CDO performance data across several vintages (different closing dates). Having attacked so ferociously the validity of the term *typical* in the context of CDO performance, an explanation is in order. Our goal is not to predict (not even with a remote hope for accuracy) what the future returns of a typical CDO equity investment will be. The objective is only to examine the behavioral trends of a specific class of CDO with a specific structure that can provide insight into the nature of CDO equity returns and their correlation with other assets or indexes.

It might be tempting to believe that by looking back and obtaining data on all of the relevant parameters of the past (e.g., funding gap, forward curves and bond spreads), one could create representative CDOs for each year from 1983 to 2003. Unfortunately, the rating agencies have changed their methodologies over that time. Also, the ever-changing tastes and appetites of investors have also evolved. This makes the so-called typical structure of one year quite atypical when judged by the trends du jour of a different year. Given that, such a comparison would look accurate, but it would be deceptively meaningless.

Considering the above-mentioned limitations, we will compromise. We will create three CDO structures, each designed around a speculative-grade collateral pool and all with three tranches: senior (Aaa), mezzanine

2. Moody's Investors Service, Inc., Global Credit Research, *Default & Recovery Rates of Corporate Bond Issuers*, January 2004.

(Baa) and equity. The tranche sizes have been determined in accordance with the Moody's CDO rating requirements (as of January 2004). The three collateral pools considered are 1) Ba3 average; 2) B1 average and 3) B1/B2 average. The asset, liability and structural assumptions are shown in Exhibit 2. We further assume that all CDOs consist of five-year bullet assets.

Exhibit 2: Structural Features of the Three CDOs Considered for Simulation

	CBO No. 1	CBO No. 2	CBO No. 3
Assets			
Collateral Par Amount ($)	97,000,000	97,000,000	97,000,000
Average Rating	Ba3	B1	B1/B2
Probability of Default in Five Years	11.0%	16.0%	18.5%
Moody's Diversity Score	40.0	40.0	40.0
Average Collateral Coupon	8.5%	9.5%	10.0%
Liabilities			
Class A Notional ($)	81,000,000	73,000,000	71,500,000
Class B Notional ($)	10,000,000	13,000,000	13,000,000
Equity Notional ($)	9,000,000	14,000,000	15,500,000
Class A Spread (bps)	50	50	50
Class B Spread (bps)	300	300	300
Structure			
Senior OC Test	1.15	1.20	1.20
Mezzanine OC Test	1.04	1.06	1.06
IC Test	None	None	None
Swap Notional	65%	70%	55%
LIBOR Curve Flat at	5.50%	5.50%	5.50%

IC: Interest coverage; OC: Overcollateralization.
Source: Wachovia Securities.

The idea is to subject the collateral pool of each of the three CDOs to the historical default and recovery rates experienced by the market during the forward five-year period starting with 1983 and ending with 1999. Exhibit 3 shows the different default rates by rating category,[3] and recovery rates that are presumed to be constant across rating categories. Then,

---

3. A quick look at the default rate data indicates how hopelessly naive were those creatures who relied on the so-called 2% per year base-case default scenario as a basis to estimate what a typical equity return could be.

we calculate the equity internal rate of return (IRR) for each five-year CDO, again, from 1983 until 1999. Because each CDO pool is subjected to the average default and recovery rates experienced during the corresponding period as dictated by the average collateral pool rating, we implicitly assume that the CDO manager is mimicking the market. In short, we assume that the manager is able to trade the collateral in such a way that the pool does neither better nor worse than the market as a whole.

It might be argued that most CDOs do not consist of five-year bullet bonds. In reality, they have amortizing collateral with average lives of 7–10 years, however, for the purpose of this study, the aforementioned

Exhibit 3: Default and Recovery Data by Year

Year	Default Rate			Recovery
	Ba3	B1	B1/B2	
1983	2.65%	0.00%	5.00%	42.0%
1984	0.00%	5.84%	12.30%	47.0%
1985	2.84%	4.38%	6.04%	47.0%
1986	3.44%	7.61%	12.14%	47.0%
1987	2.96%	4.93%	4.62%	47.0%
1988	2.58%	4.31%	5.73%	45.0%
1989	4.71%	5.76%	7.78%	40.0%
1990	3.93%	8.50%	15.57%	30.0%
1991	10.08%	5.86%	9.38%	28.0%
1992	0.73%	1.00%	1.30%	37.0%
1993	0.76%	3.24%	4.14%	44.0%
1994	0.59%	1.88%	2.82%	43.0%
1995	1.76%	4.35%	5.39%	42.0%
1996	0.00%	1.17%	0.59%	44.0%
1997	0.47%	0.00%	0.77%	47.0%
1998	1.12%	2.11%	4.83%	51.0%
1999	2.00%	3.29%	4.94%	40.0%
2000	1.04%	3.51%	3.79%	33.0%
2001	2.97%	3.42%	6.93%	25.0%
2002	1.60%	1.94%	4.27%	32.0%
2003	1.48%	0.77%	1.67%	40.0%
Average	2.27%	3.52%	5.71%	40.5%
Std. Dev.	2.21%	2.38%	3.92%	7.2%

Source: Moody's Investors Service, Inc.

Exhibit 4: Simulated Returns Data for CDO Equity and Other Indexes/Assets

Cohort	Ba3 Collateral Pool Unleveraged Pool	Ba3 Collateral Pool CDO Equity	B1 Collateral Pool Unleveraged Pool	B1 Collateral Pool CDO Equity	B1/B2 Collateral Pool Unleveraged Pool	B1/B2 Collateral Pool CDO Equity	SSB HY Index	LEH HY Index	Vanguard HY Fund	Evergreen HY Fund	Treasury Index	S&P 500	Gold	RM
1983	7.14%	12.62%	7.01%	8.48%	5.25%	-9.37%				9.01%	11.74%	16.30%	1.16%	
1984	7.19%	13.38%	6.33%	1.22%	4.98%	-10.78%		13.85%	12.38%	8.29%	11.82%	15.14%	1.42%	13.32%
1985	6.57%	3.53%	6.29%	0.72%	5.62%	-5.73%		11.94%	11.10%	6.12%	11.81%	20.17%	5.36%	13.20%
1986	6.33%	-0.70%	5.61%	-8.29%	4.23%	-38.01%	8.02%	4.81%	5.50%	-2.66%	9.43%	13.12%	3.21%	10.40%
1987	5.36%	-38.51%	5.66%	-8.75%	4.39%	-25.88%	11.04%	9.50%	7.60%	2.47%	9.35%	15.23%	-1.90%	10.83%
1988	5.40%	-24.02%	5.87%	-3.96%	4.25%	-41.06%	13.80%	11.66%	9.93%	6.78%	10.45%	15.61%	-7.13%	11.53%
1989	5.41%	-15.19%	5.84%	-3.33%	4.08%	-20.44%	14.07%	12.56%	10.82%	9.40%	11.19%	14.31%	-0.97%	11.16%
1990	5.84%	-6.47%	6.26%	1.04%	4.48%	-11.54%	12.56%	12.14%	10.03%	7.73%	7.50%	8.54%	-0.92%	7.76%
1991	6.17%	-0.58%	7.21%	10.06%	6.65%	3.45%	17.38%	18.51%	15.34%	15.29%	9.35%	16.35%	0.22%	8.88%
1992	8.01%	23.90%	8.07%	17.83%	8.22%	15.64%	12.85%	12.23%	11.62%	9.71%	6.86%	15.01%	0.81%	6.87%
1993	8.05%	24.26%	8.10%	17.79%	8.18%	15.19%	11.90%	11.64%	11.16%	8.73%	7.34%	20.04%	-2.88%	7.24%
1994	8.03%	24.03%	8.29%	19.34%	8.25%	15.77%	9.39%	8.57%	8.68%	3.25%	7.21%	23.82%	-5.90%	7.23%
1995	7.86%	22.27%	8.13%	18.11%	8.01%	14.28%	9.94%	9.31%	9.61%	7.33%	7.41%	28.28%	-5.55%	7.93%
1996	7.96%	23.59%	8.31%	19.84%	8.29%	16.35%	5.11%	4.28%	5.65%	3.73%	6.52%	18.17%	-6.80%	6.90%
1997	7.52%	18.27%	7.93%	16.94%	7.31%	9.14%	3.93%	3.11%	4.33%	2.70%	7.34%	10.61%	-5.37%	7.47%
1998	7.31%	14.91%	7.54%	13.19%	6.63%	3.07%	1.13%	0.38%	2.36%	1.08%	7.73%	-0.59%	3.78%	7.39%
1999	7.20%	12.90%	7.56%	13.08%	6.78%	4.42%	5.01%	5.23%	4.51%	5.32%	6.17%	-0.59%	7.58%	6.59%
Average*	6.90%	6.36%	7.06%	7.84%	6.21%	-3.85%	9.72%	9.36%	8.79%	6.14%	8.78%	14.68%	-0.82%	9.04%
Std. Dev.*	0.99%	18.55%	1.01%	10.20%	1.64%	18.80%	4.58%	4.70%	3.50%	4.14%	2.00%	7.37%	4.39%	2.33%

CDO: Collateralized debt obligation; HY: High yield; LEH: Lehman Brothers Holdings Inc.; RM: Residential mortgage; SSB: Salomon Smith Barney Inc.

*Due to overlapping periods, readers should not use these values to project future performance.

Source: Bloomberg L.P. and Wachovia Securities.

simplification does not alter the pertinent characteristics of the CDO equity behavior—return distribution and correlation. Furthermore, other researchers have adopted similar time frames, and to allow comparisons between our study and theirs, we have adopted a similar convention.

HISTORICAL RETURNS

Exhibit 4 shows the returns for each of the three CDO equity positions, for the corresponding collateral pools (Ba3, B1 and B1/B2) and for several indexes and funds.

A few comments are in order. First, the average CDO equity returns should not be regarded as representative of high-yield CDOs. However, what is typical is the variation of the returns, which is extremely high compared with the mean. This demonstrates that any attempt to analyze average returns to estimate the return on a potential CDO equity investment will offer little guidance. Take CDO equity backed by Ba3 collateral. The average IRR is 6.36% with a standard deviation of 18.55%. If one were to choose a CDO backed by Ba3 collateral, the probability that the IRR of that equity tranche will be close to 6.36% is so low that the average is almost meaningless. In fact, given the non-normal distribution of CDO equity returns it could be argued that an IRR close to 6.36% is perhaps one of the least likely possible scenarios (Exhibit 5). Second, the year-to-year variation of the IRR is so dramatic that it makes a compelling case for focusing almost exclusively on one's ability to guess the credit cycle and for disregarding the past.[4]

The observed volatility of returns is consistent, of course, with what one would expect from a leveraged investment. In Exhibit 4, the IRRs of the Ba3, B1 and B1/B2 (unleveraged) portfolios are stable (with a fairly small standard deviation) compared with those of the equity tranches (in the Ba3 case, for example, 0.99% versus 18.55%). The volatility we have seen, as high as it is, could be even higher if one were to account for the manager trading behavior.

IS CDO EQUITY CORRELATED WITH OTHER ASSETS?

Intuitively, we would expect

1) CDO equity returns to be highly correlated with the return of the underlying assets; and

---

4. This finding, namely the high volatility of CDO equity returns, seems to be consistent with previous reports. See, for example, Data Table 2 in "CDO Equity as an Alternative Investment" by P. Rappoport and J. Meli, J.P. Morgan, *Fixed Income Quantitative Strategy*, October 2002.

Exhibit 5: Histogram of CDO Equity Returns (Ba3 Collateral Pool)

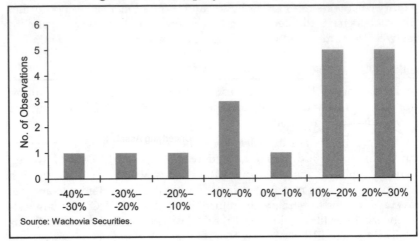

Source: Wachovia Securities.

2)   the correlation between CDO equity returns and some index to be close to the correlation between the return of the underlying CDO assets and that same index. This, of course, would be a logical consequence of 1).

These ideas are shown schematically in Exhibit 6.

Exhibit 7 shows the simulated correlation between the CDO equity returns (three cases), the unleveraged collateral pool returns (three cases) and the returns of eight relevant indexes or funds.

Regarding proposition 1), we can see that it seems to hold. The correlation between the equity returns and the underlying pools is 0.96, 0.99 and 0.94 for the Ba3, B1 and B1/B2 pools, respectively. Furthermore, these correlation values are consistent with the two arguments advanced earlier regarding the characteristics of CDO equity (highly, but not perfectly correlated with the underlying assets).

Let us examine proposition 2). The correlations between CDO equity (the Ba3 pool) and the following indexes (Salomon High-Yield Bond Index, SSB HY; Vanguard High-Yield Fund; S&P 500; and Gold) are -0.43, -0.13, 0.13 and -0.01, respectively. The correlations between the Ba3 (unleveraged) pool and the same indexes are -0.46, -0.19, 0.20 and -0.12, respectively—not that different. The same holds if we look, for example, at CDO equity (B1/B2 pool) and the Lehman (LEH HY) and Residential Mortgages indexes (-0.13 and -0.69, respectively) and at the correlations between the underlying pool (B1/B2) and the same indexes (-0.22 and

**Exhibit 6: Schematic Description of Correlations,
Two Possible Scenarios***

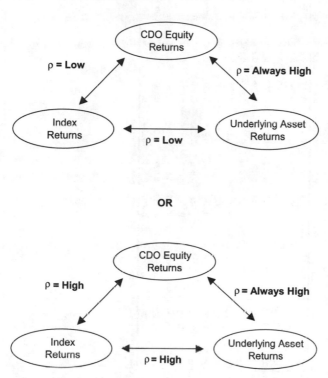

Source: Wachovia Securities.

-0.73) — a similar situation. The same holds for all the other cases. Therefore, proposition 2) holds also.

An important corollary of proposition 2) is the following: when we see a low correlation between CDO equity returns and some index, it is because the correlation between the underlying pool and that index is low. It is not due to some property of the CDO that magically makes the correlation disappear or decrease. This is extremely important to understand, as some investors have been led to believe that CDO equity is uncorrelated with major market indexes. Although frequently true, that statement is misleading. A more insightful characterization is the following: CDO equity returns will be uncorrelated to some index, for instance, the Abraxas-Demian High-Yield Index (ADHYI), only if the correlation between the underlying CDO assets and the ADHYI is low.

Exhibit 7: Correlation between CDO Equity Returns and Various Assets and Indexes

	Ba3 Collateral Pool		B1 Collateral Pool		B1/B2 Collateral Pool		SSB HY Index	LEH HY Index	Vanguard HY Fund	Evergreen HY Fund	Treasury Index	S&P 500	Gold	RM
	Unleveraged Pool	CDO Equity	Unleveraged Pool	CDO Equity	Unleveraged Pool	CDO Equity								
Ba3 Portfolio	1.000	0.957	0.896	0.886	0.886	0.848	-0.462	-0.339	-0.193	-0.067	-0.617	0.201	-0.117	-0.600
CDO Equity Ba3	0.957	1.000	0.853	0.866	0.820	0.828	-0.425	-0.281	-0.131	0.026	-0.550	0.133	-0.013	-0.571
B1 Portfolio	0.896	0.853	1.000	0.995	0.973	0.941	-0.355	-0.276	-0.160	0.101	-0.766	0.159	-0.278	-0.793
CDO Equity B1	0.886	0.866	0.995	1.000	0.955	0.946	-0.339	-0.248	-0.133	0.155	-0.743	0.131	-0.253	-0.782
B1/B2 Portfolio	0.886	0.820	0.973	0.955	1.000	0.935	-0.287	-0.216	-0.090	0.082	-0.716	0.254	-0.273	-0.733
CDO Equity B1/B2	0.848	0.828	0.941	0.946	0.935	1.000	-0.266	-0.128	-0.016	0.222	-0.655	0.167	-0.135	-0.695
SSB HY Index	-0.462	-0.425	-0.355	-0.339	-0.287	-0.266	1.000	0.977	0.954	0.744	0.535	0.471	-0.194	0.465
LEH HY Index	-0.339	-0.281	-0.276	-0.248	-0.216	-0.128	0.977	1.000	0.981	0.844	0.485	0.440	-0.035	0.416
Vanguard HY Fund	-0.193	-0.131	-0.160	-0.133	-0.090	-0.016	0.954	0.981	1.000	0.845	0.457	0.543	-0.087	0.381
Evergreen HY Fund	-0.067	0.026	0.101	0.155	0.082	0.222	0.744	0.844	0.845	1.000	0.170	0.251	-0.024	0.054
Treasury Index	-0.617	-0.550	-0.766	-0.743	-0.716	-0.655	0.535	0.485	0.457	0.170	1.000	0.187	0.191	0.973
S&P 500	0.201	0.133	0.159	0.131	0.254	0.167	0.471	0.440	0.543	0.251	0.187	1.000	-0.568	0.198
Gold	-0.117	-0.013	-0.278	-0.253	-0.273	-0.135	-0.194	-0.035	-0.087	-0.024	0.191	-0.568	1.000	0.185
Residential Mortgage	-0.600	-0.571	-0.793	-0.782	-0.733	-0.695	0.465	0.416	0.381	0.054	0.973	0.198	0.185	1.000

CDO: Collateralized debt obligation; HY: High yield; LEH: Lehman Brothers Holdings Inc.; RM: Residential mortgage; SSB: Salomon Smith Barney Inc.
Source: Bloomberg L.P. and Wachovia Securities.

An example will make this concept clear. Consider the correlation between CDO equity (B1 pool) and the Evergreen High-Yield Index, which is low (0.16). However, the correlation between the underlying pool (B1) and that index (0.10) is also low. The same is valid for CDO equity (B1/B2 pool) and the Lehman Index, where the correlation is -0.13. Between the underlying pool (B1/B2) and the same index, that value is -0.21. This holds for all cases that we studied. Furthermore, while the correlation between CDO equity (B1 pool) and Residential Mortgages is high but negative (-0.78), so is the correlation between Residential Mortgages and the return of the B1 pool (-0.79). In summary, whatever correlation exists (low or high) between the collateral pool and the index, that same correlation will characterize the relationship between the CDO equity returns and such index. Thus, investors looking to diversify should focus on the correlations between their current holdings and the underlying assets of the potential CDO investment. Using indexes as proxies for the performance of the underlying pools can be misleading.

However, there is a *surprising* observation in this study: the correlation between the underlying collateral pools and seemingly similar high-yield indexes can be low and even negative. For example, the correlation between a) the B1 pool and Lehman Index is -0.28, b) the Ba3 pool and Salomon High-Yield Index is -0.46 and c) the B1/B2 pool and Vanguard High-Yield Fund is -0.10. One might wonder why these correlations are not closer to 1. After all, should the CDO collateral pool (and therefore CDO equity) not behave like a high-yield bond index?

DIFFERENCES BETWEEN CDO POOLS AND INDEXES

Appealing to common sense, one might expect a high positive correlation between the performance of a high-yield index and an underlying collateral pool consisting of high-yield bonds. However, the truth is that these two groups of investments are quite different. First, the performance of the CDO collateral pool is driven by realized credit events, whereas the performance of the index is driven mainly by projected market risk (expectations of future credit events and interest rate risk), something of no consequence to the collateral pool. Also, the duration of the CDO pool decreases as we move forward, diminishing the influence of changing credit environments and interest rates, whereas the index duration is held relatively constant and fully exposing it to changing expectations (in a way, the index behaves like a going concern). In addition, the composition of the index is more dynamic, as new bonds are frequently added and removed from the index when their ratings move beyond certain levels (or default). Finally, although this is a minor factor, due to their composition some indexes are exposed to foreign currency risk, whereas CDO pools typically are not. Together, all of these factors explain why the index and the pool can, and often will, exhibit such different behavior.

CONCLUSIONS

Recently, CDO equity has been subjected to renewed scrutiny. Investors are no longer satisfied with tables of IRR targets based on artificial (and often dubious) default and recovery rate assumptions. Nor are they happy with estimated performance under the so-called base-case scenario (normally an illusory pie-in-the-sky, wishful thinking, groundless utopia) or, for that matter, dubious claims proclaiming the lack of correlation between CDO equity and pretty much everything else. We hope the present study clarifies some of these issues.

Our findings can be summarized as follows:

1) CDO equity investments, like any high-return investment, are subject to high volatility. Therefore, it is hopeless to look at average past returns (assuming availability of sufficient data) with the expectation of gaining some insight into what future returns of a particular CDO equity investment could be. Rather, one should concentrate on the specific merits of the transaction at hand and on one's existing portfolio, and to make an accurate estimate of the credit picture over the next few years.

2) Consistent with 1), investors unfamiliar with CDO vehicles (but who would like to invest anyway to gain exposure to a new "asset class") might be better served by investing in CDO equity through a fund. Granted, this will reduce their chances of earning a spectacular return, but it will also reduce the volatility of such returns. In other words, it will reduce the likelihood of experiencing big losses.

3) Investors seeking diversification should understand that CDO structures do not manufacture diversification. CDO equity returns are closely linked to the performance of the underlying assets. Hence, if the underlying CDO assets have low correlations with the existing assets in the investor's portfolio, then yes, that CDO equity will bring diversification. If those correlations are high, such CDO equity will add nothing in terms of diversification. Equally important, investors should not rely on some seemingly relevant index when assessing correlations (with the hope that it might capture the behavior of the CDO collateral pool). This could be misleading.

Our analysis is based on a simulation using historic high-yield bonds default and recovery data. However, the conclusions are not restricted to CDOs backed by high-yield bonds only. They can be extended to any CDO for which the underlying assets exhibit significant year-to-year default and recovery fluctuations.

One final thought: CDO equity investing is a high stakes, potentially extremely rewarding (or disastrous) exercise. Just like marriage. In fact, when George Bernard Shaw described marriage, he said it was popular because it combined the maximum of temptation with the maximum of opportunity. Clearly, this is something that could also apply to CDO equity investing. Statistics support these views. For instance, 49% of the marriages in the United States end up in divorce. In other countries, the situation is worse (e.g., Belarus 68%, Belgium 56% and the United Kingdom 53%).[5] Exhibit 4 tells a similar story. For example, in 47% of the cases shown, the B1/B2 CDO equity investors lost money. Therefore, people should approach CDO equity investments in the same way they would approach marriage — on a case-by-case basis. When it comes to high stakes decisions, averages do not help.

5. Source: *Divorce Magazine,* Americans for Divorce Reform, Infoplease and Segue Esprit Inc.

Chapter 15

Monte Carlo Methods:
The Devil Is in the Details!

EXECUTIVE SUMMARY

The use of Monte Carlo methods in financial engineering is widespread and their popularity in the CDO arena continues to grow daily. Their power is great, their flexibility tremendous and their scope in terms of potential applications virtually unlimited. However, in the hands of inexperienced users, Monte Carlo methods could be fatal for they could give an undeserved air of authority and legitimacy to what would otherwise be considered numerical garbage, thus laying the foundation for what could become a financial Chernobyl. In this chapter, we explore the *do's* and *don'ts* of Monte Carlo analysis in the context of financial problems that are relevant to credit risk modeling. Several examples are included.

INTRODUCTION

Nuclear energy can be both useful and dangerous. If managed properly it can provide a big city with virtually unlimited power but, if mismanaged, can bring the same city to extinction. Monte Carlo methods are a bit like nuclear energy: They can be used to provide great insight into many financial problems, or, if misused, they can lead to a financial Chernobyl. As investors and rating agencies rush to use this powerful tool, it would be appropriate to pause and consider the robustness of certain Monte Carlo assumptions. When it comes to Monte Carlo methods, the devil is in the details.

The purpose of this chapter, of course, is not to discredit Monte Carlo methods, as their usefulness has been well established; rather, it should serve as a warning against irresponsible use. Several examples illustrate this point.

WHY MONTE CARLOS?

Certain mathematical problems do not lend themselves to what are referred to as *closed form* solutions, that is, results cannot be produced by simply plugging numbers into a formula. Unfortunately, many financial problems fall into this category.

One approach to solving such problems is to use the so-called Monte Carlo methods. Using Monte Carlo simulations, many possible inputs are generated randomly for the problem under study (*many* could be several thousand or even a few million). After recording the results for each possible input, statistical methods are used to deduce a solution based on the distribution of outcomes. In other words, one generates several possible inputs and takes the average output as the answer.[1]

The following examples will clarify the difference between problems that may be solved in closed form and those that cannot (but can be tackled with a Monte Carlo). Consider the equation:

$$Ax = B$$

where A and B are known. Clearly, the solution is obtained by plugging in the values of A and B into the formula.

$$x = B/A$$

Hence, this is a typical case of a problem with a closed form solution.

Suppose now you have a one-foot-by-one-foot square such as the one shown in Exhibit 1.

Exhibit 1: Blind Monkey's Dartboard

Let us assume that you have been assigned a fairly peculiar task: to determine the ratio between the area of the square above the curved line and the area below the curved line without using calculus (try to hide your disappointment!). The only tools available to you are a handful of darts and a blind monkey. Because a closed form solution is unavailable, you will likely turn to Monte Carlo analysis. By training the monkey to throw a dart at the square and performing this experiment several times (e.g., 1,000), one can keep track of the number of times the dart hits the area above or below the curved line. The ratio between these two numbers is the desired result. Furthermore, increasing the number of trials will increase the precision of the result.

Using this basic strategy, Monte Carlo methods have been used successfully to solve many scientific and engineering problems. The key to using Monte Carlo methods is the ability to describe the system inputs in terms of random variables, that is, variables that follow a certain (known) probabilistic distribution. Thus, to the extent that one can simulate the behavior of those random variables, one can hope to analyze the problem using Monte Carlo methods. This is often, but not always, the case.

ARE MONTE CARLO METHODS THE ULTIMATE PANACEA?

Although Monte Carlo methods are powerful, they are not the ultimate answer and care must be exercised in their application. There is often a temptation to jump blindly into a Monte Carlo simulation without considering the implications of certain assumptions. Regrettably, most financial problems (at least most *interesting* financial problems, that is, the ones most people are interested in solving) present two difficulties. First, the random variables in question (e.g., interest rates, bond default probabilities, mortgage prepayment patterns) do not follow a normal distribution. This means that certain standard mathematical methods and results are difficult or impossible to apply because they do not work for non-normal variables. (Further elaboration on the implications of this issue is beyond the scope of this report.)

Second, and perhaps more important, the correlation among the input variables that define the behavior of the system under study (i.e., the degree to which these input variables move together) is either unknown or extremely difficult to determine. To make things worse, the correlation between variables is not constant (it changes over time) and, frequently, there are few data points available to produce reliable estimates. Finally, correlation *is not* one number; it is several numbers. For example, in a problem with five variables (e.g., a portfolio of five bonds) the correlation matrix is a 5×5 symmetric square array of numbers that involves 15 numbers. The five numbers located along the diagonal of the matrix are 1's—this is the easy part. The difficulty arises in determining the remaining 10 numbers—the so-called off-diagonal terms—for which values range from -1 to 1.[2] Thus, before performing any Monte Carlo analysis, one has to determine these 10 numbers. This is a major challenge and the chief reason many Monte Carlo simulations in finance produce results that are random combinations of garbage and nonsense.

To be clear, the difficulties in estimating correlations should not be considered an indication that Monte Carlo simulations are useless. They are merely an indication that any reasonable modeling attempt should explore the implications of the assumptions made in terms of correlation. In fact, much insight can be gained from using Monte Carlo methods correctly, that is, examining the variability of results when correlation assumptions are altered. Implementing this method without analyzing the implications of the assumptions can lead to confusion and, possibly, financial ruin. In either case, Monte Carlo simulation results always generate visually appealing graphs that look great in PowerPoint presentations.

STABILITY ANALYSIS

The idea behind stability analysis is to assess the impact of changes to key input variables on the final result. When there is uncertainty regarding the input data, this is crucial. For example, suppose we need to calculate the possible return *(IRR)* of a potential investment in a bond issued by a U.S. telecommunications conglomerate known to employ questionable accounting practices. The *IRR* depends on a number of factors, three of which are 1) the value of the coupon *(c)*, 2) the probability that the bond could default *(d)* and 3) the recovery rate in case there is a default *(r)*.

Formally,

$$IRR = f(c,d,r)$$

Suppose we know that *IRR* = 10.7% when c = 14%, d = 25% and r = 45%. Is this useful? It depends. If we are uncertain of the future value of r

---

2. These numbers, taken together, must produce a positive definite correlation matrix, that is, a matrix with positive eigenvalues. This additional mathematical complication means that, in the event that one were able to estimate these numbers, there is still one additional check that needs to be performed before declaring the potential correlation matrix admissible.

(recovery rate) but conclude that for r between 30% and 60% (a range dictated by questionable accounting practices) the *IRR* only varies between 9.5% and 11.7%, then we can likely overlook the small degree of uncertainty and accept the 10.7% estimate as representative.

But suppose that a variation in r from 30% to 60% actually implies a change in the value of the *IRR* from 0% to 7% (as it might if the default is known to occur earlier). That changes the picture quite a bit; it means that more effort should be made to estimate r more precisely. Also, and more important, it means that we should examine closely the distribution of the *IRR* as a function of r. In short, relying on the value of *IRR* for just a single value of r would be misleading and dangerous. In other words, we need to know not only the expected value of *IRR* but also its distribution (or at least its standard deviation).

EXAMPLE OF APPLICATION

In the context of CDOs, Monte Carlo methods are typically used to simulate the default behavior of a pool of assets, that is, to generate cash flows under different default scenarios. These cash flows, in turn, are used to feed the waterfall and to estimate the amount of money received by each CDO tranche. Because the probabilistic part of the problem is the default behavior of the collateral (the waterfall is deterministic, that is, known ahead of time), this example will concentrate only on the pool of assets and no CDO structure or waterfall will be included.

Consider a collateral pool made up of 100 homogeneous (equal par) leveraged bank loans having an average life of seven years, an average default probability of 24% (B2 type of pool) and a recovery rate of 75%. Moreover, assume that the loans are equally distributed over 25 industries (four loans per industry). Finally, we assume that the intra-industry asset correlation (ρ-intra) is the same for all industries and is equal to 30%. Likewise, the inter-industry asset correlation (ρ-inter) is the same in all cases and equal to 20%.[3]

The objective of this analysis is to determine the sensitivity of portfolio performance to ρ-inter and ρ-intra using a Monte Carlo simulation. Clearly, dramatic changes in the portfolio IRR distribution have important implications for the performance of any derivatives (e.g., CDOs) that may reference the portfolio.

3. The value assumed for the intra-industry correlation is in line with rating agency assumptions. The value chosen for the inter-industry correlation is roughly consistent with the values chosen by Fitch Ratings while higher than the value normally assumed by Moody's Investors Service, Inc., and Standard & Poor's Corp. (0%).

RESULTS

To explore how a variation in the values of ρ-intra and ρ-inter affect the results, we have analyzed nine cases. The base case, of course, is ρ-intra = 30% and ρ-inter = 20%. Exhibit 2 describes all nine cases studied, defined in terms of +/- 50% perturbations of the base-case values as well as the resulting portfolio IRRs graphically and in tabular form.

Exhibit 2: Response of IRR Distribution to Correlation Assumption Changes

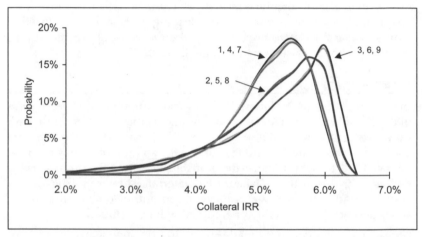

	Case 1	Case 2	Case 3	Case 4	Case 5	Case 6	Case 7	Case 8	Case 9
E[Return]	5.28%	5.27%	5.26%	5.28%	5.27%	5.26%	5.28%	5.27%	5.26%
Standard Deviation	0.60%	0.83%	1.04%	0.61%	0.84%	1.05%	0.62%	0.85%	1.06%
ρ-Intra	15%	15%	15%	30%	30%	30%	45%	45%	45%
ρ-Inter	10%	20%	30%	10%	20%	30%	10%	20%	30%

Source: Wachovia Securities.

Clearly, the average return is highly stable around 5.27% regardless of the values of ρ-intra and ρ-inter.[4] However, a prudent investor would not stop here because the distribution of the returns changes substantially depending on the value of ρ-inter. Specifically, the standard deviation of the return fluctuates between 0.597% and 1.059% for values of ρ-inter between 10% and 30%. Exhibit 2 shows this effect graphically; the changes in the distribution function shape are dictated by ρ-inter. In fact, the shape of the distribution for cases 1, 4 and 7 is virtually undistinguishable. The same holds for cases 2, 5 and 8 and for cases 3, 6 and 9.

4. This is to be expected. Changes to correlation assumptions will not change the expected IRR but rather the distribution of possible IRRs.

The key conclusion of this simulation is that much more effort should be placed on estimating ρ-inter than ρ-intra for our hypothetical, but representative, portfolio. And in the absence of a reliable ρ-inter estimate, caution should be exercised when speculating about the likelihood of the IRR exceeding a given threshold value. For instance, if ρ-inter = 10% the probability of exceeding a 6% return is about 8%; alternatively, if ρ-inter = 30% that value rises to 27%.[5] Therefore, a single Monte Carlo analysis (e.g., just the base case) would have given a fairly incomplete picture of the possible portfolio performance. Thus, the stability analysis has been successful at identifying the critical input variables, and it has provided additional insight into the range of variation of the possible outcomes. Hence, we see the importance of performing a stability analysis.

CONCLUSION

Monte Carlo methods are powerful tools for financial analyses. That said, blind application of this technique without exploring the importance of assumptions or the quality of the input data can lead to disappointments, regrets and perhaps tragedy. In the context of CDO analysis, this is even more relevant because a minor variation in certain key assumptions can under- or overestimate the cash flows generated by the collateral pool and also, therefore, significantly under- or overestimate variations in the cash flow assigned to each tranche. Obviously, equity positions will feel the brunt of these cash flow variations but all CDO investors are sensitive to the elevated risk associated with unpredictable collateral cash flow. Specifically, the sensitivity of the tranche cash flows is inversely proportional to the seniority of a tranche but the relative changes to tranche risk may not be. In essence, look at all the Monte Carlo simulations, but only trust those that come with a stability (sensitivity) analysis. Put another way: The single Monte Carlo analysis is almost always suspect absent any knowledge of the importance of key inputs. Useful Monte Carlo analyses tend to come in groups.

As rating agencies incorporate Monte Carlo methods into their CDO rating methodologies, we believe everyone would do well to study the sensitivity of rating estimates to correlation assumptions, specifically the inter-industry correlation assumptions. A popular trend these days is to assume that equity correlations are a good proxy for asset correlations, which are used in Merton-type default models. The literature that speaks

---

5. Assuming ρ-intra is held constant at 30%.

to this issue is mixed. For example, Philipp Schonbucher[6] states that the "correlation of $\rho = 11.21\%$ yields a loss distribution which is roughly consistent with historical experience. Share price correlations on the other hand are significantly higher." The same warning goes to institutional investors that set aside reserves based on supposedly accurate Monte Carlo simulations. These reserve amounts can vary wildly as a function of the inter-industry correlation assumed.

Finally, the example discussed in this chapter focuses on the inter-industry correlation. Equally compelling examples could have been made using other variables that are subject to uncertainty, for example, recovery rates or loan prepayment speeds. However, the conclusions would have been the same: When it comes to Monte Carlos, the devil is in the details.

6. Schonbucher, Philipp J. "Credit Derivatives Pricing Models" (p. 324), John Wiley & Sons, 2003.

Chapter 16

CLO Equity Performance: The Forgotten Factor

EXECUTIVE SUMMARY

Common sense dictates that CLO performance is driven chiefly by defaults and recoveries. Up to a certain point, this is true. But the influence of loan prepayment speeds—which could be either detrimental or beneficial to the transaction—cannot be ignored. In this study, we explore the effects of different reinvestment strategies and different prepayments speeds on CLO performance.

INTRODUCTION

Common sense, that is, the wisdom of the fool, is a poor adviser when it comes to science and art.[1] In science, for example, common sense would lead one to believe that heavier objects would fall faster than lighter objects. Fortunately, Galileo discredited this erroneous conception, held by Aristotle among others, for good. In art, similar situations have occurred. For instance, when Picasso completed *Les Demoiselles d'Avignon,* fellow painters and critics condemned it as ugly, shocking and monstrous. Thus, considering that investing in general, and more specifically, CDO investing, is a mix of art and science, one should be suspicious of "common sense views." With this premise in mind, we explore in this chapter the factors that drive the performance of CLO equity and challenge some commonly held views.

---

1. Einstein defined common sense (not to be confused with uncommon wisdom) as all the prejudices that accumulate in a person's mind before he or she turns 18.

BACKGROUND

Recently, CLOs have gained popularity compared with CBOs.[2] In part, this trend has been motivated by the stronger performance exhibited by bank loans relative to high-yield bonds carrying the same ratings. (Stronger performance, in this context, refers to lower defaults coupled with higher recoveries.) In part, also, this has been the result of CLOs simply doing better than CBOs in terms of downgrade percentages, Moody's Deal Score or equity returns. Finally, CLOs have not been affected by the excessive burden put on the structures by the misguided rating agency criteria that continue to drive hedge strategies.

Although we agree with these views and consider CLOs attractive investment vehicles, we believe that, in addition to default risk, investors should also pay attention to the so-called "reinvestment risk," that is, the possibility that the portfolio manager might 1) not be able to reinvest at the initial (higher) spread, 2) be "forced" to buy, for example, second-lien loans or 3) end up paying down principal if a suitable attractive investment cannot be found. Even though these factors are generally less relevant than the credit risk itself, they can become important in high prepayment rate scenarios. Therefore, in this chapter we investigate the performance of the equity tranche of CLOs as a function of the portfolio prepayment rate.

METHOD

The best way to explore the relevance of different prepayment rates and different reinvestment scenarios is to use an example. We consider the CLO structure described in Exhibit 1, which is typical. Appendix A details some relevant modeling assumptions. The idea is to examine how the equity internal rate of return (IRR) varies as a function of the portfolio prepayment rate. Specifically, we consider a base case (A) and three variations of the base case (B, C and D). The reason for choosing the equity as a proxy for the overall performance of the deal is that the equity is the most sensitive tranche in a transaction, and it reflects more quickly the strengths and weaknesses of the collateral pool.

The performance of the equity in each case is described by a rectangular array of IRR values that correspond to different constant default rates (CDRs) and different prepayment rates. It is assumed that the equity is purchased at par.

2. In this context, CBO refers to transactions backed principally by high-yield bonds and the term CLO is reserved for transactions supported mainly by leveraged bank loans.

Case A. This is the base case. It is assumed that the manager is able to reinvest repaid loans at the same initial spread, LIBOR plus 280 bps. One can think of this case as the case in which performance is driven mainly by defaults.

Case B. In this case, it is assumed that the manager cannot reinvest at the initial spread and, instead, reinvests at the minimum spread permitted by the indenture, LIBOR plus 265 bps.

Case C. Here it is assumed that the manager is not able to invest in "conventional" senior loans and buys (assuming that the indenture allows this or that the trustee/rating agencies remain unaware of it) second-lien loans. We assume that these loans, should they default, will have a lower recovery rate (30% versus 60%). In essence, the overall effect of this investment strategy is a gradual decrease in the average recovery rate of the pool.

Case D. This is the most interesting case. We assume the manager cannot find suitable investments within a year, and therefore the cash received from prepayments is paid down through the waterfall.

RESULTS

Exhibits 2–5 summarize the results. Exhibits 3–5 should be looked at in relation to the figures shown in Exhibit 2.

We begin with Case A (Exhibit 2). The equity IRR is relatively similar for low default scenarios regardless of the prepayment rate. The reason is that the loans that prepay are quickly replaced by loans offering the same spread. In a way, the transaction "does not realize" that a loan has prepaid, except during the short period between prepayment and reinvestment, when the yield suffers slightly, as cash only generates LIBOR minus 25 bps (instead of LIBOR plus 280 bps). In fact, this is the reason why in the 0% CDR scenario we observe a minor reduction in the equity IRR for higher prepayment rates (a 14.60% equity IRR for a 0% prepayment rate is reduced to a 14.30% IRR for a 40% prepayment rate).

For high default scenarios, however, the IRR varies quite a bit depending on the prepayment rate. The reason is that in high default scenarios, cash diversion tests (specifically, the overcollateralization test) will likely be violated. Thus, the high prepayment speed leaves more cash available to amortize the senior tranches, which, in turn, mitigates the losses suffered by the equity. Another factor that contributes to mitigate the losses is that the CDRs are applied as a percentage of the outstanding collateral; having less collateral outstanding due to the high prepayments leaves less collateral exposed to defaulting.

In Case B (Exhibit 3), the transaction shows the same tendencies as in Case A. Although reinvesting at a lower spread reduces the equity IRR, the effect of the defaults is generally much more significant than the reduction in spread. In a way, this shows that worries about "reinvesting at a lower spread" are often unwarranted—quality matters more than spread.

Case C (Exhibit 4), however, reveals an important reduction in IRR, which, not surprisingly, manifests itself more clearly in the high default/high prepayment rate scenarios, when low recoveries are more relevant. Thus, investors participating in transactions that have the ability to purchase second-lien loans should look at potential equity returns using lower (bond-like) recoveries for these assets.

Case D (Exhibit 5) is the most compelling. It shows that for low-default scenarios amortizing the senior notes (due to the inability to reinvest) hurts the equity significantly, as any excess cash must be passed through the waterfall to pay down liabilities rather than going directly to the equity investors. For instance, with no defaults and a 30% prepayment rate the equity IRR decreases dramatically from 14.39% (base case, Exhibit 2) to 3.68% (Exhibit 5); with a 2% CDR and 20% prepayment rate, the IRR decreases to 1.93% (Exhibit 5) from 10.31% (Exhibit 2). Intuitively, the reason is clear: Leverage is reduced and the life of the deal is shortened. Consequently, the equity feels the strongest impact of defaults in the pool. In addition, with a portion of the pool earning a coupon below the funding cost, in this case for a year, the situation is exacerbated.[3]

On the other hand, under high default situations, a high prepayment rate can benefit the equity. In a way, this is a "lesser of two evils" situation: Loans could be defaulting massively, however, the impact of this tragedy is mitigated by the ability to amortize the notes using the cash generated by a large number of loan prepayments. In short, a high prepayment rate could be either beneficial or detrimental to a transaction; it all depends on the level of defaults.

Finally, we should note that the situations described by Cases A, B, C and D represent extreme cases in the sense that, in a real-life situation, a

---

3. As explained before, in this case we have assumed that the manager waits one year before paying down the cash. This is reasonable because the manager, in all likelihood, will try, at least for some time, to find an attractive investment. That said, the equity IRR could be fairly sensitive to the length of the "waiting period"—the period during which the cash sits in a money market account earning LIBOR minus 25 bps. However, the trend demonstrated by Exhibit 5 does not change.

manager will never engage exclusively in one strategy. In other words, a manager might reinvest some cash at LIBOR plus 280 bps and some cash at LIBOR plus 265 bps, might buy a few second-lien loans and might pay down some cash. In a way, a typical behavior will most likely be characterized by a "combination" of the four cases considered rather that one case alone. Hence, a prudent investor, when looking at a potential transaction, should examine several combinations of the basic cases.

CONCLUSIONS

Conventional wisdom has led CLO equity investors to focus almost exclusively on default scenarios when assessing potential returns. Accordingly, the importance of the prepayment assumptions and, more important, the impact of managers' investment strategy on the collateral pool, is often overlooked. This study shows that different prepayment scenarios can alter the equity returns significantly.

Interestingly enough, fast prepayment speeds per se, are neither advantageous nor harmful. In certain cases, for instance, when the manager cannot reinvest and the pool is experiencing low defaults, higher prepayment rates hurt the equity performance. On the other hand, if the pool is suffering high defaults they are a blessing for they limit the negative impact of the losses.

In addition, concerns regarding the possibility that the manager might buy loans offering lower spreads seem overblown. However, the potential impact of second-lien loans (specifically, defaults of second-lien loans) is not to be neglected. These assets should be modeled using bond like recoveries.

Finally, one thing is clear: Making an assessment of the equity performance without examining different loan prepayment speeds—something frequently forgotten—is not prudent. This again proves that what applies to love and war also applies to investing: Common sense is almost always a poor guide.

Exhibit 1: CLO Capital Structure

Assets

Par = $300 Million
c = LIBOR + 280 bps
Diversity Score = 50
Maximum Average Rating Factor = 2,300
Average Life Test = 9 Years

Liabilities

Class A = $230 Million	LIBOR + 38 bps
Class B = $39 Million	LIBOR + 250 bps
Equity = $37.25	Excess Cash

Management Fee, Senior = 20 bps; Subordinate = 30 bps
Reinvestment Period = 6 Years

	Senior	Mezzanine
OC Test	1.154	1.05
IC Test	1.3	1.1

Payment Frequency = Quarterly

IC: Interest coverage test; OC: Par value coverage test.
Source: Wachovia Securities.

Exhibit 2: (Case A) Base Case, Manager Reinvests at LIBOR plus 280 bps (same spread)

CDR	Prepayment Rate								
	40%	35%	30%	25%	20%	15%	10%	5%	0%
0%	14.30	14.35	14.39	14.44	14.48	14.52	14.56	14.59	14.60
1%	12.65	12.66	12.67	12.68	12.68	12.69	12.69	12.68	12.67
2%	10.51	10.47	10.42	10.37	10.31	10.25	10.19	10.12	10.05
3%	7.76	7.63	7.49	7.35	7.20	7.04	6.88	6.72	6.55
4%	4.38	4.14	3.89	3.63	3.37	3.10	2.83	2.56	2.30
5%	0.47	0.10	-0.28	-0.66	-1.06	-1.46	-1.85	-2.22	-2.58
6%	-3.95	-4.46	-5.02	-5.61	-6.21	-6.84	-7.46	-8.07	-8.68
7%	-9.53	-10.54	-11.67	-12.78	-13.91	-15.04	-16.50	-18.07	-19.65
8%	-19.10	-20.97	-22.91	-25.08	-27.25	-29.87	-34.22	-45.91	-58.98
9%	-30.39	-33.30	-37.04	-41.52	-52.95	-63.91	-63.97	-64.72	-66.98
10%	-47.95	-56.51	-66.11	-68.31	-70.78	-73.60	-74.84	-74.90	-74.96

CDR: Constant default rate.
Source: Wachovia Securities.

Exhibit 3: (Case B) Manager Reinvests at a Lower Spread (LIBOR plus 265 bps

CDR	Prepayment Rate								
	40%	35%	30%	25%	20%	15%	10%	5%	0%
0%	13.77	13.84	13.92	14.01	14.10	14.20	14.30	14.42	14.54
1%	12.09	12.13	12.17	12.22	12.27	12.33	12.40	12.49	12.58
2%	9.73	9.72	9.71	9.71	9.72	9.74	9.78	9.83	9.90
3%	6.85	6.76	6.66	6.57	6.49	6.42	6.37	6.34	6.35
4%	3.33	3.12	2.91	2.71	2.53	2.35	2.20	2.09	2.03
5%	-0.74	-1.08	-1.42	-1.74	-2.06	-2.36	-2.61	-2.81	-2.94
6%	-5.44	-5.97	-6.52	-7.08	-7.61	-8.17	-8.63	-9.02	-9.30
7%	-11.93	-13.12	-14.25	-15.25	-16.20	-17.09	-18.38	-19.30	-20.27
8%	-23.10	-24.77	-26.59	-28.56	-30.44	-32.54	-38.87	-49.28	-59.17
9%	-35.10	-38.52	-42.60	-49.20	-64.50	64.45	-64.39	-65.02	-67.16
10%	-57.55	-65.12	-67.05	-69.20	-71.60	-74.34	-75.21	-75.16	75.10

CDR: Constant default rate.
Source: Wachovia Securities.

Exhibit 4: (Case C) Manager Reinvests in Second-Lien Loans (lower recoveries)

	Prepayment Rate								
CDR	40%	35%	30%	25%	20%	15%	10%	5%	0%
0%	14.30	14.35	14.39	14.44	14.48	14.52	14.56	14.59	14.60
1%	11.88	11.92	11.97	12.03	12.09	12.17	12.27	12.39	12.54
2%	8.15	8.17	8.22	8.30	8.42	8.60	8.84	9.16	9.58
3%	3.07	3.05	3.08	3.19	3.38	3.67	4.11	4.71	5.51
4%	-3.54	-3.64	-3.63	-3.49	-3.18	-2.68	-1.96	-0.97	0.34
5%	-14.18	-14.30	-14.17	-13.76	-13.04	-11.97	-10.55	-8.63	-6.19
6%	-30.06	-30.71	-31.08	-30.43	-28.88	-26.56	-22.73	-18.46	-14.48
7%	-49.67	-50.02	-50.34	-50.61	-50.83	-51.00	-51.11	-45.55	-37.27
8%	-57.36	-57.88	-58.39	-58.88	-59.35	-59.79	-60.22	-60.61	-60.98
9%	-63.80	-63.84	-64.38	-65.07	-65.79	-66.52	-67.27	-68.05	-68.85
10%	-74.64	-74.68	-74.72	-74.76	-74.80	-74.84	-74.88	-74.93	-74.97

CDR: Constant default rate.
Source: Wachovia Securities.

Exhibit 5: (Case D) No Reinvestment, Management Pays Down Liabilities

	Prepayment Rate								
CDR	40%	35%	30%	25%	20%	15%	10%	5%	0%
0%	2.03	2.78	3.68	4.78	6.03	7.50	9.30	11.41	13.51
1%	0.60	1.24	2.04	2.99	4.05	5.31	6.93	8.89	11.21
2%	-0.86	-0.35	0.29	1.10	1.93	2.93	4.27	6.01	8.13
3%	-2.43	-2.07	-1.54	-0.96	-0.35	0.26	1.20	2.57	4.39
4%	-4.06	-3.86	-3.50	-3.20	-2.97	-2.75	-2.51	-1.41	0.07
5%	-5.84	-5.82	-5.68	-5.64	-5.94	-6.44	-6.54	-5.83	-4.78
6%	-7.78	-7.98	-8.16	-8.63	-9.53	-10.97	-11.25	-11.14	-10.70
7%	-9.87	-10.28	-10.92	-12.13	-14.29	-16.03	-17.46	-18.13	-19.11
8%	-12.26	-13.03	-14.44	-17.15	-20.18	-23.14	-26.77	-31.70	-44.24
9%	-15.01	-16.42	-18.88	-23.41	-28.66	-37.87	-44.04	-70.38	-68.10
10%	-18.23	-20.65	-25.40	-33.31	-43.64	-64.28	-79.19	-80.42	-77.94

CDR: Constant default rate.
Source: Wachovia Securities.

APPENDIX

Modeling Assumptions

Defaults/Recoveries

1. No defaults occur during the first payment period or the first six months after the purchase during the reinvestment period.
2. Defaults occur at a constant rate on the outstanding collateral balance after the interest is received.
3. Recoveries on defaults are received immediately. Recovery rates are set at 60%.

Interest Rates/Coupons

1. The initial loan portfolio earns a spread to LIBOR of 2.80%.
2. LIBOR is equal to forward LIBOR as of June 9, 2004.

Other

1. Of the portfolio, 60% is held at closing, with the remainder purchased evenly over the next four months.
2. The initial loan portfolio purchase price is 99.875.
3. All assets purchased during the reinvestment period have a price of par (100.0).
4. No prepayments occur during the first payment period or the first six months after the purchase during the reinvestment period.

Source: Wachovia Securities.

Chapter 17

Investor's Perspective on Hedge Fund–Linked Principal-Protected Securities*

ABSTRACT

Principal-protected securities are the most popular form of structured hedge fund product and constitute the largest segment of the structured hedge fund market. Financial institutions provide guarantees for the repayment of the principal amount of the protected securities at maturity. To date, the structured hedge fund practitioners have used, by and large, the Constant Proportion Portfolio Insurance (CPPI) methodology to structure these securities, although some have used the Black-Scholes option (Option) pricing methodology as well. To the best of our knowledge, none of the practitioners has used the collateralized debt obligation (CDO) methodology in structuring these securities.

The CDO methodology has been one of the most successful and is an ever-growing methodology in the structured fixed-income securities market. The CDO methodology obviates the need for a financial institution to guarantee the principal of the securities. This chapter is designed to provide the basic structural framework, investment process and the benefit of the CDO, CPPI and Option methodologies. The preference for a methodology in structuring a protected securities transaction depends on several factors, such as target investor, leverage and cost. We believe that as the market grows and becomes more competitive, the CDO methodology will become one of the structural alternatives for the principal-protected securities transactions.

I. INTRODUCTION

The hedge fund–linked principal-protected securities (the "protected securities") are designed to provide investors with the benefit of upside while protecting the risk of downside of the loss of principal from invest-

*This chapter, written by Shanker Merchant, appeared in the *Journal of Alternative Investments*, Summer 2004 issue.

ment in hedge funds. The downside protection can be provided by collateralizing the securities with riskless assets (i.e., zero coupon U.S. Treasurys) or by a guarantee from a financial institution. In general, however, these securities carry the guarantee of a financial institution, which, in turn, protects the institution's risk by investing in riskless assets on a static or dynamic basis, depending on the structure of the transaction. The securities tend to have medium- to long-term maturity (7–15 years) depending on, among other things, the yield on the riskless assets and the expected return on the securities. Under current market conditions, the maturity of such securities can be expected to be in the range of 10 years.

Protected securities provide an attractive means of exposure to hedge fund assets to institutional and high net worth ("retail") investors. The growth in the demand for these securities has come from investors overseas. Demand for these securities in the United States has been limited for the following reasons:

- **Tax liability.** The securities are treated as issued with an original issue discount. As a result, a U.S. holder of the securities is generally required to include in its taxable income each year an amount reflecting the "comparable yield" on the securities. The yield on the securities is taxed as ordinary interest income to the holders without the distribution of income on the securities. This imposes on the holders the burden of making an additional investment each year until the maturity of the securities. In the event that the investor receives only the principal at maturity, the investor would suffer a loss in the transaction.

- **Liquidity.** There is no secondary market or ready source of liquidity for the securities. The only possible source of liquidity is the redemption of the securities. The redemption is subject to a number of constraints and carries a penalty fee, which makes them burdensome and thus less attractive to investors.

- **Long maturity.** Under the current low interest rate environment, protected securities require maturity in the range of 10 years to generate a reasonable level of return on hedge fund investments. The retail investors prefer shorter maturity, in the range of five years.

- **High protection cost.** Financial institutions currently charge approximately 1.25% per annum to guarantee the repayment of principal at the maturity of the securities. Institutional investors consider this cost to be high because the financial institution hedges its risk of repayment fully with riskless assets. For retail investors, however, this cost is generally not an issue, because they do not tend to have a look-through approach for their investment decisions.

- **Earnings volatility.** The accounting treatment of protected securities is bifurcated in terms of two components—a zero coupon bearing instrument and an option. The institutional investors are required to carry the securities on a marked-to-market basis. This creates earnings volatility (without any liquidity at such earnings). Therefore, the securities become less attractive to investors who must follow the U.S. generally accepted accounting principles (GAAP).

The protected securities can be designed to address some of these issues. However, in this chapter, we focus on the structural alternatives to protected securities transactions and their relative advantages and disadvantages.

The remainder of the chapter is organized as follows: Section II reviews the general framework used in structuring protected securities transactions and the investor perspective of the framework; Section III describes the CDO framework for protected securities transactions, which is currently not employed by the practitioners in the market; Section IV reviews the Constant Proportion Portfolio Insurance framework employed most widely in protected securities transactions; Section V discusses the Black-Scholes option pricing framework employed less frequently for hedge fund–linked protected securities transactions; and Section VI summarizes the relative advantages and disadvantages of these frameworks from the investor perspective.

II. THE PROTECTED SECURITIES

The protected securities represent equity interests in leveraged hedge fund portfolios with guaranteed return of principal at maturity. The guaranteed return of principal is supported by riskless assets or by a financial institution (the "counterparty"), which hedges its risk of the guarantee with riskless assets. The protected securities could, therefore, be considered as CDOs backed by a portfolio consisting of two classes of assets: 1) riskless assets and 2) hedge funds or funds of such hedge funds (hereinafter referred to as "risky assets"). The riskless assets account for the protection and the risky assets for the appreciation in the value of the securities. That is, at any time during the investment horizon:

Protected Securities Value = Riskless Assets Value + Risky Assets Value

(Eqn. 1)

Under the current low interest rate environment, a significantly large portion of the capital from the issuance of the protected securities is required to provide for the protection. Therefore, only the remaining relatively small portion of the capital is allocable to risky assets to provide for the return on the securities. For example, the current yield on the 10-year zero-coupon Treasurys (riskless assets) of approximately 4% per annum would require allocation of approximately 70% of the capital from the protected securities to riskless assets. The remaining 30% of the capital would be available for allocation to risky assets, which is too small to produce a meaningful return on the protected securities. Therefore, the risky assets must be leveraged to a level desired by the risk considerations of the counterparty to produce a marketable level of risk-adjusted return on the securities.

Leveraged Investment

Protected securities are designed to provide at least 100% exposure to risky assets at the inception of the transaction. That is, the capital employed in risky assets is at least equal to 100% of the principal amount of the securities. Therefore, the transaction must be leveraged to achieve a desired level of exposure to risky assets, as follows:

$$\text{Leverage} = E\% / (100\% - A\%)$$

where

$E\%$ = The desired level of exposure (as a percentage of the protected securities' capital) to risky assets at the inception of the transaction.

$A\%$ = The required level of allocation (as a percentage of the protected securities' capital) to riskless assets at the inception of the transaction.

(Eqn. 2)

The performance of the protected securities is thus linked to the performance of a leveraged portfolio of risky assets. The protected securities, therefore, represent equity interest in the portfolio. Consequently, the formula for the value of the securities, given by Eqn. 1, is modified as follows:

$$\text{Protected Securities Value} = \text{Riskless Assets Value} + \text{Risky Assets NAV}$$

(Eqn. 3)

Structural Framework

The design of the protected securities is based on the design of its two components: 1) the protection component employing riskless assets and 2) the return component employing leverage to a portfolio of risky assets. That is:

Protected Securities Structure → Protection Structure + Leverage Structure

(Eqn. 4)

The structure of the protection is designed either in the form of a static hedge or a dynamic hedge. In either case, the underlying assets providing the hedge are riskless assets (but can involve a certain level of credit risk acceptable to the holders of the securities). In a static hedge, riskless assets are allocated toward protection at the inception of the transaction in an amount that equals the principal amount of the securities at maturity. These allocated riskless assets are not altered or managed during the transaction, hence the name *static hedging*.

In a dynamic hedge, riskless assets may be allocated toward protection (or deallocated from protection) occasionally and in amounts during the life of the transaction based on the performance of the risky assets. For example: In the event of a decline in the value of risky assets, the allocation to riskless assets is increased through the liquidation of the risky assets, and if there is a subsequent improvement in the performance of risky assets, the allocation to riskless assets may be decreased through the liquidation of riskless assets. The hedge involving the allocation and deallocation of assets is based on a formula specific to the structure of the transaction and is managed dynamically during the life of the transaction, hence the name *dynamic hedging*. The most widely recognized form of dynamic hedging is portfolio insurance, which has its origins in portfolio insurance based on option pricing models.

Leverage Structure

There are three principal methodologies for leveraging an investment in a protected securities transaction: 1) the CDO methodology, 2) the Constant Proportion Portfolio Insurance (CPPI) methodology and 3) the Black-Scholes Option (the "Option") pricing methodology. The leverage determines, by and large, the cost of the protected securities transaction. The larger the leverage, the higher the cost.

The leverage level in each of these methodologies depends on, among other things, 1) the characteristics of risky assets, 2) the risk tolerance of the leverage provider and 3) the marketability to investors based on the risk/return profile of the securities. Certain characteristics of risky assets, such as high volatility combined with low and restricted liquidity, may prohibit leveraging a risky assets portfolio to 100% of the capital of the securities at the inception of the transaction. As a result, lower than 100% initial exposure to risky assets may be employed in structuring the leverage for the transaction.

Investor Perspective

The protected securities are a long-term and buy-and-hold investment. The return on the securities depends broadly on the performance of risky assets and the behavior of the interest rate during the investment horizon and, to a certain degree, on the structural framework. From an investor's perspective, the preference for the structure of a protected securities transaction is subject to one or more of the following attributes of the securities.

- **Optimal return on the protected securities.** The structural framework that enables the deployment of the highest level of leverage to a portfolio of risky assets with high volatility increases the likelihood of maximizing the return on the protected securities (and increases the potential risk of no return as well). Under current market conditions, there is a growing demand by institutional investors to use the highest possible leverage on high volatility assets to optimize the potential return on the securities.

- **Transparency of the investment process.** A lack of transparency affects the liquidity of the securities. The investable hedge fund indices, such as the MSCI Hedge Invest Index, tend to provide more transparency to the underlying hedge funds. The protected securities transactions with transparency will facilitate the liquidity of the securities, one of the most important U.S. investor considerations for investment in protected securities.

- **Mitigation of the defeasance likelihood.** Defeasance of the protected securities implies 100% allocation of the entire assets of the portfolio to riskless assets with a value at maturity equal to the principal amount of the securities, hence the name defeasance. Defeasance freezes the investment process and leads to a zero return on the protected securities. The framework based on a static hedge is subject to the volatility of return on risky assets only, whereas that based on a dynamic hedge is subject to volatility of risky assets and the interest rate, which increases the likelihood of defeasance.

- **Periodic distribution on the securities.** The protected securities are issued in the form of notes linked to the performance of or ownership interests in a portfolio of risky assets and generally do not provide for any distribution until maturity. Regardless of the form of the securities, investors have to recognize taxable income without receiving any distribution. Therefore, periodic distribution on the protected securities is an important structural consideration for U.S. investors—in particular, retail investors.

III. THE CDO FRAMEWORK

CDOs are recognized as the most efficient technology for leveraging investments in a broad range of financial assets and are structured as cash flow, market value or synthetic transactions. The application of the market value CDO technology to leverage investments in hedge fund portfolios is emerging. In the past two years, several hedge fund CDO transactions have been consummated. As the demand for leveraged investments in the hedge fund sector grows, we believe the CDO technology will gradually become a major structuring tool for such investments.

Mechanics of the CDO Structure

A special-purpose vehicle (SPV; the "Issuer") issues protected securities and invests the capital from the issuance to 1) hedge the repayment of principal of the securities through a static hedge and 2) acquire equity interests in another SPV (the "Fund"), which invests in a portfolio of risky assets.

*   **Protection component.** Under a static hedge, the Issuer uses the capital from the issuance of the securities in an amount sufficient to defease the protected securities with riskless assets (or riskier assets acceptable to investors). That is, the market value of such assets will equal the principal amount of the securities at maturity.

*   **Leverage component.** The Fund issues several classes of investment-grade debt rated AAA to BBB (the CDOs), and a class of unrated equity interests, and deploys the aggregate proceeds into risky assets to generate leveraged return on the equity interests. The initial size of the total debt, the relative sizes of the various classes of debt therein and equity interests are subject to the characteristics of the risky assets portfolio, in particular, liquidity, volatility and diversification aspects of the portfolio.

Investment Process of the Transaction

The ongoing investment in the risky assets portfolio is managed in accordance with the terms and conditions of the debt. The investment in

Exhibit 1: The CDO Transaction Schematic

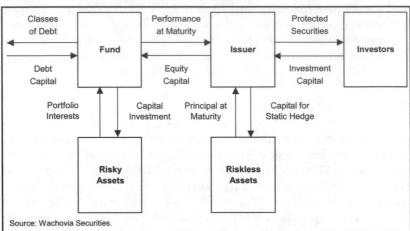

Source: Wachovia Securities.

risky assets increases and decreases based on the level of the debt, which is subject to appreciation and depreciation in the net asset value of the Fund. The level of a class of debt outstanding at any time during the investment horizon of the Fund is governed by the overcollateralization ratio (the "OC Ratio") for the class of the debt, as described in the following paragraphs.

- **OC Ratio.** The OC Ratio for a class of debt is defined as the ratio of (x) the market value of risky assets of the Fund (excluding cash equivalent assets, if any) and (y) the sum of a) the outstanding amount of that class of debt, b) the aggregate outstanding amount of all other classes of debt senior to this class and c) all applicable accrued and unpaid administration expenses and interest costs of the Fund. The required OC Ratio for each class of debt is set forth at the inception of the transaction (by the rating agencies or the provider of the debt).

The performance of the Fund determines the aggregate level of the debt outstanding at any time during the life of the Fund. If the performance is too weak to support the aggregate level of the debt outstanding, the Fund is deleveraged and may be subsequently releveraged depending on the recovery of its expected performance. The leverage (i.e., the level of debt outstanding at any time) is therefore managed dynamically during the life of the Fund, pursuant to the OC Ratio test.

- **Deleveraging of the Fund.** If the Fund fails to comply with the OC Ratio with respect to a class of debt at any time during the life of the Fund, the Fund is deleveraged by 1) liquidating a certain amount of risky assets of the Fund and 2) applying the proceeds from such liquidation to either a) reduce the debt outstanding by such amount or b) invest it in cash equivalent assets (which is viewed as reduction of the debt by such amount, and is not accounted for in the market value of risky assets of the Fund), until the resulting OC Ratio meets or exceeds its target.

- **Releveraging of the Fund.** In the event that the OC Ratio exceeds its target for a class of debt subsequent to a deleveraging event, the Fund is releveraged by allocating cash equivalent assets (if any) of the Fund to risky assets until the resulting OC Ratio is down to its target level.

- **Incremental leverage.** In the event of a significant appreciation of the equity class of the Fund, and therefore the OC Ratio exceeding its target maintenance level by a significant amount, the Issuer may either 1) issue an additional amount of each class of debt in the same proportion as the originally issued or 2) seek to employ only a senior class of debt in the form of a credit facility to the Fund in an amount and on terms acceptable to the provider of the facility. Generally, the second approach is preferred because it is less costly and can be implemented more easily.

Valuation of the Protected Securities

The protected securities are valued as the sum of the values of two components of the structure: 1) investment in riskless assets with a value equal to the principal amount (P) of the protected securities at maturity, and 2) the equity class of the CDO transaction.

The parameter affecting the value of riskless assets is the remaining time to maturity ($m - t$) and the interest rate for the corresponding period. The value of the initial investment in riskless assets grows to the principal amount of the securities at maturity, although the value may fluctuate along the way, depending on the interest rate (i). The value of riskless assets at any time (t) is given by the following:

$$(P) / (1 + i)^{(m - t)}$$

(Eqn. 5)

The value of the equity class at any time during the investment horizon is equal to the net asset value (NAV) of the Fund after the deduction for all outstanding liabilities including accrued fees and expenses of the Fund.

Risk of the Investment Process

A CDO transaction is based primarily on a set of leveraging and deleveraging covenants, pursuant to which the transaction is managed until maturity. A significant decline in the NAV could trigger a liquidation event for the Fund. In the event of such liquidation, the proceeds are used to retire the outstanding obligations of the Fund, and then the remaining proceeds (if any) are distributed to the holders of protected securities. The transaction does not involve the risk of any counterparty with respect to the repayment of principal at the maturity of the securities, because the repayment is fully hedged with riskless assets at the inception of the transaction, unlike the CPPI framework and the Option framework.

Benefits of the CDO Framework

The CDO framework for the securities combines the static hedge for the protection of principal with the traditional CDO methodology for leverage. The benefits of the framework include the AAA rating on the securities and the implied lower cost of guarantee on the securities. Furthermore, investors rely on the structure of the transaction rather than the counterparty for the protection.

- **AAA rating on the protected securities.** The protected securities will be rated AAA, because the repayment of principal on the securities is directly tied to riskless assets at the maturity of the securities. To our best knowledge, the protected securities issued to date are not rated AAA because they carry guarantees of non-triple-A rated financial institutions.

- **Lower cost of guarantee on the securities.** The framework involves only one cost—the cost of leverage (debt), which is the implied cost of the guarantee on the securities. If we assume a structure with a leverage of 4x and the cost of the debt of approximately 125 bps above LIBOR, this would then be equivalent to an implied guarantee cost of approximately 95 bps per annum on the principal amount of the securities. This cost is lower than the traditional cost of guarantee of about 125 bps per annum under both the CPPI and Option frameworks.

III. THE CPPI FRAMEWORK

Most practitioners in the structured hedge fund business view CPPI, which has its origins in "portfolio insurance theories" based on option pricing models, as the most suitable framework for protected securities transactions. The CPPI framework is designed to maximize the return on a portfolio with a downside protection. The return on the securities is maximized by allocating the maximum possible amount to risky assets at all times during the investment horizon, and the principal is protected by ensuring that proceeds from the liquidation of risky assets at any time during the investment horizon, if invested in riskless assets, will equal the principal amount of the protected securities at maturity. Therefore, CPPI requires a dynamic allocation between risky assets and riskless assets to accomplish these two objectives, simultaneously.

The maximum allowable allocation to risky assets at any time during the transaction is governed by the following formula (wherein each term, except the leverage factor, is expressed as a percentage of the principal amount of the protected securities):

$$(\text{Risky Assets Value})_{max} = (\text{Leveraged Factor}) \times (\text{Portfolio Value} - \text{Defeasance Value})$$

$$(R_t)_{max} = (F) \times (V_t - D_t)$$

$$= (F) \times (F_t)$$

(Eqn. 6)

where:

- Leverage factor (F) is a constant multiplier, which depends on the volatility and liquidity of risky assets, among other things, as determined by the counterparty providing the protection.

- Portfolio value (V_t) is the NAV of the portfolio after the deduction of all accrued and unpaid fees and expenses and outstanding liabilities associated with the transaction.

- Defeasance value (D_t) is the value of riskless assets required to defease the principal amount of the protected securities at maturity. The defeasance value is therefore a function of the interest rate for the time remaining before the maturity of the protected securities.

- Equity value (E_t) is the buffer amount to offset the possible loss in the value of risky assets in the event of the liquidation of the risky assets in the portfolio, as determined by the counterparty providing the protection.

The equity value determines the level of allocation to risky assets at any time during the transaction. The equity value may grow due to appreciation in the portfolio value, a rise in the interest rate (which will have the effect of reducing the defeasance value) or a combination thereof. Similarly, the equity value may decrease due to depreciation in the portfolio value, a decline in the interest rate (which will have the effect of increasing the defeasance value) or a combination thereof.

Mechanics of the CPPI Structure

The Issuer issues protected securities and enters into an agreement with a counterparty, pursuant to which the counterparty invests the capital in another Fund, which, in turn, invests some or all the capital in a portfolio of risky assets in an amount allowed by the CPPI formula given by Eqn. 6, and the remaining capital, if any, in a portfolio of riskless assets. Thereafter, the counterparty (assumed here to be the same as the Fund manager, for the purposes for simplicity of the description of the process) manages the allocation of the assets of the Fund (or the portfolio, used herein interchangeably) between the risky assets and riskless assets in accordance with the CPPI formula.

The counterparty guarantees the holders of securities 1) the repayment of the principal at maturity and 2) the payment of 100% of the performance of the Fund. The protection and the leverage components constituting the framework of the transaction are discussed in the following paragraphs.

- **Protection component.** The counterparty provides the protection for the repayment of principal at the maturity of the securities. Therefore, the rating on the protected securities is the same as that of the counterparty, which is generally AA or below. The counterparty hedges its risk of repayment by managing dynamically the allocation of risky assets of the portfolio to riskless assets. Alternatively, it ensures that the NAV of the portfolio at all times during the investment horizon is at least equal to the defeasance value. A failure in this allocation process exposes the counterparty to a risk of guaranteeing the securities.

- **Leverage component.** The counterparty is the implicit source of leverage in the transaction, in addition to the source of protection on the securities. This dual role of the counterparty is the result of the dynamic hedging of value of the portfolio from declining below the principal amount of the protected securities. (The transaction can be construed as the counterparty issuing put options to the holders of the protected securities with a strike price equal the principal amount of the securities at maturity, and then hedging its risk through the asset allocation process). The CPPI formula can be rewritten to show the leverage component of the transaction, as follows:

$$(R_t)_{max} / (F) \; = \; (V_t) - (D_t)$$

(Eqn. 7)

Equity   = Assets – Libabilities

Leverage   = $(V_t) \times (F) / (R_t)_{max}$

(Eqn. 8)

This characterization of the CPPI formula in terms of assets and liabilities shows the leverage implicit in the transaction.

Exhibit 2: The CPPI Transaction Schematic

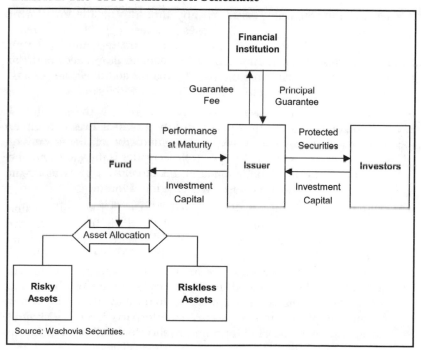

Source: Wachovia Securities.

Investment Process of the Transaction

The investment in the risky assets portfolio, on an ongoing basis, is managed in accordance with the investment guidelines of the Fund and the CPPI formula. The investment in risky assets increases or decreases through an increase or decrease in the equity value of the Fund, subject to the leverage factor, as described in the following paragraphs.

- **Leverage factor.** The leverage factor (F) is a constant number determined at the inception of the transaction based on, among other things, volatility, liquidity and the diversification of risky assets, as determined by the counterparty providing the protection. Generally, at the inception of the transaction, the leverage factor enables full allocation of the capital raised from the issuance of the securities to risky assets.

    Leverage Factor (F) = $100\% / (100\% - D_o)$

    (Eqn. 9)

- **Deallocation of risky assets.** At any time during the investment horizon, if the equity value decreases (as a result of either a decrease in the value of risky assets, an increase in interest rates or both), risky assets in the portfolio may have to be liquidated, and the proceeds from such liquidation are then allocated to riskless assets, in an amount sufficient to comply with the CPPI formula.

- **Reallocation to risky assets.** At any time during the investment horizon of the Fund, if the equity value increases (as a result of either an increase in the value of risky assets, a decrease in interest rates or both), riskless assets in the portfolio may be liquidated and the proceeds from such liquidation are then allocated to risky assets, in an amount sufficient to comply with the CPPI formula.

- **Incremental leverage.** A significant increase in the equity value during the investment horizon would reduce the risk to the counterparty of guaranteeing the protected securities and may warrant an incremental amount of explicit leverage to further enhance the return on the securities. The incremental leverage amount will depend on the continued positive performance of the Fund. Generally, the counterparty limits this amount to 50% of the principal amount of the protected securities (due to its internal risk limit considerations). The CPPI formula can then be modified as follows:

    $(R_t)_{max} = (F) \times \{V_t - (D_t + L_t)\}$

    (Eqn. 10)

where L_t is the incremental liability of the Fund, which, if owed to a party other than the counterparty, would be senior to the liability implicit in the defeasance of the protected securities. That is, in the event of a depreciation in the NAV of the Fund, this liability must be paid first before making any allocation to riskless assets in the Fund.

Valuation of the Protected Securities

Protected securities are valued at the NAV of the Fund, after the deduction for the outstanding liabilities of the Fund. The NAV at any time during the investment horizon consists of two components: 1) the value of riskless assets, if any, and 2) the value of risky assets of the Fund. The relative contribution of these two categories of assets at any time depends on the performance of the Fund, measured at such time as explained previously in the asset allocation and deallocation process of the Fund.

Risk of the Investment Process

The counterparty employs dynamic hedge to manage its exposure in the transaction. Under this hedging mechanism, the counterparty ensures that the value of the Fund allocated to risky assets does not exceed the amount given by the CPPI formula. A sudden depreciation in the value of risky assets could, for liquidity and other reasons, adversely affect the allocation of a sufficient amount of risky assets to riskless to provide for the repayment of principal at the maturity of the securities. The counterparty is therefore exposed to the so-called gap risk in managing its exposure in the transaction.

The investors, on the other hand, are not affected by the CPPI's dynamic hedging mechanism because they depend solely on the counterparty for the realization of principal at maturity. However, the investor may be adversely affected with respect to the return on the protected securities if the securities are fully defeased before maturity, because then the counterparty ceases the investment process.

Benefits of the CPPI Framework

The CPPI framework for protected securities transactions combines dynamically the protection of principal and the leverage in a formulaic approach. The relative benefits of the framework, particularly from a retail investor's perspective, include the simplicity of the approach and the likelihood of a higher return in a rising interest rate environment, as described in the following paragraphs.

- **Simplicity of the formulaic approach.** The advantage of CPPI is that it is simple to understand (which is important to investors) and does not require the use of option, although it has its roots in the option theory. The dynamic allocation between risky assets and riskless assets based on the performance of risky assets and riskless assets is the sole basis for protecting the principal and leveraging the return on the securities.

- **Likelihood of higher return in a rising interest rate environment.** Rising interest rates during the life of the transaction cause a slower growth in the defeasance value than that caused by stable interest rates. As a result, the likelihood of allocation to riskless assets is reduced, or reallocation to risky assets is increased. This contributes to the likelihood of a higher return on the protected securities.

IV. THE OPTION FRAMEWORK

Protected securities transactions are most common for assets involving publicly traded equities and investable equity indices. These assets are very liquid, and options on them are traded in the market. As a result, the application of the Black-Scholes option pricing model and other such option pricing models have become the standard for structuring equity derivatives securities, such as certificates of deposits linked to the S&P 500. However, the option models are not as easily applicable to hedge funds in creating derivatives securities because hedge funds are not as liquid, nor is there a market for options on hedge funds. However, the Option framework can be applied to structure protected securities linked to hedge funds (risky assets).

The Black-Scholes option pricing formula for a call option on a Fund that does not pay dividend is as follows:

$$\text{Option Price (p)} = s\Phi(d_1) - z\,e^{r\,t}\Phi(d_2)$$

where:

$$d_1 = \ln(s\,/\,z) + (r + 0.5{*}\sigma^2 t)\,/\,\sigma\sqrt{t}$$
$$d_2 = d_1 - \sigma\sqrt{t}$$

$\ln$ = Natural logarithm

s = NAV per share at any time during the investment horizon

z = Initial NAV per share as the strike price of the option

r = Risk-free interest rate compounding continuously

t = Time in years until the expiration of the option

σ = The volatility of the NAV per share

Φ = Standard normal cumulative distribution function

(Eqn. 11)

Mechanics of the Option Structure

The Issuer issues the protected securities and enters into an investment hedge agreement with a counterparty pursuant to which the counterparty guarantees the holders of securities 1) the repayment of the principal at maturity, and 2) the payment of 100% of the performance of the Fund, another SPV designed to make an investment in hedge funds. The protection and the leverage components constituting the transaction are discussed in the following paragraphs.

- **Protection component.** The counterparty provides the protection for the repayment of principal at the maturity of the securities. Therefore, the rating on the protected securities is the same as that of the counterparty, which is generally AA or below. The counterparty hedges its risk of repayment through a static hedge, whereby it invests, at the inception of the transaction, an amount of capital in riskless assets with a maturity value equal to the principal amount of the protected securities.

- **Leverage component.** The counterparty writes a call option on the Fund, which entitles the Issuer to provide investors with the full appreciation of the Fund above its initial NAV (the principal amount of the securities). The option is the source of leverage in the transaction, and its value during the investment horizon is determined by the application of the Black-Scholes option pricing formula, as described by Eqn. 11.

Exhibit 3: The Option Transaction Schematic

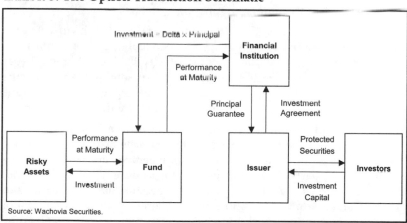

Source: Wachovia Securities.

Investment Process of the Transaction

The counterparty employs "delta" hedging to manage its exposure under the call option. Pursuant to this hedging, the counterparty acquires interests in the Fund (i.e., makes an investment in the Fund) in an amount given by the following expression:

delta × principal amount of the protected securities

The determination of the value of delta and the investment in the Fund are described in the following paragraphs.

- **Determination of delta.** The delta of an option reflects the sensitivity of the option price with respect to a change in the price of the underlying asset. In other words, delta reflects the units of change in the price of the option with respect to the per unit change in the NAV per share of the Fund.

  Mathematically, delta is the partial derivative of the option price with respect to the NAV per share of the Fund, and its value is, therefore, between 0 and 1.

  $$\Delta = \partial p \, / \, \partial s$$

  (Eqn. 12)

- **Investment in the Fund.** At the inception of the transaction, the value of delta is expected to be generally 0.5 or higher. During the investment horizon, the value of delta will change subject to the change in the NAV of the Fund. The counterparty will adjust its investment in the Fund as a function of delta.

  At maturity, if the NAV of the Fund is greater than its initial value (i.e., the strike price level), delta will be equal to 1. This implies that the counterparty will have invested the full principal amount (par amount) of the protected securities. Conversely, if at maturity the NAV is below its initial value, delta will be equal to 0. This means that there will be no investment in the Fund by the counterparty.

- **Incremental leverage.** To enhance the return on investment in the Fund beyond the level achievable through the leverage inherent in the option, an incremental amount of leverage can be deployed by the counterparty. This leverage is in the form of a loan to the Fund, which is generally equal to 50% of the amount of the investment in the Fund made by the counterparty. Therefore, the total amount of investment in the Fund during the investment horizon is given by the following:

$$(\text{NAV per share}) \times (\text{delta}) \times (\text{par amount}) \times (100\% + 50\%)$$

(Eqn. 13)

Valuation of the Protected Securities

The protected securities are valued as the sum of the two components of the structure: 1) the value of riskless assets (D_t) and 2) the value of the option. The parameters affecting the value of the riskless assets are the remaining time to maturity and the corresponding interest rate, as given by Eqn. 5.

The main parameters affecting the value of the option include NAV, time to maturity, the volatility of NAV and the interest rate, according to Eqn. 11. The value of the option at any time (t) during the investment horizon is determined by the application of Eqn. 11 for the option pricing formula.

Exhibit 4: The Option Value Schematic of Protected Securities

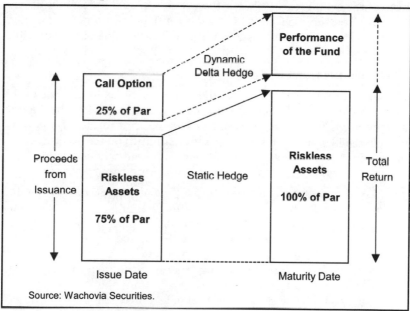

Source: Wachovia Securities.

Risk of the Investment Process

As described previously, the counterparty employs a dynamic delta hedge to manage its exposure under the option. Notwithstanding the dynamic nature of the hedge, the investment process is not risk free to the counterparty.

For example, the counterparty could be significantly underhedged in the event that the NAV goes up significantly higher than the level anticipated by delta. Similarly, the counterparty could be overhedged in the event that the NAV goes down significantly lower than the level anticipated by delta. In either case, the counterparty would be exposed to a risk of loss, depending on the extent of sudden appreciation or depreciation in the NAV.

The holders of the protected securities, on the other hand, are not affected by the hedging mechanism employed by the counterparty. The investors would receive the full appreciation of the Fund above the par amount at maturity, subject to the credit risk of the counterparty. That is, investors are indifferent to the delta hedging mechanism. However, in the event that an investor redeems the protected securities before maturity, it would be exposed to the risk of the delta hedging mechanism of the counterparty. That is, the investor would redeem the securities based on the then prevailing value of delta and other parameters affecting the option price. This could result in a value of the securities below its par amount.

Benefits of the Framework

The Option framework combines the static hedge (as in the case of the CDO framework) for the repayment of principal with the Option methodology for leveraged return. The benefits of the framework include the likelihood of achieving a higher return on the securities and, more important, the total return at maturity being independent of the investment process, as described in the following paragraphs.

- **Likelihood of a higher return.** There is always some value of the option during the investment horizon. This implies that there is no likelihood of a full and permanent defeasance of the transaction, unlike the CPPI framework. As a result, the Option framework should produce a higher level of total return on the securities than the CPPI framework. The return may be further supplemented by the fact that the Option framework enables the counterparty to employ a higher and constant level of leverage than the CPPI framework, generally.

- **Return independent of the investment process.** The advantage of the Option framework is that the return to investors at maturity does not depend on the delta hedging employed by the counterparty to protect its risk underlying the option. Investors should therefore view the Option framework as a more favorable investment process compared with the investment processes for the CDO framework and the CPPI framework.

V. COMPARISON OF THE STRUCTURAL FRAMEWORKS

The three structural alternatives to protected securities transactions described herein involve certain advantages and disadvantages to investors and entail different types of risks to the counterparty providing the protection. The major aspects of the advantages and disadvantages relating to return, risk, cost and marketability to investors are discussed in the following paragraphs:

- **Return on the securities.** The Option framework provides the likelihood of generating a higher return on the protected securities than the other structural alternatives, because it generally enables the counterparty to employ a higher level of leverage throughout the investment horizon of the transaction. The likelihood of a higher return also stems from the fact that the Option framework 1) provides a constant level of 100% exposure to risky assets throughout the investment horizon of the transaction; 2) does not involve the risk of a permanent defeasance of the securities at any time during the investment horizon, unlike that under the CPPI framework; and 3) enables the application of the incremental leverage (if any) at the inception of the transaction, which is generally not the case with the CPPI framework.

- **Risk exposure to investors.** The protected securities transactions are structured as buy-and-hold, medium- to long-term (7–15 years) transactions. The CDO framework does not involve the risk of any counterparty either for the repayment of principal at maturity or for the distribution of return on the securities. The Option framework and the CPPI framework carry the credit risk of the counterparty for the repayment of the principal at maturity and for the distribution of the return on the securities.

- **Cost of transaction.** The major element of the cost of the protected securities transaction under the CDO framework involves the cost of the leverage, which is fully transparent and market-driven. The major element of the cost of the transaction under both the CPPI framework and the Option framework is the cost of the guarantee of the principal of the securities, which is dependent solely on the counterparty, and investor perception of the risk of the counterparty, and is therefore not as market-driven. We believe the CDO framework should provide the lowest implied cost of guarantee to investors.

- **Marketability to investors.** Investors rely on a financial institution for the repayment of principal in the Option and CPPI frameworks, whereas they rely on the structure in the CDO framework. Reliance on the financial institution rather than the structure makes the securities marketable more broadly, particularly among retail investors.

From the previous points, one can discern that there is not a clear answer for the preference of a structural alternative. From the risk-adjusted return perspective, however, the CDO framework should be superior to other traditional structural alternatives.

ACKNOWLEDGEMENT

Thank you to Fabrice Hugon, vice president, Equity Derivative Group of Societe Generale, New York, for providing certain insight into the application of the Option framework for protected securities transactions.

Chapter 18

Concluding Remarks

The CDO market has experienced explosive growth since the mid-1990s. Annual domestic issuance grew from approximately $15 billion in 1996 to $60 billion at the end of 2003, peaking at $80 billion in 2000. In more recent years, domestic volume has remained somewhat stable in the $50 billion–$70 billion range (although the number of transactions per year has increased), whereas the European market (virtually nonexistent in the early to mid-1990s) now rivals the U.S. market in size. Total global volume is expected to be in excess of $100 billion by the end of 2004. All in all, CDOs continue to represent one of the largest components of the ABS market.

HERE TO STAY

In any event, those with any doubts about the permanence of the CDO market should focus on one, and only one, characteristic—its incredible growth. We believe there is no doubt that the growth in volume, in the number of different underlying asset types and in the variety of structures is a testament to the broad appeal of the product. Any counterargument suggesting that CDOs are a fad or that they have yet to endure a major crisis (cyclical or otherwise) to prove their resilience is soundly defeated by this evidence.

An equally convincing, albeit more anecdotal, indicator of the success of the CDO concept is that the number of people who proudly claim that they 1) invented CDOs, 2) structured the first CDO or 3) invested in the first CDO seems to be growing steadily.

A FEW EASY WISHES

Despite the strong performance of the CDO market and its continuous evolution, we believe there is still room for improvement. We focus on four aspects of this market that we think will benefit from fresh and innovative ideas. We do not intend to cover all of these topics in depth here, just to highlight a few relevant points.

MANAGER'S COMPENSATION

The typical compensation of a CDO manager consists of three separate fees—a senior management fee, a subordinate management fee and a participatory/incentive fee.

The senior fee is a comparatively small fee paid at the top of the waterfall that generally amounts to 10 bps–20 bps of the notional amount of collateral per year, whereas the subordinate fee (30 bps–50 bps) is more significant but paid near the mezzanine tranche level in the waterfall. This fee structure has remained more or less unaltered since the early days of the CDO market.

The thought behind this fee structure, a thought misguidedly but effectively championed by most investors, investment banks, rating agencies and monolines, was that the manager had to have "some skin in the game," and the more "skin," the better. Like so many clichés, the true meaning of this requirement is somewhat nebulous, but it is widely interpreted to mean that the collateral manager should suffer, or at least be punished, should the transaction not perform well. On the surface, this seemed like a good idea.

In reality, things have worked in a slightly different fashion, and not always to the advantage of investors. Far too frequently, when managers are faced with the possibility of losing their subordinate fee, the affected CDOs have tended to experience a frenetic amount of trading, almost always shortly before the determination date. These trades are often designed purely to pass structural safeguard tests, at least from a technical point of view, and to ensure that the subordinate management fee will be paid.

We are of the opinion that the fee structure needs major reengineering.

One possibility is to increase the senior fee substantially, eliminate or reduce the subordinate fee and provide greater investor rights. A robust senior fee, coupled with greater investor rights, mitigates the occasional conflict of interests created when small managers are forced to balance the needs of the transaction with those of the firm.

In exchange for larger senior fees and reduced returns, the process of removing the manager should be controlled by the equity investors and should be expedient. Some debtholders may cringe at this suggestion; however, we believe the inclusion of supplemental overcollateralization

(OC) tests, CCC/Caa haircuts, purchase price haircuts and other tests offer debtholders adequate protection. With these added safeguards, we believe the time has come for CDOs to adopt the corporate model whereby management decisions are (at least in theory) directed by equity holders. At the very least, the idea of appointing the manager for a certain period (e.g., 3–5 years) subject to renewal, much like the CEO of a company, is a valid suggestion. In short, it is better to pay the good managers well and quickly sack those who perform poorly. We believe a revision of current compensation arrangements is in order.

HEDGE STRUCTURE AND PHILOSOPHY

Traditionally, CDOs have been designed to provide varying degrees of protection to investors (commensurate with their position in the capital structure) from the potential adverse effect of defaults in the collateral pool. Interest rate risk has always been a secondary consideration, supposedly mitigated (if not eliminated entirely) via the use of interest rate swaps and caps. At least, that was the theory. In practice, however, many CDOs (particularly those structured in the late 1990s) have experienced unusual stress due to an unfortunate set of circumstances—high defaults and low recovery rates. The negative impact of these factors has been exacerbated by swaps with large notional amounts that were designed to hedge away risks associated with rising interest rates. In low rate environments, such as that which characterized the early 2000s, the vehicles were left paying out substantial amounts of cash to the swap counterparty, to the detriment of investors.

In broad terms, we can say that the hedge structure has almost always been driven by the rating agency criteria. Let us summarize them briefly. Standard & Poor's Corp. (S&P) demands that CDOs "pass" a given set of predetermined (not forward curve dependent) interest rate scenarios that can rise to 12% in just two years. Fitch Ratings uses two LIBOR scenarios (up and down) determined by the value of LIBOR at the closing and then adds (or subtracts) for years 1, 2 and 3 certain predefined increments to capture "stressed" situations. These increments tend to decrease in absolute value as one moves forward in time. Finally, Moody's Investors Service, Inc., uses the current forward curve as the base case scenario and then incorporates four additional cases (plus and minus one and two standard deviations). In essence, these are perturbations of the forward curve based on a volatility parameter that, incidentally, is rarely updated.

Both Moody's and Fitch implicitly recognize in their respective approaches the changing nature of interest rates (in fact, that is the reason hedges are required) by making reference to the current forward curve or the current value of LIBOR when establishing the base case. S&P, however, uses interest rate scenarios that are independent of the forward curve. Conceptually, this is somewhat difficult to grasp. In practical terms, it can lead to some distortion when structuring the hedge, and possibly even manipulation with the use of far-out-of-the-money caps.

In any event, what is really missing from the hedge analysis is a probabilistic approach. Simply put, the idea of having to pass a given set of predefined scenarios without taking into consideration the likelihood that those given scenarios could occur is both wrong and dangerous. It forces bankers to set up hedges that, by design, place the same importance on likely and unlikely events—not a prudent thing to do.

In summary, the time has come to rethink the hedging strategy. Ideally, the hedge structure should be driven by a probabilistic view of future interest rates. The notion that certain "fixed" scenarios should be "passed" at all costs should be discarded. Alternatively, if one does not want to incorporate a probabilistic approach, perhaps a compromise can be reached. One can continue the practice of passing certain scenarios as long as some leniency is granted in terms of passing less likely scenarios. Finally, the idea of using dynamic hedging and/or giving the CDO manager more discretion should be considered.

USE FORMULAS AND DIAGRAMS...PLEASE!

Words are powerful, and many words put together intelligently can convey, sometimes with beauty and clarity, great concepts and interesting ideas. The following example is not such a case; in fact, only confusion and ugliness emerge from this unfortunate prose taken from a CDO indenture.

> The Diversity Score is the fraction, rounded to the nearest integer, of which the numerator is the product of (i) the aggregate for all Collateral Securities of the product of the (x) "default probability" (as defined herein) of each Collateral Security, and (y) the principal balance of such Collateral Security, and (ii) the aggregate for all Collateral Securities of the product of (x) one minus the default probability of each Collateral Security and (y) the principal balance of such Collateral Security; and the denominator is the aggregate for all of the Collateral Securities of, with respect to each Collateral Security (Security A) the aggregate with respect to each Collateral Security (Security B) of the product of (i) the correlation (as defined herein) between Security A and Security B, (ii) the square-root of

the product of (a) the default probability of Security A, (b) one minus the default probability of Security A, (c) the default probability of Security B, and (d) one minus the default probability of Security B, (iii) the principal balance of Security A, and (iv) the principal balance of Security B.

The aim of the preceding paragraph was to "explain" the Moody's diversity score formula. And that is precisely the problem; formulas do not lend themselves to verbal explanations. They are better conveyed with mathematical notation that, incidentally, was invented to avoid the ambiguities of conventional language. A much cleaner and clearer description of the diversity score (DS) can be achieved with the following definition:

$DS = X/Y$

where

$$X = \left(\sum_{i=1}^{N} p_i F_i \right) \left(\sum_{j=1}^{N} (1 - p_j) F_j \right)$$

and

$$Y = \sum_{i=1}^{N} \sum_{j=1}^{N} \rho_{ij} F_i F_j \sqrt{Q_{ij}}$$

with $Q_{ij} = p_i p_j (1 - p_i)(1 - p_j)$

Granted, formulas might intimidate some people, but the limitations of conventional language when it comes to specifying mathematical operations succinctly and unambiguously has been accepted and documented for centuries. In fact, many other legal documents (e.g., engineering regulations, building codes, insurance-related documents) include formulas and have done so for many years. By the same token, the use of diagrams and flow charts (similar to those employed by computer programmers) in offering memorandums and other documents would do wonders for readers attempting to understand the intricacies of principal and interest waterfalls, much in the same way that their use in marketing materials helps potential investors understand CDO structures.

To be fair, some avant-garde market participants have already adopted these practices. We just need the rest of the industry to follow these leaders.

TRANSPARENCY

Transparency in terms of transaction performance information has improved a great deal since the inception of the CDO market, but there is still room for further improvement. At present, most arrangers distribute periodic reports and post data on their Web sites regarding key parameters that reflect the status of deals they have brought to market. In fact, one could argue that the recent increase in secondary trading volume has been fostered, at least in part, by the improved ease with which such data can be obtained. In general, deal reports provide a snapshot of most deal performance metrics, including par value (OC) and interest coverage (IC) ratios, current ratings, dollar or euro amounts of outstanding tranches, pool rating factor (WARF), the percentage of defaulted assets and assets having CCC/Caa ratings, collateral floating and fixed spreads and the current diversity score.

That said, there is still an area where more progress is required: the rating process, or more precisely, rating agencies' methodologies. Although the three primary rating agencies have articulated in some detail their approaches, there are still two agencies that rely on a "black box" system for the ultimate computation of the key parameters that determine the rating of a CDO tranche. And the third agency recently made a move in the wrong direction by unveiling its "black box" for synthetic deals. It might sound as though "giving away" a computer program that allegedly makes life easier for users by not burdening them with the unpleasant task of developing a model is a good idea. Actually, the opposite is true.

Most market participants would welcome a "reproducible" methodology—that is, a set of rules, assumptions, etc., that they could replicate with their own models. In fact, if the agencies were willing to discard their "black boxes" and instead spell out all of the details behind their "methodologies," CDO participants would be able to understand the driving factors behind the performance of every tranche rating. This way, for example, it would be easier to identify which aspects of a potential CDO structure should be changed to obtain a desired rating. At present, however, bankers are forced to run several "blind iterations" hoping that, for a particular set of parameters, the "black box" will produce the desired output. In short, this state of affairs is utterly counterproductive and unfair, for it leaves CDO market participants at the mercy of a set of unknown, and worse, unpredictable, rules. It is time to trash the "black boxes."

A FINAL THOUGHT

Many pundits believe the CDO market has reached a state of maturity —
a situation normally characterized by a lack of creativity and slow
growth or, perhaps, decay. On the contrary, we believe the CDO product
has only entered the "young adult" stage of its life and will continue to
evolve for years. CDO technology has proved to be resilient and flexible,
but its full power (in terms of volume and breadth) is still being developed. Like a young marathon runner, the best times are still ahead. Thus,
as we close the books on 2004, we look at the future with optimism and
a sense of anticipation. We do not know what the future will bring; in
fact, we will not even attempt to predict the future, for experience has
shown that reality always surpasses imagination. We are just happy to
be participating in this exciting market; we hope you, the reader, will
share our enthusiasm. Let us enjoy the ride, for CDOs are here to stay!

Glossary

Advance Rate: 1) With regard to an asset-based loan, the amount that can be borrowed versus the amount of pledged assets. For example, assuming a 75% advance rate and $100 million in assets, the borrower could borrow up to $75 million. Typical advance rates are 75%–85% for accounts receivable, whereas 50% would be typical for inventory. 2) In a market value CDO, the percentage of a security that can be leveraged (borrowed against).

Amortization Period: The period in which principal is returned to the note holders. The amortization period may begin at the first payment date in the case of a static pool transaction or following the reinvestment period in the case of a managed transaction.

APEX CDO: A proprietary CDO structure developed by Wachovia Securities. The structure's primary difference from other managed, cash flow CDOs is the use of the APEX swap that reimburses the transaction for principal losses on defaulted assets or on the sale of credit risk securities.

APEX Swap: A combination of three swaps that use ISDA documentation—the APEX Credit Swap, the APEX Income Swap and the APEX Balance Swap.

Arbitrage: The simultaneous buying and selling of a security at two different prices in two different markets to generate profits without risk.

Arbitrage Transaction: A transaction motivated by the desire to capitalize on the relatively high spread or yield of the underlying collateral over the relatively low spread or yield of the liabilities issued by the SPV.

Asset-Based Loan: A loan provided to a company that is fully collateralized by accounts receivable and inventory. The borrowing availability is determined based on the amount of eligible inventory and receivables, and the applicable advance rate.

AUM: Assets under Management.

Balance-Sheet Transaction: A transaction motivated by the needs of an institution to improve its return on assets by removing assets from its balance sheet. The institution gets regulatory capital relief and may also receive a fee for managing the assets. Frequently, the institution retains all below-investment-grade CDO debt.

BDC: See Business Development Company.

Beta Distribution: A probability distribution that takes values between zero and one that is often used to model random principal recovery rates.

Bond Floor: In terms of CPPI, this refers to the amount of riskless assets required to pay the principal of the protected securities at maturity.

Business Development Company (BDC): A BDC invests in private companies and is regulated by the Investment Company Act of 1940.

CADR: Constant Annual Default Rate.

Capital Structure: The unique mixture of debt and equity securities offered in a CDO transaction.

Cash Flow Loan: A loan for which the primary means of repayment is the borrower's cash flow. The borrowing availability is determined based on a multiple of cash flow, typically EBITDA.

Cash Flow Transactions: A transaction where the collateral is measured by par amount (i.e., amount due). These transactions are characterized by overcollateralization tests and interest coverage tests that, when violated, divert cash to protect investor interests.

CBO: See Collateralized Bond Obligation.

CDO: See Collateralized Debt Obligation.

CDO Debt: Fixed-income securities (bonds) offered by a CDO transaction.

CDO Liabilities: See CDO Debt.

CDO of CDOs (CDO^2): A CDO transaction primarily backed by other CDO securities.

CDO-Level Collateral: In a CDO^2 transaction, the first level of collateral (the CDOs that support the CDO2).

CDR: Cumulative Default Rate.

Cholesky Decomposition: A numerical procedure frequently used in Monte Carlo analyses to factor a correlation matrix.

Class: See Tranche.

CLO: See Collateralized Loan Obligation.

Closing: The day on which investors purchase the CDO debt (i.e., the day that money changes hands).

CMBS: See Commercial Mortgage-Backed Security.

Collateral Manager: The organization responsible for conducting the day-to-day business of a special-purpose entity, especially the maintenance of the collateral pool. The collateral manager is primarily responsible for purchasing and selling collateral and receives a management fee.

Collateral Quality Tests: Generally, cash flow CDO transactions include several tests that are designed to maintain the quality of the collateral pool. These tests include the weighted average spread test, the weighted average coupon test, the rating factor test, the weighted average life test and diversity tests.

Collateralized Bond Obligation (CBO): A structured security backed primarily by corporate bonds.

Collateralized Debt Obligation (CDO): 1) A CLO, a CBO or any structured security backed by other structured products including RMBS, CMBS, corporate debt issued by real estate investment trusts or other CDOs. In addition, CDOs include structured securities backed by credit default or total return swaps that are linked to corporate or structured product debt. 2) The transaction in a broad sense including the special-purpose vehicle, the collateral manager, the trustee, the controlling legal documents, collateral, etc.

Collateralized Loan Obligation (CLO): A structured security backed primarily by corporate loans.

Commercial Mortgage-Backed Security: A structured security backed by commercial mortgages.

Commercial Real Estate CDO (CRE CDO): A CDO primarily backed by CMBS and corporate debt issued by real estate investment trusts.

Constant Proportion Portfolio Insurance (CPPI): A form of dynamic hedging developed by Fischer Black and Robert Jones of Goldman Sachs in 1986. Portfolio assets are allocated between risky assets and riskless assets in proportion to the amount of trading equity.

Copula: A mathematical procedure to construct a joint distribution from known marginal distributions.

Coverage Tests: Collectively, the overcollateralization tests and the interest coverage tests.

CPPI: See Constant Proportion Portfolio Insurance.

CRE CDO: See Commercial Real Estate CDO.

Credit Risk Sale: In the context of a CDO, the sale of a security that, in the collateral manager's judgment, has a significant risk of declining in credit quality or, with a lapse of time, becoming a defaulted obligation.

Cumulative Distribution Function (CDF): A function that calculates the probability that a value randomly selected from a probability distribution will be less than a known constant.

Default Scenario: Schedule of collateral defaults, their recovered principal amounts and the time lag from default to recovery.

Default-Adjusted Cash Flow: Tranche cash flows that have been averaged over default scenarios for their underlying collateral.

Defeasance Assets: The assets that will be used to retire an obligation. Within the context of portfolio insurance, this generally refers to riskless assets (e.g., U.S. Treasurys).

Discount Margin: For floating-rate tranches linked to a certain index rate, the spread to the index rate that would discount future cash flows back to a known present value.

Diversity Score (DS): A measure of collateral diversity assigned by Moody's Investors Service, Inc. There are two methods for calculating diversity scores depending on the type of asset class. The method employed for transactions backed by structured products explicitly incorporates correlation, whereas transactions backed by corporate debt use a point scoring system.

DPD: Days past due on a loan's payment.

DS: See Diversity Score.

DSCR: Debt Service Coverage Ratio calculated as net operating income/debt service.

Dynamic Portfolio Hedging: A trading strategy designed to protect principal but retain the upside potential of an investment through the disciplined allocation and reallocation of funds to riskless and risky securities, depending on the performance of the overall portfolio. Also see Constant Proportion Portfolio Insurance.

Effective Date: The day on which the CDO has acquired all of the collateral needed and meets all other relevant conditions dictated by the indenture. This day marks the end of the ramp-up period.

Excess Spread: Interest proceeds that remain after payment of interest due to the CDO debt securities according to the interest waterfall.

Expected Loss: The average fraction of the present value of a future tranche cash flow stream that is lost when underlying assets default. The averaging is performed over randomly generated default scenarios.

Exponential Distribution: A probability distribution used to model the time until an asset default occurs.

Gearing Factor: In terms of CPPI, this is a multiplier that is used to determine the maximum amount permitted to be invested in risky assets.

Hedge Counterparty: The bank that provides interest rate swaps and caps to offset interest rate mismatches between CDO assets and CDO liabilities.

High-Yield Bond: A bond that is not investment grade; sometimes referred to as a junk bond.

IC Test: See Interest Coverage Test.

ICDR: See Idealized Cumulative Default Rate.

Idealized Cumulative Default Rate (ICDR): A table published by Moody's Investors Service, Inc., that contains the expected default rates for corporate securities of various ratings and maturities.

Incentive Management Fee: A fee that is paid to the collateral manager pari passu with equity after an equity return hurdle has been met.

Indenture: The controlling legal document for a CDO or other securitization that dictates deal mechanics as well as the responsibilities and obligations of all parties.

Interest Coverage Test (IC Test): An evaluation of the anticipated interest proceeds from collateral relative to interest payments due on the CDOs. Failure of this test frequently results in the sequential principal payment of the CDO notes.

Interest Proceeds: Payments from the collateral pool that represent interest.

Interest Rate Hedge: A parallel investment made with the intention of reducing the risk of payment to CDO note holders that may result from unfavorable fluctuations in interest rates.

Interest Waterfall: The priority of payments applied to interest proceeds as defined in the indenture.

ISDA: International Swaps & Derivatives Association. The ISDA sets the international contractual standards for the derivatives industry.

Letter of Credit (LOC): In the context of securitization, a form of guarantee of payment issued by a bank on behalf of a borrower that ensures the payment of interest and repayment of principal on the bond being guaranteed.

Leverage: A measure of the amount of debt financing of a pool of assets. A significant debt-to-equity ratio is indicative of high leverage.

Leveraged Loan: A non-investment-grade loan to a borrower that either is rated below investment grade or commands a high pricing spread vis-à-vis other investment-grade borrowers.

LIBOR: London Interbank Offered Rate. LIBOR is the rate of interest at which banks borrow funds from other banks and is the most widely used benchmark or reference rate for short-term interest rates.

Liquidity Facility: An arrangement allowing interest shortfalls to be paid using funds from a third party (liquidity provider) that are later repaid with future interest or principal proceeds.

Loan-to-Value (LTV): The percentage or portion of a loan amount relative to the value of the property.

LOC: See Letter of Credit.

Managed Transactions: A transaction in which a collateral manager is permitted to make discretionary purchases and sale decisions within the guidelines of the transaction indenture.

Market Value Transactions: A transaction where the collateral is measured by market value or advance rates for purposes of the overcollateralization tests. Typically, the collateral pools for these transactions range across many asset classes including equities.

Mark-to-Market: The value of an individual security or an entire portfolio if liquidated at current market prices.

Mezzanine CDO Debt: Bonds that are positioned below the senior-most notes in the capital structure of a CDO, but above subordinated notes and equity.

Middle-Market Companies: Small to medium-sized companies in terms of revenue and EBITDA. There is no official definition, but we define the middle market as companies with $10 million–$250 million in revenue and $5 million–$50 million in EBITDA.

Monte Carlo Simulation: A method that uses a large number of trial simulations and is designed to provide the relative probability of various outcomes (e.g., returns).

Multisector CDO: A CDO backed by an assortment of other structured products such as CMBS, RMBS, structured securities linked to aircraft leases, shipping container leases, home equity loans, auto loans, small business loans and other CDO debt.

Non-Call Period: The period in which equity investors are not permitted to unwind or terminate the transaction.

OC Test: See Overcollateralization Test.

Overcollateralization Test (OC Test): An evaluation of the par amount of collateral relative to the debt issued by the special-purpose vehicle (i.e., the CDO). Failure of this test frequently results in the sequential return of principal to the CDO liabilities.

Owner-Occupied: A unit is owner-occupied if the owner resides in the unit.

Par: The notional or face value of a security.

Pari Passu: Equal in terms of rights and priority of payment.

Pay-in-Kind (PIK): A bond that, under certain circumstances, is permitted to make interest payments to investors in the form of additional bonds, rather than with a cash payout. In other words, the security capitalizes its interest payment.

PEG: See Private Equity Group.

PIK: See Pay-in-Kind.

Placement Agent: The investment bank that markets and sells the CDO debt and equity. Typically, the placement agent is also the structurer.

Portfolio NAV: In terms of CPPI, portfolio NAV represents the net asset value of the portfolio (i.e., the value of the portfolio minus any borrowing).

Preferred Shares: The junior-most securities issued by a CDO. These securities receive payment only after all other obligations of the CDO have been paid.

Prepayment Penalty: A fine for paying off a loan partially or in full before its maturity.

Principal Proceeds: Payments from the collateral pool that represent return of principal.

Principal-Protected Security: A security that retains the upside potential of a direct investment of the underlying collateral with minimal risk of principal loss.

Principal Waterfall: The priority of payments applied to principal proceeds as dictated in the indenture.

Private Equity Group (PEG): A group that sources investment opportunities for emerging or small companies. Oftentimes, a PEG will have expertise in certain industries and will advise management.

Pro Rata Payment: Payment to multiple parties in proportion to the amount due to them.

Ramp-up Period: The time between the closing and the effective date, usually lasting 1–6 months.

Ramp-up: The process of acquiring collateral after the transaction has closed. CDO transactions will frequently close with only a portion of the collateral identified and purchased. Therefore, flush with cash from the issuance of the CDOs, the CDO transaction will use this money to purchase collateral during the ramp-up period.

Rating Agencies: Refers to Moody's Investors Service, Inc., Standard & Poor's Corp. and Fitch Ratings. The rating agencies analytically stress the CDO capital structure and assign ratings to the CDO liabilities.

Reinvestment Period: The period in which the collateral manager is permitted to purchase additional collateral with principal proceeds from the collateral pool. This term is only relevant to managed (non-static) CDO transactions.

Resecuritization: A transaction wherein the securities issued are backed, at least partially, by other structured securities. See also Multisector CDO and Structured-Finance CDO.

Reserve Fund: A pool of cash or highly liquid assets that is placed into an account to cover shortfalls of interest or principal.

Residential Mortgage-Backed Security (RMBS): A structured security backed by residential mortgages.

Restricted Investments: In an APEX CDO, high-quality (Aaa/AAA) securities with floating-rate coupons that secure the interests of the swap counterparty and then the Class C noteholders.

Revolving Loan: A loan facility that allows the borrower to draw funds up to its specified limit, repay all or a portion and then re-borrow.

Registered Investment Company (RIC): A RIC must maintain a conservative leverage of 1:1 debt to equity and distribute the majority of its income as dividends to shareholders.

RIC: See Registered Investment Company.

RMBS: See Residential Mortgage-Backed Security.

Sequential Pay: Refers to the repayment of principal to the senior-most tranche outstanding in a securitization until it is completely paid off before repaying the next most senior tranche and so on. Most CDOs are sequential pay structures.

SF CDO: See Structured-Finance CDO.

Should Opinion: Refers to the tax opinion issued by deal counsel with regard to the liabilities issued by a CDO. The opinion states that a security should be treated as debt for U.S. income tax purposes though it may be viewed as equity interest due to its subordinate position in the capital structure. Should opinions are generally issued for a CDO's mezzanine and subordinate tranches. Investors should consult their tax accountants for further details. Also see Will Opinion.

SIC Code: The Standard Industrial Classification Code is a four-digit numerical index assigned by the U.S. government to a business establishment to identify the primary business of the establishment.

SBA: See Small Business Administration.

SBLC: Small Business Lending Company.

Small Business Administration (SBA): Established in 1953 as an independent deferral agency to provide financial assistance to small businesses.

SPE: Special-Purpose Entity. Also see Special-Purpose Vehicle.

Special-Purpose Vehicle (SPV): A shell company created to issue debt and equity and purchase collateral. Typically, the SPV has no employees and is incorporated in a tax-friendly jurisdiction such as the Cayman Islands. Also known as a Special-Purpose Entity (SPE).

Spread: A percentage, measured in basis points (1/100 of a percent), over a predetermined interest rate benchmark, typically LIBOR.

SPV: See Special-Purpose Vehicle.

Standard Normal Variate: A number randomly drawn from the standard normal distribution.

Static Pool: A defined pool of assets (such as loans), backing a securitization, that will not be changed during the life of the securitization and will only decline via amortization of the assets through payment or default.

Static Portfolio Hedging: The partial allocation of an investment to risk-less securities to ensure that principal payment will be made at a future date. The balance of the investment is invested in risky securities.

Static Transaction: A transaction in which the collateral pool is not managed and remains unchanged over time. The asset manager of a static pool transaction is frequently able to sell a security if it has defaulted or is credit-impaired but may not purchase new collateral.

Structured-Finance CDO (SF CDO): CRE CDOs, multisector CDOs or CDOs of CDOs.

Structured Security: A debt obligation issued by a special-purpose vehicle and backed by the cash flow stream from a pool of assets.

Structurer: The structurer works with the collateral manager and the rating agencies to create the CDO. Typically, the structurer is also the placement agent.

Subordinate Management Fee: A fee that is paid to the collateral manager at a lower position in the cash flow waterfall than the senior management fee. Usually, the subordinate management fee is paid just before the equity or preferred share holders.

Syndicated Loan: A loan facility that is provided by a coordinated group of lending or financial institutions.

Synthetic Transactions: A transaction backed by derivative securities linked to debt securities. Synthetic transactions can be executed on a funded or unfunded basis. When a transaction is unfunded or partially funded, investors agree to pay for losses beyond a certain threshold but are not required to invest cash at closing.

Threshold Utilization Ratio: In an APEX transaction, the ratio of the APEX swap balance (the amount drawn on the swap) over the APEX swap limit (the maximum amount that can be drawn on the swap). Historically, this ratio has been set at 50%–60%. Breaching this test leads to immediate termination of the reinvestment period.

Threshold Utilization Test: In an APEX transaction, the threshold utilization test is violated if the threshold utilization ratio is greater than a predetermined value (usually 50%–60%). Breaching this test leads to immediate termination of the reinvestment period.

Trading Equity: In terms of CPPI, this is the amount by which the Portfolio NAV exceeds the bond floor.

Tranche: A collection of structured securities that share the same position within the payment waterfall. Typically, the special-purpose vehicle will issue multiple tranches of debt where each tranche is prioritized in right of payment. Securities that are a part of the same tranche have rights that are pari passu with other securities of the same tranche but have either more or less senior rights compared with securities of other tranches in accordance with the priority of payments dictated by the waterfall.

Trustee: The trustee monitors and prepares monthly reports on the collateral and collects and distributes all interest and principal payments.

Turbo: To accelerate the repayment of notes in a securitization via the use of excess spread so that the note balance declines more quickly than the underlying assets.

Underlying Collateral: In CDO^2 transactions, the second level of collateral, which includes corporate bonds, loans and leases that support the CDO-level collateral (e.g., CDOs, CMBS, RMBS and similar products).

Underwriter: A firm, typically an investment bank, that raises capital for issuers of debt and equity securities. Also see Placement Agent.

Variance Reduction: A procedure to enhance the accuracy of a simulation method.

WAC: Weighted average coupon.

Warehouse: A facility that permits the collateral manager, who may be capital constrained, to purchase collateral with funds from the warehouse provider that will be sold to the CDO at closing. The warehouse provider is typically the same institution as the structurer/placement agent.

WARF: See Weighted Average Rating Factor.

WAS: Weighted average spread.

Warm Backup Servicer: A servicer that is chosen as a backup to the original servicer and receives monthly tapes and reconciles actual cash collections to expected cash collections.

Waterfall: The interest waterfall and principal waterfall.

Weighted Average Rating Factor (WARF): A measure of collateral quality assigned by Moody's Investors Service, Inc. Under this measure, collateral ratings are converted to a numeric scale and then weighted by size of holding.

Will Opinion: Refers to the tax opinion issued by deal counsel with regard to the liabilities issued by a CDO. The opinion states that a security will be treated as debt for U.S. income tax purposes and is generally issued for a CDO's investment-grade tranches. Investors should consult their tax accountants for further details. Also see Should Opinion.

Wrap: Refers to a guarantee issued by an insurer or bank that promises payment of principal and interest. Senior CDO notes are frequently "wrapped."

Zero-Coupon Spread: The spread over the implied zero-coupon spot curve that equates present value to market price (including accrued interest).